SPRING
OFFENSIVE

By the same author
Kippenberger: an inspired New Zealand commander
Massacre at Passchendaele: the New Zealand story
Letters from the Battlefield: New Zealand soldiers write home 1914–18

SPRING OFFENSIVE

New Zealand and the
Second Battle of the Somme

GLYN HARPER

HarperCollins*Publishers*

National Library of New Zealand Cataloguing-in-Publication Data

Harper, Glyn, 1958-
Spring offensive : New Zealand and the second Battle of the
Somme / Glyn Harper.
Includes index.
ISBN 1-86950-481-X
1. New Zealand—Army—History—World War, 1914-1918.
2. Somme, 2nd Battle of the, France, 1918. 3. Ypres, 3rd Battle
of, Ieper, Belgium, 1917. 4. World War, 1914-1918—New
Zealand. 5. World War, 1914-1918—Registers of dead—New
Zealand. I. Title.
940.434—dc 21

First published 2003
HarperCollins*Publishers (New Zealand) Limited*
P.O. Box 1, Auckland

Copyright © Glyn Harper 2003

Glyn Harper asserts the moral right to be identified as the
author of this work.

ISBN 1 86950 481 X

Cover photo: New Zealanders on the front line on the
Somme, La Signy Farm. *RSA Collection, Alexander Turnbull
Library G-13092-1/2-*

Designed and typeset by Chris O'Brien/Pages LP
Printed by Griffin Press, South Australia, on 100 gsm
Publishers Offset

To the men and women of the
New Zealand Expeditionary Force, 1914–19,
for whom honour, service and courage
were more than just words.

Lest We Forget

Acknowledgements

As always, my first thanks goes to my family: my partner, Susan, and my daughters, Natalie and Rhiannon. Without their support this book could never have been completed.

Most of the primary source material for this book has been obtained from the National Archives, the Alexander Turnbull Library and the Kippenberger Archive and Research Library at the Army Museum in Waiouru. Yet again I am deeply indebted to the staff of these research institutions. In particular, I wish to thank the staff of the Manuscripts and Archives section of the Alexander Turnbull Library in Wellington and Dolores Ho of the Kippenberger Archive and Research Library. The World War I Oral Archive created by Jane Tolerton and Nicholas Boyack, part of the collection of the National Library of New Zealand's Oral History Centre, was an invaluable source of information. I wish to thank Vicki Hughes and Linda Evans of the Oral History Centre for their help in accessing this historical treasure trove.

Paul Lumsden produced the excellent maps from his home in Nelson. Anna Rogers edited the manuscript from her home in the 'garden city'. The book is certainly the better for her care and diligence. I would also like to thank Christine Wallworth for her assistance in compiling the first of the appendices.

Finally, I wish to thank Lorain Day and Sue Page of HarperCollins for their belief in this project and for their unstinting support. This was our fourth venture together and I hope there will be many more to follow.

Glyn Harper
Palmerston North
August 2003

Foreword

'Still in the trenches. I am tired, sore and heart broken
of this Hellish life . . .'

These poignant words, with so many others in this book, reveal
the stories of young New Zealand men who found themselves
knee deep in mud and human remains, waging the trench warfare of the Second Battle of the Somme in March and April 1918.

Nearly 1000 New Zealanders died during their two-month
battle against the Michael Offensive, Germany's most audacious
campaign during the First World War. Another 2700 were injured, captured or missing at the end of the campaign. Yet, even
today, few New Zealanders know about the battle, widely considered to be our most vital contribution to the Allied victory.

*Spring Offensive: New Zealand and the Second Battle of the
Somme* by Glyn Harper fills this glaring gap in our knowledge.
As a sequel to his *Massacre at Passchendaele*, Harper contributes
to a greater understanding of New Zealand's role in the First
World War, and to the psyche of a tiny nation that gave so much,
so many years ago.

The Second Battle of the Somme signified a coming of age for
New Zealand soldiers. It was the first time they had been involved in a defensive battle on the Western Front, and had been
on the receiving end of a full-scale German attack. It was also the
first time New Zealand soldiers had seen for themselves what
happens when ordinary men, women and children become refugees — displaced from their homes through acts of war.

Spring Offensive captures and portrays these two crucial
months of warfare in many ways. It offers a detailed, referenced
chronicle of the military strategies and manoeuvres that eventually led to the German retreat. These details reveal the courage
and intellect of the New Zealanders — the qualitative edge, the

ability to punch far above their weight, as the author observes.

But *Spring Offensive* is also an emotional tale of young men far away from home, fighting in conditions euphemistically described by some as 'not too good'.

By including excerpts from diaries and letters home, the author captures the real world of these determined young men — their perpetual optimism, their secret despondencies and their determination to protect their loved ones back home from the horrific reality of their lives.

It reveals what it means to be a New Zealander, even under such traumatic conditions. Readers will not resist a smile at the 9 March entry in the war diary of the 2nd Otago Battalion. The entry detailed a rugby game between the battalion and Welsh soldiers, with the observation that the referee's decisions were 'at times peculiar'.

Spring Offensive chronicles, objectively, the elation and horror of participation in war. Harper acknowledges the historical importance of the battle, but notes that every casualty 'represents an individual, a New Zealand soldier far from home, with dreams and aspirations, plans for the future and loved ones to whom he wished one day to return'.

Spring Offensive: New Zealand and the Second Battle of the Somme is a book for all New Zealanders.

Silvia Cartwright

The Honourable Dame Silvia Cartwright PCNZM, DBE
Governor-General and Commander-in-Chief in and over New Zealand

Contents

Introduction

Storm Warning

O n 21 March 1918, at 4.20 a.m., a storm of fire and steel was hurled against two British armies on the Western Front. The German artillery that unleashed this onslaught had been secretly assembled around St Quentin in the southern sector of the British front line. The concentration of military force for this operation was massive: some 74 infantry divisions, a number greater than the entire British Expeditionary Force, and more than 6000 artillery pieces. German morale was high and they were confident of success. One fanatical young German stormtrooper, Lieutenant Ernst Junger, felt that with this huge artillery barrage and the hundreds of thousands of infantry ready to surge forward, victory was a foregone conclusion.

> When I saw this massed might piled up, the break-through seemed to me a certainty. But was there strength in us to smash the enemy's reserves and hurl them to destruction? I was convinced of it. The decisive battle, the final advance had begun. The destiny of the nations drew to its iron conclusion and the stake was possession of the world.[1]

This battle, the *Kaiserschlacht* (Kaiser's battle) or the Michael Offensive as it is also known, was to be the Germans' supreme effort to win the war. Its initial success brought the Allies on the Western Front to the brink of defeat.

The German artillery that opened fire on the British lines that morning numbered nearly 6500 guns of all calibres and more than 2000 trench mortars. It was the heaviest artillery barrage of the war and one of the largest ever used. In the first two hours the German artillery drenched the British gun positions in front of them with mustard gas. Then for the next three hours they fired a mixture of high explosive and gas shells that targeted the British infantry's forward positions. It was indeed, as the Germans labelled it, the 'Devil's Orchestra'.[2]

This bombardment lasted five hours. It was designed to stun the defenders, destroy the front-line communications, and silence the enemy artillery by its sheer weight and ferocity. It was totally successful. Ernst Junger, one of only fourteen lieutenants to win the Pour le mérite, Imperial Germany's highest military decoration,[3] left a vivid description of this action:

> At once the hurricane broke loose. A curtain of flames was let down, followed by a sudden impetuous tumult such as was never heard, a raging thunder that swallowed up the reports even of the heaviest guns in its tremendous reverberations and made the earth tremble. This gigantic roar of annihilation from countless guns behind us was so terrific that, compared with it, all preceding battles were child's-play. What we had not dared to hope came true. The enemy artillery was silenced, put out of action by one giant blow. We could not stay any longer in the dugouts. We got on to the top and looked with wonder at the wall of fire towering over the English lines and the swaying blood-red clouds that hung above it.[4]

Young British officer Lieutenant E.C. Allfree was on the receiving end of this wall of fire:

> So intense was the bombardment that the earth around us trembled. It was a dark night, but the tongues of flame from the guns — 2500 British guns replied to the German bombardment — lit up the night sky to daylight brightness. Mixed up with the high explosive shells crashing on our trenches, were the less noisy, but deadly gas shells. Trenches collapsed, infantry in front-line positions, groping about in their gas masks, were stunned by the sudden terrific onslaught . . .
> Machine-gun posts were blown sky high — along with human limbs. Men were coughing and vomiting from the effects of gas, and men were blinded.[5]

At 9.40 a.m. the bombardment was replaced with a creeping barrage behind which advanced specially trained storm troops, equipped with numerous flame-throwers and light machine guns. Their tactic was to push forward and bypass centres of resistance. This deadly artillery and infantry combination soon overwhelmed the dazed, outnumbered British defenders in the front lines who bore the brunt of this ferocious storm. At the end of that long day the British situation on the Western Front was critical. The Fifth and Third Armies suffered 38,000 casualties and lost 500 guns. When an army loses its guns, it is a sure sign that the military situation is desperate. On 21 March the German stormtroopers managed to penetrate the front lines to a depth of 5 miles, forcing the two British armies to fall back in some confusion. Over the next six days they would be forced, in the face of renewed attack, to withdraw further, to a distance of nearly 40 miles.

In a theatre of war where gains measured in a few hundred yards were considered successful, the German rate of advance in these early days of the *Kaiserschlacht* was regarded as staggering. A withdrawal in the face of an aggressive enemy is the most difficult of military operations to perform. In the process of withdrawing the two armies, huge gaps opened up in the British lines between army and corps boundaries. The German storm troops were expert at spotting these gaps and exploiting them to the maximum. They drove through them in force, prompting further British withdrawals. The French, on the left of the British line, became so alarmed at the extent of the British casualties and at the ground being lost to the Germans that their commander considered abandoning his front-line positions and moving his armies back to protect Paris. For a time, the whole Allied line on the Western Front was in danger of collapsing. As leading First World War historian Gary Sheffield has written, the German spring offensive of 1918 'brought the allies face to face with defeat'.[6]

In order to plug these gaps in the British lines and in an attempt to stem the German advance, nine divisions were plucked from other sectors and rushed to the endangered areas. It was a last-ditch effort to hold the Germans at bay. Included were three Australian divisions and the New Zealand Division.

In March 1918 the New Zealanders were in rest areas around Cassel and Hazebrouck as part of the Second Army reserve. The previous few months had not been good ones for the New Zealanders. In October 1917 they had taken part in two large offensives in the Ypres salient at Passchendaele. The second of these, on 12 October 1917, had been an absolute catastrophe; in terms of human suffering it is the greatest disaster New Zealand has ever experienced. The massacre at Passchendaele very nearly broke the spirit of the New Zealand Division. Then, in November 1917, came another failed attack at Polderhoek Chateau, with heavy casualties. From December 1917 through to February 1918 the New Zealand Division was in the Ypres salient, a period one writer has aptly described as 'dreary weeks of trench fighting in desolate wintry places'.[7] Though little fighting occurred during those two months, New Zealand battle casualties numbered 877 — 25 per cent of them were the result of poisonous gas. But evacuations of New Zealand soldiers who fell sick during this period were much higher: some 1788, 730 of whom were suffering from trench fever.[8]

From late February 1918 the soldiers of the New Zealand Division were rested and began to recover their health and spirits. The fine weather in early March 1918 helped considerably, as did the fact they were now out of the terrible Ypres salient. Time for personal administration and periods of moderate physical training also provided welcome relief. Unfortunately it was all too brief. On the first day of the *Kaiserschlacht* the New Zealand Division was placed in Army Reserve, and two days later, on 23 March 1918, it began a long trek towards the threatened areas of the British front line. Just three days after starting this march towards the sound of the guns, the first New Zealanders were in action against an enemy flushed with victory.

So, after suffering New Zealand's worst ever military defeat five months before and spending a 'winter of discontent' in the most dangerous sector of the line, and with only a few weeks of rest from this ordeal, the New Zealand Division was facing Germany's greatest offensive of the war. Once there, they were asked to plug a huge gap in the line. This book concentrates on the division's experiences and the actions it fought against the Germans in the valley of the Ancre River in March–April 1918. It was here that the New Zealanders made their most vital contribution to the Allied victory, yet, like so many New Zealand experiences in the First World War, their ordeals and achievements during those weeks remain unknown to most New Zealanders. These New Zealand soldiers played a decisive role in stopping the German storm of fire and steel that erupted on 21 March 1918. Here, for the first time, is their story.

Chapter 1

Storm Clouds

Nineteen-seventeen was the hardest year of the war for the European Allies, a time of disasters and defeats. So severe were most of these setbacks that they altered the strategic situation in favour of Germany. All of the four major Allies — Britain, France, Russia and Italy — were seriously weakened and, in the case of Imperial Russia, the wounds inflicted proved fatal.

In 1917 Russia suffered the twin evils of disastrous defeat on the battlefield and revolution on the home front. It was more than the fragile Romanov Empire could stand. Most of Russia's armies had dissolved by the middle of 1917 and, at the end of November, the new revolutionary government, which the Germans had helped to create, formally requested an armistice. At the start of 1918, as General Max Hoffman, the German Chief of Staff in the East so graphically put it, 'The whole of Russia is no more than a vast heap of maggots.'[1] The collapse of Russia altered the military balance of power in the war. Masses of men and artillery could now be released for service on the Western Front and armaments captured from defeated Russia and Romania could also be used. From November 1917, General Erich Ludendorff, the man effectively running the German war effort, was able to transfer land forces to the Western Front at the rate of two divisions a week. This would give Germany numerical superiority and the initiative on the Western Front, something they had not held since launching the Verdun offensive at the beginning of 1916. According to Cyril Falls, the elimination of Russia 'gave Germany her first and only chance of redeeming the loss of the Battle of the Marne in 1914 by winning the war on land'.[2]

There was something equally sinister about the defeat of Russia on the Eastern Front. Hostilities between Russia and Germany were not formally concluded until the signing of the Treaty of Brest-Litovsk in March 1918. Brest-Litovsk was a conqueror's peace and it was harsh. Russia lost 34 per cent of its population, 32 per cent of its agricultural land, 54 per cent of its industry and 89 per cent of its coalmines. The treaty showed the Allies the type of peace they could expect if Germany won the war. As John Terraine has aptly commented, 'Brest-Litovsk, too often forgotten now, was, in fact, what the war was about'.[3]

If Russia's condition was terminal at the end of 1917, it appeared to many that Italy's situation was not much better. After more than two years of costly, inconclusive battles on Italy's Isonzo Front, on 24 October 1917 an Austro-Hungarian army, backed up by the German strategic reserve of six divisions, launched an offensive that routed the Italian Second Army and completely ruptured the Italian front line. Italian casualties were heavy, more than 300,000, and the Second Army lost over half its strength in less than a week. The Battle of Caporetto, as this offensive is known, came close to knocking Italy out of the war. The crisis was averted largely due to poor weather, which made it impossible for the Germans and Austrians to sustain their offensive. In an effort to prop up an ally on the verge of collapse, five British and six French divisions were sent from France to Italy, along with a large number of heavy guns, planes and other matériel. Such a large diversion of troops came at a very dangerous time. The Western Front was the decisive theatre of operations in this war. Not only were the Germans increasing their numbers there as a result of their victory over Russia, but the French and British armies were in poor shape and stretched dangerously thin.

In 1918 the French Army was recovering from three years of butchery and bloodshed. The French had suffered massive casualties since the start of the war and the failure of the much-publicised Neville Offensive of April 1917 was the final straw. It had promised so much but delivered so little and, as a result, the French Army was seriously damaged. Soldiers in 54 divisions, nearly half the army, demanded better treatment for the rank and file and an end to the butchery. They refused to take part in further offensive actions. These mutinies meant that, for a considerable period, the French Army was incapable of any more large-scale offensive operations. General Henri Pétain took over the running of the French Army during this troubled time and slowly nursed it back to health. By the beginning of 1918, French military morale had improved but the army had lost its fighting spirit. Its poor condition was reflected in Pétain's strategy for victory: to wait for the Americans and the tanks.[4]

After three failed and costly British offensives on the Western Front in 1917 the British Expeditionary Force (BEF) was also in a bad state. In January 1918, after losing the equivalent of half an army to the Italian Front, the BEF consisted of four field armies. These comprised 47 British divisions, four Canadian divisions, five Australian divisions and the New Zealand Division. There were also five cavalry divisions, an anachronism in this war, each about a third of the strength of an infantry division. The key problem, which was especially acute at the beginning of 1918 and would plague the BEF for the rest of the war, was shortage of men. At the end of 1917, the British Army Council asked for an immediate draft of 250,000 men, 95,000 of whom were needed to bring the infantry battalions in France up to strength. A further 350,000 men were required to cover wastage over the next seven months. The council was told that these numbers were excessive and that it probably would not get them. Called home to consult the War Cabinet on 7 January 1918 about his manpower requirements, Field Marshal Douglas Haig, the BEF commander, committed a crucial blunder. As Field Marshal Sir William Robertson, the Chief of the Imperial General Staff, explained to him:

> For a long time past they [the War Cabinet] have been trying to persuade me to say that the Germans may not attack this year. Unfortunately you gave as your opinion this morning that they would not do so, and I noticed as Lord Derby also did, that they jumped at the statement . . .
>
> The long and the short of it is that the cabinet think that by giving us a hundred thousand men this year in place of six hundred thousand we have asked for, you will be able to hold your own. Personally, I think that it is doubtful. My belief is that the Germans will make the heaviest attack possible this year.[5]

Two days later the notoriously inarticulate Haig[6] attempted to recover from this blunder by reversing his view. The damage was already done, however, and Haig's volte-face was exploited by a hostile Prime Minister, David Lloyd George, who asked his Cabinet, 'What is the value of a man's opinion who says one thing one day and the opposite the next?'[7]

Haig did not get the 600,000 men he requested. The Royal Navy, the newly created Royal Air Force, ship building, munitions and food production were all to have priority in terms of manpower allocation.

Haig was given 100,000 Category A men, with another 100,000 available from lower medical categories should they be needed. The irony was that the men Haig required were readily available. There was an enormous Home Army in Britain supposedly necessary in the most unlikely event of a German invasion — 1.5 million men, 449,000 of whom were medically fit and over nineteen, the official minimum age for overseas service.

There was also another barb to the War Cabinet's January decision. As Anthony Farrar-Hockley has pointed out, though he was aware of the dangers presented by the collapse of Russia, Lloyd George was 'blinded by his mistrust of Haig and Robertson . . . He fell back on the age-old remedy of administrators lacking original ideas: reorganisation.'[8] The War Cabinet directed Haig to make up his shortfall by reducing the number of cavalry divisions in the BEF and by cutting the number of battalions in an infantry division from twelve to nine. In 1916 the Germans had reorganised their divisions to contain only nine battalions and the French had soon followed their example. But Germany and France had made this change in order to form new divisions from the withdrawn regiments (of three battalions). When the BEF was ordered to carry out this reorganisation in 1918, it was not done to create new military formations, but to beef up those that remained.

The British Army Council protested about being forced to make these changes, warning of the dire consequences:

> There is every prospect of heavy fighting on the Western Front from February onwards, and the result may well be that even if the divisions successfully withstand the shock of the earlier attack, they may become so exhausted and attenuated as to be incapable of continuing the struggle until the Americans can effectually intervene. In short, the Council would regard the acceptance of the recommendations in the draft report, without further effort to provide the men they consider necessary for the maintenance of the forces in the field during 1918, as taking an unreasonably grave risk of losing the War and sacrificing to no purpose the British Army on the Western Front.[9]

The War Cabinet remained unmoved and ignored the warning, ordering the reorganisation on 10 January 1918. Effectively, 145 battalions would disappear from the British order of battle. Many British historians have been scathing about these forced changes, and their timing. John Terraine's comments are typical:

> So, as the German preparations for the greatest battle of the war remorselessly proceeded, the British Commander-in-Chief found himself forced to disband two of his five cavalry divisions (another Cabinet Committee edict) and was given a list of 145 infantry battalions out of which he was permitted to select the four which might survive and the 141 which must go.[10]

It took some time to implement these alterations. The disruption and the effect on the morale of those whose units were disestablished can only be imagined. Esprit de corps built up over years of fighting was killed off overnight with the stroke of a pen. Three of the British armies were reorganised during the last two weeks of February 1918 but the changes in the Fourth Army were not complete until 4 March, only two and a half weeks before the *Kaiserschlacht*. In all 115 battalions were disbanded, 38 were amalgamated to form nineteen new units and seven were converted to pioneer battalions. (These provided labour for digging trenches and other duties.) The British Army's peacetime training had been based on their divisions containing three brigades with four battalions in each. For three years the British had fought all their battles in this formation and now 'on the eve of the impending German offensive, they had to reorganise their thinking'.[11] They would not have had time to do so.

Even then, British divisions remained significantly understrength and the BEF was certainly incapable of mounting the large-scale offensive that was the hidden purpose behind this reorganisation. Those battalions that survived were supposed to number around 1000, but the lack of reinforcements meant that, in 1918, most were down to 600 men.

Of the ten dominion divisions, only the Australians were forced by severe manpower shortages to disband individual units, a price paid for Australia's refusal to introduce conscription. By the end of 1917, as Jeffrey Grey has noted, 'The effort of maintaining a field force of approximately 117,000 men in France was becoming too great for Australia to bear.'[12] The Canadians and New Zealanders retained twelve battalions in their infantry divisions, making them significantly stronger than their British counterparts. The New Zealand Division did disband its fourth infantry brigade but used it to provide a pool of reinforcements and to form three entrenching battalions as a divisional reserve. This restructuring made the New Zealand Division the strongest on the Western Front.[13] (For a breakdown of the structure of the New Zealand Division, see Appendix 2, page 271.)

Another factor added to the weakness of the BEF in 1918. From the last few months of 1917 Haig was under increasing pressure to extend the British line by taking over an additional sector from the French, who wanted a more equitable share of the front line. At the beginning of 1918 the French armies were holding 350 miles of trench lines with 108 divisions, each equipped with nine infantry battalions, making a total of 972 battalions. The BEF was holding 100 miles of trench line with 62 divisions, but each British division had twelve infantry battalions and a pioneer battalion, making a total of 806.[14] On paper it looked grossly unfair, but the reality was different. A large section of the French line, some 150 miles to the east of St Mihiel, was virtually inactive and only one-seventh of the French Army was garrisoned here. The British sector in northern France and Belgium was an extremely active part of the front: 69 German divisions faced the British across no-man's-land. The long French front line faced 79 German divisions. Since May 1917, the BEF had done the bulk of fighting on the Western Front; the French armies had not fought a major action. Also, a French soldier enjoyed three times the leave entitlements of his British counterpart, so the French divisions in the line were never at their full establishments.

Yet the French felt they were being cheated and that Britain was not doing her fair share. On one occasion, French Prime Minister Georges Clemenceau, known as 'The Tiger', even threatened to resign if the BEF did not extend its front line. Since increased responsibilities in France also suited the British government, it did not resist this pressure as firmly as it could have and Haig again lost the argument. On 14 December 1917 the Supreme War Council decided that Britain would take over an additional 26 miles of the French front, covering the sector opposite St Quentin and south towards Barisis. General Sir Hubert Gough, whose Fifth Army later had responsibility for this new sector, was scathing about the logic behind extending the British line and the pressure to 'equalise' the burden:

> This was an extremely superficial way of deciding on the disposi-
> tion of troops. A sound consideration should naturally take into

account the strength of the enemy in front and the importance of the bases it covered. In January 1918 there were nearly twice as many German divisions massed opposite the smaller British front, than there were opposite the French front. Moreover, behind the English front, within easy striking distance, lay the Channel ports — all vital bases of supply for our Army.[15]

The extension of the line, which was completed by the end of January, entailed the creation of a new army, the Fifth Army, under the command of General Gough. When the Fifth Army took over the additional 26 miles from the French, they found the state of the trench system extremely poor. The French assured them, however, that this was a quiet sector and that swamps on either side of the Oise River guaranteed no danger of attack. The extension meant that the BEF held the line very thinly, especially in this new sector. The Fifth Army was to hold a front of 42 miles, much longer than any held by the other British armies. The Fifth Army had the smallest number of infantry divisions — only twelve. Its 58th Division, the last BEF division on the right flank, was holding a front of 10 miles, the longest held by any British division. Spread so thinly, and without adequate reserves, the Fifth Army was an exceptionally soft target, and it would bear the brunt of the German offensive.

Why had the British government agreed to all these measures which they knew must weaken the BEF in France? The answer lies in the total breakdown of trust and confidence between the military commanders represented by Haig and Robertson, and the British government headed by Lloyd George. By the end of 1917 Lloyd George was convinced that Haig was incompetent as a military commander, yet he lacked the power to remove him. In his view, and it was not without foundation, Haig had squandered men's lives on the Somme and at Passchendaele. If Haig had his way, he would do it all again in 1918: his preferred strategy was to continue the Flanders offensive when the good weather arrived. This would renew the series of attacks that had ground to a bloody halt in the mud of Passchendaele in November 1917. Haig believed, and he was almost alone in this, that the Germans' morale was close to cracking and that one more great offensive would break them. The senior officers of France, Italy and Belgium, however, favoured remaining on the defensive in 1918 until a large United States Army was ready to take the field in 1919. This was the policy Lloyd George also favoured.

Rather than more attritional stalemates on the Western Front, with their huge and politically damaging 'butchers' bills', Lloyd George wanted to concentrate on sideshows and to knock away Germany's props of Turkey, Bulgaria and Austria. British strategic plans for 1918 were decided at the Supreme War Council in January 1918. There would be no major offensive on the Western Front until 1919 when the Allies would have masses of tanks, planes and guns and the armies of the United States. In 1918, the British would make Palestine their main offensive. The British armies in France were deliberately being kept weak in order to prevent a renewal of the offensive in Flanders.

There were several problems with this strategy. The first was that Germany was propping up its allies; they were not vital to her war effort. The second was that the Western Front, as Haig and Robertson recognised, was the decisive front of the war. Haig was also correct in his assertions that the Somme and Ypres Offensive had seriously damaged the fighting quality of the German Army. Yet now, while the Germans were concentrating their efforts on the Western Front, the BEF was being reduced in strength. Third, this strategy required the BEF to stand on the defensive for all of 1918, requiring tactics with which they were wholly unfamiliar. According to the British official war historian, Sir James Edmonds, after two and a half years of offensive warfare the BEF 'were not well trained to stand on the defensive and to deal with attacks by infiltration; they were totally untrained in the carrying out of a retreat'.[16] Finally, as the historian of the New Zealand Rifle Brigade recognised, 'It was clear that for a time the initiative must pass from the Allies to the Germans. A defensive policy was therefore adopted, and preparations were made to meet a strong and sustained hostile offensive.'[17]

The initiative did not automatically pass to the Germans on the Western Front in 1918; it was gifted to them by the Allies' chosen strategy. Though the British government was fully aware of the growing German concentration against the Allies on the Western Front, they accepted the risks associated with keeping the BEF in a weakened state. Part of their risk assessment was based on recent British failures. According to Winston Churchill, at the time munitions minister in the War Cabinet, the British government 'believed that the Germans if they attacked would encounter the same difficulties as so long baffled us, and that our armies were amply strong enough for defence'.[18] Seeking to restrict Haig's activities on the Western Front by subterfuge rather than by direct instructions to him would seriously impair the fighting effectiveness of the BEF in the early months of 1918. This was 'unlikely to avoid the merited censure of posterity'.[19]

The strategy decided upon by the Allies in 1918 recognised that the United States would eventually become a key player on the Western Front. The entry of the Americans into the war in April 1917 compensated in some respects for the Russians leaving the war at the end of the year. Historian John Mosier has christened the period from April 1917 to April 1918 'the Great Race': could the United States Army take the field before the Germans won the war in the west?[20] At the beginning of 1918, though, the Germans were clearly winning. In 1917 the United States was in no state for decisive and immediate intervention. It possessed a formidable naval fleet that could be used immediately, but its army was 'only a skeleton and to put flesh upon it was going to be a long task, which would show no results at all for some time'.[21] Raising, equipping, training and sustaining a large field army would take considerable time and effort. In April 1917, the United States Army did not have even a single division and there were serious shortages in the most basic of equipment. The American military possessed no aircraft or trained pilots and industry was not geared for war production. Added to the problems of creating a field army from scratch were the difficulties of getting this army to France. Shipping space was at a premium and added to the length of time before the United States could deploy its armies. At the beginning of 1918, there were only four American divisions in France — the 1st, 2nd, 26th and 42nd Divisions, totalling 130,000 troops. But these men had to be equipped and trained before they could take to the battlefield, and even then they could not be used. Unless it was a dire emergency, the American commander General John Pershing refused to allow his troops to be committed piecemeal. These newly raised American divisions would be allowed to fight only as part of a United States-led army. Given that it had taken Britain almost two years to raise an army capable of large-scale offensive action on the Western Front, little could be expected from the Americans until the second half of 1918.

In his brilliant history of the First World War, Cyril Falls neatly encapsulated the strategy forced upon the belligerents on the Western Front. According to him, the stronger side had no option but to carry out offensive operations: 'And if the stronger side did not attack on the Western Front it played into the hands of the weaker, which asked nothing better than it should be left in peace during the phase of weakness.'[22]

By the early months of 1918 Germany had the strongest army in France, but her military leaders knew this would not long be the case. They were determined, therefore, to exploit this temporary position of strength. General Ludendorff would make the strongest possible attack against the BEF where it was weakest. Victory here could split the Allies and win the war.

Although the German Army possessed some of the world's most talented military intellects, by 1918, its fate lay in the hands of one man, the First Quartermaster General, Erich Ludendorff. A man of mixed ability and unstable temperament, he alone dictated the army's strategy and tactics. As Churchill wrote of Ludendorff's influence in 1918, 'We must regard him at this juncture as the dominating will.'[23] Though Ludendorff was nominally subordinate to Field Marshal Paul von Hindenburg and the Kaiser, he had almost unfettered powers of command over the German Army. As he stated frankly in his memoirs, 'My sense of responsibility was far too great. I alone had to decide, of that I remained conscious throughout.'[24]

In 1918, the German Army was in a paradoxical situation. Numerically it had never been stronger, yet in terms of quality it was 'in palpable decline'.[25] The collapse of Russia and Romania meant that, for the first time, the Germans outnumbered their opponents on the Western Front. As Ludendorff later recorded, the military situation was 'more favourable to us . . . than one could have ever expected'.[26] However, three years of attritional warfare had taken a heavy toll on the German Army. Its best soldiers had become casualties and it was riddled with what Ludendorff called 'skulkers', men who disappeared during dangerous periods and reappeared when things had quietened down.[27] There was an acute shortage of men caused by an 'uncommonly high' desertion rate.[28] Tens of thousands of German deserters had fled to internment in neutral Holland and an equal number were living in Germany where sympathetic local authorities seemed happy to turn a blind eye.

It seemed, then, that the strategy of attrition initiated by the Germans at Verdun and adopted by the Allies on the Somme in 1916 and in several offensives in 1917 'was at last bearing fruit'.[29] The last thing the German High Command wanted in 1918 was a repeat of the Allied offensives of 1917, which had inflicted heavy casualties and, more importantly, drained the army's morale. In order to survive, the German army needed to attack and now had the numbers to do so, as Ludendorff made clear in his memoirs:

> Against the weight of the enemy's material the troops no longer displayed their old stubbornness; they thought with horror of fresh defensive battles and longed for a war of movement . . . As they were depressed by defence their spirits rose in the offensive. The interests of the Army were best served by the offensive; in defence it was bound gradually to succumb to the ever-increasing hostile superiority in men and material. This feeling was shared by everybody. In the West the Army pined for the offensive . . . It amounted to a definite conviction which obsessed them utterly that nothing but an offensive could win the war.[30]

Ludendorff made the decision to launch a major offensive in the spring of 1918 at a conference at Mons on 11 November 1917. As we have seen, from November 1917 the German Army started transferring infantry divisions from the east to the west at the rate of two divisions a week and by mid-March 1918 had an additional 46 divisions on the Western Front. These were fresh and at full strength. When the Germans began the offensive on 21 March they had a total of 192 divisions;[31] the Allies could field only 175. By May 1918 the number of German divisions had peaked at 208 while that of the Allies had fallen to 173.[32] In addition, the Hindenburg Industrial Scheme enabled Ludendorff to recall 123,000 men from industry to the army. By the opening day of the attack 136,618 German officers and 3,438,288 other ranks were crammed into the Western Front ready for action.[33]

A significant number of guns accompanied the million men who came from the east. These included German and Austrian artillery pieces now regarded as surplus, as well as weapons recently captured from the Russians and Italians. Some 3000 of these guns, 1000 classified as heavy, now appeared on the Western Front ready for action.

How was this mighty array of military force to be used? Though the decision about a major offensive was made on 11 November, the plans for how that offensive would unfold were not finalised until 21 January 1918. The reason for the delay was the number of options open to Ludendorff, which made it difficult to decide where to attack. There were three obvious sectors: in Flanders in the north between Ypres and Lens, on both sides of Verdun in the south, and between Arras and St Quentin in the centre of the line. After consideration Ludendorff decided to attack on both sides of the town of St Quentin. There were compelling strategic and tactical reasons for attacking at this point: 'here the attack would strike the enemy's weakest point, the ground offered no difficulties, and it was feasible in all seasons . . . If this blow succeeded the strategic result might indeed be enormous, as we could separate the bulk of the English Army from the French and crowd it up with its back to the sea.'[34]

The objective of the attack was to separate the French and British Armies at their junction some 30 miles south of Cambrai. The BEF would be then forced back to the Channel with 'little room for manoeuvre and none for escape'.[35] It would be hemmed in against the coast, leaving the Germans free to deal with the French. Both armies would be tied to their critical vulnerabilities — the BEF to the Channel ports and the French to Paris. There they could be isolated and defeated. It was hoped that the BEF and the French armies would become so exhausted during the offensive and subsequent withdrawal that they would sue for peace. An ambitious timetable was set for the offensive. It aimed to push the British back over the Somme on the first day, enforce a general retreat down the Somme Valley on the second day and take the strategic town of Arras by the third day.

This attack, given the name Michael, was to be the main effort of the German offensive and other attacks (named Mars and George) were planned to supplement it. Michael was to be an immense undertaking involving 74 divisions, three armies and a combined soldiery larger than the 1918 population of New Zealand. Orders for Michael were issued on 10 March 1918. Attacking across an enormous front of 50 miles, from the Oise to Croisilles near Arras, were three armies divided between two army groups. In the north was the Seventeenth Army newly arrived from Italy and commanded by General Otto von Below. In the centre was General von der Marwitz's Second Army. Both these armies were in the Army Group of Crown Prince Rupprecht of Bavaria and they were to make the main inroads in this attack by cutting off the Cambrai salient on each side and pushing through to Croisilles and Péronne. Protecting the left flank of Rupprecht's armies was the Eighteenth Army under General Oscar von Hutier, who had only recently arrived from the Eastern Front where he had a formidable reputation. He had been instrumental in breaking the Russian Army at Riga in September 1917 and had pioneered new artillery techniques to do so. When given his new command von Hutier insisted on bringing his artillery expert from the Eastern Front, Lieutenant Colonel Georg Bruchmüller. Von Hutier's Eighteenth Army was in the army group of the German Crown Prince.[36] The Seventeenth Army would attack in the Arras area against the BEF's Third Army. The other two armies, numbering 43 divisions, would attack the weakest of the British armies, the Fifth, then comprising only twelve divisions. Michael was an undertaking deserving of the name *Kaiserschlacht*.

The offensive aimed to pierce and break through the Allies' front line, sending them reeling back in defeat. This was what both sides on the Western Front had been attempting to do for the past three years, without success. Solving the problem of endemic trench warfare required a new sort of offensive tactics. At the end of 1917 the German Army came up with an innovative set of solutions, quite an achievement given that the Germans had not taken offensive action on the Western Front for more than a year. Reviving some of the earlier principles of offensive operations and combining them with the recent lessons of the failed Allied offensives, the Germans introduced several tactical innovations aimed at breaking the deadlock of trench warfare. As Ludendorff explained in a set of notes issued in January 1918, the success of any offensive operation depended on skilful leadership at all levels and on adaptability:

> our attack must differ essentially in this respect from the attacks hitherto undertaken by the British. The British believed in the efficacy of their skilfully worked out but rigid artillery barrage; this was to carry forward the infantry attack, which advanced without any impetus of its own. The subordinate and, still more, the higher commanders ceased to have any further influence.[37]

Although the recent British attacks — Somme, Arras, Messines, Flanders and Cambrai — had caused considerable alarm, 'the initial tactical successes, which were frequently very considerable, were not seized upon and were not usefully exploited. A defeat was eventually the outcome of this narrow-minded principle on which the conduct of the battle and the leadership was based.'[38] As British novelist, biographer and military historian, John Buchan, wrote of the 1918 offensive, Germany 'deserves all credit for a brilliant departure from routine, a true intellectual effort to rethink the main problem of modern war'.[39] The novel use of infantry soldiers and some innovative employment of artillery amounted to a revolution in military firepower.

In the German infantry companies, the light machine guns ceased to be regarded as auxiliary weapons and became standard infantry weapons. This increased firepower was further enhanced by quick-firing weapons of all kinds, plus various sorts of rifle grenades and the flame-thrower. The infantry units and sub-units were augmented by sections of heavy machine guns and light trench mortars. German infantry units were classified into three types. The best soldiers, in some cases whole battalions of them, were chosen as *Sturmabteilungen* or storm troops. Divided into mobile teams armed with light machine guns, mortars and flame-throwers, they had the task of penetrating the enemy lines where they were weakest. They would lead the assault but not in packed ranks. They acted more like skirmishers, except that there were large numbers of these small groups all closing on the enemy at speed. They would head the assault, pressing on through weakly held positions and past any centres of resistance, which would be left to the waves of infantry following them. If possible, the storm troops were to break through and threaten the enemy's artillery positions. As the vanguard of the assault, the storm troops were to be constantly kept up to strength by reinforcement and they received priority for all vital equipment — stores, horses, support weapons and rations. Behind the storm troops came the battle units. These were composed of regular infantry units, machine guns, trench mortars, engineers, field artillery and ammunition carriers. Their task was to mop up the strong points bypassed by the storm troops. In the third category were the poorer quality soldiers whose sole job was to occupy trenches.

The other main innovation involved the use of artillery, the focus of the storm troops' tactics. The German artillery for this offensive was concentrated in numbers 'in a quantity never before dreamed of, and used with great sophistication'.[40] They would be controlled by the outstanding artillerist Colonel Bruchmüller. All guns to be used in the offensive were tested for individual errors behind the lines and a simple table was constructed for each one, explaining how to adjust it when firing on a target. Ranges were accurately measured. Maps were made as accurate as possible and targets plotted on them using the techniques of flash spotting, sound ranging and aerial photography. A great deal of work had to be done before the attack. The artillery bombardment unleashed to support the offensive would be short, only a few hours long, but it would be enormous and ferocious. Ludendorff's 'battering ram' consisted of 3965 field and medium guns, 2435 heavy and 73 super-heavy guns and howitzers. By comparison, on the opening day of the Somme the BEF had used 149 heavy and 18 super-heavy guns.[41]

Once the German artillery had had sufficient time to pound the British artillery and front-line trenches, the German infantry in its forward positions would then advance behind a powerful creeping barrage. The offensive would be supported by over 700 aircraft but by very few tanks. In the vital sector of the Third and Fifth Armies there were 730 German planes, 326 of which were single-seater fighters. Opposing them was the Royal Flying Corps with 579 machines, including 261 single-seater fighters. These numbers are significant. As the British official historian later stated, 'For the first time, the German air concentration for battle on the Western Front was greater than that of the Royal Flying Corps.'[42] Tanks were a different matter. In March 1918, the German Army possessed only fifteen tanks of their own design and a small number of captured English ones. Tanks would be used on only one sector, near St Quentin. Ludendorff did not rate tanks highly as weapons of war and therefore he 'had not recognised their value or ensured their provision'.[43]

So, in essence, the German assault of 1918 involved no preliminary massing of troops. Men would be brought up by night marches only just before zero hour, thus achieving a tactical surprise. There was to be no long artillery preparation to alarm the enemy. The attack would be preceded by a short, intense bombardment that would deluge the enemy's back areas and support lines with gas shells. The infantry assault, following hard on the heels of a creeping barrage, would be made with picked troops, in small clusters, armed with many automatic weapons. Their aim was to punch small holes in the front line through which they could infiltrate, outflank and encircle. A system of flares and rockets would let the battle units know where the gaps had been made. The storm troops at the front of the offensive had unlimited objectives, rations and ammunition to last them for several days. When one unit of the storm troops tired or suffered heavy casualties, another took its place, 'like a continuous game of leap-frog'.[44] Ludendorff's tactical notes were emphatic on the use of reserves. They 'will . . . not be thrown into the battle at points where the attack has been held up by strong points and centres of resistance, and where unnecessary sacrifice is involved, but at points where the attack is still in movement and its progress can be facilitated with a view to breaking down the enemy's resistance in the neighbouring sector by rolling it up from flank and rear.'[45] Acknowledging that the position of all commanders was 'of considerable importance', Ludendorff directed that 'All staffs, including Corps staffs, must be on the battlefield, the divisional staffs being pushed well forward'.[46] In many respects, with the exception of the absence of tanks, this new method of attack had a 'modern' look.

For the last two months of 1917 and the first two months of 1918 the German Army was trained in these new techniques, 'another tremendous task', according to Ludendorff.[47] There was no time to prepare every division: only 56, and a large proportion of the German artillery, underwent this training. But all levels of command were involved, including the higher level commanders, staff officers, officers and soldiers, and it was comprehensive. In his autobiographical account of the war, Ernst Junger described the training scheme for this offensive as 'marvellously clear', with Ludendorff's directive being distributed 'even to company commands'.[48] Fourteen of the storm troop divisions trained with aircraft and practised new techniques of close air support. The training culminated in live firing exercises which included having the infantry advance behind a creeping barrage. With nearly every available slope behind the front line being used as a firing range it was little wonder that there were many casualties. Junger described the bullets as 'whistl[ing] about the country very much as in a battle' and admitted that a machine gunner in his company accidentally shot the commanding officer of another unit from his horse while that unfortunate man was reviewing his troops. 'Fortunately the wound was not mortal, and equally fortunately the deed was not clearly brought home to us.'[49] By the end of February the trained units began the lengthy process of moving into position for the attack. As Junger wrote, 'Training was over; and now we came to the business, not a wheel of the machine was to be checked.'[50]

According to John Terraine, the 1918 German offensive was 'the decisive battle of the war'.[51] The Germans understood the importance of the forthcoming offensive and the stakes involved. As Ludendorff was well aware, it was a huge gamble that would either win or lose the war.

> All that had gone before was merely a means to the one end of creating a situation that would make it a feasible operation . . . That the attack in the West would be one of the most difficult operations in history I was perfectly sure, and I did not hide the fact. The German nation too, would have to give all it had.[52]

When Ludendorff met the Kaiser and the Imperial Chancellor at Hamburg on 13 February 1918, he told them that

> The battle in the West is the greatest military task that has ever been imposed upon an army, and one in which England and France have been trying for two years to compass . . . I believe too, that I, who have to furnish the Field Marshal with the foundation on which he bases his request for His Majesty's decision, am more than anyone impressed by the immensity of the undertaking . . . The Army in the West is waiting for the opportunity to act. We must not imagine that this offensive will be like those in Gallicia or Italy; it will be an immense struggle that will begin at one point, continue at another, and take a long time; it is difficult, but it will be victorious.

Ludendorff concluded by reporting to his emperor 'that the Army was assembled and well prepared to undertake the biggest task in its history'.[53]

Because of the enormity of the task before them, the German troops were told that the Emperor was in command — this would be the *Kaiserschlacht*, his battle. It was for this reason that von Hutier's army was placed under the German Crown Prince (and would in the course of the battle compete with the other armies for the lion's share of the glory). The Kaiser and his generals were also hoping that, by giving the German people the decisive victory they craved, they would restore the waning prestige of the royal house. The future of the House of Hohenzollern and the fate of the German nation were the ultimate stakes in Ludendorff's massive gamble. To paraphrase Gary Sheffield, in 1918 the German Army risked everything to obtain victory on the Western Front. Failure could cost them everything.[54]

That there would be a great German offensive in the early months of

1918 was the worst kept military secret of the war. For example, on 16 March 1918, the German Minister of the Interior, Karl Helfferich, delivered a public lecture on Germany and England. He told his audience that the outcome of the war would be decided very soon on the battlefields of France: 'Where is Hindenburg? . . . *He stands in the West with our whole German manhood for the first time united in a single theatre of war, ready to strike with the strongest army that the world has ever known.'*[55] Allied military intelligence detected the German build-up of troops and material. In the first week of February 1918, for example, the Fifth Army's intelligence section reported that the Germans had 64 divisions, all trained and rested and within three nights' march of St Quentin, the town opposite the centre of their line. This was how the Germans had massed their forces before their successful attacks at Riga and Caporetto. The Army Commander, General Gough, passed this information on to GHQ and to his corps commanders. Gough had also discovered that von Hutier, new to the Western Front, was commanding the Germans.

Warnings also came from other sources. Early in the year, the King of Spain informed the French military attaché in Madrid that 'a great blow to end the War was intended, and that it was already imminent and likely to be struck in February'.[56] As Ludendorff noted in his memoirs, 'All the world, including the Entente, knew we were going to attack in the West.'[57]

The problem for the Allies, though, was that they did not know where or when the attack was coming. An elaborate German deception plan gave their entire front the appearance of preparing to mount a large-scale offensive in the immediate future. Meanwhile the real build-up continued, well concealed from the Allies. The Germans occupied an area of France well served by an intricate railway network, which meant they were capable of strategic surprise.

So what did the Allies, and in particular the British upon whom the mighty blow was soon to fall, do to prepare for the imminent offensive?

Forced onto the defensive by a lack of reinforcements, the British Army had some serious problems. It had fought defensive battles in 1914–15, but by 1918 the men who had conducted them were mostly gone. From 1916 to 1917 the BEF had concentrated its education and experience on offensive action. Now training and education for a defensive role was urgently required. But preparing for a withdrawal over many miles 'never entered anyone's mind'.[58] To ready itself for this new role the British Army attempted to copy the German methods of defence that had successfully thwarted their efforts over the last two years. In doing so, they misunderstood the key principles behind the German methods and applied them wrongly.

The British had captured German manuals of defensive techniques soon after they were issued in August 1917. On 14 December the BEF's GHQ issued instructions as to how their front line should be defended using the 'German' methods. The line was divided into three zones of defence: the Forward Zone (called the Outpost Zone by the Germans) the Battle Zone and the Rear Zone. The Forward Zone was the apex of the front line. Supposed to be lightly held, it relied on many machine guns for its firepower. Its task was to guard against surprise and compel the enemy to deploy strong forces in order to capture it. It was intended to drain any attack of its momentum. Behind the Forward Zone, on the ground most suited to defensive warfare, was the Battle Zone. It could be anywhere from 600 yards to as much as 3 miles from the Forward Zone but was usually 1 to 2 miles behind it. The Battle Zone was about 3000 yards deep. Designed to repulse whatever attack the enemy might make, it was heavily fortified by mutually supporting redoubts and machine-gun nests. This ground was to be held at all costs, even if meant deploying corps or army reserves.

An attack should be halted in the Battle Zone, but in case it wasn't a Rear Zone was also to be constructed as the ground of last resort, the area to which the defence could fall back if necessary. The Rear Zone was to be about 4 to 8 miles behind the Battle Zone. Owing to a shortage of labour, in 1918 the Rear Zone had only been reconnoitred and marked out for construction. In some parts of the British line, it consisted of 'the removal of a spit of turf to show where the trench should be dug'.[59]

Simply copying the enemy's methods without understanding why they worked eventually proved disastrous for the BEF. The January 1918 change of name from Outpost Zone to Forward Zone indicates how little the British understood of the German methods of defence. An Outpost Zone implied that the ground was not to be seriously contested and that there would be a withdrawal only when things got too hot for the defenders. Yet in March 1918 some of the BEF's Forward Zones were more than 2 miles wide, impeding a hasty withdrawal, making support from the Battle Zone difficult and allowing the Forward Zone to be surrounded. The troops holding the Forward Zone were instructed to 'do all in their power to maintain their ground against attack'.[60] The danger was, and it did eventuate, that good troops would be sacrificed trying to hold ground of no vital importance.

The German method of defence in depth relied on a decentralised method of control which the British, in early 1918, were ill prepared to practise. As an American historian has recently commented,

> On the one hand, the British failed to grasp the key basis of German defensive success, the holding back of most of the infantry so the attackers would be sucked into a trap, blasted by artillery, exhausted by their trek, and then wiped out by the developing counterattack. In actual practice, most British infantry were too far forward. On the other hand, British practice was such that there was no possibility of giving low-level unit commanders the authority they needed to determine when and where to fight. German tactics worked because the Germans decentralized decision making downward. Simply copying their troop dispositions hardly solved the problem.[61]

In March 1918, the British attempt to emulate the German system of defence proved a total failure.

On 10 January 1918, XVIII Corps of the Fifth Army, under Lieutenant General Sir Ivor Maxse, began the takeover of a sector of the line previously held by the French Sixth Army. This meant that the British front line was now 26 miles longer. The newly acquired portion of the front did not have the three zones of defence. Only a belt of wire marked the second, vital zone. To hold this 126-mile line, Haig had 59 divisions consisting of 47 British divisions, four Canadian, five Australian, one New Zealand and two Portuguese divisions. He also had three cavalry divisions, each the equivalent in size of an infantry brigade. Haig's dispositions showed that his main concern was his left flank and the Channel ports. From the coast to the link with the French Army Haig spread his forces as follows. The Second Army, nearest the coast, held 23 miles of front with twelve divisions. Next came the First Army, stretching to Vimy, a distance of 33 miles which it held with fourteen divisions. Third Army held its 28 miles of front with fourteen divisions. Anchoring the British right flank was the Fifth Army, which had twelve divisions (plus three cavalry divisions) to hold 42 miles of front. In addition there were eight divisions in GHQ Reserve, parcelled out two behind each army.

These reserves were wholly inadequate to cover such a long front, but there were other serious concerns for the British commanders. Not one division was at full strength. Those in General Gough's Fifth Army were typical. As Gough recorded when the attack came, 'Instead of strength of 12,000 men, none of them [his infantry divisions] could produce more than 6000.'[62] The divisional frontages of British armies were too long for the number of divisions they contained. In the Fifth Army, the average front for a division was 6750 yards. In the Third Army it was 4700 yards. The average length of frontage for German divisions at this time was 1200 yards.[63] Then there was the appalling disposition of the Fifth Army, which would soon bear the brunt of the German offensive.

Despite being one of the weakest of the British armies and still re-covering from its battering in the Third Battle of Ypres, the Fifth held the largest portion of the line. When Gough took over in 1918 it was 42 miles long and had only one line of defence, based on the old British and German trenches of 1916. It possessed only one natural feature that could be a useful obstacle in defence: the water line of the River Somme and canal, and its extension to the Oise River known as the Crozat Canal. General Gough estimated that he needed seventeen divi-sions as a minimum to hold this line. As William Moore noted, 'Never, during the First World War, had a British Army been spread so thinly.'[64] When Gough asked Haig to explain why he was being kept so weak in the south Haig replied that he expected the French to assist the Fifth Army in the event of a serious German attack. Also, the marshes of the Oise were impassable and provided Gough's army with good flank pro-tection. Haig explained further that he considered his north and central sector vital. The loss of the Channel ports in the north, he said, 'would be absolutely fatal to the British Army and probably decisive to the war'.[65] The nearest point of strategic significance in the Fifth Army's sector was the great railway centre of Amiens, nearly 40 miles behind Gough's front. This, Haig felt, could not be threatened in the foresee-able future.

During the months of February and March, Gough became increas-ingly uneasy about the front he was holding and the forces allocated to him. His intelligence sources detected in this area a huge build-up of the German Eighteenth Army. The current spell of excellent spring weather had dried out the swamps around the Oise, making them no obstacle at all to advancing troops. Gough knew that, in their current state, his troops were sitting ducks. A huge front to defend, an acute shortage of men, a German defensive doctrine hastily adopted and poorly understood, limited time for training especially in defensive tactics, lack of time to add depth to their defensive positions — little wonder Gough and other British commanders viewed the coming of the German offensive with foreboding. It is hard not to agree with the New Zealand historian who wrote that the British front in March 1918 was 'thinly held and inadequately organised'.[66]

On the night of 20 March 1918, a gentle rain, the first for eight weeks, started to fall on the British soldiers in the front line. A major in the London Regiment recalled this pleasant evening, the last that many British soldiers would ever experience, as 'strangely still and peaceful; few of war's usual discordant sounds disturbed the last quiet hours of the departing day. The whole country was instinct with the sweetness and vigour of approaching spring . . . Yet over all there was a presage of impending disaster.'[67]

Chapter 2

A Brief Interlude

October 1917 through to the middle of February 1918 was the worst of times for the New Zealand Division. A military disaster at Passchendaele on 12 October, another failed attack at Polderhoek in November and then three months wintering in the Ypres salient had taken a fearful toll, and Christmas provided no respite. On 24 December the New Zealanders were shelled for more than two hours. As Oscar Reston, a signaller in one of the Canterbury battalions, recalled many years later, 'After you stood up to that for a couple of hours, you just felt like a jelly. It's a horrible feeling I tell you.'[1] A Christmas dinner of iron rations — bully beef and biscuits — did little to improve the men's spirits. The conditions in the Ypres salient were almost indescribable. For Reston, it was 'the worst place ever I was in. It wasn't like going over the top . . . You were sort of pinned down by shellfire all the time. You never got rid of it. It was there all the time and you were likely to get blown up. You never knew when a shell was coming.'[2] Many years later Thomas Eltringham, a Lewis gunner from the 2nd Auckland Battalion, remained incredulous about the conditions he experienced in the Ypres salient:

> Mud, slush. You imagine a strip of land from the Belgium border to the Swiss border — but in the middle . . . nothing but mud & slush, dug up by shellfire . . . not a green blade of grass, not a leaf on a tree not a cat or a dog or any sort. Just mud and slush. And we had to live in it. Now that was the Ypres front . . . And we lived in that. If anyone had told me when I went to war that I would be able to stand up to that, I would have laughed at them. I would have said it's impossible.'[3]

After three months of this hell on earth the New Zealanders were in a poor state. According to James McWhirter, a veteran of the Auckland Infantry Regiment, by the beginning of 1918 the division was 'trench weary' and overdue for 'a well-earned rest'.[4] Leaving the men for so long in this sector of the line nearly broke their spirit. As the historian of the Otago battalions admitted, 'Continuous fighting under the worst possible conditions of ground and weather, such as had been experienced in the salient over the preceding few months, had produced a state of complete exhaustion.'[5] 'They'd had it', Oscar Reston recalled. 'Those who were fit to stay on, by the time they got out of Ypres and got shifted down to the Somme, they were due to go out. They'd had plenty.'[6]

On 24 February 1918, the New Zealand Division handed over its sector in the Ypres salient to the British 49th Division and passed into the Second Army's rest area. The New Zealanders did not know it then, but the division's period of active service in Flanders was over. Not all the Kiwis experienced this fortunate change of circumstance though. The Maori Pioneer Battalion remained at Ypres digging trenches and laying belts of barbed wire to protect them — a backbreaking, laborious task. They also spent some time strengthening the pillboxes. The Maori continued this work uninterrupted until 21 March 1918, when news of the German offensive reached them. The next day, after three months in the salient, the battalion was on the road heading south. Their experience was shared by the New Zealand artillery brigades, who also remained in the line at Ypres supporting the divisions of the Second Army. It would take them three to four days to pack up and start their journey south.

At the end of February 1918 the bulk of the division was billeted in pleasant villages around Cassel and Caestre. The first few days were devoted to what the army calls 'interior economy': cleaning equipment, refurbishing missing or lost equipment and reorganising individual units so that their numbers approximated what the establishment levels indicated they should be. James McWhirter, who was a member of a machine-gun crew, noted in his diary that although warned to move at five minutes' notice, 'Our first undertaking was to overhaul all our guns, spare parts, ammunition, belts, ropes & other gear'.[7] The light workloads, coupled with a spell of glorious spring weather and the attention of friendly villagers, soon revived the exhausted men's spirits. Great efforts were made to remove all traces of the Flanders mud. 'All this cleaning had its effect. As clothing and equipment became spotless and shining, the stain of the mud and blood of the autumn and winter from the salient commenced to fade from the men's minds'.[8] After the first three days out of the line, the cleaning was combined with some light training designed, as the war diary of the 2nd Brigade explained, with 'the object of smartening the men up'.[9] Other activities included inspection parades by the ever-watchful divisional commander, Major General Andrew Russell, and sporting competitions. On 9 March a football match was held between New Zealand and their great rugby rivals of the day, the Welsh. As the war diary of the 2nd Otago Battalion shows, some things never change: 'In afternoon Football match, WALES V NEW ZEALAND was held at HONDEGHEM. Game was very ragged at times, although full of incident. Wales won by 13 points to 9 and on the play deserved their win, although the referee's decisions were at times peculiar.' The New Zealanders thoroughly enjoyed being out of the line, but there was a nagging suspicion that the respite would not last very long. As Ezekiel Mawhinny wrote to his sister Laura in New Zealand on 10 March, 'as usual there isn't anything to say. We are still out for a spell and things are going all right as long as Fritz doesn't get too ostropulus somewhere and cause us to get sent back into the line again'.[10]

By the middle of March, the training programme was in full swing and it had a new focus. As well as the standard, repetitive musketry training with rifles and Lewis guns, emphasis was now placed on the use of infantry weapons in the open, in combination with machine guns, mortars and artillery fire support. Various war diaries record training for an 'attack in open warfare',[11] attacking trenches across open ground and various tactical schemes illustrating the 'Principles of Fire and Movement'.[12] The New Zealand Division, under Russell's guidance, had begun to train in the techniques of open warfare, which had not been seen on the Western Front since the opening months of the war.

Despite Russell's prescience in initiating this type of training, it was a case of too little, too late and he was unhappy with the standards reached by his division. When, on 8 March, Russell watched two battalions of the 2nd Brigade training for an advance in open country he was disappointed: it was 'extraordinary difficult to get the right idea of fire and movement carried out'. Three days later, and only ten days before the start of the German offensive, he watched the same brigade undergoing company field training. 'I was frankly disappointed, and think that it is doubtful if we can get the division up to anything like a decent standard in open warfare.' On 21 March, the day the German spring offensive began, Russell paid a surprise visit again to the 2nd Brigade 'to see what work the units of the 2nd Bde were doing — not much, chiefly competitions, instead of taking advantage of fine weather and good training ground'.[13]

The New Zealand historian of the division was in no doubt about the state of the New Zealand Division barely a month after leaving the Ypres salient: 'By the middle of March rest and training had reforged the Division into a weapon of sterling quality'.[14] The war diary of the 2nd Infantry Brigade echoed this view, although it was not quite as emphatic: 'the Brigade on the eve of offensive operations, is in the best of form, and as well trained as is possible under present conditions'.[15] Even General Russell was occasionally pleased by what he saw. On 1 March he had described the men of the 3rd (New Zealand Rifles) Brigade as 'looking well, and full of go'. On 5 March he had found the two Otago battalions 'quite satisfactory' and felt 'quite cheered and encouraged'.[16]

Yet there are several warning signs that the New Zealand Division was not as well prepared for the ordeal ahead as several commentators have suggested.[17] First, those who had been through the hell of Passchendaele were physical and emotional wrecks: 'They'd had it. Exhaustion.'[18] Then the period spent in training for open warfare was too brief — only nine days — and the division had not reached a high standard. Finally, the effects of the disasters of Passchendaele, Polderhoek and the winter in Ypres should not be underestimated. As Ormond Burton recalled, 'There is a limit to what men can endure and during the winter of 1917–18 this limit was very nearly reached.'[19] Some units in the division had been seriously affected. On 4 March Russell inspected the two Canterbury battalions and found mixed results.

> 1st Canterbury was . . . distinctly good . . . 2nd Canterbury distinctly bad — this latter suffers from a complete change of officers including C.O. who is only temporary — Stewart on leave — In everything they require bracing up — Heavy casualties in bde and at Polderhoek account for deterioration.[20]

A unit in such a poor state could not recover its fighting spirit in less than a fortnight. The New Zealand Division had no doubt benefited from its time out of the line, but it was certainly not in peak condition.

On 14 March, the New Zealanders were issued a warning order preparing them for rapid movement in case of an emergency. On 21 March the men learned that the Germans had opened their massive offensive and seemed to be carrying all before them — 'Wild stories of impossible captures and impossible losses were passed from mouth to mouth'.[21] These rumours were soon confirmed. The German Army had broken through on a wide front, the Fifth Army was falling back on the Somme and the Germans were in pursuit, surging towards Amiens in an attempt to cut railway communications, isolate the Channel ports and destroy the British Army. Edward Bibby and the rest of the division could see what lay ahead:

> We knew that the Russians had surrendered and the Germans were bringing back all their Eastern troops and massing them along the border. They knew and we knew, even the ordinary private soldier, that once the Americans got over in force they could stop the Germans. So the Germans must act quickly in spring and we knew that we would be involved. They told us that within a month we would be in a major conflict.[22]

On 21 March the division was ordered to be ready for immediate movement. The next day Russell received his instructions: 'Word has come that we are to be ready to move south at once to the Somme, to help hold up the German offensive which has been let loose on a 50 mile front — the men very pleased, I hear'.[23] Amid the laughter, tears and prayers of the local villagers, the first New Zealand units set off for the Second Battle of the Somme at dawn the following day. Up to this time the division had experienced only offensive operations in France — they had been involved in attacking the Germans. Now, for the first time in the war, they would be on the receiving end of a German Army flushed with victory. They would have their first experience of defensive operations in one of the decisive battles of the war, and it would test them to the limits.

The New Zealanders were not the only soldiers called to assist the beleaguered British divisions on the Somme. Three Australian divisions were also on the way. Brigadier W.R. McNicoll, of the 10th Brigade, made a stirring speech to his officers on the road at Campagne in Flanders:

with his map before him, he put the position plainly. He told us that the Fifth Army had been driven back, and were retreating everywhere, and that the British front was broken and the British and French Armies were in danger of separation; that the German divisions were pushing forward with great rapidity; and he added the surprising information that a long-range gun was shelling Paris. He finished by saying that we would entrain the following morning, and would go straight into action and that we would have the fight of our lives as the fate of the war now hung in the balance.[24]

Chapter 3

The Storm Breaks:
21–25 March 1918

From the evening of 18 March 1918, those German divisions selected to open the offensive began to move into position. To avoid detection they marched by night and rested during the day. After weeks of intensive training, and with the might of the German Empire on display all around them, the marching men were full of confidence. As one German officer recorded,

> The preparations have been so thoughtfully planned that failure is almost an impossibility . . . moral and general condition is very satisfactory . . . We have a colossal amount of artillery at our disposal; for instance, in our own division, of which only two regiments will be in line, we have 68 batteries and several hundred trench mortars of various calibres. Gas is to be freely used.[1]

This battle was to be a true *Materialschlacht*, involving a prodigious amount of men, matériel and heavy weaponry, artillery in particular. It 'enveloped the battlefield in a "storm of steel"'.[2]

By the evening of 20 March 1918, the German Army was ready. That night their officers read a special signal to the soldiers: 'H.M. the Kaiser and Hindenburg are on the scene of operations'. Some of the old hands muttered that they would rather have had an extra issue of cheese, a remark tactfully ignored by the officers, who recorded that the message was 'received with enthusiasm'.[3] Close to a million German troops were in position, as was a massive concentration of guns and ammunition. It was a masterpiece of planning and precision, of which Ludendorff remained justifiably proud. 'It was a remarkable achievement,' he wrote later, 'and at the same time a marvel that the enemy had neither seen anything nor heard any movement at night.'[4]

Meanwhile, back in New Zealand on this very day, a newspaper report assured its readers that the German offensive would be delayed for some considerable time. The *Otago Daily Times* reported that:

> The delay in the German offensive is probably due to the failure of their gunners to gain the ascendancy over the British batteries, which for several weeks have returned blow for blow. It is a repetition of the German failure in the air, for we have completely smashed every strong German serial offensive for the past fortnight. There has been a remarkable increase in the enemy's gun-power since Christmas, owing to the reinforcements from Russia, but the enemy's full strength in artillery has not yet been disclosed.
>
> A significant feature of the new situation is the promptness with which the British recognise and counter every manoeuvre of the German gunners in their attempt to silence our guns. British shells immediately strip the camouflage from the carefully hidden German batteries, and drench their gun crews with gas.[5]

In just a few short hours German gunners would demonstrate that they had gained absolute ascendancy over the Third and Fifth Armies.

At 4.20 a.m. on 21 March, the 'Devil's Orchestra' of 6608 artillery pieces and an almost equal number of trench mortars opened up along the entire front of the Fifth Army, along two-thirds of the Third Army and, as part of a deception plan created by the innovative Bruchmüller, along the front of the First Army too, hammering the British defenders to the full depth of their positions. By the standards of the First World War the artillery barrage was short, lasting only five hours. But it was the heaviest artillery barrage of the war and to date 'the most concentrated artillery bombardment the world has yet known'.[6] By the end of the day the German gunners had fired 3.2 million rounds, a third of which were gas shells.[7] This was ten times the number of shells that had been used on the opening day of the Somme.

The artillery fire programme had been meticulously planned. The first two hours of bombardment was devoted to neutralising the British artillery primarily by firing gas shells on their positions. Also targeted were command centres, various unit and formation headquarters, telephone exchanges, railheads and arterial roads. The Germans had spent the previous month pinpointing most of these important locations and all received direct hits. In the next three hours the weight of fire was directed against the infantry positions in the forward and battle zones.

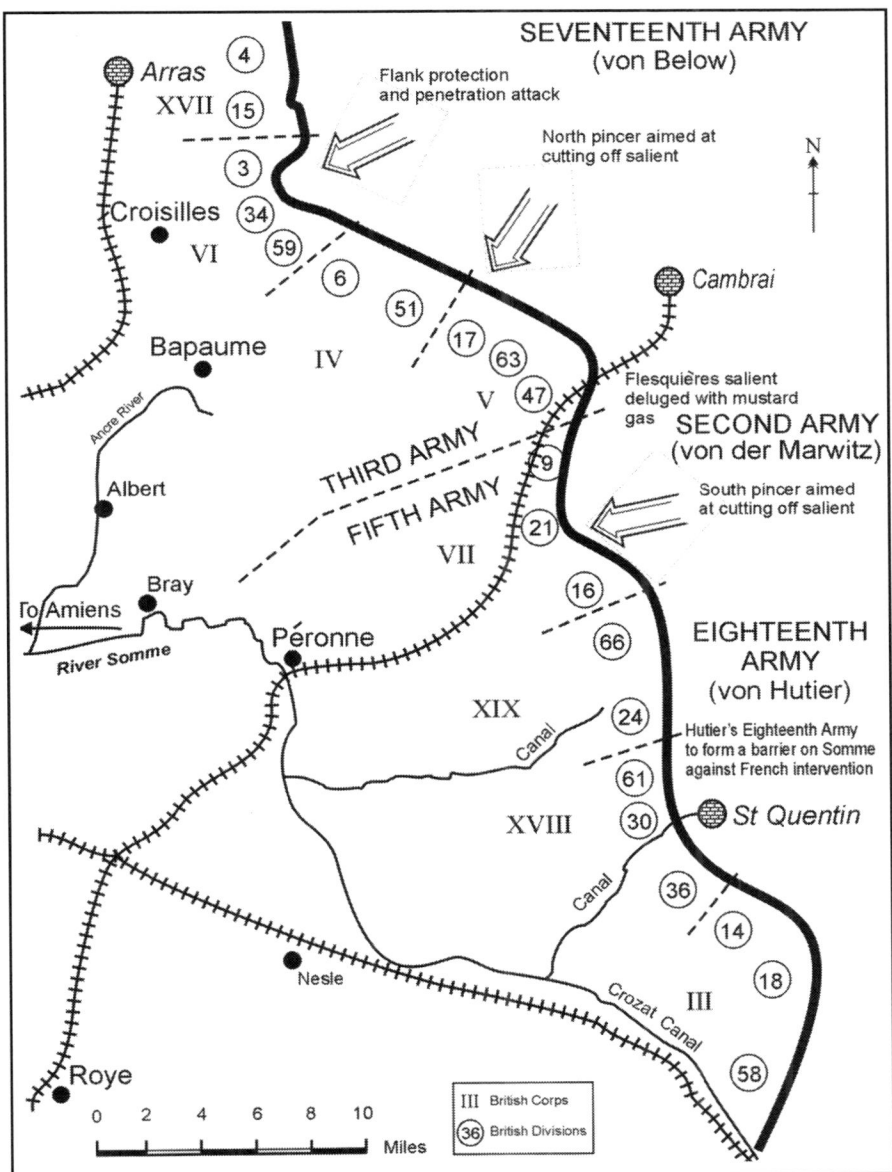

The German plan of attack, 21 March 1918

It culminated in a concentration on the frontline trench positions. Half-way through this fire programme, there was a deliberate respite when the firing paused for half an hour. It was a ploy: the Germans were hoping to lure reinforcements into the open where they could also be destroyed. After this the medium and field batteries opened fire on the British infantry positions with shrapnel and gas shells.

When the attack opened Winston Churchill was in France attending a chemical warfare conference at St Omer. He had stayed overnight with the 9th Division commanded by Major General H.H. Tudor. (In 1916 Churchill had commanded a battalion of this division.) Waking in the early morning, Churchill was an eyewitness to this storm of steel:

> Suddenly, after what seemed about half an hour, the silence was broken by six or seven very loud and very heavy explosions several miles away. I thought they were our 12-inch guns, but they were probably mines. And then, exactly as a pianist runs his hands across the keyboard from treble to bass, there rose in less than one minute the most tremendous cannonade I shall ever hear . . . Far away, both to the north and to the south, the intense roar and reverberation rolled upwards to us, while through the chinks in the carefully prepared window the flame of the bombardment lit like flickering firelight in my tiny cabin.

So loud was the noise of the German barrage that when the 9th Division's 200 guns fired in reply, Churchill could not hear them:

> From the Divisional Headquarters on the high ground of Nurlu one could see the front line for many miles. It swept around us in a wide curve of red leaping flame stretching to the north far along the front of the Third Army, as well as of the Fifth Army on the south, and quite unending in either direction. There were still two hours to daylight, and the enormous explosions of the shells upon our trenches seemed almost to touch each other, with hardly an interval in space or time. Among the bursting shells there rose at intervals, but almost continually, the much larger flames of exploding magazines. The weight and intensity of the bombardment surpassed anything which anyone had ever known before.[8]

Many of the waiting German troops were so impressed with the destructive might of their artillery that they left the safety of their trenches and dugouts and stood high on the parapets to watch the effect as the shells fell on the British lines.[9] The barrage awakened the Fifth Army commander. To Gough the artillery fire was 'so steady and sustained that it gave me an immediate impression of some crushing, smashing power'. He immediately rang his four corps commanders to find out where the artillery fire was directed. He learned that its target was his entire front.[10]

At 9.40 a.m., five hours after the opening of the bombardment, the German infantry advanced behind a creeping barrage. Thousands of machine guns had joined in the barrage, though they could scarcely be heard above the din of the artillery fire. They swept the British forward zone 'with swarm upon swarm of lead'.[11] The Kaiser, staying with his son in an Eighteenth Army observation post, watched his infantry soldiers stream past in the thick fog. All four corps of the Fifth Army and two corps of the Third Army were subjected to this attack. The Fifth Army's forward zone was swamped and overrun. The storm troops swept on though, leaving posts and redoubts still holding out in the forward zone. These were to be dealt with by the battle troops following them. Some of these British strongholds held out for two days; most survived for only a few hours. This opening phase of the offensive was a real soldier's battle on a vast scale. All told, 127 British battalions met the onslaught that morning in their forward and battle zones. Each fought its own individual, disjointed battle, often as isolated companies or platoons. Against such overwhelming odds, though, gallantry was not enough and the British front crumbled in the face of the sheer weight of high explosive shells and innovative infantry tactics.

The war diary of the 51st Highland Division is typical in its record of the day:

> 21 March Midnight to 5:00am
> No Man's Land on Div front was patrolled continuously, but no unusual enemy movement was heard. Morning reports by all three Inf Bdes & by flanking Divs . . . stated that all was quiet.
>
> 5:00am
> Very heavy bombardment opened by guns and howitzer of all calibres up to 8' on our front & also on our back areas as far as FREMICOURT. Front, support & all Intermediate line & bty posns heavily gas-shelled.

9-9.30am
Large numbers of enemy infantry appear on left flank.

11.30am
Left flank withdrew

1pm
1/6th Black Watch launch counter attack — 50% casualties already.

5pm
Withdrew to Corps line that night.[12]

General Gough received the first situation reports from his four corps at 10.00 a.m. All spoke of heavy fighting, but only III Corps on the right flank appeared to have lost significant ground. There the Germans were clear of all obstacles and making significant progress. The Oise marshes had not impeded them at all. Gough was not too concerned: 'If that is all we've lost it'll be a miracle'.[13]

There was to be no miracle though. On 21 March the Fifth Army had 20 battalions manning the forward zone. Blinded by fog, they were too far apart to support one another and their orders did not envisage a retirement. In Gregory Blaxland's words, they were 'doomed from the start'.[14] Some idea of the extent of the losses can be seen in the fate of XVIII Corps: of the eight battalions in the front line on 21 March, only 50 men survived the day to retire to the battle zone where half of them quickly became casualties.[15] Some battalions disappeared without trace. The fate of two battalions of the King's Royal Rifle Corps was not discovered until the end of the war when a few survivors were found in German hospitals recovering from their wounds.[16] By mid-morning the forward zone of the Fifth Army had ceased to exist.

That evening the situation was critical. The Germans had taken the forward zone along the front of both the Third and Fifth Armies. In the south, von Hutier was almost through Gough's battle zone, which had necessitated a retreat to the Crozat Canal. The Germans had penetrated the British positions to a depth of nearly 5 miles. The Fifth Army was falling back in considerable confusion and the Third Army would have to withdraw also or face the danger of being outflanked and encircled. Both armies were now forced to implement a withdrawal — a difficult manoeuvre for which the British were wholly untrained.

On the opening day of Ludendorff's offensive, the BEF had lost 500 guns and suffered 38,000 casualties, most from the Fifth Army.

Yet the day was not the overwhelming success the Germans had been seeking and Ludendorff was disappointed with progress.[17] The soldiers on the ground doing the actual fighting certainly felt elated with their success, as one officer noted in his diary: 'The attack was a complete success and the enemy entirely taken by surprise . . . The spirits of the troops are high . . . As Michael's attack succeeded, it seems highly probable that the further planned attack by Mars (to whom we belong) will take place.'[18] But though the Germans had inflicted heavy losses on the British and taken an unprecedented amount of enemy territory, their own losses were substantial. As Ernst Junger noted, the machine-gun nests caused particularly heavy casualties. Some positions surrendered easily, but in most cases the British defenders 'put up a superb show'.[19] The advancing storm troops also suffered heavily from the efforts of the British airmen, who met little resistance in launching their attacks. Later, the German air arm came in for much criticism for their inactivity. As William Moore has written, 'It was a mercy for the hard-pressed British ground troops that Ludendorff did not possess an aeronautical Bruchmüller to advise him.'[20] British resistance meant that the Germans were nowhere near reaching the Somme as far north as Péronne, which had been their objective on this day. In the north, the Seventeenth Army, attacking the strongest part of the line, had made little progress, barely reaching the second line of defence. In the centre the Second Army had made better progress and had actually penetrated the battle zone. Von Hutier's Eighteenth Army was the real success story, however, taking all its planned objectives. Despite initially having only a subsidiary role, the Eighteenth Army had made the greatest progress and Ludendorff now considered exploiting this success at the expense of the main thrust. His decision would depend on the progress achieved by the other two armies the next day.

Fighting was continuous on 22 March as fresh German troops entered the battle. The Fifth Army was in poor shape. Its withdrawal had actually increased its line by 4 miles but heavy casualties had reduced the infantry divisions to below half strength. By the evening of 22 March the Fifth Army had been driven completely beyond its battle zone and half was beyond its last prescribed defensive line. The Third Army was still fighting in and around its battle zone. British casualties now exceeded 100,000 men. German losses were also heavy but could be replaced by the reserves close at hand. By midday on 22 March the Germans made their first breach of the Somme, the water obstacle that was supposed to be the Fifth Army's last line of defence. This happened on the extreme right near the junction of the Oise with the Crozat Canal.

On the night of 22 March General Gough ordered the Fifth Army to withdraw behind the Somme River. The ordering of this retreat was thoroughly justified but entailed considerable risk. It would leave the flank of the Third Army exposed unless it also withdrew in concert and, as Churchill wrote, 'once the retreat of so thin a line on such a wide front had begun, it was very difficult to stop as long as the enemy pressure continued'.[21] Because the armies were withdrawing at different rates, the first significant gap in the British line opened that night. A German colonel detected the gap, sent through a sizable force and seized the village of Fins, astride an important supply route used by the Third Army. Over the next few days many more gaps would appear.

Most withdrawals were poorly handled because the British had not trained for them, but on the morning of 23 March the 50th Division carried out a textbook one. After fighting a hard and costly action on the previous evening, the troops disengaged from the enemy on the night of the 23rd without detection and had an easy passage back to the Somme. It was, according to Blaxland, 'a manoeuvre that begged more frequent use'.[22] In a retirement of this magnitude the general policy should have been to hold onto positions by day, then slip away a couple of miles or so to a new position under cover of darkness, leaving a screen behind to cover the withdrawal. It was courting disaster to remain in established positions and be found in them in the morning once the enemy knew of the location and had registered it with his artillery. The BEF learned this painful lesson, and another. When two armies withdraw, their movements must be carefully planned and coordinated. This did not happen during the Michael Offensive. Generally, the Fifth Army withdrew too quickly, while the Third Army was much too slow in leaving non-vital ground such as the Flesquières salient, which had been formed in the Cambrai Offensive. When the Third Army did withdraw, it tended to head due west without extending its flanks in an effort to maintain contact with the Fifth Army. Inevitably contact was soon lost and large gaps began appearing in the British lines. For the

Germans, though, the battle had now developed into a race to cut off as many British units as possible on the east side of the Somme and, if possible, prevent the British from destroying the bridges across the river.

General Haig visited Gough briefly on the morning of 23 March, the only person from GHQ who did so during 'Michael'. Haig was surprised to learn that much of the Fifth Army was already behind the Somme and Tortille Rivers. He was calm and cheerful and his only comment to Gough was a philosophical 'Well, Hubert, one can't fight without men'.[23] That night, back at GHQ, Haig sent an order to Gough: 'Fifth Army must hold the Somme at all costs. Third and Fifth Armies must keep in close touch in order to secure their junction and must mutually assist each other in maintaining Péronne as a pivot.'[24] But events were moving too quickly for Haig to keep up. By the time he had finished writing the order the Germans were already across the Somme in force and had taken the important railhead and communication centre of Péronne.

Worry over the gap between the two British armies forced further retirements. But the gap widened and another one of some 2 miles occurred between VII and XIX Corps in the Fifth Army. This day, 23 March 1918, was 'perhaps the most difficult in the whole annals of the British Army . . . It was open warfare with a vengeance, and often it seemed that the whole British line had lost cohesion, and had been jolted into a number of isolated detachments.'[25] That evening, German news bulletins announced the end of the first stage of the battle and claimed that a large part of the British Army had been defeated. In three days since the start of the offensive the Germans had advanced 9 miles at their deepest point.

Dawn on 24 March revealed that the Fifth Army was in a perilous position. The previous day it had been forced back an average of 4 to 6 miles everywhere along its line. Most of the Fifth Army was now behind the Somme and it had been driven back from the Crozat Canal. Its line contained several gaps and the situation was chaotic. The left flank was not in touch with the Third Army whose nearest troops were at least 3000 yards further north. The retreat of both armies continued on 24 March and, according to the official history, 'a considerable amount of ground was lost, both in the Fifth and Third Army areas'.[26] The Germans were able to cross the Somme at several places and now gained a strong foothold west of the river. After three days of battle, with

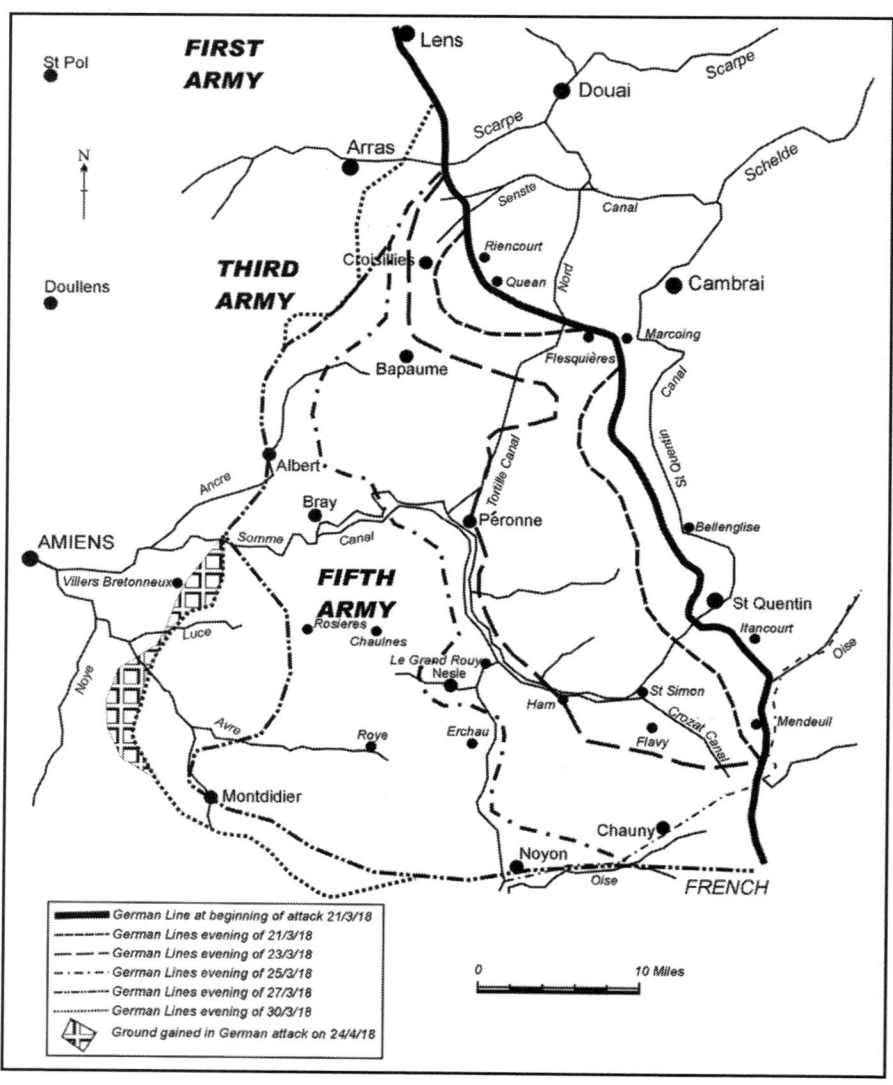

German progress, 21 March – 24 April 1918

constant fighting and much forced marching, German and British troops 'were tired almost to the limits of endurance'.[27] Short of food, ammunition and sleep, the British were so exhausted that many managed to snatch some sleep even while under artillery bombardment.

On the evening of 24 March the Germans found a gap between the two armies and launched a powerful attack on the flank of the Fifth Army, driving a deep wedge into the centre of the British front. By 10 p.m. there was a gap of more than 4 miles between the two British armies. To avoid disaster the Third Army was forced to swing its right wing back to the line of the River Ancre. Bapaume, an important junction town, had to be abandoned. This meant that, by the end of the day, the southern flank of the Third Army was nearly 17 miles west from where it had been that morning. In the north, where contact was maintained with the First Army at Arras, its line had barely moved at all. The situation was perilous. There were other gaps between IV and V Corps of the Third Army, and between many of the divisions. The Germans were freely exploiting these breaks and there was a real danger that the British front would collapse.

During the night of 24 March, the BEF underwent a dramatic reorganisation in which General Gough lost three-quarters of his army. As it was north of the Somme, VII Corps of the Fifth Army was transferred to the Third Army and XVIII and III Corps were placed under operational control of the French, leaving Gough with just XIX Corps under his direct command.

The day of 25 March was one of crisis in the Third Army as seventeen German divisions crashed into its fragile defences.[28] Another long withdrawal was needed and that afternoon the Third Army fell back to the line on the Ancre River, a tributary of the Somme and the location of the old British front of July 1916. There it would hold a line running from Bray-sur-Somme to Albert, Beaumont-Hamel, Gommecourt and through to Arras. Any reserves on hand were to occupy this line forthwith. On the evening of 25 March, in the most unfavourable of circumstances, the Third Army carried out another general retirement. The troops had to break contact with the enemy at short notice, they were already thoroughly exhausted, and the weather was stormy, with much hail and sleet. All around them buildings were on fire and the roads were congested with traffic. It was the stuff of nightmares. As the official historian commented, 'Few who took part will forget the horrors of the all-night march by the light of burning dumps and aerodromes'.[29] That night the Germans captured the town of Albert and the Third Army withdrew to take up defensive positions on the left bank of the Ancre.

By the morning of 26 March the Third Army managed to reach the new positions assigned to it, but the revised line was far from intact. Between 62 Division of IV Corps in the north at Bucquoy and 12 Division of V Corps just north of Albert there was a dangerous gap of 5 miles stretching from Puisieux-au-Mont south to Hamel. If it could not be closed before the Germans exploited it further retirements were likely. The New Zealand Division and the 4th Australian Brigade would eventually be given the task of closing this gap. The British had now lost most of the gains on the Somme battlefield that had cost them so dearly in 1916 and the enemy seemed to have Amiens within its grasp. However, fresh reinforcements were arriving and it was evident that the German thrust was weakening. The German élite units were tiring and their artillery and logistics support could not keep pace with the rapid advance.

Several other significant events occurred during the week-long retreat. First, on Saturday 23 March, Ludendorff, believing that he had decisively beaten two British armies, changed his plan of attack. He had earlier told Prince Rupprecht: 'I forbid myself to use the word strategy. We chop a hole. The rest follows.'[30] This was the method of a military opportunist. The hole (actually several) had been cut and here was an opportunity. That evening Ludendorff issued new orders to his armies:

> A considerable part of the British Army is beaten . . . The object now is to separate the French and British by a rapid advance on either side of the Somme. The Seventeenth will conduct the attack against the British north of the Somme to drive them into the sea. They will keep attacking at new places in order to bring the entire British front to ruin.[31]

Instead of cooperating in a gigantic turning movement against the British, the three German armies were now to do their own thing. Von Hutier's Eighteenth Army, originally there to provide flank protection and stand on the defence, was now to press further to the south-west and carry the offensive to the French. Von der Marwitz's Second Army was to advance on Amiens along both banks of the Somme, forming the blade that would sever the British from the French. Von Below's Seventeenth Army, reinforced by three new divisions, was to attack through Arras towards St Pol with the rather forlorn hope of driving the British into the sea. As Blaxland puts it, 'the three German armies were now to sprout forth in divergent directions like the leaves of a *fleur-de-lys*'.[32] The main thrust now was to separate the British and French armies by capturing the important junction town of Amiens. This change of plans, so soon in the offensive, was a considerable contraction of the original aim and it violated two crucial principles of war: selection and maintenance of the aim and concentration of force. Ludendorff's new direction would prove a major mistake.

Second, on the same day, as part of their policy of *Schrecklichkeit* ('frightfulness'), the Germans began shelling Paris with their long-range guns. These huge weapons, 8.26 inches in calibre, were firing from 75 miles away. This shelling was meant to demoralise the French people and demonstrate German resolve to win this war. The New Zealand newspapers reported that firing shells at such a great distance 'seems incredible'.[33] In his memoirs, Ludendorff wrote proudly of this action. The guns, designed by Krupps, were 'marvellous product[s] of technical skill and science . . . They made a great impression on Paris, and on all France. Part of the population left the capital, and so increased the alarm caused by our success.'[34]

New Zealand Brigadier Herbert Hart had been convalescing from illness in the south of France when news of the German offensive reached him. He immediately set off for the front, passing through Paris on 29 March where he witnessed the effect of the long-range shelling.

> Business as usual was the password here although there was sufficient reason to be otherwise. A fortnight ago the whole town was shaken by a munition explosion, one of the biggest in France. The town has been bombed nightly all the month, — a week ago the offensive commenced and the advance of the Germans threatens both Amiens & Paris, and at the same time Paris was bombed by the extraordinary long range gun firing a 4.5 inch shell a range of 75 miles. Each day it has fired regularly one shell every 15 minutes. Today 29 March, Good Friday, one shell hit a church at the moment the congregation was at prayer, killing 77 & wounding 90. Otherwise the casualties from the gun average about 18 daily.[35]

This shelling of a nation's capital by guns that could not be seen was a new development in the war. It was a feat that had been possible for some time, but it took a ruthless and determined enemy to perform it. As Churchill wrote, 'it was a warning to the Allies that Germany was devoting every energy to her final offensive, and would leave no method untried to break her foe'.[36]

Third, one of the many units of the BEF swallowed up by the Germans in the long withdrawal was the only formation South Africa had sent to the Western Front. The South African Brigade was part of the 9th Division, which Churchill had visited on the eve of the attack and which fought extremely hard during the German offensive. The South Africans had been given the order to 'hold at all costs' the ground west of Bouchavesnes and they 'carried out this duty to the letter'.[37] Though their commander, Brigadier General F.S. Dawson, had serious doubts about the wisdom of this order, it had been given to him personally by the divisional commander, General Tudor, so that he felt compelled to obey it. Dawson confided in his diary: 'I cannot see that under the circumstances I had any option but to remain till the end. Far better to go down fighting against heavy odds than that it should be said we failed to carry out our orders. To retire would be against all traditions of the service.'[38]

The South Africans were supposed to have a brigade on each flank in support. When the Germans attacked the position in force from 9 a.m. on 24 March, the two flank brigades, perhaps less worried about traditions of the service than keeping their units intact, withdrew in the face of the onslaught. The South Africans fought on and by noon the brigade was surrounded. The 35th Division sent to relieve them got within 2 miles of their position but could get no further. At 4 p.m. there were only 100 South Africans left unwounded and to compound problems they had run out of ammunition. When the Germans charged the position shortly afterwards the brigade's survivors had no choice but to surrender. That evening the South African brigade ceased to exist on the BEF's establishment.

Finally, there had been a resolution of a crisis that threatened to split the alliance between Britain and France, thereby assuring a German victory. During the withdrawal in the face of the *Kaiserschlacht*, there was a meeting between the commanders of the British and French armies that caused considerable alarm. On 24 March, an 'upset and very anxious . . . almost unbalanced'[39] Pétain visited Haig at Dury. Haig tried to cheer his French counterpart with some good news, as a French account of the meeting stated:

> Although his [Haig's] Third Army had, during the day, made a considerable withdrawal, he was concentrating behind it all his reserves — in the first place five divisions, of which four were solid Australian ones. Thanks to this reinforcement he was hoping to stop the enemy's progress on that front at least temporarily.[40]

But Pétain was not convinced and remained gloomy. In his view the current battle was not going to be the principal German offensive. This would be made against his front soon. Then he dropped a bombshell. If the Germans continued to press towards Amiens, Pétain would withdraw his armies to the south-west in order to cover Paris. If this had occurred, the Germans would have been successful in their aim of splitting the two armies. In Geoffrey Blaxland's words, 'It was tantamount to admitting that the war was lost.'[41]

At Haig's urgent request, a meeting of political and military leaders from both nations took place at Doullens on 26 March. As it was just 20 miles from Albert, which had fallen to the Germans the previous evening, General John Monash's 3rd Australian Division was used to provide a protective screen around the town. Described as 'a milestone of the war',[42] the meeting got off to a bad start. General Pétain — who, according to Haig, 'had a terrible look. He had the appearance of a commander who had lost his nerve'[43] — began by insulting the quality and performance of British soldiers over the last few days. 'Alas, it [the Fifth Army] no longer really exists. It is broken . . . From the first they have refused to engage the enemy . . . They have run like the Italians at Caporetto.'[44]

Pétain, however, was sidelined for the rest of the meeting. A crucial decision was taken to appoint the French general, Ferdinand Foch, as the coordinating authority for the Allies on the Western Front, in effect a supreme commander. Foch, renowned as a fighting general, immediately overruled any suggestions of falling back to Paris or of separating the two armies: 'We must fight in front of Amiens, we must fight where we are now. As we have not been able to stop the Germans on the Somme, we must not now retire a single inch.'[45] It was a policy welcomed by Haig, who had informed the meeting that he had no intention of giving up any more ground. He was determined to hold the enemy on the Somme and he was bringing forward every division he could spare. This battle would be won or lost on the line the BEF was currently holding. With Foch directing the Allied war effort, unity of effort and purpose would be achieved.

Pétain's plans to abandon the front and fall back to Paris were not the only casualty at this meeting. At Doullens Haig was told that, in order to appease the British public, the commander of the Fifth Army, General Gough, had to go. Haig defended Gough, protesting that 'Whatever the opinions at home might be, and no matter what Foch might have said, I considered that he [Gough] had dealt with a most difficult situation very well. He had never lost his head, was always cheery and fought hard.'[46] Haig was correct. In many ways his handling of the Fifth Army during this difficult withdrawal was Gough's finest military performance. This did not save him, however. The situation demanded that heads must roll and it was Gough who was unfairly made to pay the price.

It should be clear that from 21 to 26 March 1918 the BEF had suffered 'a grave disaster'.[47] There was no other way to view being forced back a distance of 15 to 20 miles to positions held at the beginning of 1916 and suffering more than 100,000 casualties in an army strapped for manpower. Yet by 26 March, the British were not beaten in the field, as Ludendorff prematurely believed. By 26 March, after six days of heavy fighting, the BEF had taken a severe battering. Even the British official history admitted that 'the opening of a breach between the French and British Armies appeared inevitable'.[48] However, in spite of the heavy casualties and the lost ground, the Allies' front line remained intact. And it was clear to many observers that the German offensive was losing momentum. The situation was precarious for both sides. Success was finely balanced, as if on a sabre's edge. It could go either way.

How had this grave disaster been reported in New Zealand? Were New Zealanders aware that the outcome of the war hung in the balance? The metropolitan newspapers stressed three main themes about Michael: that though the Germans had taken considerable ground from the British, none of it was of vital importance; that the Germans had suffered massive casualties taking this useless ground; and that the British Army had retired in good order at a rather leisurely pace. The *New*

Zealand Herald of 25 March is a good example. The thundering head-lines were followed by a Reuters account, sent from London three days before:

ENEMY GAINS OF NO GREAT STRATEGIC IMPORTANCE.

WITHDRAWALS, AFTER EXACTING FEARFUL PRICE.

DIVISIONS MELT AWAY UNDER TORRENTS OF SHELLS

. . . A correspondent at British headquarters writes: The offensive is proceeding. The weather is glorious. Definite details are still unobtainable. Despite our giving ground under the unprecedented weight of men and guns, the enemy gains are nowhere of real strategic importance. The withdrawal was carried out in an or-derly manner, at all points, after a fearful price had been exacted. The airmen report that the ground in the enemy's rear is strewn with grey corpses.[49]

The next day's headlines were in a similar vein:

HOMERIC FIGHTING

INCREASING RESISTANCE

TERRIFIC GERMAN LOSSES

BRITISH ON NEW LINE

OPENING OF TITANIC BATTLE SOUTH OF ST. QUENTIN.[50]

On the same day the *Dominion* told its readers:

BRITISH RETIRE FROM BAPAUME

LINES STILL INTACT

FEARFUL SLAUGHTER OF ENEMY TROOPS

GERMANS DRIVEN BACK OVER SOMME

Today's reports dealing with the tremendous conflict in France show that the Allies are still slowly retiring on a considerable part of the battlefront, but with lines intact and with artillery and machine-guns taking unprecedented toll on the advancing enemy masses.

TITANIC STRUGGLE CONTINUED

London, March 25

Sir Douglas Haig reports: 'The battle continues with great vio-
lence on the whole front. We heavily repulsed powerful attacks
yesterday morning and last evening north of Bapaume. The Germans only at one point reached our trenches where they were
immediately thrown out.'

BRITISH RETIRE VOLUNTARILY FROM BAPAUME

GERMANS BLEEDING AT THE MAIN ARTERIES
BRITISH RETAIN COMPLETE POWER TO
COUNTER-ATTACK

London, March 25

Even if the German claim of prisoners and guns is true, it does
not justify the despondency on our part or jubilation on the part
of the enemy. We do not hear of any division being cut off. All
the accounts suggest that the Germans are bleeding at the main
arteries. The Kaiser has apparently announced the end of the first
stage of the battle because the Germans want breathing time.[51]

Despite the positive 'spin' being placed on the events occurring in
France, most New Zealanders must have been aware of the gravity of
the situation. Buried among the optimistic accounts were some disturb-
ing facts. 'GERMAN LOSSES ENORMOUS; BRITISH CONSIDER-
ABLE' conceded a headline in the *Press* of Christchurch.[52] On 30 March
the *New Zealand Herald* carried a surprising admission that must have
alarmed its readers. Its headlines stated that the German advance was
slowing and had outpaced its artillery support, but the paper continued: 'What the German papers call the great Kaiser battle continues in
full force. The Germans in five days wiped out the results of the eight
months' battle of the Somme, which cost ourselves and the Germans a
million and a quarter casualties. Nevertheless the latest news shows
that the German advance is slowing down'.[53]

In a ministerial statement made in the House of Representatives on
Monday 15 April 1918, Prime Minister William Massey admitted that,
during the first few days of the German offensive, he had feared that
the British were losing the war. Referring to a new German offensive

against the BEF in Flanders, Massey said:

> There can be no doubt in the minds of any of us who have watched what is going on but that is the intention of the Kaiser and those who are acting with him. Their intention is to smash the British during the next two or three weeks, or during the next two or three months; but we can say so far that he has not been able to accomplish his object, and I do not for one moment imagine that he can succeed. It is his last effort. I believe that to be the case, and I feel that he knows it. Field-Marshal Sir Douglas Haig issued that famous order that we all read a few days ago — an order no doubt necessary, and issued at the right moment — in which he said to his soldiers, 'Stand fast; stop the enemy; die at your posts if necessary, but do not allow the enemy to advance.' That, Sir, was the tenor of his order. I have no doubt they will stand fast; and it is not the first time that British soldiers have been called upon in the same way, and they have never failed in hundreds of years. I am quite satisfied they will not fail now. At all events, I have a very confident feeling with regard to the outlook. I can speak for myself, and I am sure my experience is the experience of many others. I have a very different feeling with regard to the outlook to-day as compared with that I experienced some days ago.

This frank admission earned Massey an interjection from the floor:

> Mr. PAYNE.- You should not give way to hysteria.

Massey retorted:

> I am not in the habit of giving way to hysteria; I take things as they come along.[54]

Certainly many in New Zealand in March 1918 shared Massey's unease about events in France and their concerns only increased when they learned that the New Zealand Division would soon be involved in the fighting.

By 26 March, 29 British divisions had been fighting almost constantly since the start of the offensive. After six days of continuous action the men were reaching a state of exhaustion and numbers were much reduced as battle casualties, sickness and straggling took their heavy toll. Despite several large gaps the British line was still in place and the survivors of these decimated formations were determined to see that it remained so. Nine fresh divisions had arrived to help: four from the GHQ reserve and five being released by the other British armies. The first three of these reinforcements arrived on 22 March, to be followed by three more the next day. From 24 March a fresh division arrived each day and was immediately committed to the battle. Eight of the nine divisions were sent north of the Somme in order to keep the Third Army in existence. Especially significant were the arrivals of the 5th Division from Italy, of the 1st, 3rd and 4th Australian Divisions and of the New Zealand Division. None of these had undergone the reorganisation enforced on the BEF and all were thirteen battalions strong.

In 1918 the New Zealand Division was the strongest on the Western Front. It had been released from the Second Army and placed in GHQ reserve on the evening of 21 March. The next day it was marked for transfer to the Third Army. On 23 March the New Zealanders began their march to the Somme front, uncertain about where and how they would be used. All they knew for certain was that when the marching stopped, the fighting would begin.

Chapter 4

A Hurried Journey:
22–26 March 1918

General Russell's diary entry for 21 March had noted that the New Zealanders were pleased at the prospect of being involved in this deadly struggle. John Harcourt of the 1st Canterbury Battalion agreed. In his diary for 23 March he wrote: 'we expect to move any day, probably tomorrow. Everyone excited and keen. News of attack down South very scarce.'[1] The next day, however: 'News from the front rather disquieting. We heard with incredulity of the shelling of Paris by long range gun.'[2] Writing from the No. 1 General Hospital at Brockenhurst in England, a wounded Lieutenant Kenneth Luke, on the headquarters staff of the New Zealand Rifle Brigade, recalled the soldiers' reaction when they learned they were to play an active role in halting the German offensive:

> It was about Thursday 21st that we received word that we were to be withdrawn & thrown into the big scrap. At this time we were getting very meagre details of the fighting, but we were delighted at the prospect of the change as we were thoroughly sick of Ypres & its environments, having been there for six months during the worst part of the year. We gave three cheers when we heard of the change & eagerly awaited detailed orders for the shift.[3]

All unit and formation war diaries of the New Zealand Division recorded the news of the opening of the offensive on 21 or 22 March and receiving a warning order to be ready to move at short notice. The diary of the 3rd Battalion, New Zealand Rifle Brigade was typical:

22 March
Sent out 200 O/R [other ranks] on Working Parties from WEST FARM CAMP. Quiet day in camp and no enemy shelling as on

previous days. At 6 pm warned to be in readiness to move at 3 hours notice. Issued order for all ranks to be ready to move out at 1 hours notice and all gear for transport to stand ready for loading from 8pm onwards.

7pm. All night work parties cancelled by Brigade. Received orders at 8.30 p.m. to be clear of WEST FARM CAMP by 9.30 p.m. Company Commanders called up and orders issued for march to WINNIPEG camp. All Companies cleared camp by 9.45 p.m. Whole Battalion in WINNIPEG CAMP by 2am 23rd March.

23 March
Instructions for Brigade to be ready to move at 4 hours notice by bus, train or route march. Day spent in equipping whole Battalion for battle and all equipment complete by 5pm. Conference of Battalion Commanders held at Brigade at 3 pm. Our period of rest as Corps Troops cut out but men in good fettle. Had a decent night's rest without interruptions from enemy shelling. Lorries passing through the whole night with troops for the Battle Front.[4]

The New Zealand Division's artillery brigades and the Maori of the Pioneer Battalion still working in the Ypres salient also received the word to move. According to its war diary, the readying of the Pioneer Battalion for the march south presented additional problems:

On 21st March news came through of the Germans offensive in the Cambrai Area. From the reports it appeared they had met with little success but we got orders to stop all work and prepare for an immediate shift. Steps were taken at once to get ready for the road and the amount of extra blankets and gear our young gentlemen had collected round themselves during our nearly three months stay in Ypres was appalling. We got it all away and were ready waiting first thing on the morning of the 22nd.[5]

The Pioneer Battalion set off for the Somme at 7 o'clock that evening. The next day the diary recorded that 'Ammo was brought up to strength and officers kits down to reasonable proportions'. Joining up with the Rifle Brigade on 24 March the Maori troops learned that the first reports were wrong: 'News from the South much more serious'.[6]

Bombardier N. Bailey from Little Akaloa on the Banks Peninsula was a member of the New Zealand Field Artillery, responsible for the

General Russell (standing) watches a brigade on field operations in early March 1918. Kippenberger Military Archive and Research Library H434

General Russell inspects an Otago Battalion on 5 March 1918. He wrote in his diary that the two Otago Battalions were 'quite satisfactory. I feel quite cheered and encouraged.' From Russell this was high praise indeed. Kippenberger Military Archive and Research Library H439

The caption to this cartoon in Chronicles of the N.Z.E.F. *read 'Trouble is blooming in Picardy.' The New Zealand Division were to find themselves in the thick of that trouble.*

New Zealand machine gunners, such as these men in the fields near Colincamps, inflicted massive casualties on the advancing Germans. RSA COLLECTION, ALEXANDER TURNBULL LIBRARY G-13258-¹/₂

That a great German offensive was coming in 1918 was the worst kept military secret of the war. Yet the Allies were still not prepared for it when it happened. As this cartoon shows, some people had become a little blasé about the coming offensive. By the time this cartoon appeared in New Zealand the offensive had started and the Allied line was crumbling under its weight. NZ HERALD 23 MARCH 1918

Their world 'tumbling into ruins', French refugees, wearing their best clothes, flee from the advancing Germans. This was the first time New Zealand soldiers encountered refugees in a war zone, and it made a deep impression on them.
KIPPENBERGER MILITARY ARCHIVE AND RESEARCH LIBRARY

New Zealand engineers dig a strong point at Colincamps. KIPPENBERGER MILITARY ARCHIVE AND RESEARCH LIBRARY H465

Wounded New Zealand soldiers are placed into an ambulance at a Casualty Clearing Station. KIPPENBERGER MILITARY ARCHIVE AND RESEARCH LIBRARY H479

loading and distribution of ammunition for the New Zealand guns. On 21 March 1918, he wrote in his diary:

> This evening at about 7.pm we got word to prepare to move out early in the morning to an unknown destination to entrain in the near future. Rumoured that Fritz has broken through on the 3rd & 5th Army fronts and also on part of the French Front. Plenty of work and preparation going on.

The artillery units moved out of the front line the next day, which was beautifully fine and warm. 'At 9.30 am we had a mobilization parade, and all spare gear, extra blankets etc were collared and sent to salvage . . . We are down to summer issue and marching order kits.' On 24 March the artillery ammunition arrived and was loaded on horse-drawn wagons. Bailey's unit set off to Caestre at 1.30 p.m. 25 March. 'There are all sorts of rumours flying around that Fritz has advanced for miles and that he has bombed the railway bridge at Amiens, hence the delay in trains.' The ammunition was loaded onto a train in the early hours of 26 March. That afternoon Bailey and his comrades reached Ailly-sur-Somme where the ammunition had to be unloaded. 'All along the road we passed Frenchies fleeing for their lives away from Fritz. Rumours galore floating around.'[7]

These fresh reports from the battlefront, 'which alters rather too fast' as Russell noted in his diary on 24 March[8], caused the New Zealand Division to be issued four different sets of orders in the first 24 hours of the march. At first the division was to concentrate on the left flank of the Third Army at Le Cauroy, some 12 miles east of Arras. They would be part of that army's XVII Corps. On 24 March this order was cancelled and the New Zealanders were diverted to the Fifth Army area where they would concentrate at Bray as part of VII Corps. Russell set up his divisional headquarters at Corbie in preparation for this move. At 1 a.m. on 25 March the orders were changed again: the division was to concentrate around three small villages on the outskirts of Amiens. At 10 p.m. came fresh instructions. As Russell recorded, 'Orders came late in the evening that whole Div was to move northwards and shifted HQ to Hedauville, where we concentrate to fill a gap to the North.'[9]

Even these orders were altered. The 10 p.m. orders stated that Russell was to establish a line from Hamel to Puisieux, where there was a gap in the line. At 2 a.m. on 26 March, though, fresh orders arrived from

Lieutenant General G.M. Harper, whose IV Corps now included the New Zealand Division (see Appendix 3, page 249). The division was to move further north through the village of Mailly-Maillet to the line of Hamel-Serre and close the gap there. If the Germans reached this line first they were to be pushed back and every effort was to be made to connect the line up with the right flank of 62nd Division. If the Germans could not be pushed back then the New Zealanders were to check their advance and establish and hold a line from Colincamps–Hébuterne, some 3 miles to the rear of Hamel–Serre. Russell did not need to shift his headquarters again; he remained at Hédauville, some 4 miles north-west of Albert, which was now held by the Germans. He eagerly awaited the arrival of the units of the New Zealand Division.

The constantly changing orders clearly reflected the fluctuations of battle. The Germans still retained the initiative and the British had to react to the shifting situation. They also reflected a degree of panic in the higher levels of the BEF and a lack of clear direction. So many different directives in one day also had an adverse effect on the New Zealand Division. They caused much confusion and anger, as well as additional fatigue, and ensured the division was strung out over many miles. This contributed to the delay in concentrating it for action.

Getting to Hédauville proved a nightmare for most of the New Zealand soldiers. The men travelled to the Somme by train, then by lorry — the first time large numbers of Kiwi troops had moved on operations in motorised transport — and then by forced march. The train journey was uncomfortable. The soldiers travelled in cattle cars displaying a sign that indicated they were suitable for carrying either 40 men or eight horses. Ira Robinson of the Rifle Brigade described the experience to his sister Lizzie:

> Well, we marched out of that camp and after walking most of the night we reached another camp near the railway and the town of Poperinghe. There we rested all one day and those who had not made wills were compelled to make one out. The following, or at least the same night, we packed up and marched out again, and after walking two or three miles we entrained and started on an all night ride. It was not by any means a pleasant one as we were told off in lots of thirty and bundled into covered vans and told to make ourselves as comfortable as possible on the floor. It was one tangled mass of legs, arms, boots, rifles and equipment, steel

hats and gas helmets, but in spite of all that I managed to get a few hours' sleep. I can sleep on a brick now and not even get a little bit stiff. The only thing that would keep me awake would be a decent bed, which I have not seen for months and months.[10]

Captain George Tuck of the 2nd Auckland Battalion travelled with the battalion's headquarters group. 'In the train on the way south towards Amiens. Have been travelling all night & still a long journey before us . . . In the carriage with Hdqtrs are Col. Allen, Major Shepherd, self, Wolow, Padre, Lts Stewart & Eccles. How many of us will return I wonder.'[11] His commanding officer, Lieutenant Colonel S.S. Allen, had had a similar thought during the church parade on Sunday 24 March. That service was 'unusually impressive from the thought that must have been present with everyone that to many it would be their last'.[12]

The march to the Somme front was a long, hard one for men who had wintered in the trenches of Flanders. The lack of available transport required most of the New Zealanders to march a considerable distance — between 25 and 30 miles if the trains had deposited them south of Amiens. The men marched in light fighting order, which required them to leave their packs, blankets and greatcoats behind. They carried 220 rounds of ammunition, extra ammunition for the Lewis guns and three days' water and rations. For the next two weeks the New Zealanders had to live, sleep and fight in their uniforms. They lacked shelter and warm clothing and the spring weather was unpredictable, with extremely cold nights. The war diary of the 2nd Otago Battalion summed up the conditions:

> Battalion detrained at HANGEST at 4 p.m. and received orders to proceed in fighting kit at once. All surplus gear dumped and left under charge of guard. Had evening meal and set off at 8 p.m. Bivouacked for night near BRIELLY — bitterly cold, no blankets or overcoats and hence little sleep.[13]

As they marched through the Somme district the New Zealand soldiers were struck by the beauty of a landscape which, so far, had escaped the damage of war. This would soon change, as one veteran recalled many years later: 'When we went up to the Somme, there was grass that high, whole of the Somme country, grass all over it. When I went out of the line there wasn't a bit of grass left, it was all mud with bombs, so you'd wonder how anybody lived there.'[14]

The soldiers also thought it strange that the countryside 'appeared to be curiously deserted',[15] but this altered as they reached Hédauville. Large fires in the direction of Albert were visible throughout the night. As one diary recorded, on the morning of 26 March, 'The whole countryside is aglow with burning villages and the roar of the artillery is awful.'[16] Along the road one of the Auckland battalions experienced an unusual event which William Knight, one of three brothers killed in the war, described to his parents:

> I have been trying to write before but we are in for very hard times from pillar to post but we are to settle here to dig trenches in case we had to fall back . . . As we were having dinner on the road side, coats off, boots off etc, the King, on a tour, got out of his car, & walked along past us & we gave him a cheer for company as he went past.[17]

Every account of this journey describes it as extremely tough. For example, Corporal Gerald Beattie of the 1st Otago Battalion recorded in his diary for 25 March that:

> We marched in Battle Order not even carrying greatcoats. Were issued with extra ammo and rations and then marched on until 8.30 when we were billeted in a row of crippled motor lorries along the roadside . . . It was a hard frost and we were very miserable without any blankets, but we had to make the best of a bad job.

On the next day came a forced march of 25 miles, 'a record for the New Zealand Division'. That night the battalion 'had to doss down in an open field in a heavy frost with only an oilsheet . . . Another most miserable night.'[18]

Another soldier recalled:

> Hell! But I am weary this morning! Had a most wearisome march last night. We seemed to cover fifty miles or so, but we learned this morning it was only eighteen . . . Half the boys dropped out of the ranks during the night, and ducked into the hedges for a rest and sleep. I plodded steadily, or perhaps I should say unsteadily along the weary road, but I must say it was hard going

made harder by the officers informing us every now and again that there was only a kilometre or two further to go. After about five more kilometres had been covered the same would be told; the march seemed endless. At some unearthly hour during the night, we halted on the cobblestones in some dingy dark town, where we remained for perhaps an hour, while there was bustling to and fro by the officers who seemed to be completely at sea to us as to where we were or where we were going and when. Discipline went by the board and the boys were in an evil temper, shouting and calling the officers all the B.B.B.'s they could lay their tongues to.[19]

John Coleman neatly captured the experience in a letter to his sister Mary:

Our company was out in billets for a few weeks' spell, but old Fritz started making things pretty merry, and we were moved away in rather a hurry to quite a different part of the line. We had about eighteen hours' train journey, stayed the night in a village, where we got off the train. Spent most of the night waiting for transport. We made huge fires in the streets and sat around them until I went to sleep, and when I woke up again our fire was out and all the fellows were asleep, huddled up to each other in all sorts of attitudes. Well, we had a good rest in the morning and finally got in the motor lorries at two in the afternoon. We travelled in the lorries for about two hours and then marched about ten miles, where we camped in an open field for the night, but were fortunate enough to get some straw which we nestled in like pigs. There was a fairly hard frost, but we cuddled up close to each other and kept fairly warm.[20]

Such a difficult journey meant that the New Zealand soldiers arrived at Hédauville footsore, tired and hungry. They were exhausted before they had even met the Germans. As the War Diary of the 2nd Auckland Battalion admitted on 26 March:

2 a.m. Battalion proceeded by motor lorries to PONT NOYELLES debussing at 5 a.m. and marched to HEDAUVILLE . . . where the Division assembled. Arrived at 12.30 p.m. During this march which was very long the Battalion displayed the greatest endurance. Only one man fell out. The men were very tired after travelling constantly without sleep for 38 hours.[21]

It was certainly not an ideal state for soldiers who were about to have the fight of their lives.

As the New Zealand and Australian soldiers neared the front line they came across thousands of retreating soldiers, mainly from the Fifth Army. They were not at all impressed by what they witnessed. Bernard Cottrell wrote home to his father:

> I suppose you have wondered at how events have shaped recently, well we also were very surprised, you will get details later & will be in a better position to judge still there was some damnable mistakes somewhere, as we came up everyone was clearing for their lives, many did not know what was doing, others gave very vivid descriptions, but one look at their clothes was sufficient. They had never been in the line. There were told what was thought of them in very forcible language.[22]

Charlie Lawrence from Greymouth served in 13 Company, 1st Canterbury Battalion, which encountered a large group of retreating British soldiers. 'They said to us: "Don't go over there chum, you'll get killed." That's what they said: "Don't go Chum, you'll get killed." We said: "Turn around, you bastards and go the other way." . . . It was a bad affair that was.'[23] Although he moved to the Somme behind the infantry, Sergeant Leonard Hutchinson of the 15th Howitzer Battery, New Zealand Field Artillery, still formed a thoroughly negative impression of the British soldiers.

> Our batteries moving up fast & will go into action tonight . . . Civilians evacuating all along the road from Amiens to Picquigny. The sight is awful. Old men and women carrying packs & almost praying of the lorry drivers to give them a lift. We were full up, but carried 4 ladies & 2 children on the back. They were that thankful that they wanted to pay us, but we refused. The Tommy soldiers have behaved shamefully, deserting the line and going into the civilian's houses & looting — absolutely wanton destruction.[24]

Corporal Claude Wysocki of the 2nd Battalion, New Zealand Rifle Brigade was disgusted with the soldiers of the Fifth Army and had no sympathy for them.

It was General Gough's Fifth Army, God Bless 'em. General Gough's Fifth Army was the most disorganised, out-of-tune, poor silly sips that you ever had anything to do with . . . At 3 o'clock in the afternoon at Amiens, that's when the war really started on the Second Somme. Previous to this, all you had was General Gough's Fifth Army in disarray. They'd been running all night long from the front line, which was the front line in their case, . . . you never saw such a spectacle in all your life. Nothing ever appeared in the newspapers concerning that. They had absolutely no heart for it and they were the cause of more trouble than enough . . . They never marched past, they ran![25]

In a letter to his sister, John Bartle recounted a popular joke in the New Zealand Division. 'A Tommy O. [officer] asked a Maori what he was doing here one day, & he said, "Oh putting up plenty of barb wire to stop the Germans getting through & stop the Tommy's from running back". He got seven days CB [confined to barracks].'[26]

Vincent Jervis of 12 Platoon, C Company, 2nd Battalion, New Zealand Rifle Brigade, was in hospital with a high temperature when the New Zealand Division marched to the Somme: 'I wonder what the NZ Div is doing. I should like to be with the boys if they go into it.'[27] As he had more news from the wounded New Zealand soldiers passing through his hospital, Vincent Jervis formed a poor opinion of the British soldiers' performance. He would not have been alone.

Very nice day. Fritz seems to be doing what he likes. I don't believe the British are putting up as big a stand as they might . . . Saw Fitzsimmons out of C Coy. Hear Sgt Dobson & Mick Dellow were killed. When our division went into the line down Amiens way they reckon they had to fill a gap of about 6000 yds. The Aussies and NZ's have been sent up to the Bailleul front, they get shoved into all the hot spots. I'll bet it is because they don't run away.[28]

Some New Zealanders, while not excusing the retreating British soldiers, did express some sympathy for them. William Jamieson, a runner in the New Zealand Field Artillery was one:

Some of them came down the road as we were going in. They said to us: 'They're coming over in thousands. They're coming over in thousands.' But a lot of these little blokes, they were not much more than schoolboys. The Tommy Army had been there for four years and they were just about wiped all out, by that time they were not much more than damn kids. At least that's what they looked like to me.[29]

Corporal Gerald Beattie of the 1st Otago Battalion, who survived the war and lived to the age of 103, dying in Rangiora in 1994, recorded the popular opinion of the British two days before he was wounded by a German artillery shell:

> The Froggie flight from these parts had been very precipitate, showing the speed of the Huns advance . . . The Tommies put up no fight at all against Fritz, but turned and fled, and our Dinks [soldiers of the New Zealand Rifle Brigade] coming up on Monday when just about 400 yards beyond Mailly Maillet, met a battalion of Fritzies marching in column of route with a band playing, the dinks spread out and got well sunk into Fritz and he turned round and got chased back a mile or so. Prisoners said the New Zealanders were the first to offer any resistance. Fritz is a fine soldier when the enemy is running away, but he won't have a go at us in the open at all.[30]

According to C.E.W. Bean, the Australian war correspondent and official historian, the widespread judgement that British soldiers were greatly inferior to Australians and New Zealanders derived largely from these experiences of 1918. Unfortunately the Anzac soldiers took this harsh view back to their respective countries where it gained a widespread following. As Bean himself recognised, the verdict was inaccurate and unfair:

> It may be taken as an axiom that, when an army is in the grip of a desperate struggle, any one moving in its rear tends to be unduly impressed with the disorganisation, the struggling, the anxiety of the staffs, and other inevitable incidents of such a battle; he sees the exhausted and also the less stubborn fragments of the force, and is impressed with their statements, while the more virile and faithful element, mainly fighting out in front, ignorant or heedless of all such weakness in rear, is largely beyond his view.[31]

As the New Zealanders marched south and then east the roads were crowded with stragglers, vehicles and French refugees fleeing from the advancing Germans. The refugees were dressed in their best clothes and carried their most valuable possessions. They were worn out, frightened and in a state of bewildered despair as their world tumbled into ruins. John Coleman described them to his sister:

> We marched the next evening to a village that the French had just deserted for the second time, poor beggars. You see some rotten sights on the battlefield, but one is so hardened to them now that you really don't take much notice of what occurs now. All along the road as we came up here we passed continual streams of these poor peasants beating a hasty retreat. This is what touches the soft part of a fellow's heart, to see the poor women and children hurrying along the road with terror-stricken faces. They have all sorts of old-fashioned vehicles moving their happy homes, some with mules drawing them, others horses and some smaller carts drawn by dogs. And what a collection are in some of the carts, furniture, poultry, calves and the cows are generally tied behind like we would lead a horse. Other women might have four or five cows tied coupled together, leading them. Lots of old people, who might be seventy or eighty years old, were wheeling barrows with their goods and chattels. Women, too, and they must have travelled miles.[32]

As Lieutenant Kenneth Luke remembered, near Amiens 'along the high road beyond one saw evidence of the big push coming our way. We met hundreds of refugees pushing, wheeling & carrying their scanty possessions. Some of their valuables would make you laugh, at other times make you feel mad with the hideous war.'[33] All surviving accounts of New Zealand soldiers comment on the refugees' plight. Harold Muschamp of the Machine Gun Battalion: 'We saw some pitiful sights on our march. Old men and women and children all fleeing for their lives.'[34] And Corporal Beattie, writing on 26 March: 'on the road we passed dozens of people moving back with all the possessions they could carry. It was truly a pitiful sight'.[35] For Padre Ronald Watson of the 1st Otago Battalion, 'Two of the saddest things I have seen lately have been the plight and sorrow of refugees and destroyed homes. New Zealand is indeed a happy country to be spared the sight of so much sadness and desolation as poor old France has known.'[36] Cecil Jepson of the 2nd Wellington Battalion wrote in his pocket diary that 'Heartbreaking sights are here seen' but added that 'many of our boys are wheeling barrows and carts and carrying bundles for the refugees who are passing through here day & night'.[37]

This was the first time ever that New Zealand soldiers had seen refugees fleeing from a war zone and it made a lasting impression on them. According to Ormond Burton, the New Zealand soldiers felt compassion for the suffering French, but also a hardened resolution to halt the Germans.[38] As Ira Robinson told his sister Lizzie,

> Man, it made regular savages of our boys and Fritz has paid the price since . . . This last stint has made me very bitter towards Fritz and I will never think of him as anything but a savage again and will treat him as such. I am on a gun capable of firing 700 shots a minute and if it would fire 1400 shots a minute it would not be going too quickly for me.[39]

For many New Zealand soldiers this was also a chance to avenge their suffering at Passchendaele the previous year. This was certainly James McWhirter's thought as he watched a large group of Germans march into the killing zone of his machine-gun crew. 'Oh what a target, men & transport in marching order, we were all eager to have a bit of our own back for what we got at Passcendaele [sic].'[40]

A considerable mythology has arisen, especially in Australia, about the role of the four Anzac divisions that arrived to help stem the German advance. Some accounts have exaggerated their role, suggesting that they were almost solely responsible for the German offensive grinding to a halt.[41] Nearly every Australian account of the *Kaiserschlacht* contains two quotes from Bean's official history that have passed into Australian folklore. As the men of the 4th Australian Division moved southwest of Arras, they were recognised despite the fact they had never served in the region before. At Barly, the villagers were loading their most precious possessions onto wagons and carts and making ready to abandon their homes to the Germans. When they saw the Australians, they stopped and took up the call, 'Les Australiens'. One old man said to the soldiers of the 13th Battalion, whose lorry had halted, 'Pas necessaire maintenant — vous les tiendrez.' (It's not necessary now — you'll hold them.) A digger is said to have replied, 'We'll have to see the old bloke isn't disappointed.'[42] Similarly, a 'grim digger' of the Australian 3rd Division, cleaning his rifle in the village of Heilly, said to a woman in broken French, 'Fini retreat, Madame. Fini retreat — beaucoup Australiens ici.'[43]

Contemporary New Zealand accounts carried similar tales although they did not receive as wide an audience as the Australian ones quoted above. When asked why the French civilians had halted their flight from the Germans at Amiens, the answer, attributed to a French general no less, was obvious:

> they had learnt that the troops they had just passed were the New Zealanders moving in and so there was no need for them to move out & so the evacuation came to an end. Yes, he [the French general] said, such was the reputation of the New Zealanders.[44]

In a letter to his father, Bernard Cottrell emphasised the role of the New Zealanders:

> The most pitiful sight was the poor French people getting out of it with their worldly goods stacked on a cart followed by cows, pigs & goats. By the way the French authorities are supposed to be taking this retreat pretty badly (and every reason) & French papers give us the credit for stopping the 'British rot'. I haven't seen the English equivalent for it yet though I think a certain amount of credit must come eventually to us.[45]

Newspaper reports in Australia and New Zealand echoed the theme that Australia and New Zealand had saved the situation on the Western Front and tended to exaggerate their performance. The account featured in the *Otago Daily Times* by the distinguished correspondent Philip Gibbs is typical. It is featured below with its evocative headlines:

A BREATHING SPACE

AUSTRALASIANS IN BATTLE-LINE

MR PHILIP GIBBS ENTHUSIASTIC

DASHING ATTACK BY NEW ZEALAND

BRILLIANT SUCCESS ACHIEVED

ENEMY SURPRISE ATTACK FORESTALLED BY
AUSTRALIANS AND NEW ZEALANDERS

EAGER WELCOME BY THE VILLAGERS

THEN 'THERE WAS SOMETHING DOING.'

... The enemy in the next tussle will meet men who are not tired, whose resolution is as great as that of those they met in the first on-slaught. The Australians and New Zealanders have come into the line, fresh and keen, uplifted by a fierce enthusiasm, stirred by emotions which make these fellows very dangerous. I saw them coming to relieve hard-pressed troops, and the sight made the pulse beat. It gave a sense of security. The Australians came swinging down towards the old Somme battlefield with the spirit of men coming to the rescue of a great cause. Is not this blasted field of Pozieres hallowed to them by memorials of their own dead and the graves of many comrades? 'We will take Pozieres back,' they said; 'it is our job.' News that the enemy had come pouring back over the ground at Bapaume and Le Sars, where the Australians bitterly fought a year ago, was a shock and a challenge. They waited impatiently for the call to come, saying, 'It's a damned shame we are not on the way.' ...

The New Zealanders followed spick and span, debonair lads who have already seen many adventures. It was a glorious night on the road.

After reaching the battle line there were things doing. They sent out patrols, clearing 'No Man's Land,' caught the Germans in ambushes, raking stragglers with bullets; slaughtered the enemy in several small attacks; drove them out of woods and villages, scaring them horribly day and night.

Mr Gibbs says he saw slightly wounded Australians and New Zealanders, who remarked: 'We were a bit rash to put our heads into it.' All are certain the enemy will not get further.[46]

Yet, as with most mythology, there is some truth in these accounts. Certainly by 1918 the Australian divisions in France had established a formidable reputation, while the New Zealand Division, as Keith Murdoch reported in the *New Zealand Herald*, 'is known everywhere as one of the hardest-working and hardest-fighting Divisions in France'.[47] There is plenty of evidence to suggest that soldiers of this calibre must have been welcome during the Allies' darkest hour.

On 24 March two official Australian correspondents (probably Bean and Murdoch) went to the press headquarters of the BEF, now at Amiens, to gain information about the progress of the German offensive. There the chief censor, Major the Honourable Neville Lytton, and a press officer, Lieutenant Colonel C.R. Cadge, gave them an overview of the situation. Both Australian correspondents were shocked to learn that the Germans were now past Combles and on the old Somme bat-tlefield. Part of the conversation went as follows:

> 'Where's the nearest point they have got to?' I asked.
> 'Delville Wood,' he [Lytton] said.
> That was a staggerer.
> 'Haven't we any reserves — surely we must have!' I asked.
> 'No — I don't think there's a division between the Germans and here,' Cadge said.
> We said our divisions would surely be coming and the N.Z's.
> 'How can they get here in time?' he asked.

Both Australian correspondents were somewhat despondent on hear-ing this news. But the next morning (25 March) troops were passing through Amiens heading towards the advancing Germans and one of the correspondents recorded in his diary: 'They were New Zealanders. I can't say how glad I was to see them . . . They are the solidest, calmest looking troops in France.'[48] An Australian battalion history reported a similar experience. On the trip south the Australians stopped at Doullens, where they saw many British wounded and stragglers. 'There was a most depressing atmosphere of hopelessness about them all, but we saw some New Zealanders who told us that their division had gone down, and that the 4th Australian Division was also on the way, so we bucked up considerably.'[49]

Kenneth Luke described the effect of the Anzac troops arriving to plug the gaps in the line: 'We met remnants of the Divisions that had fought from the beginning of the terrible battle struggling along the road, & everywhere our peaked hats were espied the anxious question was asked "Are the ANZACS coming?" and cheers & smiles met us everywhere.' Watching the troops of his brigade's 1st Battalion go into action was inspiring: 'It did my heart good & stirred my blood to see our boys swing by. They did look a fit lot after their month's rest and went in to fight with great spirit.'[50]

At 10 p.m. on the evening of 25 March General Russell received orders from the Third Army to move his division into the ever-widen-ing gap between IV and V Corps. The New Zealanders were to establish a line running from Hamel in the south and bending northeast through Beaumont-Hamel to Puisieux-au-Mont, a distance of just over 4 miles. This would place the division on high ground overlooking the Ancre

Valley and facing almost due east. It was also 'the most vulnerable and fluid part of the front'.[51] There they would be part of IV Corps under command of Lieutenant General G.M. Harper and provide the link between 62 Division of IV Corps at Puisieux and 12 Division of V Corps at Hamel. In a further complication, the 4th Australian Brigade was allocated to the depleted 62 Division in order to help with securing and holding the important junction town of Hébuterne. The command arrangements were complicated, but the task allocated the New Zealanders was not:

> 1. Gap exists in line from Hamel to Puiseux au Mont. The NZ Division will occupy this gap, both villages inclusive — second Brigade on the right, 1st Brigade on the left. Dividing line L of BEAUMONT HAMEL.

> 2. All units in the Brigade Group . . . will proceed by shortest route forthwith, to HEDAUVILLE.[52]

Orders issued to the individual units contained more information and explained what their task would be once they were involved:

> The enemy last night reached the line of the ANCRE from MIR-AU-MONT to BEAUCOURT where he is believed to have crossed the river. The 12th Divn. has been ordered last night to occupy the line of the ANCRE from ALBERT to HAMEL. The 62nd Divn. are retiring from the ANCRE North of MIR-AU-MONT to the line PUISIEUX-AU-MONT-BOCQUOY, where they will fight today remnants of 5th Corps on collecting about ANGEL BELMER and of the 4th Corps at SAILLY AU BOIS. N.Z. Division will occupy and hold the line HAMEL–SERRE and close the gap between the right of the 62nd Divn. and the left of the 12th Divn . . .
> Should the enemy be encountered he must be pushed Eastwards and every endeavor made to get touch with the Right of the 62nd Divn and cover their flank.[53]

By the early morning of 26 March Russell had established his headquarters at Hédauville and the first of the New Zealand units was arriving. But the division was strung out on the road for many miles so that, as they arrived at Hédauville, the units had to be committed piecemeal to the battle. There was no time for reconnaissance and a lack of information about the exact location of the advancing Germans and their numbers. A plan was hastily worked out. The first battalion to arrive at Hédauville would be sent through the village of Mailly-Maillet to occupy an outpost on the dominant Engelbelmer–Auchonvillers Ridge. Here it could protect the New Zealand Division's right flank as it advanced to contact the Germans. Then two infantry brigades would make the main advance to Serre and Hamel — one to occupy Hamel and link up with V Corps, the other to secure the road north from Beaumont-Hamel to Hébuterne, swinging back to Serre and linking up with IV Corps at Puisieux. When it arrived the third brigade would extend the line north to hold the high ground from Colincamps to Hébuterne. It was an ambitious plan and Russell soon realised that he lacked the resources to carry it out. He stressed, however, that if the New Zealand brigades encountered superior numbers of the enemy they were to check their progress and manoeuvre to establish a solid line of defence on favourable ground. 'The definitely affirmed principle on which these operations were based was that whatever the development of the enemy offensive, the New Zealand Division was to set itself as an impassable barrier to the German onslaught.'[54]

The first unit to arrive at Russell's new headquarters, at 2 a.m. on 26 March, was the 1st Battalion of the New Zealand Rifle Brigade (hereafter, the 1st Rifles), after a 10-mile march from Pont Noyelles. After resting for four hours, the battalion set out at 6 o'clock to occupy Englebelmer and Auchonvillers and the connecting ridge line. This, it was hoped, would cover the advance of the rest of the division. By mid-morning only four other complete battalions had reached Hédauville: the 1st and 2nd Auckland, and the 1st and 2nd Canterbury battalions. Three companies of the 2nd Battalion of the Rifle Brigade (hereafter, the 2nd Rifles) and two machine-gun companies had also arrived. Russell, aware of the urgency of the situation and how little time he had to concentrate his division, formed these battalions into two composite brigade groups, each containing two battalions and a machine-gun company. The 1st and 2nd Canterbury Battalions were designated the 2nd Brigade; the two Auckland battalions and the companies of the Rifle battalion formed the 1st Brigade. In the afternoon both brigades moved forward to fill the gap between Hamel and Puisieux.

The New Zealand soldiers were heading for a large hole in the British lines through which the Germans were advancing. For four days now the Germans had met with no serious opposition and they were 'flushed with victory'.[55] They had now passed the old front lines of 1916 and were capturing new French towns and villages. The city of Amiens was within their grasp. Shortly, without its artillery support, the New Zealand Division would have to fight the advancing Germans with only the weapons they carried. The two infantry brigades were at half their normal strength and the division's flanks were exposed. As soon as the marching stopped, a hard fight could be expected. All told, it was a very risky prospect as General Russell well recognised. 'The Division came on in the nick of time. There was a big gap and by dint of hard marching we managed to fill it just in time . . . I was not sure that we were not in for a catastrophe.'[56]

Russell was certainly risking the fate of his prized division, but the situation was desperate. Though the German offensive was slowing, it was far from a spent force. Pushing the New Zealand Division piecemeal into the large gap in the Third Army was a leap in the dark. If the Germans could not be halted on this new line the New Zealanders might well suffer the same fate as the South African Brigade.

Chapter 5

Into the Storm:
26 March 1918

The 1st Rifles had a number of important tasks to perform on that fine spring morning in March 1918. First, it was to advance through Mailly-Maillet, in the scenic Picardy region of the Somme, ensuring that the village was clear of enemy troops. Then the battalion had to establish an outpost line on the Auchonvillers Ridge, an important piece of high ground. In doing so it was to establish contact with 12 Division of V Corps at Englebelmer, while covering the deployment of the 2nd and 1st Infantry Brigades in their advance to Hamel and Serre. To help them achieve these tasks the 1st Rifles had been allocated two sections of the Canterbury Company of the Machine Gun Battalion. By the end of the day these two sections would more than prove their worth.

At 6.30 a.m. the 1st Rifles, with their two sections of machine guns, moved from Hédauville, up gentle slopes northeast towards Mailly-Maillet. Using a company well in advance as a protective screen the battalion advanced in open formation; they passed through Mailly-Maillet just after 9 a.m. An advanced brigade headquarters was established in the village. It was not until 11 a.m. that the New Zealanders encountered the Germans, some 500 yards east of Auchonvillers. The battalion's screening company bumped into several German patrols which had skirted around the open flank of 12 Division and were pushing westward. These patrols were easily driven off by Lewis gun and rifle fire from the centre platoon of the screening company. Many casualties were inflicted on the fleeing Germans. This company then pushed forward to the road leading to Hébuterne and started to advance along it. At the major crossroad to Serre stood a sugar refinery and here the company engaged a strong enemy position. The fighting was fierce and at close range — sometimes less than 20 yards separated the combatants. One rifleman accounted for fourteen Germans, including two

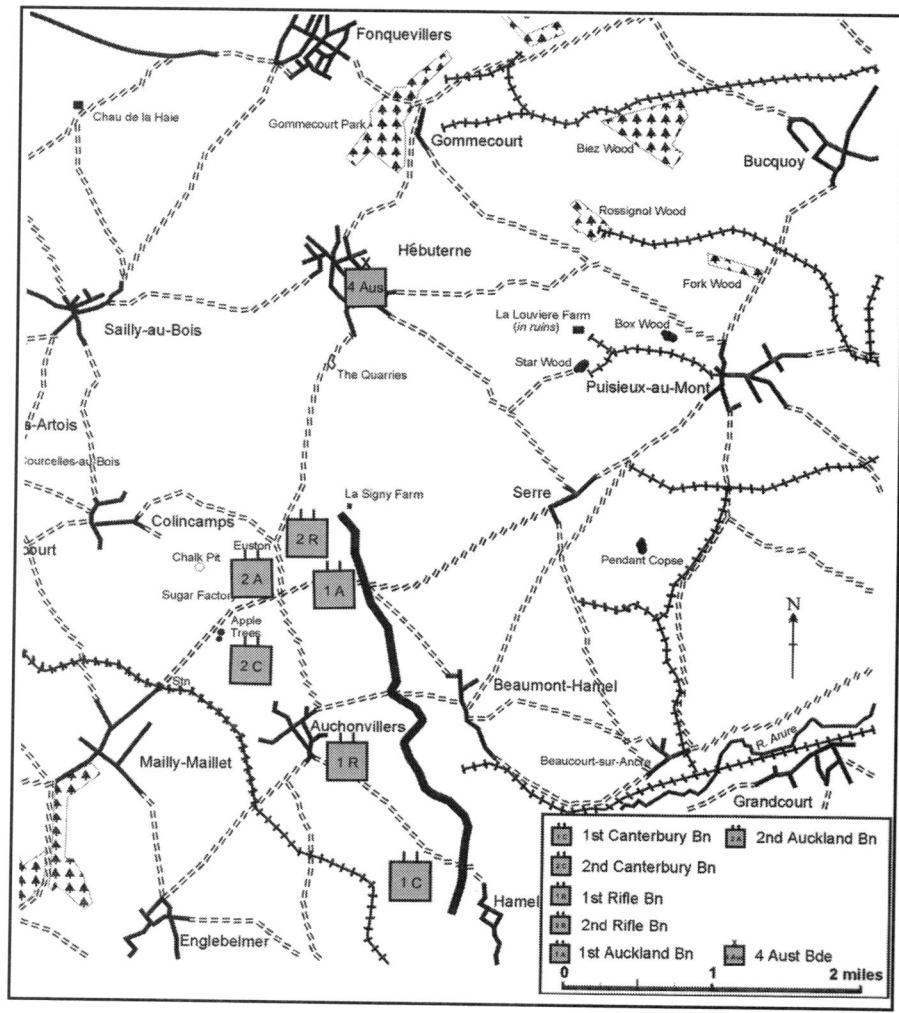

Where NZ Division was committed on 26 March 1918

officers, while the Lewis gun section of this company accounted for a further 90 enemy soldiers.[1]

The odds, however, were against this isolated company and it was nearly overrun. At the last moment, two other companies of the 1st Rifles arrived and occupied the high ground of the Auchonvillers Ridge, meeting little resistance. One company of the battalion was held in reserve. The company occupying the right portion of the ridge pushed out patrols to a distance of 2 miles and easily linked up with 12 Division of V Corps at Hamel. Things remained relatively quiet on this right flank and in the centre of the ridge. Meanwhile, though, the two rifle platoons on the extreme left were fighting for their lives, trying to prevent the enemy from advancing up the sunken road from the sugar factory. Machine-gun and rifle fire coming from Hébuterne was also severe. The enemy surrounded the sugar factory in force. There were about 300 Germans now in position across the Serre Road and fresh troops could be seen marching westwards from Serre. The Germans called upon the platoon on the extreme left to surrender. Though cut off from the rest of the company, this platoon refused to give in and kept fighting. Only the support provided by two machine guns prevented the New Zealanders from being routed. By 1 p.m. the situation was desperate and the battalion commander committed half his reserve and his support company to hold this flank open. The Germans were held up at the sugar factory, but they remained a potent threat.

Rifleman Fred Avery of the battalion's C Company was hit in the shoulder and hand by a German machine gun while fighting at the factory. From a strict Catholic family, he had departed New Zealand with a stern warning from his father: 'The Germans won't be your enemy, it will be women, so be careful'. On the Serre Road, Rifleman Avery learned that the Germans were equally dangerous:

> Well, it [was] mostly a train ride, and then a long walk. I remember I had a sleep . . . on the steps of the Amiens Cathedral. And we were there till we got the orders to go in. Into a bit of a ditch and the sunken roads. We'd call them a hollow here . . . Then we had to attack a sugar refinery near Colincamps. And that's where I got my [wound]. There was so much stuff flying you don't know what hit you. You don't know whether it was machine guns or shell burst. You couldn't tell what hit you. It was raining and mud & slush at the time. I didn't come conscious until I woke up in Walton-on-Thames, London . . . It was wet & cold and I was in a lot of pain.[2]

Between 3 and 4 p.m. the two Canterbury Battalions of the 2nd Brigade advancing to their objectives passed through the positions of the 1st Rifles and turned the tide against the Germans on the sunken road. With 1st Rifle's left flank now secure, the New Zealand Division's outpost line was firmly established and doing its job of covering the deployment of the two infantry brigades. As well as this, the division's right flank was anchored to V Corps.

During this hotly contested engagement, the Germans, a battalion of the 4th Division, had attacked with great courage and their losses were severe. As the historian of the Rifle Brigade recorded

> The fearlessness displayed by the German leaders evoked the unbounded admiration of our men. Possibly they were unduly flushed with the victories of the past few days, for they repeatedly dashed forward with what appeared to be the utmost foolhardiness, and it was clear that a realization of the fact that they were now striking at a line practically immovable had not yet dawned upon their minds.[3]

The 1st Rifles had had a remarkable day. It now became part of the 2nd Brigade.

The New Zealand infantry brigades that advanced to meet the Germans on the afternoon of 26 March had been cobbled together from units as they arrived at Hédauville. The first brigade to set off was the 2nd Brigade (temporarily designated A Brigade) under the command of Brigadier Robert Young. It consisted of the 1st and 2nd Canterbury Battalions plus a machine-gun company, about half its normal battle strength. After the redistribution of equipment and ammunition, the insertion of detonators into the Mills bombs and a hot meal hurriedly eaten, the brigade set out from Hédauville at noon. Its task was to occupy the ridge line overlooking the Ancre from Hamel in the south, northwest to Beaumont-Hamel.

The 2nd Canterbury Battalion led the way, advancing in artillery formation with platoons spread out at 100-yard intervals and with a protective screen of scouts in front. The battalion advanced down the Mailly-Maillet Road, reaching the village without opposition. Knowing nothing of the situation to its north and with many enemy troops in the sunken road, 2nd Canterbury sent one company down the Serre Road to assist the hard-pressed left flank of the 1st Rifles. This company took up a position on a stretch of high ground known as the Apple Trees, about a half-mile northeast of Mailly-Maillet. It would protect the left flank of 2nd Brigade as it advanced.

Meanwhile the 1st Canterbury Battalion, also in artillery formation, moved southeast of Mailly-Maillet in an attempt to link up with the

12th Division on the New Zealand Division's right flank. Young Lieutenant John Harcourt found this movement impressive. It was 'carried out exactly as if on parade and was a great sight — must be about the only occasion on record that such a stunt had been carried out according to textbook'.[4] At 4 p.m. 1st Canterbury moved through the outpost line established by the 1st Rifles and on to the brigade's objective, establishing a line west of Hamel and southwest of Beaumont-Hamel. It experienced some light shelling, but took its objectives easily. Harcourt, a platoon commander of the 13th North Canterbury and Westland Company, recorded the experience in his diary:

> On our left we could see the 1st Bde [it was actually the 1st Rifles] having a good scrap but we found a few Tommies holding some old trenches (the old British Line on the Somme) in front of us. Occupied these. The Hun could be seen retiring over a hill some distance in front and we peppered him with rifle & MG fire. At the time we could have advanced almost unopposed but the 'Heads' decided to stay there.[5]

The 2nd Canterbury Battalion attempted to do the same on the left of the line but experienced considerable difficulties. At Auchonvillers the battalion came under heavy machine-gun fire and light shelling. It took the village, moved through it and continued to its objective, the old British trench line of 1916.

Private William Morris of the 12th Nelson Company remembered this day more than 70 years later. The time spent in training for open warfare had been well worth the effort. After three days on the march:

> We ended up on a hillside like that one there and it was a nice sunny day . . . and we had our first hot food — a plate of porridge. Not much of a feed, was it? Then we started off and it was all rolling downs . . . And there were Australians on that side and New Zealanders on this side. All in order, one section here, one here and so on. I said to the bloke in front of me, 'Good Lord, it doesn't look like there is a war on'. I just got the words out of my mouth and old Jerry turned a machine gun on us. Well, there wasn't a second and there wasn't a bloke standing up, they all went down like a shot. We were trained to do that, you see. We never got any casualties then.

When his company reached the old British trenches, Private Morris was confronted by a German soldier there and was forced to bayonet him. 'It was the only time I used a bayonet. I'm glad it was the last. I was nearly sick. It was a terrible thing to do.'[6]

A new defensive line had been formed, about 3000 yards in advance of the outpost line of the 1st Rifles and about 1000 yards northeast of Auchonvillers. On the left the 2nd Canterbury Battalion was occupying a portion of the old British trenches while further south, 1st Canterbury was on the high ground and had linked up with the 12th Division. The situation was far from secure, though. From the ridge they now held the New Zealanders overlooked the Ancre Valley as far back as Thiepval. It was full of German soldiers on the move. To their north, they could see the 4th German Division in Beaumont-Hamel and heading towards Auchonvillers. The New Zealand machine gunners soon took a heavy toll on the advancing Germans, forcing them to take cover. The left flank of 2nd Canterbury, resting on the Apple Trees, was 'up in the air'. Its casualties were few but 'flank connection was not good'.[7] The Germans were in possession of One Tree Hill between Beaumont-Hamel and Colincamps, which was reported to be in enemy hands. There was considerable opposition on the left flank and the brigade lacked a reserve to deal with it. Fresh New Zealand units were eagerly awaited.

The 1st Canterbury Battalion had had a much easier time, as its war diary reveals:

> Reveille: 2 a.m. Marched to HEDAUVILLE, where we arrived about 9 a.m., and where we found the greater portion of the Division already assembled. A hot meal, and a short rest, and orders for the attack were explained to all ranks. One bomb per man was issued, 'B' Teams told off and final preparations made. The task allotted to this Battalion was that of filling the gap which existed between BEAUMONT HAMEL on the left and the village of HAMEL on the right. 2nd Canty. were on our left. Shortly after noon the Battalion moved off by Platoons at intervals . . . On coming under close range Artillery and Machine Gun fire the attackers deployed and arrived at the objective with practically no casualties. Consolidation was not difficult as a complete system of trenches in good order already existed and almost coincided with the proposed line. Touch was secured on both flanks, and with three platoons per Coy. in the front line

and a reserve platoon some 200 yards in rear the night passed quietly. The general situation to the right of HAMEL was obscure. Battalion H.Q. was established at . . . with Brigade H.Q. at a Chateau in MAILLY-MALLET. There was no covering artillery. Much movement on the part of the Enemy could be observed across the ANCRE on the opposite crest.[8]

The 2nd Brigade had advanced just in time to prevent the Germans from occupying the old British trenches in considerable strength and thereby holding much of the high ground in the area. As Brigadier Young recorded, 'It was apparent that I had occupied my position only just in time, as the enemy had crossed the ANCRE in places, and occupied part of the trench system in the vicinity of the Northern half of my objective'.[9] The 1916 trenches were in reasonably good condition, considering that they had been abandoned for 20 months. The precarious situation north of the 2nd Brigade was resolved by the arrival of the 1st Brigade in the early evening of 26 March. This brigade linked up with 2nd Canterbury's left flank and it was 1st Brigade's turn to have its flank 'up in the air' for a while. The night of 26 March 'passed quietly'[10] for the 2nd Brigade. It faced some light shelling and machine-gun fire but consolidated its line by intensive digging and by sending out fighting patrols. As John Harcourt noted in his diary, 'The night passed uneventfully except for a smoke bomb dump left over from the 1916 being exploded by a Lewis gun shot & rather putting the wind up everyone including the Hun.'[11]

The 1st Brigade, consisting of the 1st and 2nd Auckland Battalions, three companies of 2nd Rifles and a machine-gun company (and temporarily designated as B Brigade), and under the command of Brigadier General C.W. Melvill, did not set off from Hédauville until 2 p.m. This brigade was delayed from joining the other New Zealand units on the high ground because of the news that the Germans had taken Colincamps. The village had to be cleared because it was well to the rear of where the New Zealanders were attempting to establish their new line of defence. Once Colincamps was free of the enemy, 1st Brigade could continue its advance. It hoped to reach as far east as Serre, some $3^1/_2$ miles from Mailly-Maillet.

The brigade set off with 1st Auckland on the right, 2nd Rifles on the left and with 2nd Auckland in support. The road to Serre provided a clear direction of the attack and was the dividing line for both battalions. When the 1st Brigade reached the flank of 1st Rifles on the Auchonvillers Ridge it came under heavy fire. There was fierce opposition at the sugar factory and the enemy was across the Serre Road and holding it in force. Both leading battalions of the brigade immediately went into action.

The 1st Auckland Battalion had been advancing cautiously along the Serre road. As the men neared a large windmill two German machine guns fired on them. The Aucklanders immediately swung half-right and moved into position to attack this threat. With two infantry companies leading and another holding the Serre Road as its left flank, they advanced in artillery formation towards the Apple Trees and a long hedge running in front of them. The German machine-gun fire was intense and a number of men were wounded. From the hedge the ground fell away for some distance and then, after a small level section, rose again to the Serre Ridge. At the foot of the ridge, just to the right of the sugar refinery, one of the Auckland companies was checked in its advance. The machine-gun barrage was too heavy to continue the assault, so the company halted in the sunken road. The men gained a short respite while their officers looked for a way to continue the advance. Meantime the other company had been successful in their attack and were well forward and deep into the enemy positions. They took three machine guns, killed many Germans and put the rest to flight.

Private Jesse Stayte, who was 43 years old in 1918, wrote a vivid account of this attack in his diary. The battalion had moved out from Mailly-Maillet at 4.30 p.m. and was just past the windmill when the men were ordered to fix bayonets and move into artillery formation. They advanced up a gentle crest with a hedge running across its top. They had just broken through the hedge when:

> all at once we were under arty fire from Fritz's guns. The shells dropped right amongst us & we at once got the order to charge. Many were hit before we left the assembly place, but soon we were off got to the hedge and trees and it was here that we first got into the fight proper. Fritz seemed to have the range to a yard and his shells and bullets from machine guns and rifles simply deafened one. The screech of bullets was awful and our men began to fall rapidly. We had 800 yards to go down a slope before we could get cover. Fritz was on the ridge in front. However we went on and got to the bottom where there was a trench which

was our objective and we took it but we left a trail of dead and wounded all down that slope.

Then came word that the Germans were preparing a counterattack so another bayonet charge was needed, 'and we went over to them again and this time we were on more even terms and got among them with the Bayonet and drove them back and so spoiled their chance of a counter attack just then'. These attacks were nerve-wracking experiences for Private Stayte.

> This was my first time over the top and I hope I may never again have to go over. We were all naturally nervous at the start but once we started and saw our mates going down all fear vanished and our aim was to get to them with our Bayonets, and when we did get there they ran like a flock of sheep and it was simply a matter of shooting them as they ran.[12]

Jesse Stayte, whose brother Ollie had been killed in January 1918, did not see the end of the war. He was killed on 1 October that year, leaving a wife and six children in New Zealand to cope without him.

After more than 70 years of reflection Thomas Eltringham, a Lewis gunner in the 2nd Auckland Battalion, knew what had sustained him and the other soldiers during the terrible ordeal of close combat.

> I was never fitter in my life than when I was training . . . that stands you in pretty good stead . . . helps you a lot later on . . . and you could never find better cobbers than the jokers you were in the line with . . . Never let your mates down, that was a good motto . . . People used to say to me, 'Was you scared?' Yes, who wouldn't be? But, I said my biggest worry was not to let my mates think I was scared. Mustn't let them down.[13]

The 1st Auckland was in a precarious position. One of its rifle companies was now well ahead of the other and isolated in enemy territory. It could withdraw or the other company could renew its attack. The latter option was chosen. The stalled company was reinforced and preparations were made to renew the attack at nightfall. By dusk, everything was ready.

As darkness fell, the company commander, Captain H.R. Vercoe, gave the signal to attack and led the way, yelling, 'Come on, boys; rush them, rush them!' The men surged up the gentle slope and pressed their attack hard, despite heavy machine-gun fire. 'The Aucklanders closed in with the cold steel, and in a few moments the Huns were a crowd of panic-stricken fugitives. It was in vain that their officers endeavoured to rally them — a few were taken prisoner, many were killed and the remainder ran.'[14] The battalion's war diary simply recorded that 'The 16th and 3rd companies advanced & took this point, capturing 40 prisoners & 8 MG's [machine guns] . . . Our line was now reasonably secure and the MG fire slackened considerably.'[15]

Between the sunken road and the Serre Ridge lay only 120 yards of open gentle slope. Yet this attack demonstrated the fighting spirit and great courage of the New Zealand officers and soldiers. Taking the ridge was a significant achievement as it enabled 1st Auckland to link up with the 2nd Canterbury Battalion on their right flank.

North of the Serre Road, 2nd Rifles tried to advance to a road just northwest of Serre village. Its advance was rapid and steady until it struck heavy enemy opposition at the sugar factory. This German stronghold had been a thorn in the New Zealand Division's side all day. The 2nd Rifles' advance was concealed by the smoke of a burning ammunition dump, so that it was able to advance to a prominent hedgerow about 1000 yards east of the refinery, finally in New Zealand possession, and just south of La Signy Farm. The Germans made two unsuccessful attempts to force 2nd Rifles off this site. The left company managed to clear the Germans from the Hébuterne Road where, as a measure of protection, it established a flank guard along the road from Colincamps. The 2nd Rifles captured 37 prisoners and four machine guns in the fighting that night. The sugar refinery, scene of intense fighting all day, was set on fire by German artillery, and burned luridly, making for 'a wild night'.[16]

At 7 p.m., the left flank of 1st Auckland moved forward some 300 yards to connect with the right of the 2nd Rifles. At 10 p.m. the 2nd Auckland Battalion joined its sister battalion on the ridge line. 'The night was bitterly cold and all ranks were in battle order without greatcoats a very trying time was experienced.'[17] Years later Thomas Eltringham remembered this advance:

> Our battalion pushed them back and came to a stall at La Signy Farm which happened to be on higher ground and easily defended

... That is where we had to dig in & settle and reorganise and wait for the next attack ... La Signy Farm was of such a value, being on higher ground and with a good view right to the rear of whoever held it. We must have it or else.[18]

During the morning of 26 March, fourteen Whippet tanks had cleared Colincamps. This was the first time these light tanks had been used in action and their success meant that the New Zealand Division did not have to devote large numbers of soldiers to its rear security. It could focus solely on the enemy in front.

Despite 1st Brigade's achievements, the New Zealand commanders could see instantly that reaching Serre that night, or in the immediate future, was out of the question. The New Zealand line was linked up, but no connection had been established with 4 Australian Brigade, now at Hébuterne. The heights of La Signy Farm, a significant weak point in the New Zealand position, also required urgent attention.

Just after 2 p.m. on 26 March, 4th Australian Brigade of the 4th Australian Division was ordered to Hébuterne, which was reported to have fallen to the Germans. The brigade commander, Brigadier C.H. Brand, directed his four battalions to concentrate near an old windmill while he went forward on horseback to the village with a small reconnaissance party. It was a courageous move. Hébuterne was thought to be in German hands and there were rumours of German armoured cars raiding all along the roads of Picardy. At 3.30 p.m. Brigadier Brand came cantering back and gathered his men around him. He had ridden right into Hébuterne and the village was empty. But, well aware that his troops had not eaten all day, Brand ordered up the brigade cookers and gave his soldiers a hot meal before ordering them to take the village. So the soldiers of 4th Brigade did not set off to occupy the village until 5.40 p.m. C.E.W. Bean was critical of this delay: 'considering the tension of the situation and the vast issues at stake, he [Brand] was indeed a cool commander — the future student may think too cool'.[19] It was well after nightfall when the 4th Brigade reached Hébuterne and the Germans had beaten them to it. They were not there in force, however, and were easily driven out. The fighting that night and in subsequent days completely destroyed what had been a large village. As one New Zealand soldier recorded in his diary, Hébuterne 'is just a heap of ruins now'.[20] By midnight on 26 March, Hébuterne had been taken by the Australians and would provide a solid left flank for the New Zealand Division.

Brigadier Brand's 4th Brigade now became part of the 62nd Division. Brand was informed that the New Zealand Division was immediately south of him and would attempt to swing up and close the gap on his exposed right flank. The brigadier directed his 16th Battalion to swing round towards the east and extend the brigade's flank towards the New Zealanders. The link should be made in the next few hours. Until that gap was closed, it was a cause for considerable anxiety.

The night of 26 March was a quiet one for the New Zealanders now forming part of the Third Army's new line of defence. But the spring temperatures were bitterly cold and there was plenty of work to do as the New Zealanders consolidated their new positions. Fortunately the old British trenches most occupied did not require much repair work. As they always did when occupying new territory, the New Zealanders sent out fighting patrols along the whole of their front to establish where the Germans were and to learn what they were up to. The enemy was occupying Beaumont-Hamel and using their 1916 front-line trenches, but they were up to very little. This was a situation that was not expected to last.

At the end of this first day of action the New Zealand troops committed to the fray occupied a strong and continuous line from just west of Hamel to north of the Serre Road. The southern portion of the gap between IV and V Corps was closed. Observation on the 2nd Brigade front, based primarily on the Auchonvillers Ridge, was excellent, but north of Serre Road it was poor. Here the Germans still held the high ground and overlooked the New Zealand positions. At La Signy Farm the situation was particularly bad.

The main problem for the Allies was that, though much reduced by the day's activities, the gap had still not been closed. Between 4th Australian Brigade at Hébuterne and the left flank of the New Zealand line at La Signy Farm its northern portion was now about a mile and half long. If the Third Army was to make a stand on its current lines of defence, this gap must be closed without delay. This task would be the responsibility of those New Zealand units not yet committed to the battle.

On 26 March things improved dramatically for the British Army. Though the 29 British divisions that had been in the line since 21 March were exhausted and their numbers much reduced, the spirit of

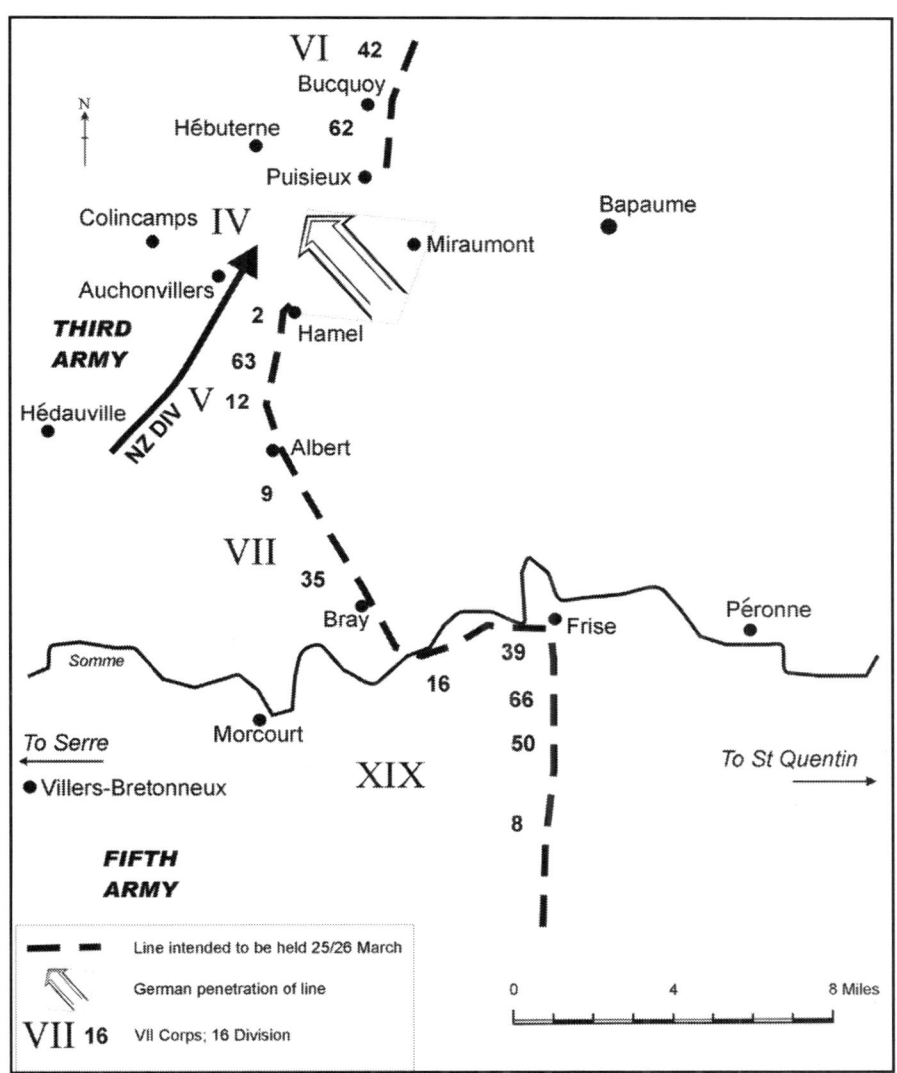

The gap in the Allied line on the evening of 26 March 1918

the survivors remained strong and there was considerable fight left in them. This was remarkable given the force that had been thrown against them. But the key to survival for the British was the nine fresh divisions, all of which had been committed to battle by 26 March, eight of them north of the Somme. There they were making a telling difference. The new line they had helped establish was almost continuous and was holding well. 'The battle was now becoming stabilised, and after the 26th March the enemy, although he made desperate and despairing efforts, gained from the British no ground worth mentioning. Reinforcements had now appeared and the idea of defeat, never very potent, was fading away.'[21]

The same could not be said for the Germans. There were plenty of indications that they, too, were tiring, lacked food and ammunition, and had outpaced their artillery support. As each new German attack failed, with ever-increasing casualty lists, morale began to plummet. For the first time the German soldiers began to doubt whether the *Kaiserschlacht* would succeed.[22]

There is little doubt that the New Zealand Division played a key role in this reversal of fortune, though the credit for halting the Germans on 26 March has to be shared with other divisions in the line. John Coleman was correct in his assessment:

> So the little New Zealand division has again made history in this rotten war. I may tell you that there was absolutely no defence on the two-mile front against old Fritz, which we are at present holding. So our boys did not know where the enemy was, one just had to march on until they ran right into them. Then the fight began and our boys must have absolutely cut the Hun to pieces. Our company was supposed to be up here first, but we were delayed on the way. When we went in to hold the lines there were Huns lying dead in all directions.[23]

Initially the Germans were delighted by the progress they were making in their offensive and believed that the British Army was in a state of collapse. 'If it goes on like this, in 14 days we'll reach the sea,' noted a German officer of the 49th Infantry Regiment on 24 March. But two days later, near Bucquoy and Serre, it was a very different story:

> Now we lay close to the edge of the devastated zone and could already gaze on the promised land. To the right ahead of us, lay

the village of Hébuterne. But two kilometres before this region untouched by war the Englishman holds his last trench ahead of us with colossal toughness . . . The resistance had so strengthened that we could no longer generally break it down. Unfortunately neither could the troops who relieved us.

As Charles Bean concluded, 'The "colossal toughness" was presumably largely that of the New Zealand Division, and the adjective does not exaggerate its quality.' He was, however, quick to point out that the German was also referring to the defensive efforts of 19th, 62nd and 42nd British Divisions.[24] It would be another 22 years before an advancing German Army finally reached the sea and the New Zealand Division had indeed helped to make history on 26 March 1918. It had, though, already lost 150 men while doing so.[25]

Chapter 6

Stopping the Storm: 27 March 1918

O n the night of 26 March there was still a large gap in the newly
established line. More than a mile wide, it stretched from the
New Zealand 1st Brigade position at La Signy Farm to the 4th Australian Brigade now firmly established at Hébuterne. The importance of
closing this gap was obvious to General Russell and the New Zealand
staff officers. As more New Zealand battalions arrived at Hédauville
they were immediately gathered up and formed into a composite brigade under the command of Lieutenant Colonel A.E. Stewart of the
New Zealand Rifle Brigade. A real mixture of units, the brigade consisted of the headquarters of the Rifle Brigade, the 3rd Battalion New
Zealand Rifle Brigade (hereafter 3rd Rifles), the 2nd Wellington and
2nd Otago Battalions. The Wellington Machine Gun Company was
also part of the brigade. General Russell kept the last two battalions to
arrive at Hédauville that night as a divisional reserve. They would be
sorely needed in the following days. Stewart's orders were to extend the
New Zealand line north to the Hébuterne Road and link up with the
Australians there. At 1 a.m. on the morning of 27 March Stewart's
composite brigade set off to find the Australians and close the gap.

The night was perfect for marching. It was cold and clear, the moonlight so bright that maps could be clearly read. There had been no time
to issue written orders, so each unit was given its instructions while on
the move. The brigade marched through Mailly-Maillet and reached
Colincamps safely at 4 a.m. There, headquarters were quickly established. The moon had now set so that the battalions, led by the 2nd
Otago, moved out from Colincamps quickly in order to take advantage
of the short period of darkness. The 2nd Otago Battalion marched directly east in order to screen the advance of the rest of the brigade. The
2nd Wellingtons on the right was to link up with the 1st Brigade at La

Signy Farm while the 3rd Rifles, marching northeast along the road to Hébuterne, would provide the link with the Australians. Once past the outskirts of Colincamps the New Zealanders came under heavy machine-gun fire that forced them to deploy in skirmishing order. In other words, they thinned out the numbers with gaps between individual soldiers and larger spaces between sections of infantry.

After spending only fifteen minutes in Colincamps, the 3rd Rifles moved off as fast as they could. After making contact with the Australians at Hébuterne, the riflemen would turn to the right. Two companies would then be sent in attack formation to the high ground east of the Hébuterne road while the other company formed a support line in a strong defensive position 100 yards east of the road. There it could cover the whole battalion front with fire. According to the history of the Rifle Brigade, the plan 'was carried out with clockwork precision'.[1] The 3rd Rifles, under the command of Lieutenant Colonel Edward Puttick, who would be severely wounded just after midday, advanced in perfect order against machine-gun and rifle fire of moderate intensity. When the battalion linked with the Australians just south of Hébuterne, two companies set off for the high ground east of the village. The company on the left gained the crest of a ridge some 600 yards away. With this flank extended, the other advancing company came up level with it so that by 6.45 a.m. the battalion had secured its objective. This important ridge was in New Zealand hands and the link-up with the Australians was secure. The fighting had not been severe despite the enemy outnumbering them. The Germans had not been expecting an attack and most fled from the ridge. Only at one point had there been any resistance and the determined riflemen charged this location with fixed bayonets, which soon dispersed the German defenders.

Bernard Cottrell witnessed the attack and described it in a letter to his parents:

> Just a few lines, not so hurried this time, but still am not yet able to write much, censorship will now be very strict on account of the serious position we were in, how serious very few realise . . . The battle & situations leading up to it I will leave later, but we spent 3 freezing nights up in the trenches & that together with travelling made 4 or 5 nights without rest. Many things happened one outstanding feature was a bayonet charge, quite like a moving picture show & quite the old style of things, it resulted in

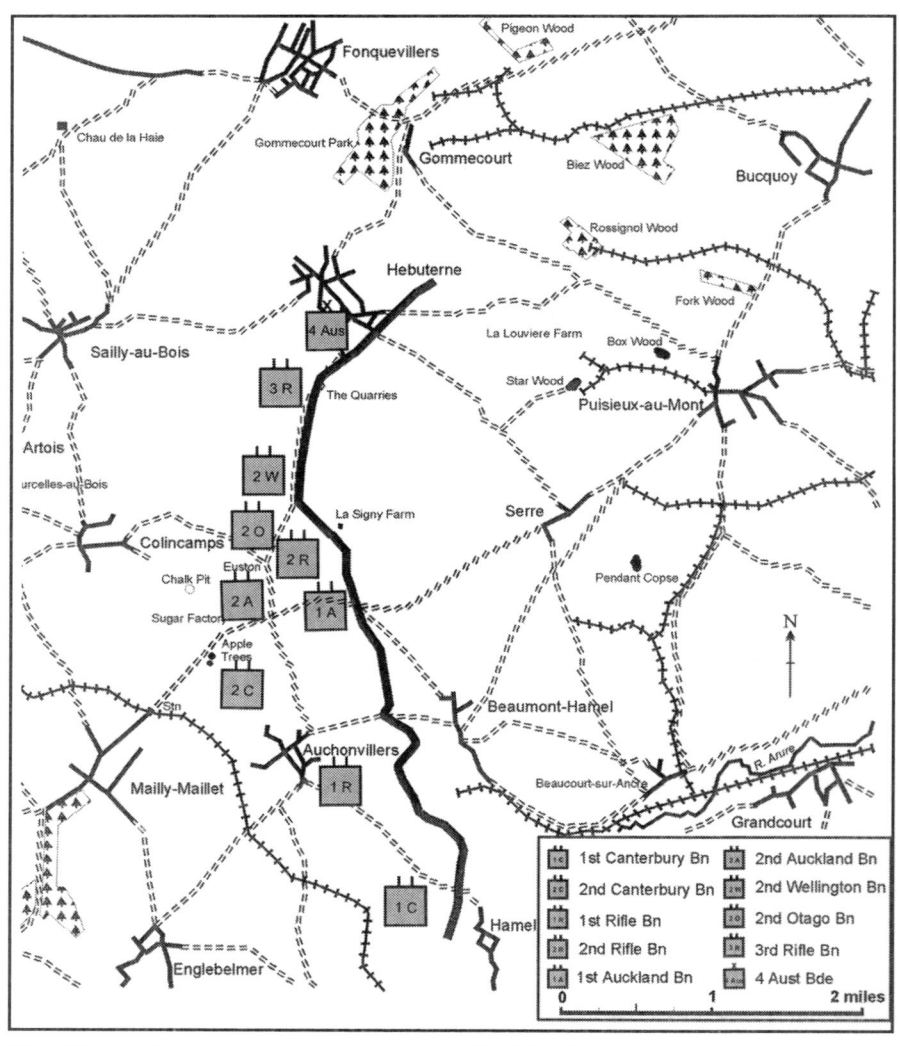

New Zealand positions on the morning of 27 March 1918

bringing in 17 machine guns. I viewed it from the front line, it was as bright as day, moonlight & Fritz light the dry grass in front so everything stood out very vividly. Our losses were not great in killed but taken together with wounded amounted to a fair number. Things are not all finished yet, but wait & you will get all news, & don't worry for me as things are quite alright with me now.[2]

The 3rd Rifles' attack succeeded because of the speed with which it was launched and the tactical surprise it achieved. By 7 a.m. on 27 March the northern portion of the gap had been closed.

Unfortunately, the 2nd Wellington Battalion on the brigade's right flank had a much tougher time and failed to reach its objective. It ran into heavy German machine-gun fire from near La Signy Farm. One of the companies attacked an enemy outpost there, killing fourteen Germans and capturing 53 others. But the intensity of the fire from the ridge in front of La Signy Farm halted further progress and the 2nd Wellingtons were forced to dig in some 400 yards west of the Hébuterne Road, which had been their final objective. Though the Germans still held the high ground and overlooked Colincamps, it made little difference to the final outcome. Despite falling short of their final objective the 2nd Wellington Battalion managed to link up with the 3rd Rifles on their left and the 2nd Rifles on their right at the road junction.

The composite brigade hastily formed on the night of 26 March had fulfilled the task assigned to it with relative ease. It had made contact with the Australians and secured the important ridge between La Signy Farm and Hébuterne. The dangerous gap on the division's northern flank had been closed. More significantly, the new British front now extended in an unbroken line from Hébuterne to Hamel. The open gate had been slammed shut. Now it needed to be firmly secured.

On 27 March, except for the area in front of La Signy Farm, the Australians and New Zealanders occupied a considerable portion of high ground overlooking much of the old Somme battlefield. They had an especially good view over the several spurs and gullies leading towards the hidden valley of the Ancre, despite the long grass that was now growing there. The village of Hébuterne, now occupied by the Australians, was also on high ground. Due south on the same ridge as Hébuterne was Auchonvillers, now held by the New Zealand Division. Southeast, 2 miles away on the plateau beyond the nearest depression stood 'the bare stump of Serre'.[3] A mile northeast of Serre in a gully leading to the Ancre was Puisieux. On the heights, $1^1/_2$ miles northeast of this lay Bucquoy, held by the remnants of the British 62nd Division. So the Australian and New Zealand soldiers had the distinct tactical advantage of being able to see for some considerable distance to their front. Everywhere they looked on the morning of 27 March, their front was alive with the movement of German troops making ready to resume their advance. The Germans were exposed and vulnerable. As Bean noted, this was a sight 'such as Australian infantry had never before watched from their front trenches',[4] and New Zealand veteran and historian Ormond Burton wrote that 'Such an opportunity had not come to most of them [the New Zealand soldiers in the line] during the whole war'.[5]

The Germans must have believed that the gap in front of them was still open: they began advancing towards the New Zealand and Australian positions as if on parade and 'without the slightest attempt at concealment'.[6] For a brief moment the New Zealanders and Australians were stunned by the sheer audacity of their opponents. 'Look at the bloody bastards coming up the road,' shouted a soldier in the 2nd Auckland Battalion as the Germans marched in four columns down the Serre Road.[7] Then every man capable of firing a rifle or machine gun opened up on the advancing Germans. They took a fearful toll on their enemy that morning and inflicted thousands of casualties in the space of a few minutes, as James McWhirter recorded: 'As we watched we could see the enemy coming marching up the road, some smoking, some laughing, as if they were marching on to Paris. What an eye opener they would get in a few minutes, everyone was eager to shoot, but we must wait till we get orders.' The Germans were allowed to get to within 50 yards of the New Zealand front line before the order was given to open fire:

> It was like corn before the sicle [*sic*], machine guns cracked every-
> one of the enemy fell like ninepins, horses struggled on the ground,
> those who did escape flew in a panic and there was congestion all
> along the road. The dead were heaped on top of one another, the
> German red-cross were carrying away the corpses for three days
> afterwards.[8]

Oscar Reston, a signaller in one of the Canterbury Battalions, told a similar story. On the morning of 27 March 1918, his battalion 'met

Fritzy coming up the road in columns of four. We got stuck into them with machine guns and rifles . . . The New Zealanders had the drop on them. We were waiting for them to come down the road. We kept quiet until they got within shooting distance and then tore into them.'[9] And William Morris of the 12th Nelson Company, 2nd Canterbury Battalion, was haunted for the rest of his life by the killing that occurred on that fateful morning.

> The Germans come over three times. Three times the next day in close formation. As close as you and I. And they just wiped them down. Wiped them down. And he sent another lot and he got wiped down the same. Terrible! One lot of Australian soldiers when we were going up there, they met a whole regiment of Germans coming along a sunken road — they had the Colonel right along in the front coming along the sunken road and they came to the top of the hill and there they were. They just wiped the whole lot out. They had four deep, cleared the whole thing. Terrible! A terrible thing to happen, isn't it? Just murder.

But, as Morris realised, 'It was you or them.'[10]

The killing continued throughout the day. In an attempt to get their advance moving again, the Germans abandoned their tactics of infiltration in favour of full frontal infantry attacks supported by heavy artillery and machine-gun fire. The New Zealanders were aided by the fact that their position formed the boundary line for two German armies — the Second and the Seventeenth — so that, according to the British official historian, 'the enemy's efforts were not well combined'.[11] Still, the New Zealanders in the front line on that day knew they were in for a tough time, but they were determined not to be ejected from their newly established positions. Captain George Tuck of the 2nd Auckland Battalion kept a detailed diary of events. That crucial morning he caught the determination of the New Zealand troops:

> We took a section of trench over this morning at 5 am. Fritz has been massing all morning in our immediate front where he had been allowed to cross the Ancre. Consequence is he intends to develop his advantage here where we threw him back some distance yesterday & closed the gap. The preliminary bombardment is down on us, we ourselves have practically no artillery & we expect him to launch his offensive at any moment. He will get the surprise of his life.[12]

The fighting was continuous from midday, but the Germans launched four large counterattacks against the New Zealand positions that afternoon. The first came just after noon; the others followed at 1 p.m., 3.30 p.m. and at 7 p.m. Only in the last counterattack did the Germans succeed in capturing any ground from the hard-pressed New Zealanders. They attacked on a front of 1500 yards midway between the sugar refinery and Hébuterne. The 2nd Wellington Battalion was forced back off its defensive position to a distance 500 yards from the road. At 8.50 p.m. the reserve company, from Hawke's Bay, tried to counterattack in an effort to regain the ground, but it made little headway against the enemy party now well established on the Wellingtons' old position, protected by machine guns and holding a section of the Hébuterne–sugar factory road. The New Zealanders fought hard, killing about 60 of the enemy and capturing five machine guns. But their own casualties were heavy and they could not re-establish the 2nd Wellington's original line. The battalion's casualties on this day were four officers and 69 soldiers.

This loss of ground had the potential to cause a huge disruption along the New Zealand line. That it did not was the result of fast and courageous action by the men of the 3rd Rifle Battalion. The forcing back of 2nd Wellington's position had left the flank of the 3rd Rifles exposed. The latter immediately altered its position to form a defensive flank, but it could spare only one platoon to carry out this vital task. This soon came under intense pressure from the Germans and the platoon's officer was killed in an early exchange of fire. A sergeant and then a corporal took charge of the platoon and held the Germans at bay. This pressured flank was reinforced first by the reserve platoon, then by the bulk of C Company, which had been detained on duty at Amiens. The exposed flank was now secure and managed to regain contact with the 2nd Wellington Battalion.

There were other times throughout the day when the situation hung in the balance. One occurred in the centre of the line at La Signy Farm. There, a young, inexperienced officer in the 2nd Auckland Battalion, after an attack where his platoon's position had been pelted with German stick grenades, decided it was time to withdraw, despite the fact that his men had not suffered any casualties. 'It was a critical moment. The whole army was depending on the New Zealand Division to hold its ground. 2/Auckland were holding the most delicate portion of the divisional front, and the left post of the 15th Company was the key to the whole position.'[13] The situation was soon restored. Captain George Tuck, from the battalion's headquarters, saw the retirement, ran from his position and ordered the men to turn back. He was obeyed and with the sergeant now leading it, the platoon rushed back and retook their trench from the enemy who had just arrived in it. A new officer was immediately assigned and the platoon put up a determined resistance for the rest of the afternoon.

Because the fighting was continuous and the New Zealanders occupied most of the high ground, German casualties mounted steadily throughout the day. In the absence of any artillery support, the New Zealand machine gunners provided the infantry with much-needed fire support and inflicted the bulk of the casualties. For the New Zealand machine-gunners, 27 March 1918 was a red-letter day. The Wellington Company in support of the composite brigade opened the account. It was occupying a superb position on the division's left flank with a commanding view over the whole brigade front. At 10.30 a.m. an enemy battalion was observed at 1800 yards' range moving from near Hébuterne. The Wellington Company's machine guns at once opened up on them and soon found the range. This 'had the effect of scattering and thoroughly disorganising the enemy. Casualties could not be observed but the action of the enemy in breaking and scattering in all directions made it evident that casualties had been inflicted.'[14]

At noon the situation was repeated, though this time the deadly effect of the machine-gun fire could be observed: 'Two guns at a range of 700 yards engaged two companies of the enemy in mass formation. The enemy was literally mowed down and stretcher-bearers were observed working at the point for three hours afterwards.'[15] The latter were not fired upon as they went about their life-saving work.

But still the Germans kept coming. Mid-afternoon the next target appeared: two long advancing columns of enemy infantry 1600 yards away and gradually converging over the Serre Ridge. Although the Germans were well within the range of the New Zealand machine guns, the order was passed not to open fire until the enemy was within 1000 yards. 'Probably no better target presented itself to the New Zealand Machine Gun Corps in France, and the fullest advantage was taken of it.'[16] The machine guns played havoc.

With the second burst of fire about 50 of the enemy were seen to fall, a long burst was then fired into the mass and a very great number fell, the remainder broke and took cover in shell holes or undulations. As a meagre estimate 300 casualties were inflicted in this instance and until nightfall the ground was observed to be littered with bodies.[17]

The Germans now turned their full attention on these troublesome machine-gunners. Twelve enemy machine-gun crews attempted to move across the open towards an old trench, presumably to establish a machine-gun nest there. They were seen and fired on. Some teams were killed outright; the rest fled, leaving behind their precious guns. When the Germans tried to recover their weapons, more were killed and wounded.

Just after 2 p.m., under cover of artillery fire, some small groups of Germans advanced through an old communication trench and rushed three of the Wellington Company's guns. The commander of A Gun stood his ground and kept firing as ten Germans attempted to seize the weapon. All were killed. C Gun managed to carry out an orderly withdrawal but a party of 30 Germans rushed B Gun. Ten of the attacking Germans were killed before the New Zealand firer was wounded and the gun taken. This was the first time a New Zealand machine gun had fallen into enemy hands, but not for long. A sergeant and some men of the Ruahine Company of the 2nd Wellington Battalion charged the Germans, killing most of them and regaining the lost weapon. In the process the Wellington soldiers captured a German light machine gun.

Still the Germans came on. At 3.30 p.m. they again attacked the composite brigade's position, this time taking the precaution of advancing in open order. They were seen as they came over the ridge some 1200 yards away. The Wellington Company's guns opened up and many of the enemy fell immediately. The rest took cover. For some time afterwards, isolated groups of Germans were seen trying to crawl back over the ridge.

At 4 p.m., when 2nd Wellington was forced back, the gun on the right flank of the Wellington Company was ordered to withdraw. The whole gun team was wounded while doing so and the gun was dismantled and left behind, minus its crucial firing mechanism. This was recovered the next day. The machine guns and rifle fire had inflicted massive casualties on the Germans. '[U]ntil nightfall' the ground in front of the composite brigade was 'littered with dead Huns'.[18]

At 9.10 p.m. on 27 March 1918 Captain George Tuck wrote an entry in his diary that neatly summed up what had been 'a stressing day':

> The Hun has been attacking us all day by all means. Things happened of which I dare not write. Haven't had 10 seconds to myself all the time. We are just holding the bounder but we have suffered pretty heavily — but he more so. If he doesn't put in an attack before the next hour I think all will be well. A thousand pities he was allowed to cross the line of the Ancre.[19]

It had been a real soldier's battle, in which nearly every New Zealander then in the line took part. It was their tenacity and courage as well as the superb leadership skills shown by non-commissioned and junior officers that held the New Zealand line intact. 'The bravery display by all ranks . . . during these attacks was beyond all praise and it was purely due to this that the Hun failed entirely in his efforts.'[20]

Captain Harry Highet was the only officer of his battalion to survive the Passchendaele disaster. Even then he had required hospitalisation in England, having suffered gas inhalation. He returned to the New Zealand Division in time to serve on the Somme in 1918, where his company was occupying part of the old British trenches in 'a very nasty position'. On the morning of 27 March, his company seemed to be alone on the battlefield.

> I got up to this place and there wasn't anybody on the left. So I set out with a man to go way out on the left which I shouldn't have done. I should have sent someone else. But I wanted to have a look. Didn't see anybody. On the way back suddenly the chap with me found that he had a big splinter taken off his rifle, the woodwork of his rifle. Sniper! From then on it was 'Up', go for your life, and down again, until we got to a place out of sight of the sniper. That was a pretty near squeak that was.

Highet's company was under considerable shellfire but his orders were explicit: 'We had word not to move'. But a runner from a Scottish battalion in front of his position brought word that his CO wanted the New Zealanders to move close to the Scots' position as the Germans were going to attack. 'What the hell do we do?' asked Highet. So off he went to the Scots, again risking artillery and rifle fire. By checking the

105

situation personally, Highet decided that there was no need to move his company. The return trip was extremely dangerous. 'On the way back, shell fire was pretty tough. I reckon I was doing 100 yards in 10 seconds.' Highet reached the safety of his trenches just as a shell did. He was covered with dirt, but unscathed.[21]

Like Harry Highet, James Frederick Blakemore was a Passchendaele survivor. In March 1918 he was a sergeant major in one of the Canterbury battalions. On 27 March an incident on the Serre Ridge stirred him to action:

> The Germans were waving a white flag. And when they [New Zealand soldiers] hopped out, three Sergeants got shot. It was a gag, to show themselves. That made me really mad. I lost control of myself. We went from shell-hole to shell-hole . . . to within 30 yards of this strongpoint . . . I had one bomb . . . Mills grenade — I rushed to this crowd . . . and I shot a pair in the head . . . Some were wounded . . . they surrendered.

Blakemore's company commander then came up, called him 'a bloody fool' and recommended him for the Military Medal. It was subsequently awarded.[22]

Conditions in the front line were hard. The day was clear but, in John Harcourt's words, 'dull and cold'. In an effort to keep warm he wrapped a thick towel around him and wore it under his tunic.[23] Private Jesse Stayte of the 1st Auckland Battalion, dug in forward of Mailly-Maillet, described the conditions in his diary: 'The weather is fine and cold, but we have no greatcoats. The food is very poor and water we have none . . . We have not had a cup of tea or anything hot since Sunday morning and we have been shivering all day.'[24] Over the next few days, conditions in the front line would get worse.

The German attacks along the front of IV Corps were unsuccessful, except at Rossignol Wood, north of Hébuterne, and on the corps' right boundary where ground near the village of Hamel was lost. As a result of this development, the 2nd Brigade reinforced their right flank and extended it towards Hamel. Elsewhere along the British front the situation was much the same. On 27 March, the Third Army had been attacked all day by two German armies (the Second and Seventeenth). Losses were heavy on both sides but the Germans did not take a single objective. Ground, none of it significant, had been lost in only four places — north of Albert, north of Ablainzevelle, west of Serre and at Rossignol Wood. The price of these minor gains was dead and wounded German soldiers numbering in their thousands. In most New Zealand units casualties were light. The 2nd Wellington and both Canterbury battalions had suffered the heaviest losses: more than 70 each. In the evening of 27 March, the New Zealand wounded collected from the regimental aid posts (RAPs), the first-line medical treatment centres, numbered just under 300. Also collected from the RAPs were about 100 wounded British soldiers and an equal number of wounded Germans.[25] All the wounded were sent for further treatment and processing at the New Zealand advanced dressing station (ADS) at Mailly-Maillet.

The New Zealanders were elated with their success on 27 March. The 1st Brigade held the difficult centre section of the line and had taken more than 100 German prisoners from five different regiments. Though its left flank had suffered badly, the brigade's war diary could record that 'The operation has left our men in excellent spirits with absolute confidence in themselves and their leaders'.[26] The New Zealand soldiers had every reason to feel this way.

During the night there was a considerable lull in activity along the New Zealand front. General Russell was able to reorganise brigades so that each unit was in its proper parent formation. In the northern sector of the line the rifle battalions were now in the New Zealand Rifle Brigade. Brigadier H.T. Fulton arrived that night to take over command from Lieutenant Colonel Stewart. In the centre of the line the North Island units formed the 1st Brigade, while in the south the battalions from the South Island formed the 2nd New Zealand Infantry Brigade. During this reorganisation, Russell was able to relieve those units that had suffered most from the German attacks and replace them with fresh ones. The 1st Otago Battalion, for example, moved into the line on the Englebelmer-Auchonvillers Ridge to relieve the 1st Rifles, the first New Zealand unit committed to action. As the medical officer of the 1st Rifles noted, this relief was welcome.

> Wednesday 27 March
> Worked all thru last night & got to bed this morning about 3 and rested until nine. Our chaps continue to hold on and casualties are somewhat less. The Battalion was withdrawn during the afternoon and we changed our position . . . now going to bed in hope of a good night's rest.[27]

Many years later Private Edward Bibby, a battalion runner with the 1st Otagos, remembered how difficult this relief was. The first task of Otago soldiers was to deepen the trench the 1st Rifles had been holding. According to Bibby, it was 'one of the hardest jobs I had, you see, being really hungry and trying to dig this gummy stuff on the bottom of the trench'. But by dawn on 28 March the task had been accomplished just in time to put the trenches to good use.[28] Further north at La Signy Farm the 4th Rifles, the last infantry unit to reach Hédauville, took over from the depleted 2nd Wellington Battalion. In the following days the 4th Rifles would make four attempts to recover the lost ground and take the heights of La Signy Farm.

The lull also permitted the completion of a reserve line of defence known as the Purple Line, which would add considerable depth to the New Zealand line. The soldiers from the New Zealand Engineers, the Pioneer Battalion and from three Light Trench Mortar batteries started work on the new position on the afternoon of 27 March and worked throughout the night. The Purple Line ran to the rear of Mailly-Maillet, Colincamps and Hébuterne. Lack of time and manpower made it impossible to build a continuous line of defence so the units allocated to this task concentrated on establishing a series of strong points that offered mutual support. Each could hold 40 men and had at least six firebays, and included adequate drainage, duckboard flooring and barbed wire obstacles to their front. This was backbreaking construction work in uncomfortable and often dangerous conditions.

William Milne was a sapper in the 1st Field Company, New Zealand Engineers. After stand-to on the morning of 27 March, his company marched from Bertrancourt to Mailly-Maillet, where they began to dig five strong points. The task was finished just after 10 p.m. and then the company manned the strong points until dawn. As Milne noted in his diary, 'All in light marching dress — bitterly cold night & all practically frozen.' The company was relieved by an infantry company the next day and marched back to Bertrancourt to collect their packs. By then Milne recorded he was 'Feeling unwell — probably cold & lack of sleep'.[29] For the next few days he was sick and confined to bed.

William Bertrand (also known as William Tume), of Ngati Awa descent, served in the Maori Pioneer Battalion. He was wounded on the Somme by German artillery fire. 'I got wounded in the hip ... How did it happen? If you are out in the rain and a drop of rain hits you, you don't describe it. You just take it for granted.' Digging the strong points on the night of 27–28 March remained a vivid memory:

> I had to lie down, I don't know how many times, to avoid the bullets from machine gun fire sweeping across. The Germans knew we were there. Every chance we got, they'd have flares up in the air. It was just like daylight. When there was a chance came, you hopped out and dug. Dug a hole. When you can get into this hole well you're right. You can carry on digging. It didn't take long to dig a hole that you can get down into when there's bullets flying about.'[30]

Bill Bertrand survived the war but returned to New Zealand to find that his guardians, the Tumes of Urenui, had died in the influenza epidemic. 'It wasn't a very happy home-coming.'

The initial plan had been for the Purple Line to be completed by 5 a.m. on 28 March and be capable of holding two infantry battalions and a machine-gun company. All the strong points were completed well ahead of time, before midnight on 27 March. Within the next four days some 60 such posts were constructed.

The New Zealand position was further strengthened by the arrival of the first units of the division's artillery: four 18-pounder batteries and one howitzer battery. The Divisional Ammunition Column had been hard at work on 26 and 27 March moving a total of 10,000 artillery rounds into the New Zealand front line. As the war diary of one of the artillery brigades states, 'Headquarters and Batteries moved into line at Mailly-Mallet [sic]. All Batteries reported in action by 11 pm.'[31] The artillery had not had time to register their guns so most of this firing was for the psychological effect it produced on both sides. The New Zealand guns kept up a harassing fire on the enemy's forward areas all night, targeting likely German concentration areas around Serre. At 4 a.m. the next day the gunners fired the first counter battery fire, which lasted for just over two hours. As soon as dawn broke on 28 March the New Zealand artillery lost no time in registering their guns along the whole New Zealand front. With excellent observation over the enemy line the New Zealand gunners made their deadly presence felt, especially as the Germans 'showed themselves very freely during the first few days, and could even be seen in bivouacs on the slopes of the ridges behind Beaumont-Hamel'.[32] The early hours of 28 March permitted 'some splendid shooting, which no one enjoyed more than the infantry in the line'.[33]

During the night of 27 March, General Russell moved the New Zealand Division's headquarters from Hédauville to the Chateau at Bus-les-Artois. Almost directly west of Colincamps, Bus-les-Artois was only 4 miles from the New Zealand front-line positions. Russell also took the opportunity to inspect his men. In general he was happy with the New Zealanders' position, though he was concerned about the ground lost near Hamel on the division's southern flank:

> 27 March
> Attacked in two places but held them off — visited Colincamps and looked over position — it is, here a strong one. To the South not so good, and down on left not sticking well — Confusion, some great, on detraining at odd places and altered destination, now being overcome. Artillery of Div just up tonight.[34]

The Germans had far greater reason for concern. Only one German army, the Eighteenth, made any significant progress on 27 March. The Second Army, which had been expected to make the greatest inroads on this day and 'on whose advance the operation mainly depended',[35] made no progress at all. The Second Army had been expecting to find only weak rearguards in its path, but had crashed into a new line defended by fresh New Zealand and Australian troops. The Germans had been made to pay dearly for this wishful thinking. As William Moore has written, 'What had been the most dangerous spot on the front of the Third Army now appeared to have been sealed.'[36] Many German sources regard the lack of progress on 27 March as the decisive moment in the Michael Offensive. This was certainly the view of the commander of the northern group of armies, Crown Prince Rupprecht of Bavaria.[37] When Rupprecht learned of the Second Army's lack of progress he ordered three of the German High Command's reserve divisions to attack Hébuterne the next day with the aim of breaking through to Doullens. No sooner had Rupprecht issued this order than Ludendorff countermanded it, sending the three divisions south of the Somme instead. On learning of this decision the prince cried, 'Then we have lost the war.' Ever after he referred to 27 March 1918 as 'this fateful day'.[38] But though the storm had been stopped in its tracks, it was far from a spent force.

Chapter 7

Holding the Storm: 28–30 March 1918

When it became evident that their offensive was slowing down, the Germans launched a new attack north of the Somme on 28 March with the codename Mars. The British know this offensive as the The First Battle of Arras 1918. First, the Germans wanted to split the two British armies defending the Arras sector of the line. Second, they wanted to recapture the vital position of Vimy Ridge that they had lost to the Canadians in April 1917. This would lead on to taking more significant ground. The final 'astoundingly ambitious' objective given for Mars was the city of Boulogne, some 72 miles from Arras.[1] Ultimately, though, the Germans wanted to reinvigorate their Second and Seventeenth Armies fighting on the Somme in order to restore the momentum of the *Kaiserschlacht*. According to Cyril Falls, 'If this had gone as well as the attack of March 21 the war might have been as nearly good as won.'[2]

There is considerable confusion in the many accounts of this battle over how many divisions the Germans used and what area they attacked. These range from 29 divisions (with another 16 in support) over a 33-mile front to just seven divisions along a front of 8 miles due east of Arras.[3] Churchill's history of the war has a 20/20 formula stating that 20 German divisions attacked a 20-mile section of the front then held by eight British divisions.[4] All the histories agree, however, on the outcome of the battle. In a static defensive battle of this kind the advantage lay with the defenders and the British made full use of it. The weather on 28 March was clear, allowing the Germans no chance of concealment. The British had learnt from the mistakes of a week before and used the new system of defence perfectly. The defences of the British Third and First Army divisions were elastic, well prepared and resolute. British artillery and machine-gun fire cut the attacking Germans to shreds.

Though the German infantry managed to penetrate the British Forward Zone in places they made no impression on the main line of defence. The Battle Zone remained untouched.

> The Germans came on time after time with the greatest bravery, sometimes almost shoulder to shoulder, assured that it required but one more effort to break the British front, only to be held and repulsed by the combined fire of guns, machine guns and rifles. They suffered severe losses, the total of which has never been divulged.[5]

For the British, the Mars Offensive was a model defensive battle; for the Germans it was a dismal failure. That evening a bitterly disappointed Ludendorff called it off.

It was not only the Germans who carried out an attack on 28 March 1918. On the night of 27 March, the New Zealand infantry carried out an offensive of their own, albeit on a much smaller scale and on the morning of 28 March they made two local attacks in an attempt to improve their line. The two attacks had quite different outcomes.

On the left flank of the New Zealand position, the 3rd Rifles had sent out reconnaissance patrols during the night and in the early morning of 28 March. As a result of the knowledge gained, 3rd Rifles decided to attack the German position in a series of quarries 500 yards south of Hébuterne and a short distance in front of their lines. The Battalion's D Company carried out the attack in the late morning and was supported by the machine guns and trench mortars of the Australians on their flank. The quarries were easily captured, along with a quantity of arms, provisions and equipment. It was an important success as the quarries gave excellent observation to the southeast for up to 3000 yards. This new position was large enough to hold a full company in its defence and had a good source of water, an important consideration in defensive warfare. The dead Germans at the quarries were searched for documents (and were also 'ratted' for warm clothing, food and souvenirs). The information obtained revealed that they came from two German divisions, the 20th and the 4th. This company attack by the 3rd Rifles had been a relatively easy affair: the objective was taken quickly and without loss. The other New Zealand attack did not meet with anything like this degree of success.

In the early morning of 28 March, the 4th Rifles had replaced the

2nd Wellington Battalion in front of La Signy Farm. The position was a poor one. The battalion did not hold any of the Hébuterne Road, which was a prime defensive position; the Germans on the high ground at La Signy Farm overlooked them and the connection with the 3rd Rifles on their left flank was tenuous. An attempt by 4th Rifles to close the gap on the Hébuterne Road soon after their arrival ground to a halt some 50 yards from the start line.

On the afternoon of 28 March, the 4th Rifles tried again to capture the high ground at the Hébuterne Road. The attack began at 4 p.m., just as heavy rain started to fall. The 4th Rifles used three companies for this attack: B Company was on the right, A Company on the left and D Company was held in reserve. The 3rd Rifles on the high ground were to assist in the attack by extending their line south to make it easier to establish the connection between the two rifle battalions.

The attacking infantry had good artillery protection provided by the New Zealand gunners, but from the moment the two companies set off they encountered withering machine-gun fire. On the right, B Company was successful in gaining part of the ridge along which the road ran, but a small party of Germans from the 24th (Saxon) Division, strongly entrenched along a huge timber dump, held up its left flank. Meanwhile A Company on the left experienced problems too. Two platoons on the right flank were held up while the remaining two attempted to storm the ridge. It proved to be a difficult task. The machine-gun fire had been so intense that only two officers and twelve men were left to assault the ridge, held by at least 50 Germans. The New Zealanders pressed home the attack, though, and drove the Germans out, capturing six heavy and two light machine guns. This success allowed the 4th Rifles to make contact with the 3rd Rifles on the ridge. But the situation was far from satisfactory, since the two platoons on the right were still held up, leaving those on the left flank isolated and exposed. The much-depleted platoons on the ridge stayed put, however, and dug a trench along their exposed flank to give a measure of protection. The attack had been only partially successful, reducing the enemy salient on the high ground and taking about another 100 yards of the Hébuterne Road. But the 4th Rifle soldiers now on the ridge were weak in numbers and terribly vulnerable with their open right flank. Clearly, another attack would soon be necessary.

The Mars Offensive around Arras and the two New Zealand attacks should not imply that the Germans were inactive across the IV Corps front. They had used the night of 27 March to send out many patrols that pressed up against the British front looking for weak spots. On 28 March, the remnants of nine German divisions attacked the four divisions of IV Corps, holding the 'great re-entrant' in the line around Hébuterne. A further five German divisions were held in reserve in case the front could be cracked open. The whole IV Corps front was harassed by German artillery and machine-gun fire and the British official history describes 28 March as 'a hard day's fighting' for the corps.[6]

The New Zealand sector of the front was under almost constant attack throughout the day until 10 o'clock that night. The New Zealand artillery and machine gunners repulsed all attacks, inflicting heavy casualties on the Germans. As the war diary of the 3rd Brigade, New Zealand Artillery, reported, 'All Batteries fired counter preparation for 2 hours as per instructions from DA [Director, Artillery]. During the day all Batteries engaged in registration and much harassing fire carried out. All Batteries reported being shelled intermittently throughout the afternoon.'[7]

In the early afternoon, two brigades of German infantry were reported moving down the valley from Serre towards the Ancre. They were immediately subjected to an hour-long barrage from every available New Zealand gun. As the artillery history records, the German infantry 'were not seen again'.[8]

The 2nd New Zealand Infantry Brigade experienced most of this German activity and was thankful for the support provided by the gunners of the 3rd Brigade, who 'during the day did some very good shooting, which was much appreciated by all ranks in the line. During the later part of the day all enemy was much more cautious in his movement than formerly thus proving the efficacy of our artillery fire.' But the German artillery was 'much more active, especially during the afternoon'.[9]

The New Zealand machine gunners started the day quietly but spent a busy afternoon firing on numerous targets. The Germans again captured a New Zealand machine gun, but once more it was recovered by the machine gunners. There were attacks at 10 a.m., noon and 3 p.m. All were repulsed. When the machine gun was captured, 'Bombs were obtained and the gun team bombed up the sap and recovered the gun . . . Many casualties were inflicted upon the enemy during these advances.'[10]

One of the busiest sections of the line was at the troublesome La Signy Farm, which actually formed part of a brigade boundary for the New Zealand Division. The Germans here were in superior numbers, well supplied with bombs, machine guns and mortars. The 2nd Auckland Battalion shared responsibility for this unhealthy sector with the hard-pressed 4th Rifles. The Aucklanders' war diary reveals that 28 March was a busy day:

> During the day the Hun made repeated attacks on our right from the direction of LA SIGNY FARM. Approximate times — 9 a.m., 12.30 p.m., 1.30 p.m., and 4 p.m. During these attacks the enemy suffered severe casualties. Ours were light . . . At 10 p.m. another attack was beaten off, his tactics being slightly different on this occasion. He attacked both up the saps and over the top. He was beaten off and left several dead in our hands. His machine gun barrage was very heavy. An inter-company relief took place on the night of the 28th/29th . . . Relief was carried out satisfactorily without casualties.[11]

Heavy casualties made it necessary for the battalion's 15th Company to be relieved that night.

German attention was not confined solely to La Signy Farm. The New Zealand right flank at Hamel was another obvious weak spot and here the 1st Canterbury Battalion also experienced a tough time.

> 28 March
> At about 1 a.m. our right was reinforced by 6 Officers 50 OR, and 10 Lewis Guns, of the Eighth Battalion Tank Corps. This was made necessary by reason of the obscure situation existing South of HAMEL. During the day the Enemy pounded our trench system from close range inflicting fairly heavy casualties. 10 O.R. Killed, 2nd. Lt. G.J. Hawkins and 45 O.R. Wounded. Much movement of Artillery, Transport and men, on the Enemy's side was noticeable, but the situation was relieved by the arrival of part of our own Artillery, and offensive action by Lewis Guns and Snipers.[12]

The New Zealand Rifle Brigade, holding the northern sector of the New Zealand position near the Australians at Hébuterne, also shared in the action. Gallipoli veteran Les Hearns remembered this day forever. The artillery and machine-gun fire was deafening: 'I never heard such a racket in all my life. It was terrible. That's when I was wounded.'[13] Around 11 o'clock that morning Hearns was hit in the leg by shell fragments. That night he was evacuated from the front line and eventually reached a field hospital that consisted of one big tent. There his leg was operated on. It was the end of Les Hearns's war.

Throughout the night the New Zealand casualties continued to mount and tragedy soon struck the New Zealand Rifle Brigade. A 5.9-inch German shell scored a direct hit on the brigade's headquarters, which had been established in a cellar in Colincamps. The whole headquarters was wrecked, eleven men were killed and another fourteen were wounded. One of the officers killed instantly was one of the most popular and talented officers in the division, Major R.G. Purdy, aptly described as 'fearless in the presence of danger, and every inch a soldier'.[14] Brigadier Fulton died of concussion the next day while being conveyed to the casualty clearing station (CCS) at Doullens. He was the third and last of the New Zealand Brigadiers to fall in action. As General Russell noted in his diary, 'Fulton & Purdy killed by an unlucky shell . . . Both a severe loss to the division. Stewart replaces Fulton.'[15] Writing to Defence Minister Sir James Allen in New Zealand, Lieutenant General Alexander Godley, commander of the New Zealand Expeditionary Force of which the division was a part, showed a little more emotion about the loss of Purdy and Fulton: 'I am very sorry about Fulton. He was an excellent Brigadier, and his loss is keenly felt by us all. Also young Purdy . . . one of the most promising officers of the Staff Corps.'[16] Lieutenant Colonel Stewart again assumed command of the Rifle Brigade, shifting its headquarters from Colincamps to Courcelles.

While the New Zealand infantry were in action on 28 March, soldiers from the Pioneer Battalion and the Engineers continued the tough task of building strong posts behind the New Zealand front line. By that night 'there was a line of posts dug right across the New Zealand Divisional area'.[17] The sappers and pioneers then started converting these posts into continuous trench lines, preparing deep dugouts for various headquarters and siting and digging machine-gun posts all over the divisional back area. The New Zealanders were not about to be easily shifted from their current location.

The situation on the Third Army front was now much improved though it 'remained full of anxiety'.[18] On the IV Corps front the situation was relatively stable, as a message to the troops on the evening of

28 March indicated:

> The Corps Commander congratulates the 42nd, 62nd, and the New Zealand Divisions and the 4th Australian Brigade on their magnificent behaviour during the last few days' fighting. Numerous heavy attacks by the enemy have been completely repulsed with heavy loss and the capture of prisoners and machine guns. He heartily thanks the troops for their courage and endurance and is confident that they will continue to hold the line against all attacks.[19]

British confidence was high, but the Germans opposite them were plummeting to the depths of despair. The diary of a German officer who would be killed on 5 April described his men as 'dog tired' and the German attacks on IV Corps as in a state of 'much confusion and great disorder'. With the enemy in front of him in strong defensive positions and in considerable numbers, he lamented, 'It seems that there will be a return to trench warfare.'[20]

The German officer was right. On the evening of 28 March heavy rain set in, bringing with it the inevitable mud and the misery of trench warfare. Those troops using the old British trenches suffered the most. After nearly two years these trenches were still reasonably intact but in no condition to withstand a deluge and it was too late to construct adequate drainage. Some collapsed in on the men sheltering in them. Those that did not soon flooded so that sentries standing at their posts, usually for two, but sometimes for up to four hours, had to do so in thigh-deep mud and water. Food was scarce and the New Zealand soldiers were without their cold weather clothing. When relieved, craving rest and sleep, they crawled into filthy, shallow holes scooped out of the sides of the trenches. It was a nightmare existence like that endured in the Ypres salient.

> Wrapped in an old bag or blanket or dead German's groundsheet, unshaven, and caked with mud and filth, men lumbered heavily along the trenches by night or lay huddled in these holes in the ground, more resembling beasts than human beings. The written impressions of a French correspondent during a visit by night to a front line trench fairly describe the conditions obtaining in this unwholesome place. 'A sinuous ditch bottomed with mud, and foul [sic] with human refuse. There are holes in its

sides from which as you lean over there comes a foul breath. Misty, shadowy things are emerging from these side caverns, and moving about in shapeless bulk like bears that shamble and growl. They are the squad.' With the substitution of the word platoon for squad, the description stands.[21]

The early morning rum ration was regarded as a lifesaver.

The New Zealand soldiers did not allow these deplorable conditions to affect their morale. They also resorted to searching the deserted French houses looking for food and warm clothing. This was often a dangerous practice, as Bernard Cottrell soon found out:

> I wondered what you did Easter Sunday. As for me, well as tucker was running pretty low two other chaps & myself decided to visit an evacuated house and made some chips and some stray rice . . . Everything was going swimmingly till Jerry lobbed one outside and killed two soldiers and a horse, we bolted for the cellar.[22]

Food was desperately short, as Private Edward Bibby of the 1st Otago Battalion remembered: 'We were down to one loaf for 10 or 12 men'. The soldiers were also issued with iron rations — a quarter of a pound of hard biscuit, some bully beef, tea and sugar — to be used only in an emergency. Bibby was with a group of soldiers sent to Mailly-Maillet to forage for food. They found some tins of bully beef, then entered a French house and looked in the cellar for food. There they got the shock of their lives: 'And didn't we get a blast. There was a French Family there taking refuge. We withdrew hastily.' When they left the trenches some days later they were 'covered with mud'.[23]

Compared with what had come before it, 29 March was a quiet day for the New Zealanders, but it was by no means easy. Conditions in the front-line trenches deteriorated further as the bad weather continued. Food remained in short supply, and the enemy, although quieter, was still active. The 4th Rifles again carried out an attack to improve their position at La Signy Farm.

At 11 a.m. a large working party of Germans was seen on a ridge in front of the New Zealand position. The Germans were 2500 yards away, well within range of the New Zealand machine guns which opened fire. There were some German casualties; the rest of the working party scattered. The New Zealand artillery continued harassing fire throughout the day and received plenty of the same in retaliation. The war diary of the 3rd New Zealand Field Artillery described the German artillery fire as '"lively" especially in village Mailly-Mallet'.[24] Bombardier Bailey and his unit took much-needed ammunition to the infantry brigades in the front line. 'Altogether we carted 575,000 rounds of SAA [small arms ammunition] and about 3000 hand grenades to the infantry.'[25]

The village of Mailly-Maillet suffered heavily during this offensive, and not all the damage was caused by the Germans. William Robson of C Section, No. 2 Field Ambulance, walked around the village on 29 March, looking for food. 'It has been knocked about a good deal by Fritz but the place has been wrecked by the Tommy in search for booze and money. Houses have been pulled inside out and it is an absolute disgrace.'[26] But New Zealand soldiers were responsible for a large proportion of the havoc, as John Coleman explained to his sister:

> We camped just behind the village where these people I speak of had deserted the first night we came up. All the fellows had a pretty gay time as, of course, they ransacked the place, and in lots of the cellars there was champagne and wine galore, so you can imagine all hands had a royal time. Of course, I daren't say where we are, but no doubt you have seen in your papers.[27]

The village was Mailly-Maillet.

Harold Muschamp of the Machine Gun Battalion had a similar experience of looting. 'There is plenty of wine & champagne in the villages & some of the boys are making a welter of it. Also the hen & pigs are getting a sad hearing from our boys, we are living high, a piece of good fresh pork is a great change these times. Vegetables are plentiful too.'[28]

Just after daylight the 4th Rifles made a renewed effort to improve their position at La Signy Farm and establish a firmer link with the 1st Brigade. Bitter fighting ensued with heavy casualties on both sides. The 4th Rifles made little progress. An attack by a bombing section cleared 200 yards of trench towards the junction of the farm track and the Hébuterne Road, but the men ran out of bombs and could not hold the ground. Later in the morning a German bombing party from La Signy Farm attacked the 2nd Auckland Battalion, which repulsed the enemy. But this action, coupled with the failure of the 4th Rifles to improve their position, prompted the two battalion commanders to plan for a larger, concerted attack next day to deal with the troublesome La Signy Farm once and for all.

The day in question was 30 March 1918, Easter Sunday. The New Zealanders had carried out valuable reconnaissance work the previous night to pinpoint where the deadly German machine guns were. The day dawned mild but there were constant rain showers. Little activity from the Germans during the morning left the New Zealanders free to prepare their attack. Although only a small-scale venture in comparison with others on the Western Front, it was a significant action and the stakes were high. Three brigades of field artillery and three battalions of infantry would be used in this attack. Before it was over another two infantry battalions would also be used. If the New Zealanders succeeded, the important position of La Signy Farm would be theirs. The spur dominated the left brigade's sector and, as the highest ground for many miles, it gave the Germans a wide field of observation. On the crest of the spur ran the hedge that the 2nd Rifles had reached on 26 March. The hedge ran for 1000 yards from northwest across La Signy Farm to the Hébuterne Road. In front of the hedge was a system of dugouts and trenches riddled with German snipers and machine-gun nests. This trench line was only 300 yards in front of the New Zealand positions; taking it would not be easy. The German defenders were mainly from the 20th Division, though remnants of several other formations were also present. By 30 March, though, the German defenders were tired and short of supplies. Their own food had long been exhausted and for the last few days they had been living on captured British iron rations. The last thing they expected on Easter Sunday was a daytime attack by the enemy to their front.

The New Zealand plan was for the three infantry battalions to advance on a front of about 1200 yards up the slopes to La Signy Farm. This would occur after a short artillery barrage designed to drive the German defenders underground. The 1st Wellington would be on the right, some distance from the farm. Their advance was to provide a solid platform for the attack by protecting the flank of the 2nd Auckland Battalion, who would be in the vulnerable centre of the attack and directly facing the hedge trench. The 4th Rifles on the left planned to advance to the Hébuterne Road, capture the section held by the Germans and link up with the 2nd Rifles on their left flank.

At 2 p.m. a 'beautifully accurate' shrapnel and machine-gun barrage forced the German defenders to take cover in the trenches.[29] The German sentries were careless. Not expecting an attack, they all took cover, keeping their heads well below the parapet as the shelling continued. The German defenders not on duty were asleep in their dugouts. As Ormond Burton has commented, 'It was the most impossible and most improbable time for an attack to take place.'[30] When the German sentries emerged after the barrage, soldiers from three New Zealand infantry battalions had crossed the dangerous open ground and were right on their positions. It was too late to organise effective resistance. On the right, the centre and left companies of the 1st Wellington advanced their line 500 yards from One Tree Hill to the southern point of the hedge above the Serre Road. This was an important gain: now the New Zealanders were nearly 1000 yards east of the sugar refinery and with an uninterrupted view along the valleys south and west of the Serre. During their advance the Wellingtons had taken 74 prisoners and 22 machine guns.[31]

In the centre of the attack, two companies of the 2nd Auckland Battalion advanced towards the hedgerow under cover of machine-gun and artillery fire 'as if on parade'.[32] Their attack completely surprised the enemy and the Auckland battalion took most of the objective within seven minutes. The 2nd Auckland infantry entered the trenches with rifles, bayonets and bombs at the ready and the slaughter of the surprised Germans was fearful. Many were killed in the trenches, some surrendered, others bolted. The Aucklanders encountered strong opposition in only two places. In the centre of the line a redoubt sheltering a machine-gun crew held out and resisted all attempts to take it, preventing the 2nd Auckland Battalion from linking up with the 1st Wellingtons on their right. A platoon from the Waikato Company tried to take this redoubt but their line of advance was exposed to direct fire from the German machine guns and fourteen men fell, every one of them shot through the head. For Lieutenant Colonel Allen of the 2nd Aucklands, it was 'the most ghastly sight I have ever seen in all my experience in the war'.[33] When more men were killed and wounded, including the company commander, Allen moved forward, bringing with him a trench mortar officer who managed to bring one of the mortars into action. The Germans in the redoubt soon surrendered. The other problem area was on the extreme right near the Serre Road. A German machine-gun post held out for a considerable time until subdued by a bombing party.

The New Zealanders took La Signy Farm. More than 140 dead Germans were counted in the 2nd Auckland Battalion position and a further 156 were taken prisoner. Captured war matériel included 43 machine guns, two mortars and three bicycles.[34]

It had been a hard fight and the Aucklanders were exhausted. Lieutenant Colonel Allen feared they were ripe for a German counterattack 'but none came'.[35] Just after 6 p.m. he reported the situation to his brigade headquarters:

> We are now in touch with 1/Wellington having captured the strong point on our right. We are not quite in touch with 4/N.Z.R.B. but expect to be soon. Our line now runs from . . . along fence to . . . The line is strong, well wired in front and with good observation. The dangerous flank is the right, where enemy can collect in . . . under cover of hedge and I should like artillery to strafe it periodically during the night and occasionally with a few on LA SIGNY FARM. We have captured a large number of machine guns estimated at 30 and at least one light Minenwerfer [trench mortar]. I have all my men in the front line except about three platoons. 2/Wellington are going to carry for us and I shall keep two platoons of theirs here for the night. The men are very tired and will not stand many heavy counter attacks. Communications with you are very bad. The Hun is now shelling us heavily without doing much damage but is probably working himself up for a counter attack. If he does I shall make for Brigade Headquarters as I have no reserves to fall back on and will leave my staff to master the situation . . . Our casualties during the attack were 7 Officers Wounded, 30 O/Rs Killed and 75 O/Rs.Wounded . . . The enemy's casualties were very heavy 140 dead being counted in the trench. All the wounded were evacuated during the attack without further mishap.[36]

Meanwhile, on the left, the 4th Rifles were experiencing considerable difficulties. Only after hard fighting all afternoon was the battalion able to link up with the 2nd Auckland Battalion on the spur and this did not occur until after 11 p.m. During this attack the 4th Rifles were dogged by persistent bad luck. Like the other battalions, they attacked with two companies of infantry, but because of their depleted strength through the previous attacks, both had to be strengthened with a platoon from the 3rd Rifles. The lone group in touch with the 2nd Rifles from the previous day stayed put on the ridge while the rest of the battalion tried to end their isolation. From the start of the atttack there was extremely heavy resistance from bombs and machine guns about La Signy Farm. Part of the company on the right reached their objective, but the remainder was held up by many Germans on the feature called Woodstacks just short of the Hébuterne Road. Again the riflemen ran out of bombs and were forced to take shelter in the shell holes there. There was another attempt at nightfall with a fresh company supported by soldiers of the 2nd and 3rd Rifle Battalions. In the face of this pressure the Germans finally abandoned the position and withdrew. The crest where the La Signy Farm track left the Hébuterne Road was occupied at last.

That night, the 2nd Rifles extended their flank by carrying out a 'brilliant minor operation'.[37] Under Captain H.E. Barrowclough, who would serve as a major general in the Second World War, two platoons struck out to their south and east to clear the gap on their right flank and gain the last of the high ground on the spur. After a brief, intense firefight the Germans fled. The 2nd Rifles managed to recover the whole of the position lost on 27 March and then took even more ground to their front. In doing so they killed many Germans, captured 22 and also took sixteen machine guns. Two New Zealanders were wounded in this venture; one subsequently died of his wounds.

The net effect of these different operations was some 300 dead Germans plus 300 captured. In fact, the 20th Division's losses were so heavy that it was withdrawn from the German front line and later disbanded. A significant amount of war matériel was also captured, including 110 machine guns and fifteen mortars.[38] Most important, the New Zealanders had significantly altered their tactical position. Their line was no longer broken and overlooked by the Germans. Instead it ran continuously from One Tree Hill in the south along the ridge to the quarries near Hébuterne. Occupying all the high ground in the location, the New Zealanders now had excellent observation over the Germans who had been forced down into the valley. A report by the Brigade Major W.I.K. Jennings of the 1st Brigade emphasised the importance of these gains:

Yesterday's operation has improved our line out of all knowledge and we now completely dominate the enemy's positions along two thirds of our front . . . The success of our attack seems to have been due to the speed with which it was carried out. Our men state that in many cases the enemy were lying down in the trench and that they were on top of them before the enemy could stand to. The men themselves are in great heart and only ask to be allowed to go on and push the enemy back again.[39]

The New Zealand history of the division in France emphasised that, apart from the 4th Rifles, who had experienced the greatest difficulties during their part of the operation, losses in the other battalions were light. When John Coleman wrote home of this attack, he stressed its success and how few New Zealanders were lost:

> After we had been there for a couple of days there was a piece of the line wanted straightening, so the boys 'hopped the bags' at two o'clock in the afternoon and caught old Fritz napping. They captured some over a hundred machine guns, 200 prisoners and Lord knows how many were killed, as they were lying about in all directions. Lots of them must have been killed whilst asleep in their bivvys. This was, I think, the most successful little stunt our boys have had, as our casualties were extremely low — small, considering what we gained.[40]

But the three attacking battalions *had* suffered and they would have to be withdrawn from the line over the next two days. A good many New Zealanders had been killed or wounded to secure La Signy Farm, as Ira Robinson acknowledged in a letter home:

> Of course we lost a lot of good men and also officers, but not as many as one might expect under the circumstances, and we have been reinforced a good deal since and are now stronger than ever. So far I thank God I have not received a scratch, although five of my mates were killed by one shell and I was standing in the middle of them, so you see your prayers are not in vain after all.[41]

The 2nd Auckland Battalion had suffered 130 casualties, 30 of whom had been killed. Captain George Tuck had been up most of the previous night writing the battalion's operation order for the attack, finally finishing it at 2.30 on the morning of the assault. That evening he reflected on its success in his diary:

> All is over for the time. We lost severely; the poor Waikatos losing more than 70% of their men. In one sap there are several Waikato jambed shoulder to shoulder all shot thru the head. We

hold all the line attacked. It is a much improved position & is well wired with a splendid field of view. Fritz was determined to hold it as it is such a fine defensive position for us. There was a mg [machine gun] every 10 yards & we captured about thirty or more. We also took 160 prisoners and killed hundreds of Huns. It was costly but well worth it. A splendid position which he will no doubt make a big effort to recapture if he can organise in time. We took men of many units so he must be a bit mixed after his great advance.[42]

The casualties of the 4th Rifles numbered almost 200; over 50 men had been killed. The 1st Wellington Battalion, allocated a minor role in this attack, lost 22 men and had more than 50 wounded.[43]

One of the 4th Rifles' deaths was that of Second Lieutenant George Malcolm. His brother, William, a soldier in the 2nd Auckland Battalion, had reached the Somme on 30 March, the day George died. William Malcolm did not, however, learn of the tragedy until 3 April 1918 and then spent hours trying to locate his brother's grave.

Poor old Mum & Dad. I don't know how you can bear it but remember that George was a son who was an honour to you. Even although I am his brother I must tell you that I know very few boys who lived a cleaner life . . . We were camped near an old sugar refinery or what was left of it. McKenzie had told me that George's grave was about 500 yds north along a sunken road. On three different days I searched for nearly a mile along and in from the road, but although I found many 4th Bttn chaps there I could not find him. I found Harry Cottingham within a couple of hundred yds of the factory. He was knocked out on the 6th. Poor old Harry. I had seen him about a week before.[44]

It was to be another two months before William Malcolm located the site where his brother was buried. He erected a cross over George's final resting place.[45]

The result of this attack on 30 March offered a much better view over the Ancre Valley to Thiepval, Pozières and the Albert–Bapaume road. Ahead lay the town of Flers, so well known to the New Zealand soldiers of 1916 and now only 7½ miles away. To the northeast, about the same distance away, was the large town of Bapaume, which would become very familiar to the New Zealanders later in the year. The New Zealand Division had carried out an attack of some significance and congratulatory messages flowed in from Generals Birdwood, Plumer, Godley, Monash and many others. As Ormond Burton wrote:

> This operation was surely one of the most successful surprise attacks of the war. When it is considered that the attackers were greatly fatigued and were part of an army that had been heavily defeated, and that the Huns were flushed with victory, the full merit of the achievement becomes obvious. Small as the operation was, compared with the mighty happenings of those critical days, it was yet the first successful attack made by Allied troops since the opening of the German offensive.[46]

Yet the New Zealand history of the division was almost dismissive of the success of this attack and downplays its significance:

> Care must be taken not to overestimate the general moral effect of this success. In conjunction, however, with the stiffening resistance all along the front and with the gallant and remunerative enterprises carried out by the Australians at Hebuterne and by the 32nd Division 6 miles at Ayette a few days later, it was unquestionable opportune and acceptable to the British Staff after days of unrelieved if stubbornly resisted reverses. It helped too, to demonstrate to the German Army that north of the Somme the British line had become established.[47]

Though such caution is an admirable quality in a military historian, the significance of the New Zealand attack on 30 March was lost in his restraint. This attack was *the* first offensive taken by the BEF on the Western Front since the start of the Michael Offensive nine days earlier. Its success stunned the Germans and provided considerable encouragement to the soldiers of the Third Army. The Australian official historian, the astute Charles Bean, recognised the importance of the New Zealand attack: 'small though the operation was, the news of it came in those dark days like a tonic to the whole of the British Army and to the Empire'.[48] James Edmonds, the British official historian, wrote: 'at the time it was said that, simultaneously with the arrival of the Australians and New Zealanders, as a result of the heavy losses inflicted by Fifth and Third Armies the initiative had passed out of the hands of the enemy'.[49] The successful New Zealand attack was the first indication that this was so.

126

By the end of March 1918 Ludendorff knew that his offensive was failing. One reason for this was that the German storm troops and battle units had outpaced their artillery and logistical support. Ludendorff therefore ordered a postponement of further operations until 4 April. He also announced another change of strategy: the city of Amiens was now the objective of the attack. There would be a pause of three to four days while newly constructed light railways took stores forward to feed the war machine. Battlefield communications would also be restored and the vital artillery moved forward with thousands of shells stockpiled for their use. This, it was hoped, would get the offensive rolling forward again. When he was ready Ludendorff would hurl his armies forward again to take Amiens. Now occupying a solid defensive position less than 20 miles northeast of this city, the New Zealand Division and the other divisions of IV Corps would be on the receiving end of a renewed German offensive within a matter of days.

Chapter 8

A Lull:
31 March–4 April 1918

Compared with the frantic period of 23–30 March 1918, the next five days were quiet, a time of minimal activity. The lull was a welcome relief. It gave the New Zealand soldiers in the front line a chance to catch their breath and to consolidate their hard-won positions. Both sides used 31 March, a day of heavy rains and thunderstorms, to bury the dead whose bodies could be retrieved without risk. Those who had been killed in the narrow no-man's-land remained where they had fallen.

The 2nd New Zealand Infantry Brigade was holding the line west of Beaumont-Hamel with the two Otago battalions in the line and the two Canterbury battalions in reserve. On 1 April its war diary recorded that 'The enemy's inactivity was most marked during the day, no movement being seen and only very scattered shelling experienced'. The next day was the same. There was the 'Usual scattered shelling', but no enemy movement. The diary made a prescient comment: 'The situation has developed almost into trench warfare'.[1] On 1 April the 1st Otago Battalion

> was in the line in front of Auchonvillers and the day passed quietly. Our artillery periodically shelled targets in enemy's forward areas, the Serre Road and Beaumont Hamel receiving special attention. A number of Stokes shells were fired at the crater, silencing an enemy machine gun which had been causing trouble to our front line. Enemy artillery was fairly active — periodically shelling our front line with 77 m.m guns, and heavier shells to the Bowery and Auchonvillers. During the afternoon rain again fell, making movement in the front line and communication trenches very difficult.

On 2 April

A New Zealand soldier using a captured German machine gun at La Signy Farm. KIPPENBERGER MILITARY ARCHIVE AND RESEARCH LIBRARY H484

Bringing in the wounded under shellfire near Courcelles village in early April, 1918. KIPPENBERGER MILITARY ARCHIVE AND RESEARCH LIBRARY H485

Members of the Maori Pioneer Battalion constructing a barbed wire entanglement near Colincamps. The work of the Pioneers was hard, back-breaking and often dangerous. There was always more to be done, too. KIPPENBERGER MILITARY ARCHIVE AND RESEARCH LIBRARY H516

A New Zealand howitzer in action. KIPPENBERGER MILITARY ARCHIVE AND RESEARCH LIBRARY H513

Loading a New Zealand trench mortar near Colincamps. Trench mortars were deadly over a short range. KIPPENBERGER MILITARY ARCHIVE AND RESEARCH LIBRARY H504

This building in Colincamps had been the headquarters of the New Zealand Rifle Brigade. On 28 March it received a direct hit from a German artillery shell, killing Brigadier Fulton, Major Purdy and several others. KIPPENBERGER MILITARY ARCHIVE AND RESEARCH LIBRARY H491

The work of the military chaplains was crucial to maintaining morale. A padre of the Rifle Brigade has set up a canteen only 300 yards from the front line. Note the stretchers in the right of the photograph, ready for action. KIPPENBERGER MILITARY ARCHIVE AND RESEARCH LIBRARY H473

Meal time for the New Zealand Rifle Brigade. This trench is at La Signy Farm and is only 250 yards from the German front-line positions. KIPPENBERGER MILITARY ARCHIVE AND RESEARCH LIBRARY H468

Our artillery was much more active particularly on the Serre Road and on village of Beaumont Hamel. Enemy artillery was normal, periodically during the day, shelling our right Coy in the front line. Heavier shells were used on Auchonvillers, the Bowery, Sugar Factory, and Mailly-Maillet. Enemy snipers, were much quieter, and except for an occasional burst from an enemy machine gun in the crater, they also were much below the normal activity. Enemy movement in the forward areas was very scarce — Rifle and Lewis Gun fire being brought to bear as soon as any targets presented themselves.[2]

Its sister battalion in the line also reflected the drop off in German activity. On 3 April, for example, its war diary recorded 'Enemy activity below normal. Usual sniping from our side, several hits being claimed.'[3] Lieutenant Roderick Toomath, the Medical Officer of 1st Rifles, had found the front-line trenches 'in a bad state', but he described the 1 to 4 April period as 'very quiet'. He described 1 April as 'an awfully lazy time'.[4] After the frenetic activity of 26 March and the days that followed, the 1st Rifles, the first infantry battalion to encounter the advancing Germans, certainly deserved a peaceful spell in the trenches.

The Germans may have been quiet during this period, but they were far from inactive. At a IV Corps conference on 2 April, the silver-haired, avuncular Lieutenant General Sir George Harper (his nickname was 'Uncle') succinctly outlined the current tactical situation: 'The enemy in front are much messed up and disorganised. He is at present quiescent, reorganising and waiting to see what will transpire to the south and north. When ready he will attack.' Harper believed that the Germans would most likely attack at Bucquoy and Hamel.[5]

From 1 to 3 April there was much activity behind the German lines as they prepared to launch a fresh attack in the Somme region. Some 60 German railway construction companies laboured day and night to build, repair and restore the communication and transport facilities necessary to support a large attack on Amiens, described by one historian as 'one of the major cities of France'.[6] The Germans planned to advance on both sides on the Somme River in an effort to take this vital rail and supply centre. The New Zealanders were sure an attack was looming when they saw German observation balloons rise into the sky. Nor was this attack the only one the Germans were planning. Aware that the

British had moved a number of divisions down from Flanders to the Somme in order to cover the vulnerable sectors exposed by their offensive, the Germans were also preparing to strike a new blow in the north.

The New Zealanders were not inactive either. Daylight patrolling began early on 31 March in order to pinpoint the forward positions of the enemy. Units also pushed out forward posts to cover any dead ground, that is, ground that could not be seen from the ridge line, and strengthened them with barbed-wire obstacles. They were eventually connected up to form a continuous trench.

West of La Signy Farm a lone daylight patrol by Lance Corporal R. McMurray of the 1st Rifles captured a German sentry who, under interrogation, revealed the location of two German strong points. These were attacked and captured that evening. Over the next two days more New Zealand posts were established all around the farm and 150 yards east of it. There was also activity to the south of the New Zealand line. On 1 April the war diary of the 1st Otagos recorded that:

> A very good and daring daylight patrol was carried out by Cpl. Marshall of 8th Company and a comrade, from the left of 8th Corps Sector. The patrol worked up a C.T. [Communication Trench] leading from our line, in enemy's direction, for about 250-300 yards. After working up and down a number of C.T's and gaining valuable information about this ground, the patrol suddenly saw an enemy block a short distance away. Cpl Marshall worked up to within 12 yards of sentry, who was guarding the block and shot him.[7]

As a result of the patrol, the 1st Otagos rushed a German trench and easily captured it. Further north a patrol from the 1st Wellingtons captured six prisoners, including a wounded German officer. Private Jesse Stayte was given the task of escorting the German prisoners to the brigade headquarters at Mailly-Maillet.

> When I got them there some of our Boys souveniered them thoroughly. They made them empty their pockets and took all they (the Fritzs) had. I could not bring myself to rob a man's pockets even though he is a Fritz, but some of the Boys did it with as little regard as though that was their trade (and perhaps it was). I don't mind looking him over after he is dead but not till then. I even saw them take Family Photos away from the Fritz.[8]

The minor engagements fought by the New Zealanders in the first four days of April 1918 were both successful and important. Though they made only a slight improvement to the New Zealand line, they did ensure that the New Zealand soldiers did not lose their hard-won initiative.

From 31 March the New Zealanders were in a fairly positive position. Their line was regular and continuous and the advantage of being on high ground was all too obvious. Observation was good, especially in the northern sector of the line from One Tree Hill to Hébuterne where the New Zealanders completely overlooked the enemy opposite them. Their line, however, was a long one and it needed all three New Zealand brigades in line to hold it. This situation could not be sustained. Accordingly, on the night of 2–3 April, the Australian 4th Brigade extended their flank so that it was now 500 yards south of the quarries and completely covering Hébuterne. On the night of 4–5 April, the 1st Brigade in the centre of the New Zealand position was withdrawn and became the reserve brigade. The Rifle Brigade sidestepped to the right and took over the sector vacated by the 1st Brigade. The latter's new line was now 3200 yards long. The Rifle Brigade placed the 3rd Battalion on the right from One Tree Hill to the Serre Road, the 4th Battalion in the centre with its flank on the hedge trench north of La Signy Farm and the 1st Battalion on the left linking with the Australians at Hébuterne. The New Zealand Division now had a normal two-brigade front and the changes were completed just in time to meet the next German attack.

The lull also provided an opportunity to rest the units that had borne the brunt of four days of heavy fighting. On 31 March, 2nd Wellington relieved the 2nd Auckland Battalion, who had not had their boots off for over a week and had not slept during their time in the trenches because the fighting 'had been severe and continuous'.[9] Many were suffering from the first stages of trench foot; they were hungry and dog-tired. Captain George Tuck caught the mood in his diary:

> 1/4/1918
> Out at last. Tho' we have been in only 4 days the Battalion has spent just about the hardest week in its history. Practically no sleep from Sunday to Sunday. No blankets or overcoats. Raining the last two days which turned the trenches into clay baths. How the men stood the terrible strain I cannot tell. There were

forty-two machine guns in the trench we took and more put out of action just in front.[10]

The 4th Rifles had also experienced heavy fighting. After nightfall on 31 March they were relieved by the 1st Rifles and enjoyed a three-day break from the trenches.

> 1 April
> Took over from 4th Battn. N.Z.R.B. in Right Subsector of Brigade Front at COLINCAMPS during last night. Very large number of enemy dead lying about as the result of the raid recently. Very active patrolling being carried out. Received reports from Australian Brigade on our left that the enemy was assembling, but nothing came of it. Battn. and Company Snipers and Observers very active and have accounted for many of the enemy. Transport is able to get up quite close to Companies so that water and rations are distributed with little trouble.[11]

During April the Maori Pioneer Battalion spent nearly every day constructing defensive works around the New Zealand front line. The men dug many miles of trenches, built strong posts and drainage and carried out a host of other tasks associated with 'all the paraphernalia of the filthy trench warfare'. As the battalion's war diary stated, it was 'not an exciting job at all as we have been for the most part working on reverse slopes and away from the enemy's observation'. It was also one that involved considerable risk. That month there were 45 casualties: four men were killed and two more later died of their wounds.[12]

The rain that had started to fall on the evening of 28 March continued unabated in the early days of April. The conditions of the trenches remained deplorable and it was an ordeal to remain in them for any length of time. In Jesse Stayte's words, 'The trenches are in a shocking condition with mud and rain . . . The place is littered with dead Fritz and the stench is very bad. It rained all evening.' After his battalion relieved a Rifle Brigade unit in the line on 2 April he and his fellow soldiers were only 70 yards from the German trenches. On Wednesday 3 April Stayte wrote, 'There is nothing doing during the day only sniping so we live like wild beasts, we sleep in our holes or trenches at day and go out to maim and kill at night.' That evening Stayte was on guard duty watching over a sap. He stood on a platform made from dead bodies and covered with earth.

It is a good stand but rather gruesome when one is on guard standing on it through the night. There is a dead Fritz officer just on the other side of the block and about 50 yards further on Fritz has a block in the same sap and I suppose his sentry is watching me from his block.

On 4 April Stayte noted that 'It has been raining nearly all day and things are very dirty in the trench'. That night, though, the Aucklanders were relieved by a battalion from the Rifle Brigade and trudged wearily back to Mailly-Maillet. 'We were wet through and quite exhausted when we got to the place. We had a good feed and a nip of rum and lay down anywhere and went to sleep.'[13]

All brigade and battalion war diaries commented on the poor state of the trenches and the terrible living conditions. The 2nd Otago Battalion found their trenches 'very muddy and dirty — very shallow in places. Poor accommodation. Posts very scattered owing to large frontage. Dispositions: — 4 Companies in line, one platoon of each company in close support.' The diary also noted that there was a 'Considerable amount of enemy movement. Much sniping on our side. Enemy snipers fairly active.'[14] The war diary of the 2nd Canterbury Battalion recorded a similar experience:

Trenches and C.Ts in very bad condition, both falling in on slightest provocation. Sniping active from our side. Hun using Light Minnenwerfer and Granatenwerfer [grenade projector] from the crater in front of Centre Company Sector. There is an occasional Pineapple [finned mortar bomb].[15]

The 2nd Wellington Battalion spent a quiet few days in front of La Signy Farm although they could see considerable German activity behind the front line. The state of the trenches caused them some concern:

Weather fine . . . Battalion in line . . . in front of LA SIGNY FARM. Enemy quiet all day, but a lot of individual movement seen in back areas. Owing to recent rain trenches very muddy and difficult to walk through. Casualties Nil. Evacuations Nil. Reinforcements Nil. Ration strength 28 Off. 748 O/Ranks.[16]

New Zealand gunner Bert Stokes hinted at the unpleasant conditions in a letter to his parents:

I'll just tell you that during the past three or four days I had had a touch of the 'Flu' & have not felt too bright . . . These times particularly we get no time to ourselves at all, and conditions are not too good either. I am writing this in a small bivvie, just a canvas one, round us is our ever present enemy — MUD. It has rained incessantly for days & days, consequently things are in a horrible mess. But of course I forgot, you don't want to hear all this do you now? I expect you imagine all too vividly as it is.[17]

Surprisingly, though the men's health suffered, their morale remained high throughout the German offensive. This is confirmed by both official and private sources. For Brigadier R. Young of the 2nd New Zealand Infantry Brigade,

The behaviour of the men throughout these operations has been excellent. They have maintained a cheerful spirit throughout, and have been eagerly awaiting an attack by the enemy, being quite confident in their ability to repel such an attack with their machine guns and rifles. This feeling of superiority became more apparent than ever when the attack on the 27th had been successfully beaten off. The men are still in good spirits, but the exposure to the mud of the trenches is beginning to affect their feet.[18]

The brigadier finished his report by noting that the battalions were using whale oil and clean socks to fix the problem of the men's feet.

Ronald Watson was the padre of the 1st Otago Battalion. Later in the year he would win the Military Cross for his bravery in caring for the wounded at Bapaume. Padre Watson's correspondence supported Young's assessment. A letter written on 9 April 1918 described the terrible condition of the trenches and the men's unbroken spirit:

In the Field.
Tuesday, April 9th. 1918.
My last budget was dated the 1st April. We have had quite a deal of rain lately, and there is plenty of mud about. Life is very full of incident, where we are. You will know now by the papers of our sector. Our boys are doing most excellent work. Really their spirit is a thing to marvel at — their cheerfulness in spite of all the mud and uncertainty. I do love these chaps. They are so supremely worthwhile. Nothing that one can attempt seems too much. I am

trying to do all I can for them. Here is a typical day of mine yesterday — Plenty of rain in morning. In the morning, I buried one of our boys, and then Campbell (my batman) and I went into a village in our rear, to see what I could fix up with the Y.M.C.A. for the boys. I landed some cigs., chocolate and toffee. I saw Frank Cameron in the Y.M. there. In afternoon, Campbell and I went the round of one company and distributed the gifts. In places, I went into mud up to my knees. It took us 4½ hrs. to do the trip. Men in great heart and very pleased to see me, and I them. A smile is a big thing, I am certain. I came on a section of one company in the Line the other day. Evidently someone said, 'Here's the Padre.' I heard, 'And I bet he's smiling.' I don't like going around empty-handed. I believe in laying hands on all I can to give away. By all sorts of means and from different sources I get newspapers, mags. (new and old), cigs., sweets, etc. and dole them out. One feels that these chaps deserve such a great deal. Several days ago, we had some hours of a fearful strafe from Fritz. I sheltered for several hours, then Campbell and I went out with a stretcher round two of our companies to see what we could do. We were out and managed to dodge everything for 3-4 hours. I am getting my nerve very much improved, I am glad to say. Our casualties have been very light, considering. We seem to have the upper hand of Fritz in these parts. Already our boys have shaken him up goodoh. Please don't expect too much in the way of letters. I find so very much to do these days. Time is not nearly sufficient for all I see I can do up here. We are a happy band of brothers.
Cheeroh.
Much love from
RONALD[19]

Echoing this view, Major Lindsay Inglis, an officer with the machine gunners and a major general in the next world war, found the spirit of the men infectious. As he wrote to Agnes May Todd, his fiancée in New Zealand,

Nobody seems to be worrying his head about the Hun much, everybody in the best of spirits — even to one company that lost two thirds of its strength from MG fire a couple of days ago. Our outfit has never been more full of fight. Beginning to catch the atmosphere myself again and feel like a warhorse once more. Wish they'd finish it off though.[20]

One letter, however, hinted that things were not quite as rosy. Bernard Cottrell wrote to his father on 10 April 1918:

> Things are somewhat 'patchy' as yet. Tucker a bit low & every-thing messy & muddy and we are doing more than our share in holding on, consequently everyone discontented, we haven't been paid yet, still that doesn't matter much seeing that there are not any places to buy anything at.[21]

Private Ernest Painter's diary also showed the reality of trench war-fare for the New Zealand soldiers.

> Still in the trenches. I am tired, sore and heart broken of this Hellish life. Just one continual roar of guns and shell and bullets flying all around everywhere . . . I have not had my clothes off for 2 months or more now, no blankets now only Great coats and as lousy as a coocoo [sic]. God knows when it will come to an end this Hellish life.[22]

With the poor conditions in the trenches, limited food, no pay or creature comforts, it is not surprising that the New Zealand soldiers were discontented. Soldiers can, however, be inveterate grumblers and grumbling should not be mistaken for a low state of morale. Both the evidence and the subsequent performance of the division indicate that the spirits of the New Zealand soldiers remained high throughout 1918. Even months of 'filthy trench warfare' could not change this.

Soldiers who joined the division in the middle of this operation found the experience hard. Rifleman Arthur Leslie Ross, known as Les, who eventually joined B Company of the 2nd Rifles, had left Etaples on 1 April and, with other reinforcements, travelled by train to the Somme. Then came a hard march of 16 miles to join the New Zealand Division. Their loads were heavy and food was scarce. 'Our rations were poor, a lot of the bake houses had been lost and bread was scarce. We found a stack of beans, they were a bit mouldy but we ate the lot we were really hungry, the troops holding the line got preference and rightly so.' On an overnight stop Ross set off with three friends in an attempt to buy some bread.

> We could not talk French but old Jack said he could make him-self understood but there was a surprise in store for him. A woman

was standing at a door and Jack went up to her he took a ten franc note out of his pocket gave it to her and said bread, bread. She nodded and motioned him in & we could almost taste the bread, but Jack was out in ten seconds. She had thought he wanted to go to bed and Jack was not having any.

The reinforcements finally reached the New Zealand Division where Les Ross ended up in a trench at La Signy Farm. It had been raining solidly for two days and 'the result was that we were in a foot of mud and water.' The New Zealanders did not, however, lose their sense of humour. A suspected German spy in a British officer's uniform had inspected the front at La Signy Farm and advised a corporal there to pull his men back 100 yards if they were shelled by the Germans. After this security scare the men instituted the use of a nightly password which all their soldiers had to remember.

> Some of the passwords were really funny. They would start to undress a girl. The first night the word would be Blouse, the next, skirt, petticoat, chemise, stocking panties would all follow, we would have the poor girl stripped in ten days. Then the reverse, it took longer to dress her as she would have a overcoat and hat on.[23]

Rifleman Ross and the newly arrived reinforcements remained in the front line at La Signy farm for two weeks.

If it was hard for reinforcements to slot into their units while they were in action, it was doubly so for newly commissioned officers. Lieutenant Marcus Smith, a lawyer from Sanson near Palmerston North, had not reached Britain until mid-December 1917 and there he remained for the next two months. On Sunday 17 March he wrote a reassuring letter to his widowed mother in Waipukurau:

> I believe I am to go overseas with a draft next Weds which will mean some time at our base in France as they don't seem to require officers at present, our division will probably be put in a quiet sector . . . we may not be in a big fight again, the Division could not stand another Passchendaele.[24]

Normally, Lieutenant Smith would have spent some time at the base camp, as he indicated in his letter. But these were far from normal times.

By the time Marcus Smith reached France the New Zealand Division was again in the thick of the action and the Rifle Brigade was desperately short of officers. His next letter to his mother was written in pencil on two pages of a field notebook rather than with the fountain pen and fine writing paper he been recently using.

> I wrote to you just after reaching France & was pushed straight into it, did some heavy marching & suddenly found myself in an attack . . . I feel very lonely among strangers & the conditions are awful, at present I have just moved back from the line & am in a fairly dry dug out. Fritz is straffing all round with shells & my nerves are on edge, he occasionally gets a dugout, one landed a few yds from mine yesterday & shook me up, also had a bullet through my coat sleeve on the first stunt, oh if it had been a blighty.
>
> This morning while walking through a newly captured trench I saw poor Mathew lying dead in the mud, he was killed in a raid the day before, he was one of my original subalterns & went right through with me, he was a very brave man in the line. I took a cigarette case from him & will sent it to his wife if I get the chance. A 'q' [small artillery shell] just landed very closed, it is hard . . . not having had a chance to get used to it first & being shoved right into bloody fighting . . .
>
> Another shell very close, I suppose I shall get used to it. Much love to you all. I will write from Blighty.
> Marcus[25]

It was certainly a tough experience for a young officer. It was not surprising, perhaps, that Marcus Smith's next letter to his mother was written from the Medical Depot at Etaples, far from the fighting on the Somme.

On the morning of 4 April a heavy German bombardment announced an end to the quiet period. It also marked the beginning of the last stage of the great March offensive. The attack on 4 April was not made on the front where the New Zealand Division was situated but rather south of the Somme on a 15-mile front. The Germans used seventeen divisions, six of them for the first time in the offensive. Twelve divisions attacked the French Army on a 9-mile front while five divisions attacked the remnants of the British Fifth Army, now renamed the Fourth Army, on a front of 6 miles. The very muddy ground the Germans had to cross greatly inhibited their movement, but they still managed to drive back the British Fourth Army along its entire front, in some places for nearly 2 miles. The French XXXVI Corps was also driven back as far as 2 miles beyond the Avres River to Senecat Wood from where the attacking Germans could clearly see the outskirts of Amiens. The Germans captured Hamel in the morning, but a new defensive Allied line was formed west of the village. A renewed attack that afternoon reached the outskirts of Villers-Brétonneux, less than 10 miles east of Amiens and the key to the defence of the city. For a time it seemed likely that the town would fall to the Germans, but a spirited charge by the Australian 36th Battalion and the remnants of two British companies saved the day. The Australians had been lying in wait in a hollow south of the town and on sighting the Germans made 'a spectacular charge' with fixed bayonets.[26] The Germans hesitated, then ran, taking up a new position in old trenches a mile from the town. The Australian 36th Battalion lost 150 men in this attack — a quarter of its current strength and more than half of its officers.[27] For a time the situation hung in the balance, but reinforcements arrived to plug the gaps in the defences. The southern approach to Amiens remained blocked.

Though significant ground had been taken the Germans finished the day well short of their objectives and their casualties were heavy. Yet this limited success was enough to encourage them to renew their attempts the following day. Believing that the front south of the Somme would crumble if subjected to enough pressure elsewhere, the Germans planned to strike on 5 April at various points north of the Somme in an effort to take Amiens from that direction. One of the areas selected for close attention was the village of Hébuterne and the region immediately to its south.

Chapter 9

Weathering the Storm: 5 April 1918

On 5 April 1918 the Germans made a last desperate effort to open the road to Amiens. Though the Second and Seventeenth Armies planned to launch a general offensive against the whole front of the British Third Army, such a large-scale operation proved impossible to mount so only isolated attacks took place. Between Dernancourt and Bucquoy, using ten infantry divisions heavily supported by artillery, three main attacks took place on 5 April at Colincamps, at Albert against the 12th and 63rd Divisions, and at Dernancourt, where the hardest fighting took place. At Dernancourt, two brigades of the 4th Australian Division held three German divisions at bay, suffering more than 1000 casualties while doing so. For the entrenched Australians, 5 April began with the heaviest artillery bombardment they had experienced 'since the worst days of the Somme'.[1] The depleted Australian brigades were forced to give ground, though the Germans gained only about 2000 yards by the end of the day. The extent of the Australian losses made it necessary to withdraw the 4th Division from the line when the fighting died away that evening.

The New Zealand Division and the 4th Australian Brigade also had their share of heavy fighting on 5 April. One of the locations singled out for attention by the Germans was just south of Hébuterne, where two German divisions attempted to batter their way through the defences. Their immediate objective was the long stretch of high ground behind the New Zealanders, the site of the village of Colincamps, just over a mile behind the New Zealand front line. Pencil sketch-maps found on the bodies of German officers showed where the enemy would locate their brigade and battalion headquarters once Colincamps was taken. A German prisoner taken that morning confirmed that their intention was to capture and hold Colincamps. The German soldiers at

Hébuterne were carrying full packs loaded with ammunition and enough rations to last three to four days. As one New Zealand historian has commented, these maps and the loaded packs suggested that 'a successful issue was, in his [the enemy's] mind, a foregone conclusion'.[2] If this was the case, then the German commanders were about to be bitterly disappointed.

Around 5 a.m. on that day, in a blanket of mist and light rain, the storm erupted again on the New Zealand Division as the Germans attempted to revitalise their flagging offensive. It was a cold, dull day with low overhanging clouds. This bleak weather tended to favour the defenders as it prevented the Germans from using their observation balloons. The German attack started with an 'extraordinarily vehement'[3] artillery bombardment, probably the heaviest and most sustained barrage the New Zealand Division experienced during the war.[4] The German artillery fire was constant throughout the day, but the initial barrage lasted for three hours and extended across the whole New Zealand front line and on the right half of the Australian 4th Brigade at Hébuterne.

The Germans used guns of all calibres, including some as heavy as 21 centimetres (12 inches). The main areas targeted were the forward trenches, the support and rear positions as far back as Bertrancourt, Colincamps and Bus-les-Artois. The German gunners paid particular attention to the dead ground and valleys in front of the New Zealand line where strong points had been recently constructed. These areas 'were almost deluged with high explosive, and swept with shrapnel'.[5] In an attempt to neutralise the division's artillery batteries, the New Zealand artillery positions were hit with a high proportion of mustard gas shells.[6] This 'storm of steel' severed all the ground wires from the various observation posts to the battalion and brigade headquarters. Throughout the day communications remained 'difficult and uncertain'.[7] Despite this, the New Zealand artillery was soon active, firing on known troop concentration points and engaging in some counterbattery fire of their own.

All those on the receiving end of this barrage commented on its severity. According to James McWhirter, 'the shells seemed to drop like hail, it was terrific and caused many casualties'.[8] Captain George Tuck found little rest away from the front line on this 'very tiring day':

At about 4.00 a.m. this morning, the Hun started to shell these areas with every kind of gun including our own 18 pounders. He never stopped for 11 hours and then continued intermittently. All windows were blown in my orderly room the sashes came in with the windows and much stuff was knocked off the ceiling and walls. We were very lucky though.[9]

The war diary of the 2nd Canterbury Battalion reflected Tuck's thoughts:

5 April
Dirty day. At 6 a.m. enemy commenced to shell AUCHON-VILLERS with guns of all calibres, and to a lesser extent, the Front and Support Lines. This continued without a lull until 4.30 p.m. Casualties were light — but AUCHONVILLERS torn to rags. Night was quiet. Patrols reported no enemy movement.[10]

Despite the intensity of the barrage, the New Zealanders were indeed lucky: casualties were surprisingly light, as all unit and formation war diaries recorded with a sense of relief. That of the 2nd Auckland Battalion, Captain Tuck's unit, is typical:

5 April
Early in the morning of the 5th the enemy unsuccessfully attacked the Rifle Brigade in the front line positions and from 5:30 a.m. until 2.30 p.m. our positions in Divisional Reserve were heavily shelled, especially COURCELLES AU BOIS and the positions occupied by the 16th Coy. However in spite of the heavy shelling our casualties were very slight.[11]

The diary of the 1st Canterbury Battalion, which had borne the brunt of the German barrage in the southern sector of the line, recorded: 'Our casualties, in face of so heavy a bombardment, were very light'.[12] Lieutenant John Harcourt was a company commander in the 1st Canterbury Battalion. Like most of the New Zealander officers that day, he was both surprised and delighted that the battalion's casualties were not heavier and he had a convincing explanation:

5 April
A memorable day which broke very chill. The trench was full of mud & movement along them difficult in consequence . . . I had

two men wounded, both lightly, but how I got off so lightly, still remains a miracle. McFadden on my left had 5 or 6 killed and several wounded. This artillery barrage was one — if not the most — prolonged bombardment with big shells yet experienced by the New Zealanders and our casualties were very light. For this we can thank the soft ground and the bad shooting of the enemy most of whose artillery had been brought up secretly and was firing without having registered on our trenches.[13]

One New Zealand soldier wounded that morning was Edward Bibby. When recalling the experience just over 70 years later he was in no doubt that the German barrage of 5 April was the 'heaviest bombardment of the war . . . they hammered us all day'. In front of the 1st Otago billets was a paddock of thick grass. At the end of the day, not a blade of grass remained: 'it had been ploughed'. A shell splinter hit Bibby early in the morning, but he could not be moved until just after 2 p.m. when there was a slight decrease in the barrage's intensity. Bibby set off for Mailly-Maillet where he found things 'a real classic, it would suit the war pictures. There were ambulances coming and going. There were shells going off, the wounded streaming in . . . It was an interesting experience.'[14]

The depth and intensity of the opening barrage indicated that the Germans were likely to launch an attack soon, so the New Zealanders in the front line steeled themselves. 'The enemy could be plainly seen in his trenches watching the effect of his shelling and in such numbers as to suggest his following up the bombardment with an infantry attack.'[15] After three hours the German barrage began to creep forward, a sure sign that the infantry were advancing behind it. The New Zealanders did not have to wait long until their suspicions were confirmed.

In line that morning were the 2nd New Zealand Infantry Brigade on the right and the Rifle Brigade, linking with the Australian 4th Brigade on the left. German infantry attacked both New Zealand brigades on two separate occasions. The German commanders had intended to synchronise these attacks, but owing to the disorganisation on the German front, they were launched at different times. In fact, the last two attacks were separated by as much as four hours.

The first German infantry attack was made just after 8.30 a.m. when a regiment from the 26th German Division advanced against the Rifle Brigade, barring their way to Colincamps. The German infantry suffered heavily under the New Zealanders' withering machine-gun and rifle fire. As they closed in on the Rifle Brigade, New Zealand bombers operating from the saps also took a heavy toll on the German infantry. Still they came on, managing to get within 30 yards of the Rifle Brigade's trenches before they were finally driven off. The war diary of the 1st Rifles records the details of this attack:

> The night of 4/5th April was quiet except for sounds of talking and whistle signals coming from the enemy lines. Patrols reported nothing else unusual.
>
> At about 5.15 A.M. on the 5th April the enemy commenced a heavy shelling of our front line which continued without cessation until about 8.30 A.M., when the barrage lifted to the hollow and ridge in rear of the front line. Shortly afterwards the enemy were seen through the haze all along the line advancing to the attack. It was general on all three front Company sectors but he appeared to be in greatest strength on the right in the direction of RED COTTAGE to LA SIGNY FARM.
>
> The S.O.S. rocket signal was put up and the artillery response was good.
>
> Our three Companies had the situation well in hand from the commencement. In no case did any advanced posts give way, but there were several cases of individual and collective movements forward to meet parties of the enemy. Waves in the open made excellent targets and bombing forward down the C.T's was exceedingly well done, the enemy being driven back through these or forced to leave them and be dealt with by Lewis Gun and Rifle fire. In every respect our men displayed fine fighting spirit. It is worthy of note that while the action was in progress, Company Cooks brought up tea for the men in the front line and posts.[16]

The next assault on the Rifle Brigade was made at 10 a.m. and it met with more success. The Germans succeeded in capturing an advanced outpost manned by a small garrison of men from the 4th Rifles. 'An advance post at LA SIGNY FARM was rushed by the enemy under cover of fog. 1 sector with a Lewis gun evaded the flanking movement by the enemy but the remainder of the garrison 14 in all were either killed or captured.'[17]

Using this position as a lever the German attackers went on to take La Signy Farm. Hoping to use the farm as a pivot to capture the New Zealand trenches, the Germans turned trench mortars on the New Zealand positions and then pushed as many parties of infantry as they could up old saps towards the New Zealand lines. The forward posts of the 4th Rifles inflicted massive casualties on the German infantry and foiled their attempt to reach the New Zealand lines. 'Never before had the Lewis gunners of the 4th Battalion had such targets as on this day and of their opportunities they made full use.'[18] With the Germans in possession of La Signy Farm, the 1st Rifles were exposed to dangerous enfilade fire, but the problem was solved by having its C Company form one defensive flank along the hedge that ran beyond the farm and another across the main line in case the Germans launched a frontal assault. Moving forward down the saps and attacking the enemy there could easily defeat any assault made against the front of 1st Rifles.

By noon the situation was restored and this attack petered out. There were no further attacks on the Rifle Brigade that day. From 1 to 12 April 1918, the Rifle Brigade's casualties were recorded as 96 men killed, 311 wounded and three missing.[19] Most of these casualties were sustained on 5 April. German losses were higher, conservatively estimated to be more than 500 on 5 April.[20] As the 4th Rifles' war diary noted, 'The enemy losses appear to have been heavy as all that day his stretcher bearers were engaged in carrying out wounded.'[21] German accounts of this action claim that the attack was halted by New Zealand machine-gun fire from the flanks and centre. The 10th Bavarian Infantry Regiment 'lost 190 officers and men. The attack had no prospect whatsoever of success unless the enfilade fire of enemy machine-guns were eliminated by the preliminary bombardment and by the barrage.'[22] La Signy Farm remained in German hands but it was kept under constant fire by the New Zealand artillery. At dusk on 5 April the New Zealanders struck back with the 3rd Rifles south of the Serre Road, advancing their line by some 150 yards.

On the right of the New Zealand line, German infantry attacked the 2nd New Zealand Infantry Brigade in the morning and afternoon of 5 April. The brigade was holding the line with the two Canterbury battalions. Of these, only the 1st Canterbury Battalion was attacked that day. The attack in the morning came just on 9 a.m. with German infantry working up the saps leading to the front-line trenches. The 1st Canterbury Battalion established blocking positions in the saps, forcing the Germans into the open where they were overcome with rifle, Lewis gun and machine-gun fire. German losses were heavy. The war diary of the 1st Canterbury Battalion made only a brief mention of this first attack:

Weather dull. Enemy opened an intense bombardment the whole of our system about 7.15 a.m., which he maintained all day, and during which he concentrated bodies of troops in saps leading towards our Front Line. At 9 a.m. his first attempt to come across was quickly repulsed, our fellows being, if anything, too keen.[23]

Lieutenant John Harcourt of the 1st Canterbury Battalion was visiting battalion headquarters at 9 a.m. when a runner from his platoon arrived to inform him that:

> Fritz was coming over the top. I rushed straight back to the front line and found that Sgt Carter had put up the S.O.S. in my absence and that the Light Trench Mortars had at once opened fire and caught the Hun waves right on the S.O.S. line dispersing them immediately.[24]

Harcourt had missed the German attack against his battalion that morning, but in the afternoon he would be in the thick of the action when the Germans struck again.

The Germans renewed their attack around 2 p.m. If anything, it was more of a nonevent than the previous one and achieved nothing but heavy casualties for the Germans. The British official historian described it as a 'final but feeble effort'[25] while the history of the Canterbury battalions said it was launched 'in a half-hearted way'.[26] For a while it seemed as if the Germans might make some progress on the New Zealand right flank, but an enterprising Corporal White of 2 Company quickly organised a bombing party to halt the Germans and captured ten prisoners. The attack was easily driven off. One of the many German casualties was a plane.

> An enemy Contact Plane, flying low over our front trench system, nearly all the morning, and doing invaluable work for the enemy was brought down by 12th. Company Lewis Gunners. The Pilot, badly wounded, and the Observer, unwounded, were both taken prisoners. Our much esteemed M.O. [medical officer], Dr. Harris was killed about 40 yards from the R.A.P.[27]

Harris was killed by the shellfire that had continued unabated throughout the attack.

Lieutenant Harcourt's platoon was on the receiving end of an intense bombardment. It caused much damage to his trench but his casualties were light: only two of his men were slightly wounded. Harcourt regarded this 'as a miracle':

> My trench was blown in many places and one section of mine had a circle of big shell holes right around them only a few yards away. I did my best to keep the men cheerful despite the rather rattled feeling I had myself . . . The Hun did not get more than 50 yards before giving it up as our rifle and MG fire was too hot.[28]

The 2nd Otago Battalion was one of the reserve battalions of the 2nd New Zealand Infantry Brigade. Its war diary gave a succinct summary of the day's action on their brigade front:

> 5 April
> Heavy enemy bombardment opened up at 5 a.m. which lasted for 10 hours. Shells of all calibres were used and all villages received special attention. Companies had to quit their bivouac shelters and dig in clear of the village. This bombardment was of a very intense nature and was used to cover his attack further north. Enemy did attempt in a feeble sort of way to attack on our front but it was easily repulsed. Wet. Poor observation.[29]

When it was clear that this last attack had failed, the German artillery fire died down to become almost nonexistent from 3.30 p.m.

Dr Harris of the 1st Canterbury Battalion was not the only Medical Corps casualty that day. At Hédauville the 2nd New Zealand Field Ambulance was in reserve. It had dispatched 50 of its stretcher-bearers to the 1st Field Ambulance, which was responsible for evacuating stretcher cases from the ADS at Mailly-Maillet. Although in reserve, the 2nd Field Ambulance had more casualties than the 1st Field Ambulance, operating near the front line. Remaining in the villages behind the New Zealand front line did not mean protection from danger. The German artillery had clearly selected the 2nd Field Ambulance as a prime target and continued shelling the unit throughout the day with a mixture of high explosive, gas and shrapnel shells. In the afternoon a prisoner of war compound in Hédauville received a direct hit and several captured Germans were killed. The 2nd Field Ambulance suffered six casualties; one soldier was killed.[30] Meanwhile, at Mailly-Maillet, the 1st Field Ambulance, busy evacuating wounded soldiers away from the front line, also came under artillery fire.

5 April 1918

Enemy attacked — 230 casualties being passed through A.D.S. RAPs on left flank had to shift back slightly, on account of heavy shelling, but all evacuations carried out satisfactorily. Two ambulance cars put out of action by shellfire. The unit had 3 casualties during the day — all slight wounds.[31]

The New Zealand artillery batteries received considerable attention from the German gunners and some suffered heavy losses, as Bombardier Bailey's diary recorded:

Fritz started shelling the heavy batteries in the next village of Bertrancourt. He pasted them all the morning. My word the big H.E. [high explosive shells] did come in . . . There was heavy artillery fire all day and some of our batteries suffered. The news reached us that the 10th Battery was blown out and some of the others had casualties . . .

Fritz is supposed to have made three separate attacks during the day and sent over three waves of infantry with each attack. Our boys must have stopped him alright though we had a lot of casualties; the ambulances being kept very busy.[32]

It would seem that the New Zealand Machine Gunners were responsible for most of the German casualties. At 8.30 a.m. the Wellington Company of the Machine Gun Battalion, in support of the Rifle Brigade, caught the advancing Germans with 'a perfect hurricane of fire'.[33] The machine gunners estimated that they accounted for about half of the advancing force. When the second attack was made on the Rifle Brigade at 10 a.m., the machine gunners once more assailed the Germans with withering fire. One gun kept up a fire that lasted for more than four hours and prevented the German infantry from reaching an old communication trench. In the southern sector of the line that afternoon, the situation was similar.

Enemy again attempted to advance and were engaged at a range of 600 yards . . . 70 or 80 casualties were observed . . . Very many small targets were engaged throughout the day and machine gun fire brought to bear upon all approaches and points where enemy might assemble unobserved.[34]

This New Zealand machine-gun fire took a heavy toll on the German infantry and was primarily responsible for the failure of the enemy attacks. In a letter home Major Lindsay Inglis described the effect of his guns in support of the 2nd New Zealand Infantry Brigade:

> Things are much the same as they were in my last letter, the only events of note being a heavy attack by Fritz two days ago — he came a stomacher as we all predicted he would. Two guns of mine had him at 80 to 100 yards range in considerable lumps and the others had him at various ranges — the bag was quite satisfactory and I don't think he'll come at it again here unless at the very greatest strength he can muster. I doubt if it will be worth his while even then.[35]

Captured Germans, too, testified to the effect of the New Zealand machine guns. An officer interrogated at General Headquarters gave two reasons for the failure of the 5 April attack:

1. The intensity of our [the New Zealanders] machine gun barrage.
2. The fact that some of the attacking troops did not leave their front line until ten minutes after the assault had been launched.[36]

A German prisoner from the 4th Company, 1st Battalion, 119th Grenadier Regiment, which had been part of the attacking force on 5 April, made a graphic and tragic entry in his diary:

> At 9.am we attacked. Many comrades find a hero's death, others writhe in their wounds. Primarily it was due to machine gun fire from the right and left flanks. The losses are very great. Many wounded are lying in the open. At night the battalion returns to its starting point. During day we are withdrawn to Battalion Battle Headquarters, but here also we are under fairly heavy fire. Thank God we are relieved here.[37]

Those New Zealanders who had weathered the storm of 5 April were full of confidence and relief.

> I do not think any man who was through today's happenings will ever forget it. We were all a bit shaken but our morale was very high after our double victory over the attacking Hun . . . It was a

very trying and nerve-racking day — although exciting at times. The men were in great spirits after the show and would have gone after the Boche had they been allowed.[38]

The German onslaught of 5 April 1918 was an event of considerable significance for several reasons. First, according to the historian of the Rifle Brigade, 'The attack was unique in the respect that it was the only one of major importance that the New Zealand Division ever sustained.'[39] Second, for the first time in this war, the New Zealanders were not at a disadvantage in terms of the terrain on which they were fighting. They enjoyed the novelty of dealing with an attack in force while occupying a superior defensive position. Their efforts to secure all the high ground over the previous week had clearly paid off. Third, as a result of the failure of the 5 April assaults, Ludendorff took the painful decision to abandon the Michael Offensive.

> These actions were indecisive. It was an established fact that the enemy's resistance was beyond our strength. We must not get drawn into a battle of exhaustion. This would not accord neither with the strategical or tactical situation. In agreement with the commanders concerned, G.H.Q. had to take the extremely difficult decision to abandon the attack on Amiens for good.[40]

So, after sixteen days, the German offensive on the Somme ground to a halt. After experiencing spectacular success at the beginning, it lost momentum and petered out in a series of spasmodic attacks. As in all the Allied offensives that had taken place to date, there was a break-in, but no breakthrough and the situation had deteriorated to the point of stalemate. After the failure of the assaults on 5 April Ludendorff decided that, in order to make any further progress, he needed to attack the BEF elsewhere. This would occur in the north in four days' time. But the Michael Offensive, the *Kaiserschlact*, 'the most formidable onslaught of the war',[41] was over. The storm on the Somme had caused considerable damage to those who had stood in its path. It remained now to count the cost.

Chapter 10

Damage Assessment

Casualty figures for military campaigns are notoriously unreliable. There are often huge discrepancies in the numbers given for dead and wounded, and the German Michael Offensive is no exception. The figures given for German casualties in the *Kaiserschlacht* vary enormously from 105,000 to 300,000,[1] and it is now impossible to be sure just how many Germans were injured and killed in the period from 21 March to 5 April. It is possible, however, to note two significant details. First, the Germans did not lose as many men as the Allies, which was rare for an attacking force during the First World War. Describing his casualties as 'not inconsiderable', Ludendorff took considerable comfort from the fact that his enemies' casualties were higher: 'We had been attacking and had come off well, even in the matter of casualties'.[2] The second point is that though the Germans had fewer casualties than the BEF and the French, they came from those units that had done the heaviest fighting: the élite storm troops and the attack formations that followed them. Germany lost many of its best soldiers, men chosen for their initiative, fitness and ability, men the Kaiser could least afford to lose. As William Moore has commented, 'the losses in numbers could be counted, the losses in quality were incalculable'.[3] This would become all too evident in the later stages of the war.

Losses in the BEF were undoubtedly heavy — around 180,000, of whom half were missing.[4] Unlike previous battles of the war, however, where a high proportion of the dead were never recovered, most of the missing were in fact prisoners of war. The British Fifth Army suffered most during the Michael Offensive. It had disappeared from the BEF establishment and needed to be rebuilt as a fighting formation. These losses were indeed serious, but the BEF was not 'virtually finished as a fighting force', as one historian has recently claimed.[5]

New Zealand losses were considerable, despite the extraordinary claim made in the division's history that the casualty list was 'by no means an unduly heavy one'.[6] By 1918, the New Zealand government knew that any involvement in operations in France inevitably meant a large list of dead and wounded would soon follow. The Minister for Defence, Sir James Allen, clearly expressed this point to General Godley in early April 1918:

> I cannot conclude this letter without referring to the great fight that is now on. We are watching from day to day with eagerness for news, and I cannot tell you how much we admire the pluck and staying power of the British Army against the attacks of the masses that are brought against them. We are hoping that you have them held and will soon turn the tables. I fear casualty lists will be heavy, but there is some consolation to us as we are informed at the same time that the lists of our enemies are heavier still.[7]

There is considerable variation in the casualty figures given for the New Zealand Division in this offensive. The *Oxford Companion to New Zealand Military History* fudges the figures somewhat by stating that the casualties were more than 500 New Zealanders killed and 1800 wounded.[8] Stewart lists the casualties as 530 men killed, 1800 wounded and another 60 missing.[9] The British official history offers different figures again: 511 men killed, 1845 wounded and a further 63 men missing, making a total of 2419. Carbery's medical history of New Zealand's involvement in the war contains a full list of New Zealand casualties month by month. For the two months of the Michael Offensive the figures are a total of 448 in March (79 dead and 369 wounded) and a total of 3201 in April (885 dead, 2300 wounded and sixteen missing or captured).[10]

The total casualties for April 1918 are among the highest for the war, surpassed only by the months of September 1916 (the Somme), June 1917 (Messines), October 1917 (Passchendaele) and September 1918. As A.E. Byrne wrote in his history of the Otago battalions, 'This high total affords some indication of the severity of the period.'[11] Carbery's figures are probably the most accurate, especially if measured against the names in the casualty reports for this period. These list all the New Zealand soldiers reported as casualties from 23 March to 30 April 1918: 811 were killed or died of wounds; 2181 were wounded.[12] And it should never be forgotten, as Appendix 1 shows, that each of these numbers represents an individual, a New Zealand soldier far from home with dreams and aspirations, plans for the future and loved ones to whom he wished one day to return.

For the Germans, the Michael Offensive was both a success and a failure. It is best summed up in the words of Cyril Falls, as 'a magnificent tactical victory, but not a strategic success to anything like the same extent'.[13] The Germans' success in the *Kaiserschlacht* was outstanding. When Ludendorff broke off the offensive on 5 April, the Germans had seized more ground than the Allies gained during the entire war. They had also inflicted some 250,000 casualties on the enemy. More than this, the Germans had done what many at the time thought was impossible: they had found a way to break the deadlock of trench warfare, something the British and the French had been struggling desperately to achieve for the last three years. Charles Bean summed up this remarkable success:

> If, however, Ludendorff failed to grasp the human problem involved, he solved most brilliantly some of the tactical and strategical ones. By solving the extraordinary difficult problem of achieving a large measure of surprise in one of these great, long prepared offensive, and by inventing a tactical method — infiltration — which freed the German infantry from the rigidity that had hitherto bound the tactics of the Allies, Ludendorff presented his opponents with a problem to which — so far as resistance in their prepared trench-systems was concerned — there was no answer. Even with his army weakened through the policy of Lloyd George, Haig had been confident of at least holding the Germans for many days before they reached the Somme. But Ludendorff, by deceiving his opponents with preparations in three sectors — and more — and then by flinging his whole strength against one of these, had actually placed it beyond the power even of a Napoleon to stop the rapidity of his advance in the first stages.[14]

Later in the year, the Allies copied Ludendorff's methods while adding some variations of their own. This initiative finally brought them victory on the Western Front.

The German victories shook the British establishment to its core and left its forces in a desperate situation. After 5 April, Haig was left with only a single division in reserve (from a total of 60). Sixteen of his divisions were being made up with drafts of youths aged eighteen or nineteen. The German triumphs also implied that, for the first time on the Western Front, the British forces in the field had been attacked and defeated. As John Buchan noted, there is no escaping the fact that the days of retreat from 21 to 26 March had all the hallmarks of defeat: 'for defeat it is, when two armies fall back thirty miles with heavy losses, and have the enemy's will imposed on them'.[15] The performance of British troops during those dark days produced a crisis of confidence at home and the demand for a scapegoat, which the government duly provided in the form of General Gough.

The atmosphere and mood in Britain is reflected in the letters that passed between General Godley and the King's private secretary, Colonel Clive Wigram. In a letter marked 'Private and Confidential' Wigram lamented the mood of pessimism that had swept the country and, in his view, had emanated from Parliament:

> The spirit of the men must indeed be marvellous . . . The misery is that with all this sacrifice and keeping up the honour of the Old Country, there is so much bickering and snarling at home, and tendency to decry what the British soldier has done and is doing on the Western Front. Why does not the Prime Minister or some Member of Cabinet get up and tell the people how magnificently our Armies have been fighting against heavy odds, and how thinly the Fifth Army front had to be held, and render to DH [Haig] and his commanders the tribute due to them?

A recent debate in the House of Commons had left the public with the impression that the British and Germans had been equal in strength during this offensive and that the British soldiers, especially those in the Fifth Army, had run away without offering any effective resistance. Wigram deeply resented this insinuation: 'Now you and I know this to be a false suggestion and a suppression of the truth, to which the accounts of all the correspondents now bear witness. I cannot understand the attitude of a Britisher who prefers to think that foreign methods, plans, leadership and staff work are better than our own.' He felt that Lloyd George had misled the British people in an effort to deflect criticism away from the government. 'I think that L.G. is the best man we could have to win the war, but his methods are rather un-English.' What was lacking, according to Wigram, was more military control in the

154

government: 'A war can only be won where there is military control in military affairs, and, alas, the Boches are expert at this'.[16]

Yet, as Ludendorff acknowledged, the Michael Offensive was a strategic failure.[17] Though, in comparison with what had gone before it, Michael had made substantial territorial gains, this was not enough. In war, a withdrawal in the face of enemy pressure does not necessarily lead to defeat, and nor does an advance mean that victory automatically follows. The offensive had not fulfilled any of its key aims. The Germans had not turned the flank of the British armies and had not separated the armies of Britain and France. The strategically important towns of Arras and Amiens were still in British control. In fact, some historians of note came to regard the Michael Offensive as a decisive defeat for the Germans. This was certainly the view of Winston Churchill:

> Contrary to the generally accepted verdict, I hold that the Germans, judged by the hard test of gains and losses, were decisively defeated. Ludendorff failed to achieve a single strategic object . . . What then had been gained? The Germans had reoccupied their old battlefields and the regions they had so cruelly devastated and ruined a year before. Once again they entered into possession of those grisly trophies. No fertile province, no wealthy cities, no river or mountain barrier, no new untapped resources were their reward. Only the crater-fields extending abominably wherever the eye could turn, the old trenches, the vast graveyards, the skeletons, the blasted trees and the pulverised villages — these from Arras to Montdidier and from St Quentin to Vilers-Bretonneux, were the Dead Sea fruits of the mightiest military conception and the most terrific onslaught which the annals of war record.[18]

In a recent publication historian Gary Sheffield echoes Churchill's view, but rather than seeing the March–April battles as defeats, Sheffield views them as successes for the BEF: 'In terms of sheer scale these battles rate as the greatest British defensive victories in history, for victories they were'.[19] If this is so, and there is good cause to argue this case, the British victory during the Michael Offensive, with its loss of territory and heavy casualties, must be described as Pyrrhic — triumph won at too great a cost.

Certainly the New Zealand soldiers in 1918 knew that they had taken part in a victory and their morale was high. The men also felt that, after

5 April 1918, the Germans were a spent force. Though the reality was a little different, as the Germans would soon show in their next attack, this optimism was widespread in the New Zealand Division in 1918. The war diary of the 1st Canterbury Battalion reflected this view in its entry for 6 April — 'Opened fine and quiet. Enemy evidently having had enough of it for the time being'.[20] — and on 22 April Captain George Tuck of the 2nd Auckland Battalion told his parents:

> Conditions have not been for the best this last month, but they might have been worse. No one seems pessimistic and I think that most of us regard the present enemy effort as being what is colloquially known as 'shooting his bolt'. Personally I am quite optimistic about the whole state of affairs.[21]

A few days earlier Tuck had written: 'In direct proportion to the Hun's success so the spirit of our men is rising. Everyone is laughing and joking about the whole thing.'[22] Success certainly bred confidence and in April 1918 the New Zealand Division had this in abundance. As Carbery's medical history noted, 'The morale of the Division had never been more exalted and our infantry were well prepared, even eager, to meet any assault the enemy might choose to fling upon them.'[23] Fortunately, though, it would be some months before the division was again involved in heavy fighting.

The Germans were far from a spent force after 5 April. They had, however, been checked on the Somme and could not break through the hastily formed British defences there. To make any further progress they needed to strike elsewhere. As the Second Battle of the Somme ended the Germans switched their efforts further north to the Lys Valley, south of Ypres. This second drive, codenamed Georgette, lasted from 9 to 29 April. Two days before the attack the Germans launched a massive mustard-gas barrage on the British positions. The New Zealander's old haunt of Armentières was saturated with more than 40,000 of these shells. Operation Georgette used two armies with 35 divisions advancing behind a Bruchmüller barrage that achieved a density of 100 guns per kilometre, their greatest artillery concentration of the war. Like the Michael Offensive, Georgette had initial tactical success but soon lost momentum. None of its aims were achieved either. The German attack advanced about 9 miles before grinding to a halt at the end of April.

The ground captured by the Germans included much of the Ypres salient, including Messines and Passchendaele. News of the loss of these two ruined villages, scene of much savage fighting the previous year, greatly distressed the New Zealanders.[24] Writing from the Medical Depot at Etaples, Lieutenant Marcus Smith caught the mood of the New Zealand soldiers:

> The position is right on the edge & if Fritz gets another mile or two we may have to withdraw from the historic Ypres Salient, already the line has withdrawn from Passchendaele Ridge where one cannot put a spade in without digging up an Australian, New Zealander, or Canadian & is the place of our enormous casualty lists of October last year. As I have told you before we were pushed up to stop a rout & have learned a lot since then & do not wonder why everybody's hearts are breaking. We have wonderful troops, far better fighters than the Hun, but it is known right through the army that our staffs have . . . failed from the beginning.[25]

Yet, the loss of this ground did not seriously damage the Allies' cause and the German targets of strategic significance, the channel ports and the town of Hazebrouck, remained in British hands.

In May 1918 came the third German offensive drive. Codenamed Roland, it struck against the French in the Aisne Valley and at the Chemin des Dames, using 41 divisions. Two smaller operations followed in Noyon–Montdidier and the Champagne–Marne area but, like the previous offensives, they achieved only limited success. By 17 July 1918 the German offensives in this war had run their course. Ludendorff's hammer blows failed to achieve a single strategic objective. Worse than this, though, was the effect they had on the German Army. They bled it white, resulted in 'almost a million casualties between March and July 1918 [and] led to a vicious spiral of collapse thereafter'.[26] The fighting spirit of those German soldiers who survived these offensives was severely affected. Even a soldier as fanatically dedicated to the cause as Ernst Junger was could admit, in June 1918:

> At such moments there crept over me a mood I had never known before: a certain war-weariness occasioned by the length of time I had been exposed to the war's excitements. Nothing but war and danger; not a night that was not convulsed with shells. Winter

came and then summer, and one was always in the war. Tired of it and used to it, one was all the more dispirited and fed up with it just because one was used to it.[27]

Ludendorff's offensives, which had promised so much, finally cost Germany the war.

Some New Zealand units were involved in the fighting during Operation Georgette, though they were not part of the New Zealand Division and were under the command of General Godley in the New Zealand Expeditionary Force. The units used included the 2nd Entrenching Battalion, the Otago Mounted Rifles and the Cyclist Battalion, some artillery units and the New Zealand Tunnellers based at Arras. As Godley explained to Sir James Allen while the offensive was at its height, the BEF had 'had very strenuous times' in the north so that:

> Anything that we could lay our hands on had to be pressed into the fight, among them the 2nd New Zealand Entrenching Battalion made up of reinforcements and remnants of the 4th Brigade. Under command of Major Tonkin . . . they did excellent service, and I sent Malcolm Ross to see the Commander of the Division to which they were attached, and he received from him a most eulogistic account of what they had done.[28]

Though the New Zealanders played a useful role in this offensive, their limited numbers ensured that it remained a minor one. Disaster struck one of the units involved. On 16 April the Germans seized the village of Meteren, surrounding two companies of the 2nd New Zealand Entrenching Battalion. Efforts by a Royal Engineer unit helped one of the companies to escape but the other was captured *en masse*, all 210 men. It was 'the largest haul of the New Zealanders taken by the Germans during the war'.[29]

On 25 March, in the midst of the great crisis then unfolding in northern France, Field Marshal Sir Douglas Haig received the following telegram from Lloyd George:

> The British Cabinet wishes to express to the Army the thanks of the Nation for its splendid defence. The whole Empire is filled with pride as it watches the heroic resistance offered by its brave troops to overwhelming odds. Knowing their steadfastness and

courage whenever the honour of their country depends on their valour, the Empire awaits with confidence the result of this struggle to defeat the enemy's last desperate effort to trample down the free nations of the world. At home we are prepared to do all in our power to help in the true spirit of comradeship. The men necessary to replace all casualties and the guns and machine guns required to make good those lost are either now in France or already on their way, and still further reinforcements of men and guns are ready to be thrown into the battle.[30]

Haig, who published the telegram in a special order of the day 'for the information of all ranks', replied to the Prime Minister the next day: 'All ranks of the British Army in France have received with gratitude the message of confidence which you have sent me on behalf of the British cabinet. The assurance that no effort will be spared at home to give us all assistance is of great encouragement to us.'[31]

Perhaps spurred on by a guilty conscience, Lloyd George was as good as his word. During the days of the military crisis in France he worked tirelessly to redeem the situation (and to deflect criticism from himself). By 7 April he had managed to persuade the War Office and the Shipping Controller to send 150,000 men across the Channel, more than double the normal amount. But a good proportion of these soldiers were untrained youths: some 50,000 of them were six months or less shy of their nineteenth birthday. On Wednesday 10 April 1918, a bill passed in the House of Commons by a majority of 223 votes reflected just how seriously the military situation was regarded. Under this new legislation the military age limit was raised to 50, the government's power to abolish ordinary exemptions was increased and conscription was extended to Ireland. The policy of keeping a Home Army for defence against invasion was abandoned and within a month from 21 March, 355,000 men had been sent across the Channel to serve in France. In addition to these measures two divisions and sundry other units were transferred from Palestine to France. The success of the German offensive brought home to Lloyd George and his government just how vitally important it was to maintain the BEF on the Western Front. Starving Haig of manpower had proved costly and brought the Allies to the brink of defeat.

Measures were also taken to expedite the transport of American troops to the Western Front. This had been a painfully slow process to date, but in April and May 1918, 120,000 American troops arrived in France, making a total of 240,000 new arrivals. The soldiers were much-needed infantry and machine gunners. In France a 'big comb-out was commenced' in the BEF.[32] Army Service Corps men were transferred to the infantry and the Royal Engineers who worked on the canal barges suffered a similar fate. The BEF's military prisons were also emptied.

As well as scouring Britain for more men, Lloyd George appealed to the countries of the Empire to do more. This request caused some resentment in New Zealand where the government felt the dominion was doing more than its share in maintaining a division to full establishment in France, along with the nondivisional units there, as well as a mounted rifle brigade in Palestine. As Defence Minister Allen wrote to General Godley in early April:

> I telegraphed you the other day asking if you could supply a rough estimate of casualties. Owing to Lloyd George's appeal for men which I believe to be made more for Australia and Canada than New Zealand, it is possible that our Reserves may be utilised for other purposes than those for which they were devised, namely to reinforce the Division. I have said New Zealand will do its duty if we keep the Division up to its full strength until the war ends.[33]

In another letter written two weeks later Allen admitted, 'You can well imagine we have been much disturbed over the recent developments and the demand for extra reinforcements.'[34] The government sought advice from Britain, who requested that New Zealand create a New Zealand tank battalion and double their number of reinforcements to 1600 per month. The New Zealand government agreed, so long as the shipping was available to take the reinforcements to France. It hoped to dispatch around 3000 men by the middle of May 1918 in two reinforcement drafts. As Allen pointed out to Godley, no doubt knowing that he would pass it on to his imperial masters, 'You will realise, therefore, that New Zealand is doing all that she can do to keep the Division up to full strength.'[35] Towards the end of May, as the crisis on the Western Front eased, Allen was in a more relaxed frame of mind when he reported New Zealand's progress to Godley:

> We have been speeding up our Reinforcements and sending away as many men as we can find accommodation for in the available

160

ships. I sincerely hope that they will arrive in time to make up all your casualties and keep the Division up to its full strength. Of course we have had our troubles in this speeding up. Men have been called into Camp earlier than they expected, and some of them resent this. However, the spirit is still sound.[36]

The improvement of the military situation in France and the end of the war curtailed the formation of a New Zealand tank battalion.

On 20 July 1918 Haig noted that 'With the failure of his attacks on the 4th and 5th April the enemy's offensive on the Somme battle front ceased for the time being, and conditions rapidly began to approximate to the normal type of trench warfare, broken only by occasional local attacks on either side.'[37] The German attack on 5 April was the last by Germans in this region of the Somme. There were several occasions when a German attack did seem possible, especially on 13 and 17 April, but they proved to be false alarms. For the New Zealanders in the front line the impasse of 'filthy trench warfare' and all its routines returned. The New Zealand Division remained in the front throughout the wet months of April and May. 'The Battalion has been in the line all this week and has had a very rough spin,' wrote 2nd Lieutenant Roderick Toomath. 'The rain has made the trenches in a terrible condition and we have evacuated many with bad feet.'[38]

Though the Germans were less active during this phase of trench warfare, New Zealand battle casualties from shellfire numbered about 40 per day.[39] In May, General Godley visited the New Zealand Division on the Somme and found them 'all very flourishing in "Uncle" Harper's Corp, who I think is looking after them well'.[40] But conditions in the trenches remained dreadful and one is left wondering how close Godley went to them before he made his report.

On 24 April there was a significant action south of the New Zealand position. The Germans varied their offensive programme by making a sudden strike at Amiens. In the only tank engagement of the war they managed to capture the key to the city, the town of Villers-Brétonneux. Outside the town thirteen German tanks clashed head on with an equal number of British tanks. The world's first tank battle had opened that morning when a British 'male' tank scored three hits on a German opponent forcing its crew to abandon it. Four British Whippet tanks were put out of action by German tanks later in the day. In an action that has been described as 'one of the finest feats of the war',[41] two Australian brigades and two battalions of the British 8th Division recovered Villers-Brétonneux in a daring moonlight counterattack. Fighting continued into the early hours of the next day as the Australians fought from house to house in the town. On the third anniversary of Anzac Day, the gap created by this surprise attack was closed, so that this offensive, like the last attack here on 4 April, ended in failure. For the Germans, the road to Amiens remained blocked and could not be forced open.

On 21 August 1918, the New Zealand Division, in strength the equivalent of a British Corps of three divisions, advanced from their trenches on the Somme. The New Zealand soldiers never returned to them. The tough Battle of Bapaume was ahead of them, but 'for the next eleven weeks the New Zealanders were constantly moving forward'.[42] Well trained, equally skilled in open warfare, trench warfare and the set-piece battle, the New Zealand Division was a superb fighting machine. For the remainder of the war, now thankfully only months away, it was used as one of the spearhead divisions of the British Third Army. Field Marshal Haig visited the New Zealanders during this advance and was impressed with what he saw:

> I spent some time with General Russell and also saw his GSO 1 [the principal staff officer, Henry Maitland Wilson]. The NZ Division has come all the way from Hebuterne [more than 60 miles or 96 kilometres] to the present front on the Selle without a rest. A fine performance.[43]

But 'stopping the storm' on the Somme in March and April of 1918 was also a fine performance, as was recognised at the time. Glowing tributes poured in from generals, politicians and even governments. At the end of the war, General Harper of IV Corps wrote a farewell letter to Russell:

> The [New Zealand] Division joined the IV Corps at a critical time on the 26th March 1918, when it completely checked the enemy's advance at Beaumont-Hamel and Colincamps, and thus closed the gap between the IV and V Corps. By a brilliant stroke it drove enemy from the commanding ground at La Signy Farm and gained observation over the enemy's lines, which greatly assisted in his defeat on the 5th April 1918, when he made his last and final effort to break our front.

Harper went on to say that though the New Zealanders experienced a very tough time while holding their portion of the Somme line — a combination of bad weather and constant harassment by enemy shell-fire and raids — 'During this period I never had the least anxiety about the security of this portion of the front.'[44]

On 9 April 1918, Field Marshal Haig received a telegram from the New Zealand Governor, Lord Liverpool, expressing the nation's 'most intense admiration for the heroism of our soldiers and the utmost confidence in the officers and men of the British Forces, as well as the Forces of our Allies'. New Zealand was 'heart and soul with Britain' and 'nothing will be left undone to support our fighting men and assist in bringing about the deserved victory and permanent peace we all earnestly desire'. Replying the next day, Haig said the message had 'been deeply appreciated'. More than this, though, 'The Empire is proud of the part which New Zealand is playing in this war, and no troops could have fought more gallantly than the New Zealand Division.'[45] There is little reason to question the sincerity of Haig's reply.

More than a year after the event the New Zealand Division was still receiving accolades for its performance on the Somme in 1918. In the War Ministry of the Republic of France on 28 November 1919, Major General Sir Andrew Russell's name was recorded in Army Orders with the following explanation:

> Has led to countless victories a splendid Division whose exploits have not been equalled and whose reputation was such that on the arrival of the Division on the Somme Battle Field during the critical days of March, 1918, the departure of the inhabitants was stopped immediately.
>
> The Division covered itself with fresh glory during the battles of the Ancre a la Sambre, at Puisieux au Mont, Bapaume, Crevecoeur, and Le Quesnoy.[46]

It is somewhat ironic that Russell was named by the French, because the only people critical of the New Zealand performance on the Somme were the New Zealand commanders, especially Russell and Godley. Russell, the most outspoken critic, demanded 'something better still . . . I certainly do expect the New Zealand Infantry both in thought and action, to be at least 50 per cent quicker than the new Armies'.[47] At the beginning of April 1918, he told his father and sister in England:

I don't know that we as a whole have done as well as we might in this first round of the battle. Some troops, of course, fought well — most did — but some want training badly — training and then more training — we all want it. You can practise in war only what you have learnt in peace. It is a grand mistake to think that the battlefield is to be the school room. It is too expensive.[48]

Russell communicated his concerns to General Godley, who duly passed them on to the New Zealand government, writing to the Minister for Defence at the end of April 1918:

Since I last wrote you will have heard that the New Zealand Division went South, and arrived just in time to help to stem the Boche advance there . . . I hear very good accounts of what they did, and their first attempt, since the landing at Gallipoli, of what was practically open warfare, seems to have been on the whole quite successful, though naturally after all these years of trench warfare, they were not as quick as they should have been, and Russell very rightly has issued criticisms and instructions on the subject.[49]

Lieutenant Colonel S.S. Allen, one of the officers on the receiving end of Russell's criticisms, offered a defence in his short history of the 2nd Auckland Battalion:

I suppose all the Commanding Officers were like myself, not so well used to acting quickly on our orders as we became later in the year; we had no previous experience of open warfare, and that is probably the reason for much of the delay in attacking which ensued. The 2nd Brigade were moving first, and they seemed the worst offenders.[50]

Lieutenant Colonel Allen's excuses (and his finger pointing) were unnecessary. Godley and Russell were wrong. It is no mean achievement to force march 20 to 30 miles, fight and defeat a skilled, determined enemy for eleven days without respite, in just the clothes you are wearing and in the most appalling weather. The New Zealand soldiers who fought on the Somme in 1918 performed a magnificent feat of arms, perhaps their finest of the war. They also made a crucial difference to the outcome of the battle. Their achievement deserves recognition.

Conclusion

The distinguished British military historian, Professor Richard Holmes, believes that, after so many years, it is possible to make balanced judgements about the First World War.[1] Such an approach is especially needed in the case of New Zealand. The First World War is the bloodiest conflict in which New Zealand has ever been involved. As for the other nations of the British Empire, the losses left New Zealanders in 'a profound state of shock that has shaped perceptions of the war ever since'.[2] Starting with the landing at Gallipoli, those long, usually inconclusive and costly battles of attrition seemed to have no point. With no recent experience of total war, and fed a strict diet of imperial rhetoric about the glories of the Empire, the New Zealanders were soon disillusioned. The current crop of British generals did not seem to know how to do their job, which, put simply, was to win on the battlefield. Worse than this, they seemed to be uncaring, inept and stupid. How else could they keep making the same terrible mistakes again and again, resulting in the deaths of millions? And this conflict came to be trumpeted as the 'war to end all wars'. When, 20 years later, another great conflict erupted, it made all the deaths and sufferings of the previous war seem futile. To lose a loved one (and sometimes more than one) was bad enough. To feel they had died for nothing must have been almost unbearable. Little wonder the bitterness took root and grew. But in all this pain and anguish, which even after 80 years is still felt intensely by the families who lost loved ones, it is easy to lose sight of what the soldiers from this nation achieved on those distant battlefields and for what purpose.

Though the First World War is generally accepted as a pivotal event in New Zealand's history, the New Zealand public has not been well served in this field by its historians. Even now, the country still does not have an official history of the conflict. The last detailed account of the war was Ormond Burton's *The Silent Division*, which appeared nearly

70 years ago. Few New Zealand academic historians work on this topic, despite its importance to the development of the nation. As a result, New Zealand's involvement in the conflict has become, to use the words of Brian Bond, 'a no man's land in the historical landscape'.[3] The lack of a balanced assessment of New Zealand's involvement in the First World War, such as has recently occurred in Britain, Canada and Australia, only adds to the extent of the tragedy for this nation.

New Zealand's involvement in the German spring offensive of 1918 was significant for a number of reasons. In terms of military operations, there were a number of 'firsts' involved. It was the first time large numbers of New Zealand troops were moved by motor transport. It was the first time New Zealand soldiers witnessed the plight of refugees. It was the first and only time New Zealand soldiers were involved in a defensive battle on the Western Front and it was the first time that the New Zealand Division was on the receiving end of a full-scale German attack. In this Second Battle of the Somme, the New Zealanders also experienced what many believe was their heaviest artillery barrage of the war. These are important events in this country's history.

More importantly, though, in March–April 1918 the New Zealand Division played a decisive part in halting the Kaiser's battle, thereby helping prevent Germany from winning the war. As Ernst Junger wrote, 'After forty-four months of hard fighting they [the German soldiers] threw themselves upon the enemy with all the enthusiasm of August 1914. No wonder it needed a world in arms to bring such a storm-flood to a standstill.'[4]

In 1918, the New Zealand Division was an important player in this 'world in arms'. The Australians also played a key role in halting the German offensive of March–April 1918, as did many of the British formations in the front line. However, at a time when well-trained, high-quality soldiers were desperately needed, the New Zealand Division, widely acclaimed as one of the best Allied divisions in France, was thrown into the thick of the action in the most dangerous sector of the line. There, between Hébuterne and Beaumont-Hamel, they brought the German advance to a standstill. It was one of the turning points of the battle and a feat of arms that could have been achieved only by the finest troops. As Charles Bean commented, 'no one who came into contact with them [the Australians] or with the New Zealanders in those dark days will deny that there was a special value in their presence.'

What impressed the British soldiers and commanders about the Australians and New Zealanders was 'the abounding willingness and virility of the troops themselves, and the calibre of their officers, largely men promoted from the ranks'. Even the Germans who came up against the soldiers of the two dominions 'were aware of a special spirit in all of them'.[5] German intelligence reports confirm that they had considerable respect for the fighting qualities of the Australian and New Zealand formations. A German report captured at Hébuterne had this to say about the New Zealand Division:

> A particularly good assault Division. Its characteristics are a very strongly developed individual self-confidence or enterprise, characteristic of the colonial British, and a specially pronounced hatred of the Germans. The Division prides itself on taking few prisoners. A captured officer taken at the end of April did not hesitate to boast of this while in the prisoner's cage. It is improbable that the New Zealand Division, which is qualitatively and quantitatively much stronger than the _th Division, should have taken over only the small sector occupied by the latter.[6]

From 26 March to 5 April 1918, and later in the year, these superb soldiers from Australia and New Zealand made their presence felt wherever they were used. In modern military jargon, they had a qualitative edge — the ability to punch far above their weight.

It is a tragedy that New Zealand's role in the German spring offensive is virtually unknown in the country that produced those fine soldiers. It is hardly surprising, however, given the lack of an official history. The British official history after the war devoted the better part of two lengthy volumes to the Second Battle of the Somme. Charles Bean devoted some 418 pages, half a volume of an impressive twelve-volume history, to the events of the Michael Offensive. Bean's account was widely read. It first appeared in 1937 and by 1943 was already into its tenth edition. By comparison, the semi-official New Zealand history by Stewart deals with New Zealand's involvement in the events of March–April 1918 in 36 pages of dense prose, and the conclusion makes no assessment of the role played by the New Zealand Division.[7] Bean devotes 40 pages to the New Zealand contribution, and his assessment is much nearer the mark than Stewart's. It is no wonder that New Zealanders in general know little about the events of March–April 1918.

Most soldiers of the British Empire did not think they were fighting a futile war. The outpourings of novelists in the interwar years should not be taken as typical or as being universally accepted. Captain Cyril Falls was a decorated veteran who served for three years on the Western Front. He later became an outstanding military historian, retiring as the Chichele Professor of the History of War at Oxford University in 1953.[8] He had this to say about the values and achievements of the First World War:

> The flood of antimilitarist literature, for the greater part fiction, which poured from the presses, deriding leadership from top to bottom, treating patriotism as a vice when not as a fraud, as it were bathed in blood and rolled in mud, was astonishing. It was far from being representative but it was assuredly symptomatic of widespread disillusion. Despite many reckless and brutal deeds done in high places, this terrible war of material was for the most part directed by statesmen and conducted by commanders who, for all their faults and errors and despite the trammels of nationalist and racialist bigotry, did not altogether lose their sense of the meaning and value of civilisation, and according to their lights, warred for a future in which civilisation should not cease to flourish.[9]

Cyril Falls had made a similar point much earlier in 1922, in the preface to his first book on the war, *The History of the 36th (Ulster) Division*, the formation in which he had served for much of the war:

> The picture now so often painted, representing the war as a single scene in a torture chamber, whence men emerged physical or mental wrecks, may be good anti-militarist propaganda, but it is false, because incomplete. From these experiences many men have emerged happy and strong. Many knew how to snatch some happiness even from their midst. A far greater number can see, in retrospect, that they played a part in one of the most dramatic, as well as one of the most terrible tragedies in history. That stands for something good, amid all its evil, in any man's life.[10]

Falls' opinion was shared by Cecil Malthus, a New Zealand First World War veteran and later Professor of Modern Languages at Canterbury University. Malthus also believed that the conflict had been fought for a just cause. He felt that the war was not 'just a useless, unjustifiable slaughter' but that 'all men of good will [must] be pre-pared to fight for justice and freedom'. According to Malthus, 'The worst casualty of this unhappy twentieth century has perhaps been the concept of honour and courage.'[11] This is indeed a tragedy. But as the eminent historians Professor Trevor Wilson and Professor Robin Prior wrote in 1995, the survival of liberal values and the system of repre-sentative government 'were not light matters, and in 1914 and the ensuing years they seemed worth fighting for'.[12]

The New Zealand Division played its part on the world stage in 'one of the most dramatic, as well as one of the most terrible tragedies in history'. The official historian of the 2nd New Zealand Division's final campaigns in North Africa in 1943 ended his account with these memo-rable words: 'Not for nothing had these men come ten thousand miles from their homeland in the new world to play their part in restoring a balance in the old.'[13] This line is also appropriate to describe New Zea-land's efforts in the war of 1914–18. It was not for nothing that New Zealanders had come to France 'From the Uttermost Ends of the Earth'.[14]

In an earlier volume dealing with his experience on Gallipoli, Malthus had these words of wisdom about the nature of war, 'War is a tragedy, of course, that we must always hope to avoid, but like most tragedies it underlines all that is finest in the human spirit.'[15] It is true that war does bring out the best and the worst in its participants. In March and April 1918, after a long, hard march, New Zealand soldiers met the German advance head on in the valley of the Ancre River and halted it with just the weapons they were carrying. They then stayed in the front line lightly clad, lacking food and water, enduring the most appalling of living con-ditions while holding their portion of the line. There they resisted the renewed German attempts to break open the British front again as they tried to restore momentum to a failing offensive. During these actions in this Second Battle of the Somme, these fine New Zealand soldiers made a vital and impressive contribution to the outcome of the First World War.

Endnotes

Abbreviations

ANZ   Archives New Zealand
ATL   Alexander Turnbull Library
KMARL   Kippenberger Military Archive and Research Library

Introduction

1   Ernst Junger, *The Storm of Steel. From the Diary of a German Storm-troop Officer on the Western Front*, London, 1929, pp. 253–4.
2   Gary Sheffield, *Forgotten Victory. The First World War: Myths and Realities*, London, 2001, p. 189.
3   Gerhard Loose, *Ernst Junger*, New York, 1974, p. 22. The decoration was instituted by Frederick the Great of Prussia, who preferred the French language to German.
4   Junger, p. 250.
5   Lieutenant E.C. Allfree, quoted in J.H. Johnson, *1918. The Unexpected Victory*, London, 1997, p. 27.
6   Sheffield, p. 60.
7   A.D. Carbery, *The New Zealand Medical Service in the Great War 1914–1918*, Auckland, 1924, p. 383.
8   *ibid.*

Chapter 1

1   Quoted in John Terraine, *To Win a War. 1918 The Year of Victory*, London, 1978, p. 27.
2   Cyril Falls, *The Great War*, New York, 1959, p. 255.
3   Terraine, p. 37.
4   John Coates, *An Atlas of Australia's Wars*, Melbourne, 2001, p. 72.
5   Quoted in Anthony Farrar-Hockley, *Goughie. The Life of General Sir Hubert Gough CGB, GCMG, KCVO*, London, 1975, p. 243.
6   He had once addressed a victorious army cross-country team: 'I congratulate you on your running. I hope you will run as well in the presence of the enemy.' Haig remained unaware of his *faux pas*. (Used as the frontispiece for William Moore's *See How They Ran*, Sphere Books, London, 1975.)
7   Farrar-Hockley, p. 243.
8   Farrar-Hockley, p. 242.
9   Sir James Edmonds, *History of the Great War. Military Operations in France and Belgium, 1918 Volume I*, London, 1935, p. 53.
10   Terraine, p. 49.
11   William Moore, *See How They Ran. The British Retreat of 1918*, London, 1975, p. 41.
12   Jeffrey Grey, *A Military History of Australia*, Melbourne, 1999, pp. 108–9.
13   G.D. Sheffield, 'The Indispensable Factor: The Performance of British Troops in 1918', in Peter Dennis and Jeffrey Grey (eds), *1918. Defining Victory*, Canberra, 1999, p. 77.
14   Figures are from Edmonds, p. 24.
15   General Sir Hubert Gough, *Soldiering On*, London, 1954, p. 146.
16   Edmonds, p. vii.
17   W.S. Austin, *The Official History of the New Zealand Rifle Brigade*, Wellington, 1924, p. 271.
18   Winston Churchill, *The World Crisis 1914–1918 Part II*, London, 1927, p. 385.
19   C.E.W. Bean, *Official History of Australia in the War of 1914–18. Vol. V. The A.I.F. in France: December 1917–May 1918*, Sydney, 1943, p. 671.
20   John Mosier, *The Myth of the Great War. A New Military History of World War I*, New York, 2001, pp. 312–14.
21   Falls, p. 259.
22   Falls, p. 180.
23   Churchill, p. 405.

24 General Ludendorff, *My War Memories 1914–18, Volume II*, London, 1919, p. 542.
25 Terraine, p. 35.
26 Ludendorff, p. 537.
27 *ibid.*, p. 542.
28 *ibid.*, p. 585.
29 Terraine, p. 35.
30 Ludendorff, p. 542.
31 There is remarkable agreement on these figures among the sources. Stewart, Edmonds, Churchill, Bean and Terraine agree that the Germans began the offensive with 192 infantry divisions and over 6000 artillery pieces.
32 Terraine, p. 37.
33 Barrie Pitt, 'Germany: 1918. New strategy, new tactics', in *History of the First World War*, Volume 6, Number 14, London, 1971, p. 2616.
34 Ludendorff, p. 590.
35 Pitt, p. 2616.
36 For most of the war the German front was organised into three army groups under the command of a royal prince. This was a Prussian, and later German, tradition. In 1918 the Army Group commanders were the Bavarian Crown Prince (Rupprecht), the German Crown Prince Wilhelm and Duke Albrecht of Wurttemberg. Later three Army Groups proved insufficient so another smaller one was created under General von Gallwitz.
37 Notes on the Offensive Battle, GHQ 25-1-18, WA 20/3 Box 2, Translation of German Documents 1/29/261, Archives New Zealand (ANZ).
38 *ibid.*
39 John Buchan, *Nelson's History of the War. Volume XXII The Darkest Hour*, London, n.d., p. 17.
40 Terraine, p. 38.
41 Farrar-Hockley, p. 250.
42 Edmonds, p. 118.
43 Bean, *Official History. Vol V*, p. 105.
44 Buchan, p. 19.
45 Notes on the Offensive Battle, GHQ 25-1-18. WA 20/3 ANZ.
46 *ibid.*
47 Ludendorff, p. 573.
48 Junger, p. 240.
49 *ibid.*, p. 240.
50 *ibid.*, p. 244.
51 Terraine, p. 39.
52 Ludendorff, p. 543.

53 *ibid.*, pp. 587–8.
54 Sheffield, p. 61.
55 Quoted in Buchan, p. 12. Italics original.
56 Edmonds, p. 71.
57 Ludendorff, p. 594.
58 Edmonds, p. 39.
59 Falls, p. 332.
60 Gregory Blaxland, *Amiens: 1918*, London, 1981, p. 23.
61 Mosier, pp. 314–15.
62 Gough, p. 151.
63 Austin, p. 272.
64 Moore, p. 42.
65 Farrar-Hockley, p. 265.
66 Colonel H. Stewart, *The New Zealand Division 1916–1919*, Auckland, 1921, p. 335.
67 Major W.E. Grey, quoted in Blaxland, pp. 33–4.

Chapter 2

1 Oscar Glen Reston, interview, 21 October 1989, OH Int 006/69, Oral History Centre, Alexander Turnbull Library (ATL), Wellington. All interviews in this book attributed to the ATL were conducted by Jane Tolerton and Nicholas Boyack.
2 *ibid.*
3 Thomas Eltringham, interview, 2 October 1988, OH Int 0006/29, ATL.
4 James McWhirter, Diary of the Great War (Written about 1920.), MSX 4915, ATL.
5 A.E. Byrne, *Official History of the Otago Regiment, N.Z.E.F. in the Great War 1914–1918*, Dunedin, 1921, p. 270.
6 Reston interview, ATL.
7 McWhirter diary, ATL.
8 O.E. Burton, *The Silent Division. New Zealanders at the Front: 1914–1919*, Sydney, 1935, p. 263.
9 War Diary, 2nd NZ Infantry Brigade, March 1918, WA76/1, ANZ.
10 Ezekiel Mawhinny, letter to Bill and Laura, 10 March 1918, MS Papers 1687 Mawhinny Family, ATL.
11 War Diary, 2nd NZ Infantry Brigade, 12–21 March 1918, WA76/1, ANZ.
12 War Diary, 2nd Battalion Otago Regiment, 2nd NZ Infantry Brigade, March 1918, WA80/1, ANZ.
13 Extracts from the Diary of Sir Andrew Russell, 'The Russell Family Saga, Vol III', MS Papers QMS0822, ATL.
14 Stewart, p. 338.

15 War Diary, 2nd NZ Infantry Brigade 23 March 1918, WA76/1, ANZ.
16 Russell diary, ATL.
17 See for example Chris Pugsley, 'Russell of the New Zealand Division' in *New Zealand Strategic Management*, Autumn 1995.
18 Reston interview, ATL.
19 Burton, *Silent Division*, p. 253.
20 Russell diary, 4 March 1918, ATL.
21 Burton, *Silent Division*, p. 264.
22 Edward Stuart Bibby, interview, 19 May 1988, OH Int 0006/09, Oral History Centre, ATL.
23 Russell diary, 22 March 1918, ATL.
24 Bean, *Official History. Vol. V*, p. 116.

Chapter 3
1 Diary of an Officer of the 119 Infantry Regiment (26 Division), 18 March 1918, WA 20/3 Box 2, Translation of German Documents (1/29/261), ANZ.
2 Loose, p. 23.
3 Moore, p. 59. Junger, p. 250, states that the message 'was greeted with enthusiasm'.
4 Ludendorff, p. 596.
5 *Otago Daily Times*, 20 March 1918.
6 Barrie Pitt, 'The Ludendorff Offensive Phase 1', in *History of the First War*, Volume 6, Number 15, London, 1971, p. 2638.
7 Jonathan B.A. Bailey, 'The First World War and the birth of Modern Warfare', in M. Knox and W. Murray (eds), *The Dynamics of Military Revolution 1300–2050*, Cambridge, Cambridge Press, 2001, p. 144.
8 Churchill, p. 411.
9 Moore, p. 64.
10 Gough, p. 153.
11 Junger, p. 251.
12 War Diary 51 (Highland) Division, 21 March 1918, WA241/21, ANZ.
13 Farrar-Hockley, p. 276.
14 Blaxland, p. 112.
15 Pitt, p. 2639.
16 *ibid.*, p. 2639–43.
17 Ludendorff, p. 598.
18 Diary of an Officer of the 119 Infantry Regiment (26 Division), WA20/3, ANZ.
19 Quoted in Moore, p. 73.
20 Moore, p. 90.
21 Churchill, p. 417.
22 Blaxland, p. 63.
23 Gough, p. 160.

24 Quoted in Blaxland, p. 68.
25 Buchan, p. 40.
26 Edmonds, Vol. I, p. 399.
27 Edmonds, Vol. I, p. 400.
28 Moore, p. 152.
29 Edmonds, Vol. I, p. 489.
30 Quoted in Blaxland, p. 70.
31 Quoted in Farrar-Hockley, p. 294.
32 Blaxland, p. 69.
33 *Otago Daily Times*, 25 March 1918.
34 Ludendorff, p. 604.
35 Brigadier General Sir Herbert Hart KBE, CB, CMG, DSO, diary entry, 29 March 1918, MS 0552 (Micro), ATL.
36 Churchill, p. 43.
37 Bean, *Official History. Vol. V*, p. 243.
38 Quoted in Moore, p. 137.
39 Bean, *Official History. Vol. V*, p. 256.
40 *ibid.* This is from *La Crise du Commandement Unique*, p.154. As Bean explains: 'The narrative as often happens, wrongly includes the New Zealand Division as "Australian". The word should be "Anzac".'
41 Blaxland, p. 71.
42 Falls, p. 335.
43 Quoted in Farrar-Hockley, p. 302.
44 *ibid.*
45 J.H. Johnson, *1918. The Unexpected Victory*, London, 1997, p. 46.
46 Quoted in Farrar-Hockley, p. 306.
47 Carbery, p. 386.
48 Edmonds, Vol. II, p. 1.
49 *New Zealand Herald*, 25 March 1918.
50 *New Zealand Herald*, 26 March 1918.
51 *Dominion*, 27 March 1918.
52 *Press*, 25 March 1918.
53 *New Zealand Herald*, 30 March 1918.
54 Ministerial Statement, House of Representatives, 15 April 1918, New Zealand Parliamentary Debates, 182nd Volume.

Chapter 4
1 John Gordon Harcourt, diary entry, 23 March 1918, MS Papers 6293, ATL.
2 *ibid.*
3 Kenneth Luke, letter to My Dear People, March/April 1918, Letters of Kenneth Ewart Luke, MS Papers 6027, ATL.
4 War Diary, 3rd Battalion New Zealand Rifle Brigade, March 1918, WA 84/1, ANZ.
5 War Diary, NZ (Maori) Pioneer Battalion, 21–25 March 1918, WA97/1, ANZ.
6 *ibid.*, 23 and 24 March 1918, ANZ.

7   Diary of Bombardier N. Bailey, SAA
    Section, NZFA, 1999–1010
    Kippenberger Military Archive and
    Research Library (KMARL).
8   Russell diary, 24 March 1918, ATL.
9   *ibid.*, 25 March 1918.
10 Ira Robinson, letter to Lizzie, 12 April
    1918, in Chrissie Ward (ed.), *Dear
    Lizzie*, Auckland, 2000, p. 87.
11 Captain George Albert Tuck, diary entry,
    25 March 1918, MS Papers 2164-2166
    (Micro 0052), ATL.
12 Lieutenant Colonel S.S. Allen, *2/
    Auckland, 1918*, Auckland, Whitcombe
    & Tombs Ltd, 1920, p. 25.
13 War Diary, 2nd Battalion Otago
    Regiment, 2nd NZ Infantry Brigade, 25
    March 1918, WA80/1, ANZ.
14 William Murray Morris, interview, 4
    July 1989, OH Int 006/58, Oral History
    Centre, ATL.
15 Burton, *Silent Division*, p. 267.
16 Jesse Williams Stayte, Rough Notes from
    my Diary, 26 March 1918, MS Papers
    7198, ATL.
17 William Douglas Knight, letter to
    Mother and Father, Easter Sunday, 1918,
    MS Papers 5548-08, ATL.
18 Corporal Gerald Beattie, diary entry, 25
    March 1918, MS Papers 3908 Folder 3,
    Diary of Gerald Craig Beattie, ATL.
19 From N.M. Ingram, 'Anzac Diary, A
    Nonentity in Khaki', p. 91, quoted in
    Christopher Pugsley, *On the Fringe of
    Hell*, Auckland, 1991, p. 269.
20 John Coleman, letter to My Dear Mary,
    29 April 1918, quoted in Glyn Harper
    (ed.), *Letters from the Battlefield*,
    Auckland, 2001, p. 137.
21 War Diary, 2nd Auckland Battalion, WA
    72/1, ANZ.
22 Bernard Victor Cottrell, letter to Dad, 10
    April 1918, MS Papers 1389, Papers of
    Bernard Cottrell, ATL.
23 Charlie Lawrence, interview, 9 October
    1989, OH Int 0006/47, Oral History
    Centre, ATL.
24 Sergeant Leonard William Hutchinson,
    diary entry, 2000-64, KMARL.
25 Claude Sheenan Wysocki, interviews, 19
    October and 22 October 1988, OH AB
    526, Oral History Centre, ATL.
26 John Ralph Bartle, letter to Nita, 27
    June 1918, MS Papers 1630, ATL.
27 Vincent Jervis, diary entries for 24 and
    27 March 1918, MS Papers 2241, ATL.

28 *ibid.*, 13 and 17 April 1918.
29 William Jamieson, interview, 3 July
    1989, OH Int 0006/43, Oral History
    Centre, ATL.
30 Beattie diary, 29 March 1918, ATL.
31 Bean, *Official History. Vol. V*, p. 236.
32 John Coleman, letter to My Dear Mary,
    29 April 1918, quoted in Harper (ed.),
    p. 137.
33 Kenneth Luke letters, ATL.
34 Harold Sinclair Muschamp, diary entry,
    25 March 1918, 9110221 9, KMARL.
35 Beattie diary, 26 March 1918, ATL.
36 Ronald Watson, letter 'In the Field',
    Monday April 1st. 1918, *Letters from a
    Padre. A Record of the War Service of
    RONALD S WATSON M.C. ED. MA.*,
    p. 27.
37 Cecil Jepson, 1918 Pocket Diary,
    Tuesday 26 March 1918, MS Papers
    1480 Cecil John Jepson, ATL.
38 Burton, *Silent Division*, p. 266.
39 Ira Robinson, letter to Lizzie, 12 April
    1918, Ward (ed.), p. 89.
40 McWhirter diary, ATL.
41 See for example, William Donovan
    Joynt, *Saving the Channel Ports*, Wren
    Publishing, Melbourne, 1975.
42 Bean, *Official History. Vol. V*, p. 120.
43 C.E.W. Bean, *Anzac to Amiens*,
    Melbourne, 1993, p. 415.
44 Alfred Stratten, manuscript, 'First World
    War 1916–1918 In France After
    Gallipoli', MS Papers 3283 Stratton
    Alfred Thomas, ATL.
45 Bernard Cottrell, letter to Dad, 10 April
    1918, ATL.
46 *Otago Daily Times*, 4 April 1918.
47 Reported in *New Zealand Herald*, 1
    April 1918.
48 Bean, *Official History. Vol. V*, p. 118.
49 *The Fortieth* by F.C. Green, p. 113,
    quoted in Bean, *Official History. Vol. V*,
    p. 145.
50 Kenneth Luke letters, ATL.
51 Moore, p. 157.
52 2nd NZ Infantry Brigade Order No. 132
    – 26 March 1918, War Diary 2nd NZ
    Infantry Brigade, WA76/1, ANZ.
53 Extract of Appendix 1. 3rd Battalion New
    Zealand Rifle Brigade, WA 84/1, ANZ.
54 A.E. Byrne, p. 278.
55 O.E. Burton, *The Auckland Regiment*,
    Auckland, 1922, p. 197.
56 Quoted in Pugsley, 'Russell of the New
    Zealand Division', p. 48.

Chapter 5
1 Stewart, p. 343.
2 Frederick Avery, interview, 23 November 1989, OH Int 0006/02, Ora. History Centre, ATL.
3 A.E. Byrne, p. 279.
4 Harcourt diary, ATL.
5 *ibid.*
6 Morris interview, ATL.
7 War Diary, 2nd Battalion Canterbury Regiment, 26 March 1918, WA78/1, ANZ.
8 War Diary, 1st Battalion Canterbury Regiment., 2nd NZ Infantry Brigade, 26 March 1918, WA77/1, ANZ
9 War Diary, 2nd NZ Infantry Brigade, 26 March 1918, WA76/1, ANZ.
10 *ibid.*
11 Harcourt diary, ATL.
12 Stayte diary, ATL.
13 Eltringham interview, ATL.
14 Burton, *The Auckland Regiment*, p. 199.
15 War Diary, 1st Auckland Battalion, 26 March 1918, WA71/1, ANZ.
16 Burton, *The Auckland Regiment*, p. 199.
17 War Diary 2nd Battalion Auckland Regiment, 26 March 1918, WA72/1, ANZ.
18 Eltringham interview, ATL.
19 Bean, *Official History. Vol. V* p. 126.
20 Diary of Private Ernest John Painter, 8 Southland Company, 2 Otago Battalion, 2000-654, KMARL.
21 Edmonds, Vol. I, p. 534.
22 Edmonds, Vol. II, p. 9.
23 John Douglas Coleman, letter to My dear Mary, 29 April 1918, in Harper (ed.), p. 138.
24 Bean, *Official History. Vol. V*, pp. 269–70.
25 Stewart, p. 349.

Chapter 6
1 Austin, p. 286.
2 Bernard Cottrell, letter, Dear Mother & Father, 2 April, Papers of Bernard Cottrell, ATL.
3 Bean, *Official History. Vol. V*, p. 129.
4 *ibid.*
5 Burton, *The Silent Division*, p. 270.
6 *ibid.*
7 Burton, *The Auckland Regiment*, p. 201.
8 McWhirter diary, ATL.
9 Reston interview, ATL.
10 Morris interview, ATL.
11 Edmonds, Vol. II, p. 35.
12 Tuck diary, 27 March 1918, ATL.

13 Burton, *The Auckland Regiment*, p. 203.
14 War Diary, NZ Machine Gun Battalion, 27 March 1918, WA98/1, ANZ.
15 *ibid.*
16 J.H. Luxford, *With the Machine Gunners in France and Palestine*, Auckland, 1923, p. 118.
17 War Diary, NZ Machine Gun Battalion, 27 March 1918, WA98/1, ANZ.
18 Luxford, p. 118.
19 Tuck diary, 27 March 1918, ATL.
20 War Diary, 2nd Battalion Auckland Regiment, 27 March 1918, WA72/1, ANZ.
21 Harry Highet, interview, 8 June 1988, OH Int 0006/36, Oral History Centre, ATL.
22 James Frederick Blakemore, interview, 5 August 1988, OH 0006/11, Oral History Centre, ATL.
23 Harcourt diary, 27 March 1918, ATL.
24 Stayte diary, 27–28 March 1918, ATL.
25 Carbery, p. 389.
26 War Diary, 1st NZ Infantry Brigade, 27 March 1918, WA 70/1, ANZ.
27 Roderick William Toomath, diary, MS Papers 2301, ATL.
28 Bibby interview, ATL.
29 William Horne Milne, diary entries March 1918, MS Papers 1879, ATL.
30 William Bertrand, interview, 3 November 1989, OH Int 0006/06, Oral History Centre, ATL.
31 War Diary, 3 NZ Field Artillery, 27 March 1918, WA53/1, ANZ.
32 J.R. Byrne, *New Zealand Artillery in the Field 1914–18*, Auckland, 1922, p. 222.
33 Stewart, p. 356.
34 Russell diary, ATL.
35 Edmonds, Vol. II, p. 41.
36 Moore, p. 160.
37 Edmonds, Vol. II, p. 40.
38 Bean, *Official History. Vol. V*, pp.286–7; Edmonds, Vol. II, p. 41.

Chapter 7
1 Falls, p. 336.
2 *ibid.*
3 Edmonds, Vol. II, p. 53; Bean, *Official History. Vol. V*, p. 288; Blaxland, p. 84. Blaxland's figures for the number of German formations used are nine fresh divisions with a further two in support.
4 Churchill, p. 419.
5 Edmonds, Vol. II, p. 53.
6 Edmonds, Vol. II, p. 56.

7 War Diary, 3 NZ Field Artillery, January – December 1918, WA53/1, ANZ.
8 J.R. Byrne, p. 223.
9 War Diary, 2nd New Zealand Infantry Brigade, 28 March 1918, WA76/1, ANZ.
10 War Diary, New Zealand Machine Gun Battalion, 28 March 1918.
11 War Diary, 2nd Auckland Battalion, WA72/1, ANZ.
12 War Diary, 1st Canterbury Battalion, WA77/1, ANZ.
13 Leslie Frederick Hearns, interview, 7 August 1988, OH Int0006/34, Oral History Centre, ATL.
14 Austin, p. 299.
15 Russell diary, ATL.
16 Godley, letter to Sir James Allen, 22 April 1918 WA 252/5, ANZ.
17 James Cowan, 'Te Hokowhitu a Tu': The Maoris in the Great War, Auckland, 1926. p. 136.
18 Edmonds, Vol. II, p. 58.
19 Quoted in Stewart, p. 357.
20 Diary of an Officer of the 119 Infantry Regiment (26 Division), ANZ.
21 A.E. Byrne. p. 282.
22 Bernard Cottrell, letter to Dear Mother & Father, 2 April 1918, Papers of Bernard Cottrell, ATL.
23 Bibby interview, ATL.
24 War Diary, 3 New Zealand Field Artillery, 29 March 1918, WA53/1, ANZ.
25 Bailey diary, 29 March 1918, KMARL.
26 William Roy Robson, diary entries, MSX 3484, ATL.
27 John Coleman, letter to Mary, 29 April 1918, in Harper (ed.), p. 138.
28 Harold Sinclair Muschamp, diary entry, 91102219 KMARL.
29 Allen, p. 44.
30 Burton, The Auckland Regiment, p. 204.
31 Stewart, p. 363.
32 Allen, p. 44.
33 ibid., p. 45.
34 Stewart, p. 365.
35 Allen, p. 46.
36 War Diary, 2nd Auckland Battalion, WA72/1, ANZ.
37 Stewart, p. 366.
38 ibid., p. 367.
39 Report on Line Captured by 1st NZ Infantry Brigade on 30 March 1918 by Brigade Major, dated 31 March 1918, WA 70/1, ANZ.
40 John Coleman, letter to Mary, 29 April 1918, in Harper (ed.)., p. 138.
41 Ira Robinson, letter to Lizzie, 12 April 1918, in Ward (ed.), p. 90.
42 Tuck diary, 9.50 p.m. 30 March 1918, ATL.
43 Stewart, pp. 363, 366.
44 Private William Malcolm, letter to 'Poor Dad and You', 18 April 1918, 1991-2782 KMARL.
45 Private William Malcolm, letter to Mum, 12 June 1918, in Harper (ed.), p. 145.
46 Burton, The Auckland Regiment, p. 206.
47 Stewart, p. 367.
48 Bean, Official History. Vol. V, p. 141.
49 Edmonds Vol. II, p. 96.

Chapter 8
1 War Diary, 2nd NZ Infantry Brigade, 1 and 2 April 1918, WA76/1, ANZ.
2 War Diary, 1st Battalion Otago Regiment, 2nd NZ Infantry Brigade April 1918, WA 79/1, ANZ.
3 War Diary of 2nd Battalion Otago Infantry Regiment, 2nd NZ Infantry Brigade, April 1918, WA80/1, ANZ.
4 Roderick William Toomath , diary entries 1–4 April 1918, MS Papers 2301, ATL.
5 Report of Conference held at Souastre 2 April 1918, Notes of Conferences, WA 20/3 Box 8, ANZ.
6 Moore, p. 160.
7 War Diary, 1st Otago Battalion, 1 April 1918, WA79/1, ANZ.
8 Stayte diary, ATL.
9 Burton, The Auckland Regiment, p. 206.
10 Tuck diary, ATL.
11 War Diary, 1st Battalion New Zealand Rifle Brigade, April 1918, WA 82/1, ANZ.
12 War Diary, NZ (Maori) Pioneer Battalion, April 1918, WA 97/1, ANZ.
13 Stayte diary, ATL.
14 War Diary of 2nd Battalion Otago Regiment, 2nd NZ Infantry Brigade, March 1918, WA 80/1, ANZ.
15 War Diary, 2nd Battalion Canterbury Regiment, 2ndNZ Infantry Brigade, 3 April 1918, WA 78/1, ANZ.
16 War Diary, 2nd Battalion Wellington Regiment, 1st NZ Infantry Brigade, 1 April 1918, WA 74/1, ANZ.
17 Bert Stokes, letter to My Dearest Mum & Dad , 7 April 1918, MS Papers 4683 Folder 9, ATL.
18 War Diary, 2nd New Zealand Infantry

Brigade, 31 March 1918, WA76/1, ANZ.

19 Quoted in Nigel M. Watson (ed.), *Letters from a Padre. A Record of the War Service of Ronald S. Watson, MC, ED, MA, 1891–1959*, Melbourne, 1970, p. 27.

20 Lindsay Merrit Inglis, letter to Dearest Old Lady, 31 March 1918, MS Papers 0421, ATL.

21 Bernard Cottrell, letter to Dad, 10 April 1918, Papers of Bernard Cottrell, ATL.

22 Painter diary, KMARL.

23 Arthur Leslie Ross, diary extracts, 2000-589, KMARL.

24 Lieutenant Marcus Smith, letter to Mrs Georgina A. Smith, 17 March 1918, 2003-69, KMARL.

25 Smith, letter to Mrs Georgina A. Smith, 30 March 1918, KMARL.

26 Bean, *Amiens*, p. 423.

27 Bean, *Official History. Vol. V*, p. 344.

Chapter 9

1 Moore, p. 195.

2 Austin, p. 306.

3 Bean, *Official History. Vol. V*, p. 414.

4 Stewart, p. 369; A.E. Byrne, p. 285; Luxford, p. 124.

5 J.R. Byrne, p. 225.

6 War Diary, 3 NZ Field Artillery, WA 53/1, ANZ.

7 J.R. Byrne, p. 225.

8 McWhirter diary, 5 March 1918 [McWhirter has confused the month here], ATL.

9 Tuck diary, ATL.

10 War Diary, 2nd Canterbury Battalion, 2nd NZ Infantry Brigade, WA78/1, ANZ.

11 War Diary, 2nd Auckland Battalion, ANZ.

12 War Diary, 1st Canterbury Battalion, 2nd NZ Infantry Brigade, WA77/1, ANZ.

13 Harcourt diary entry, ATL.

14 Bibby interview, ATL.

15 War Diary, 2nd NZ Infantry Brigade, 5 April 1918.

16 Narrative of Operations at Colincamps on 5th April 1918, War Diary 1 Battalion, New Zealand Rifle Brigade, WA82/1, ANZ.

17 War Diary, 4th Battalion New Zealand Rifle Brigade, 5 April 1918, WA85/1, ANZ.

18 Austin, p. 304.

19 War Diary, 3 New Zealand Rifle Brigade, WA81/1, ANZ.

20 Austin, p. 305.

21 War Diary, 4th Battalion New Zealand Rifle Brigade, 5 April 1918, WA85/1, ANZ.

22 Quoted in Bean, *Official History. Vol. V*, p. 416.

23 War Diary, 1st Canterbury Battalion, 2nd NZ Infantry Brigade, 5 April 1918, WA77/1, ANZ.

24 Harcourt diary, ATL.

25 Edmonds, p. 135.

26 Ferguson, p. 234.

27 War Diary, 1st Canterbury Battalion, 2nd NZ Infantry Brigade, 5 April 1918, WA77/1, ANZ.

28 Harcourt diary, ATL.

29 War Diary, 2nd Otago Battalion, WA80/1, ANZ.

30 War Diary, 2nd NZ Field Ambulance, 5 April 1918, WA 120/1 ANZ.

31 War Diary, 1st NZ Field Ambulance, WA119/1, ANZ.

32 Bailey diary, 5 April 1918, KMARL.

33 Luxford, p.124.

34 War Diary, NZ Machine Gun Battalion, 5 April 1918, WA98/1, ANZ.

35 Major Lindsay Inglis, letter to 'Dearest Old Pal' 7 April 1918, MS Papers 0421, ATL.

36 GHQ Summary 8-4-18, quoted in War Diary, NZ Machine Gun Battalion, 5 April, 1918, WA98/1, ANZ.

37 *ibid*. This extract is also quoted in Stewart, p. 370 and Luxford, pp. 125–6.

38 Harcourt diary, ATL.

39 Austin, p. 305.

40 Ludendorff, p. 600.

41 Edmond, Vol. II, p. 136.

Chapter 10

1 Mosier, p. 318; Sheffield, p. 195; Blaxland, p. 107.

2 Ludendorff, p. 602. One of the casualties was Ludendorff's stepson, a pilot killed on 23 March. Ludendorff had 'the sad task' of identifying the body. Like many other parents, Ludendorff could write, with some bitterness, 'The war has spared me nothing.'

3 Moore, p. 197.

4 Blaxland, p. 107.

5 Mosier, p. 318.

6 Stewart, p. 372.

7 Allen, letter to Godley, 2 April 1918, Letters to Colonel Sir James Allen Jan

1918–1920, Godley Correspondence, WA252/5, ANZ.

8   Ian McGibbon (ed.), *The Oxford Companion to New Zealand Military History*, Auckland, 2000, p. 606.

9   Stewart, p. 372.

10 Carbery, p. 538.

11 A.E. Byrne, p. 288.

12 From *New Zealand Expeditionary Force, Book XII List of Casualties and a Summary of Casualties in order of Units, Reported from 15th February to 14th May, 1918*, Wellington, Government Printer, 1918.

13 Falls, p. 337.

14 Bean, *Official History. Vol. V*, p. 665.

15 Buchan, p. 71.

16 Wigram, letter to Godley, 11 May 1918, WA252/14 Colonel Clive Wigram, ANZ.

17 Ludendorff, p. 600.

18 Churchill, p. 421.

19 Sheffield, p. 196.

20 War Diary, 1st Canterbury Battalion, 6 April 1918, WA77/1, ANZ.

21 George Albert Tuck, letter 'To My Dear Father and Mother', 22 April 1918, MS Papers MS2164-2166 Tuck (Micro 0052), ATL.

22 George Albert Tuck, letter 'To My Dear Father and Mother', 14 April 1918, ATL.

23 Carbery, p. 395.

24 Austin, p. 309.

25 Lieutenant Marcus Smith, letter to Mrs Georgina A. Smith, 18 April 1918, KMARL.

26 Bailey, in Knox and Murray, p. 145.

27 Junger, pp. 285–6.

28 Godley, letter to Allen, 22 April 1918, ANZ, WA252/5, ANZ.

29 Moore, p. 228.

30 Telegram, To F-M Sir Douglas Haig from the PM, 25-3-18, WA 1/5 NZEF Routine Orders and Special Orders Vol. 2 Field Marshal Sir Douglas Haig, ANZ.

31 Telegram, To PM from F-M Sir Douglas Haig, 26-3-18, WA1/5, ANZ.

32 Moore, p. 241.

33 Allen, letter to Godley, 11 April 1918, WA252/5, ANZ.

34 Allen, letter to Godley, 26 April 1918, WA252/5, ANZ.

35 *ibid.*

36 Allen, letter to Godley, 21 May 1918, WA252/5, ANZ.

37 Quoted in Ferguson, p. 235.

38 Toomath, Memorandum, 7 April 1918, ATL.

39 Carbery, p. 395.

40 Godley, letter to Lord Liverpool, 27 May 1918, WA252/8, His Excellency the Earl of Liverpool Oct 1914 – Oct 1918, Godley Papers and Correspondence, ANZ.

41 Moore, p. 236.

42 Burton, *Silent Division*, p. 298.

43 Haig's Diary, 12 October 1918, quoted in Pugsley, *Fringe of Hell*, p. 277.

44 Quoted in Russell diary, ATL.

45 Telegrams, To Field Marshal Sir Douglas Haig from the Governor of New Zealand and Haig's reply, 9 April 1918 and 10 April 1918, WA 1/5, ANZ.

46 A copy of this order is on Russell's Personal File, Personnel Archives, Wellington. It also appears in Ferguson, pp. 235–6.

47 Quoted in Pugsley, 'Russell of the New Zealand Division', p. 49.

48 Russell, letter to 'My dear Milly & Gwen', 4 April 1918, MS QMS0822, ATL.

49 Godley, letter to Allen, 22 April 1918, WA252/5, ANZ.

50 Allen, p. 32.

Conclusion

1   Richard Holmes, *The Western Front*, London, 1999, pp. 14–16.

2   Sheffield, p. xii.

3   Brian Bond (ed.), *The First World War and British Military History*, Oxford, 1991, p. 1.

4   Junger, p. 242.

5   Bean, *Official History. Vol. V*, pp. 674, 675.

6   Quoted in Stewart, pp. 617–18. Stewart points out in a footnote that 'Undue importance must not be attached to this remark', that is, to the officer's claim that the New Zealand Division took few German prisoners.

7   Stewart, pp. 372–3. This volume, like the others in the series, was a sponsored project of the New Zealand Army.

8   Hew Strachan, 'The Real War': Liddell Hart, Cruttwell and Falls', in Bond (ed.), *The First World War and British Military History*, pp. 61–2. Cyril Falls was twice mentioned in dispatches and awarded the Croix de Guerre.

9   Falls, p. 421.

10 Quoted in Strachan, 'The Real War', in Bond (ed.), *The First World War and British Military History*, pp. 62–3.

11 Cecil Malthus, *Armentieres and the Somme*, Auckland, 2002, pp. 14, 15.

12 Robin Prior and Trevor Wilson, 'Was Britain's sacrifice necessary?', in Craig Wilcox (ed.), *The Great War. Gains and Losses – ANZAC and Empire*, Canberra, 1995, p. 170.

13 W. Stevens, *Official History of New Zealand in the Second World War 1939–45. Bardia to Enfidaville*, Wellington, 1962, p. 383.

14 This inscription is prominent on three of New Zealand's battlefield memorials in France. See Ian McGibbon, *New Zealand Battlefields and Memorials of the Western Front*, Auckland, 2001, pp. 6–7.

15 Cecil Malthus, *ANZAC. A Retrospect*, Auckland, 2002, p. 100.

Appendix 1

Roll of Honour

As a tribute to the New Zealanders who fell making this vital contribution to the outcome of the First World War, we offer their names and details below. The information has been obtained from the Casualty Lists of 1918 and the database of the Commonwealth War Graves Commission (CWGC). It lists those who were killed or died from wounds between 23 March and 30 April 1918 and who are buried in cemeteries in either France or Belgium (spellings of New Zealand locations remain as presented in the CWGC database). This includes not only those who fought against the Michael Offensive, but also those who took part in the later action, the Georgette Offensive. Both assaults were part of the German spring offensive. We are aware that, despite our best efforts, some names may be missing. May the memory of their deeds live on and never be forgotten.

ABBOTT, Sapper, MARCUS CLAUDE, 37596, Tunnelling Company, NZ Engineers. Died 31 March 1918. Age 29. Son of Mr E.F. Abbott, of 11 Ravenswood Rd, Walthamstow, England. Faubourg D'amiens Cemetery, Arras, Pas de Calais, France. Grave or panel number: VII.C.27.

ABSOLUM, Private, NORMAN WILLIAM LESLIE, 42731. 1st Battalion, Auckland Regiment, NZEF. Died 26 March 1918. Age 33. Son of Abraham and Georgjean Absolum, of Battery Rd, Napier. Born at Ross, Greymouth. Grevilliers (NZ) Memorial, Pas de Calais, France.

ADAM, Private, DAVID NORRIE, 47296. 2nd Battalion, Canterbury Regiment, NZEF. Died 5 April 1918. Age 35. Son of Mrs S. M. Adam, of Turfachie Kirriemuir, Scotland. Grevillers (NZ) Memorial, Pas de Calais, France.

ADAMSON, Lance Corporal, MICHAEL IAN, 6/2520. 2nd Battalion, Canterbury Regiment, NZEF. Died 30 March 1918. Age 23. Son of Henry and M. Burke Adamson, of Canterbury. Etaples Military Cemetery, Pas de Calais, France. Grave or panel number: XXXIII.A.3.

ADDISON, Private, JOHN BAXTER, 62222. 1st Battalion, Canterbury Regiment, NZEF. Died 20 April 1918. Age 42. Son of Thomas and Jane Addison, of

179

Big Omaha, North Auckland. Native of Portland, Oregon, USA. Sucrerie Military Cemetery, Colincamps, Somme, France. Grave or panel number: I.AA.7.

AFFLECK, Private, DAVID, 14916. 2nd Battalion, Canterbury Regiment, NZEF. Died 25 April 1918. Age 20. Son of Robert and Jessie Affleck, of Opunake, Taranaki. Doullens Communal Cemetery Extension No. 1, Somme, France. Grave or panel number: VI.B.75.

AITKEN, Private, ROBERT FRANCIS, 14044. 1st Battalion, Canterbury Regiment, NZEF. Died 5 April 1918. Age 23. Son of Robert and Barbara Aitken, of Pleasant Point, Timaru. Martinsart British Cemetery, Somme, France. Grave or panel number: I.H.39.

AITKEN, Lance Corporal, STEWART ALEX, 9/108, MM. Otago Mounted Rifles, NZEF. Died 29 April 1918. Age 27. Son of James A. and Ellen S. Aitken, of Waikaka Valley, Southland. Also served at Gallipoli. Buttes New British Cemetery (NZ) Memorial, Polygon Wood, Zonnebeke, West-Vlaanderen, Belgium.

ALDRED, Corporal, ERNEST, 28847. 2nd Battalion, Otago Regiment, NZEF. Died 24 April 1918. Age 28. Twice Mentioned in Despatches. Son of James and Christina Aldred, of Dunedin; husband of Mrs E. E. Aldred (now Hunt), of 46 Queen St, Onehunga, Auckland. Sucrerie Military Cemetery, Colincamps, Somme, France. Grave or panel number: I.J.40.

ALLAN, Second Lieutenant, J., 6/1446. 1st Battalion, Auckland Regiment, NZEF. Died 27 March 1918. Age 25. Husband of Isabella Allan, of Doune Tce, Kelty, Fife. Euston Road Cemetery, Colincamps, Somme, France. Grave or panel number: III.B.5.

AMOS, Gunner, THOMAS ALFRED, 17604. NZ Field Artillery. Died 18 April 1918. Son of Charles and Annie Amos, of Greytown, Wellington. Englebelmer Communal Cemetery Extension, Somme, France. Grave or panel number: F.8.

ANDERSON, Private, ALBERT PERCY, 63707. Canterbury Regiment, NZEF. Died 21 April 1918. Age 20. Son of Mr P. Anderson, of Clive, Hawke's Bay. Etaples Military Cemetery, Pas de Calais, France. Grave or panel number: XXIX.J.8.

ANDERSON, Lance Corporal, HENRY ROBERT RICHARD, R/378. 2nd Battalion, Auckland Regiment, NZEF. Died 30 March 1918. Age 31. Son of John and Catherine Anderson, of Kennedy's Bay, Coromandel. Grevilliers (NZ) Memorial, Pas de Calais, France.

ANDERSON, Private, JOHN, 14547. 1st Battalion, Auckland Regiment, NZEF. Died 26 March 1918. Husband of Mrs M.E. Millen (formerly Anderson), of Melbourne, Australia. Grevilliers (NZ) Memorial, Pas de Calais, France.

ANDERSON, Private, WILLIAM, 52552. 2nd Battalion, Wellington Regiment, NZEF. Died 5 April 1918. Age 32. Only son of Robert and Barbara Anderson, of Staveley, Canterbury. Courcelles-au-Bois Communal Cemetery Extension, Somme, France. Grave or panel number: F.7.

ANSELL, Gunner, WILLIAM HENRY, 18254. NZ Field Artillery. Died 10 April 1918. Age 21. Son of Alberta Amelia Horner (formerly Ansell), of 13 Lawrence St, Dominion Rd, Mt Eden, Auckland, and the late Frederic James Ansell. Born at Napier. Trois Arbres Cemetery, Steenwerck, Nord, France. Grave or panel number: II.I.22.

ANSENNE, Private, HAROLD MONTROSE MONTIE, 38643. 2nd Battalion, Auckland Regiment, NZEF. Died 30 March 1918. Age 24. Son of Joe and Alice Ansenne, of Auckland. Doullens Communal Cemetery Extension No. 1, Somme, France. Grave or panel number: V.D.14.

APPLEYARD, Private, WILLIAM JOSEPH, 12/3240. 2nd Battalion, Auckland Regiment, NZEF. Died 27 March 1918. Son of Mrs Eleanor J. Appleyard, of Long Drive, St. Helier's Bay, Auckland. Grevilliers (NZ) Memorial, Pas de Calais, France.

ARMIGER, Corporal, ROBERT HENRY WHITNALL, 35538. NZ Field Artillery. Died 20 April 1918. Age 23. Son of Robert and Emma Armiger, of 20 Ardmore Rd, Ponsonby, Auckland; husband of L. T. K. Armiger, of Auckland. Lijssenthoek Military Cemetery, Poperinge, West-Vlaanderen, Belgium. Grave or panel number: XXVI.GG.4A.

ARMSTRONG, Lieutenant, PURVIS FORD, 18581. 4th Battalion, 3rd NZ Rifle Brigade. Died 6 April 1918. Age 25. Son of Walter and Ruth Armstrong, of Greytown. Grevillers (NZ) Memorial, Pas de Calais, France.

ARNOLD, Corporal, CLAUDE JAMES, 28951, MM. 4th Battalion, 3rd NZ Rifle Brigade. Died 21 April 1918. Age 32. Son of Fred and Drucilla Arnold; husband of Annie Arnold, of 24 Leydon St, Linwood, Christchurch. Born at Lyttelton. Serre Road Cemetery No. 1, Pas de Calais, France. Grave or panel number: I.K.13.

ARTHUR, Lance Sergeant, ERNEST WILLIAM, 31455, MM. 2nd Battalion, Canterbury Regiment, NZEF. Died 8 April 1918. Age 47. Son of Thomas M. Arthur, of Kimberley, Canterbury. Doullens Communal Cemetery Extension No. 1, Somme, France. Grave or panel number: VI.C.5.

ASHTON, Private, GEORGE, 27197. 2nd Battalion, Canterbury Regiment, NZEF. Died 28 March 1918. Age 22. Son of William and Mary A. Ashton, of Ashburton. Doullens Communal Cemetery Extension No. 1, Somme, France. Grave or panel number: V.D.9.

ASKEW, Private, LAWRENCE MANSON, 21640. 1st Battalion, Canterbury Regiment, NZEF. Died 23 April 1918. Age 21. Son of Samuel Manson Askew and Margaret Askew, of Riwaka, Nelson. Colincamps Communal Cemetery, Somme, France.

ASTBURY, Private, HORACE VERNON, 59580. Canterbury Regiment, NZEF. Died 29 April 1918. Age 20. Son of Henry E. and Elizabeth Astbury, of Wanganui. Born at Palmerston North. Arneke British Cemetery, Nord, France. Grave or panel number: II.A.16.

AUSTIN, Private, ALBERT HENRY, 6/1454. 2nd Battalion, Canterbury Regiment, NZEF. Died 28 March 1918. Age 22. Son of A.W. and Jane Austin, of 22 Rose St, Timaru. Born at Oamaru. Also served at Gallipoli. Grevilliers (NZ) Memorial, Pas de Calais, France.

BAGNALL, Private, LEMUEL JOHN, 15093. 1st Battalion, Auckland Regiment, NZEF. Died 26 March 1918. Son of Horatio Nelson Bagnall and Jessie Bagnall, of 26 Mason's Ave, Ponsonby, Auckland. Grevilliers (NZ) Memorial, Pas de Calais, France.

BAIGENT, Private, JOHN WALLACE, 46221. 2nd Battalion, Canterbury Regiment, NZEF. Died 29 March 1918. Son of Mr and Mrs Henry Baigent, of 78 Waimea St, Nelson. Grevilliers (NZ) Memorial, Pas de Calais, France.

BAIKIE, Rifleman, ROBERT SHERER, 38484. 4th Battalion, 3rd NZ Rifle Brigade. Died 28 March 1918. Son of Peter and Janet Baikie, of 9th Ave, Tauranga. Grevillers (NZ) Memorial, Pas de Calais, France.

BAIRD, Private, WALTER SNELLING, 56530. 1st Battalion, Auckland Regiment, NZEF. Died 26 March 1918. Age 30. Son of the late William and Ann Matilda Hooper Baird; husband of Olive Daiton Clarke (formerly Baird), of 24 Seymour St, Ponsonby, Auckland. Grevilliers (NZ) Memorial, Pas de Calais, France.

BAKER, Rifleman, JOSEPH, 52359. 3rd Battalion, 3rd NZ Rifle Brigade. Died 21 April 1918. Son of Mrs Rosie Brown, of Stratford. St Sever Cemetery Extension, Rouen, Seine-Maritime, France. Grave or panel number: P.VII.A.2A.

BALLARD, Private, WALTER JAMES, 28648. 2nd Battalion, Auckland Regiment, NZEF. Died 30 March 1918. Age 40. Son of the late James and Emily Ballard. Born at Nelson. Grevilliers (NZ) Memorial, Pas de Calais, France.

BARCLAY, Private, ALLAN HUNT, 29723. 2nd Battalion, Auckland Regiment, NZEF. Died 25 April 1918. Son of Donald Hunt Barclay and Georgina Jane Barclay, of Waikato. Grootebeek British Cemetery, Poperinge, West-Vlaanderen, Belgium. Grave or panel number: B.5.

BARKER, Gunner, FREDERICK HARROLD, 12896. 11th Battery, NZ Field Artillery. Died 5 April 1918. Forceville Communal Cemetery and Extension, Somme, France. Grave or panel number: 3.E.12.

BARKER, Rifleman, GEORGE THOMAS, 28954. 1st Battalion, 3rd NZ Rifle Brigade. Died 5 April 1918. Age 41. Son of Henry and Emma Barker, of 9 Rata St, St. Martin's, Christchurch. Born at Canterbury. Grevillers (NZ) Memorial, Pas de Calais, France.

BARKER, Private, JOHN LEONARD, 36303. 2nd Battalion, Canterbury Regiment, NZEF. Died 28 March 1918. Age 30. Son of Henry and Emma Barker, of Rata St, St Martins, Christchurch. His brother, George Thomas, also fell. St Hilaire Cemetery, Frevent, Pas de Calais, France. Grave or panel number: IV.A.6.

BARLOW, Private, JAMES ROY, 48614. 2nd Battalion, Auckland Regiment, NZEF. Died 27 March 1918. Age 22. Son of Albert Edwin and Mary Muir Barlow of 28 King St, Frankton Junction, Hamilton; formerly of Invercargill. Grevilliers (NZ) Memorial, Pas de Calais, France.

BARNARD, Private, JOHN CLIFFORD, 41466. 2nd Battalion, Canterbury Regiment, NZEF. Died 8 April 1918. Age 21. Son of Frederick and Annie Barnard, of Lower Hutt. Doullens Communal Cemetery Extension No. 1, Somme, France. Grave or panel number: VI.C.II.

BARNETT, Private, GODFREY HARRY STEEL, 49503. 1st Battalion, Canterbury Regiment, NZEF. Died 27 March 1918. Age 24. Son of Laura Barnett, of Miller St, Oamaru, North Otago, and the late Abraham Morris Barnett. Born at Waitahuna Gully. Grevilliers (NZ) Memorial, Pas de Calais, France.

BARRETT, Sergeant, GEORGE ARMITAGE, 31768. 2nd Battalion, Canterbury Regiment, NZEF. Died 28 March 1918. Age 31. Son of H.A. Barrett, of 188 Fore St, Upper Edmonton, London, England; husband of Gertrude E. Barrett, of 3 Holland Rd, Exeter, England. Grevilliers (NZ) Memorial, Pas de Calais, France.

BARRETT, Private, GEORGE EDWARD, 61121. 2nd NZ Entrenching Battalion, NZEF. Died 29 April 1918. Age 28. Son of W.G. and A. Barrett. Born at Blenheim. Perth Cemetery (China Wall), Ypres, West-Vlaanderen, Belgium. Grave or panel number: VI.E.2.

BARRY, Private, GARRETT, 60053. 1st Battalion, Auckland Regiment, NZEF. Died 20 April 1918. Age 40. Son of Ellen and the late Garrett Barry, of Tamaki West, Auckland. Bertrancourt Military Cemetery, Somme, France. Grave or panel number: 2.A.1.

BARTHOLOMEW, Rifleman, KENNETH MILLER, 56717. 4th Battalion, 3rd NZ Rifle Brigade. Died 29 March 1918. Age 33. Son of George and Ellen Bartholomew, of Feilding; husband of Annie Te Mann Bartholomew, of 23 Nelson St, Feilding. Euston Road Cemetery, Colincamps, Somme, France. Grave or panel number: Lonely Brit. Cem. No. 2 Memorial.

BARTLETT, Private, STANLEY ALBERT, 49138. 2nd Battalion, Wellington Regiment, NZEF. Died 27 March 1918. Son of Mr and Mrs Joseph Bartlett, of Napier. Euston Road Cemetery, Colincamps, Somme, France. Grave or panel number: II.D.9.

BARTON, Private, FEODOR ELFICK, 46813. No. 16 Waikato Company, 2nd Battalion, Auckland Regiment, NZEF. Died 30 March 1918. Age 37. Son of Arthur Edmund and Eliza Beelby Barton (nee Leeckie), of 9 Edensor Rd, Eastbourne, England. Grevilliers (NZ) Memorial, Pas de Calais, France.

BARTRUM, Corporal, CYRIL FREDERICK, 24/40. 2nd Battalion, 3rd NZ Rifle Brigade. Died 5 April 1918. Brother of John Arthur Bartrum, of Auckland University, Auckland. Euston Road Cemetery, Colincamps, Somme, France. Grave or panel number: II.A.1.

BATER, Sergeant, RICHARD NORMAN, 12/2639. 16th Waikato Company, 1st Battalion, Auckland Regiment, NZEF. Died 26 March 1918. Age 23. Son of Charles and Mary Francis Bater, of 87 Richmond Rd, Ponsonby, Auckland. Grevilliers (NZ) Memorial, Pas de Calais, France.

BAXTER, Rifleman, EDGAR GEORGE, 33815. 1st Battalion, 3rd NZ Rifle Brigade. Died 5 April 1918. Age 44. Son of the late George and Rachel Baxter; husband of Annie Baxter, of Hillsborough, Horsmonden, Kent, England. Born at Bedford, England. Grevillers (NZ) Memorial, Pas de Calais, France.

BAYNE, Rifleman, JAMES JOHN, 48896. 2nd Battalion, 3rd NZ Rifle Brigade. Died 27 March 1918. Age 29. Son of William and Emma Bayne, of Kent, England; husband of Mary Elizabeth Bayne, of Christchurch. Euston Road Cemetery, Colincamps, Somme, France. Grave or panel number: II.E.7.

BEARE, Private, HARVEY, 63816. 1st Battalion, Auckland Regiment, NZEF. Died 8 April 1918. Age 25. Son of Edwin and Selina Beare, of Sladesbridge, Wadebridge, Cornwall, England. Etaples Military Cemetery, Pas de Calais, France. Grave or panel number: XXXIII.E.9A.

BEATON, Private, JAMES, 40763. 2nd Battalion, Canterbury Regiment, NZEF. Died 24 April 1918. Son of Mrs E. Beaton, of Polsen St, Addington, Christchurch. Sucrerie Military Cemetery, Colincamps, Somme, France. Grave or panel number: I.J.41.

BEATTIE, Lance Corporal, DONALD, 22919. 3rd Battalion, 3rd NZ Rifle Brigade. Died 8 April 1918. Grevillers (NZ) Memorial, Pas de Calais, France.

BEATTIE, Private, PHILLIP EDWARD, 47844. 2nd Battalion, Wellington Regiment, NZEF. Died 27 March 1918. Age 29. Son of Mary J. Reid (formerly Beattie), and the late Thomas E. Beattie. Native of Napier. Euston Road Cemetery, Colincamps, Somme, France. Grave or panel number: V.C.9.

BEATTY, Private, ARTHUR, IO/2853. 1st Battalion, Wellington Regiment, NZEF. Died 30 March 1918. Age 24. Son of the late Alexander Beatty and Jessie Beatty, of Fowcliffe, Hinds, New Zealand. Euston Road Cemetery, Colincamps, Somme, France. Grave or panel number: III.C.5.

BEATTY, Lance Corporal, GEORGE, 41718. 4th Battalion, 3rd NZ Rifle Brigade. Died 30 March 1918. Age 31. Son of George and Ellen Beatty, of Umutaoroa, Dannevirke. Grevillers (NZ) Memorial, Pas de Calais, France.

BEATY, Private, JOHN SCOTT, 34009. 2nd NZ Entrenching Battalion, NZEF. Died 13 April 1918. Age 21. Son of George Henry Shaw Beaty, of 'Grimstone', Wem, Salop, England. Messines Ridge (NZ) Memorial, Mesen, West-Vlaanderen, Belgium.

BEAUMONT, Private, GEORGE, 29591. 2nd Battalion, Otago Regiment, NZEF. Died 2 April 1918. Son of Mr and Mrs George Beaumont, of Campbelltown Rd, Liverpool, New South Wales, Australia. Knightsbridge Cemetery, Mesnil-Martinsart, Somme, France. Grave or panel number: A.15.

BEEHAN, Second Lieutenant, ANSELM JEROME, 22909. 3rd Battalion, 3rd NZ Rifle Brigade. Died 27 March 1918. Age 22. Son of William and Annie Theresa Beehan, of 86 Grafton Rd, Auckland. Grevillers (NZ) Memorial, Pas de Calais, France.

BEEHRE, Sergeant, HENRY MALCOLM, 12/2947, MM. 1st Battalion, Auckland Regiment, NZEF. Died 17 April 1918. Age 21. Son of Samuel and Mary Ann Beehre, of Third Avenue, Whangarei. Etaples Military Cemetery, Pas de Calais, France. Grave or panel number: XXIX.F.29A.

BELCHER, Private, GEORGE, 28655. 2nd Battalion, Auckland Regiment, NZEF. Died 30 March 1918. Euston Road Cemetery, Colincamps, Somme, France. Grave or panel number: II.C.5.

BELL, Private, RICHARD, 38646. 2nd Battalion, Wellington Regiment, NZEF. Died 27 March 1918. Age 27. Son of Richard and Louisa Bell, of Grand Vue Rd, Manurewa, Auckland. Euston Road Cemetery, Colincamps, Somme, France. Grave or panel number: III.D.9.

BELLISS, Rifleman, REGINALD HERBERT, 26/437. 4th Battalion, 3rd NZ Rifle Brigade. Died 6 April 1918. Age 25. Son of James Belliss and the late Jean Belliss, of Taihape. Euston Road Cemetery, Colincamps, Somme, France. Grave or panel number: V.B.3.

BENNETT, Private, EDWIN, 45976. 3rd Battalion, Auckland Regiment, NZEF. Died 16 April 1918. Age 20. Son of E.W.C.N. Bennett, of Taradale. Meteren Military Cemetery, Nord, France. Grave or panel number: II.M.324.

BENTLEY, Private, JOHN ROBERT, 56234. 1st Battalion, Auckland Regiment, NZEF. Died 26 March 1918. Age 36. Son of Thomas and Elizabeth Bentley, of Hay Lane Farm, Foston, Derby, England. Grevilliers (NZ) Memorial, Pas de Calais, France.

BERENDT, Lance Corporal, GEORGE PHILIP, 25/91. 3rd Battalion, 3rd NZ Rifle Brigade. Died 31 March 1918. Son of Conrad and Louisa Berendt. Born at Hokitika. Grevillers (NZ) Memorial, Pas de Calais, France.

BERRY, Private, JOHN ARTHUR, 30164. 2nd NZ Entrenching Battalion, NZEF. Died 14 April 1918. Age 41. Son of John and Ellen Berry, of Sheffield, England; husband of Alice Evelyn Robinson (formerly Berry), of Mangahume, Te Keri, Eltham Rd, Taranaki. Native of Sheffield. Messines Ridge (NZ) Memorial, Mesen, West-Vlaanderen, Belgium.

BERRY, Rifleman, JOSEPH, 47110. 2nd Battalion, 3rd NZ Rifle Brigade. Died 26 March 1918. Age 32. Son of John and Alice Berry, of Airton, Bell Busk, Leeds, England. Sucrerie Military Cemetery, Colincamps, Somme, France. Grave or panel number: I.J.54.

BETHELL, Private, ROBERT, 45461. 2nd Battalion, Auckland Regiment, NZEF. Died 31 March 1918. Age 37. Son of Joseph and Mary Bethell, of Bay of Islands. Gezaincourt Communal Cemetery Extension, Somme, France. Grave or panel number: II.H.19.

BETTELEY, Private, FREDERICK, 15671. 2nd Battalion, Wellington Regiment, NZEF. Died 5 April 1918. Age 29. Son of George and Elizabeth Betteley, of Wallasey, Cheshire, England; husband of the late Lily Betteley. Sucrerie Military Cemetery, Colincamps, Somme, France. Grave or panel number: I.J.48.

BEWLEY, Rifleman, JOSEPH, 47966. 3rd Battalion, 3rd NZ Rifle Brigade. Died 5 April 1918. Age 32. Son of Joseph and Sarah Bewley, of 112 Main St, Westington, England; husband of Jessie Edith Milham (formerly Bewley), of Kakaramea, Wellington. Grevillers (NZ) Memorial, Pas de Calais, France.

BIDDLE, Gunner, EDWARD JOHN, 10539. 6th/2nd Brigade, NZ Field Artillery. Died 17 April 1918. Age 24. Son of Edward and Frances Biddle, of Carterton. Westoutre British Cemetery, Heuvelland, West-Vlaanderen, Belgium. Grave or panel number: F.8.

BIDMEAD, Private, JOHN VERNE, 41713. 1st Battalion, Wellington Regiment, NZEF. Died 30 March 1918. Grevilliers (NZ) Memorial, Pas de Calais, France.

BILLING, Lance Corporal, ERNEST ALFRED, IO/3832, MM. 1st Battalion, Wellington Regiment, NZEF. Died 12 April 1918. Age 27. Son of Thomas John and Emma Jane Billing, of Hine St, New Plymouth. Native of Rahotu, New Zealand. Gezaincourt Communal Cemetery Extension, Somme, France. Grave or panel number: I.L.19.

BILLING, Private, ROY GWEN, 31060. NZ Machine Gun Battalion. Died 20 April 1918. Englebelmer Communal Cemetery Extension, Somme, France. Grave or panel number: D.19.

BIRCH, Rifleman, JAMES FREDERICK, 54724. 1st Battalion, 3rd NZ Rifle Brigade. Died 5 April 1918. Age 28. Son of George Frederick and Eliza Birch, of Victoria St, Dargaville. Euston Road Cemetery, Colincamps, Somme, France. Grave or panel number: V.D.2.

BIRCHALL, Lance Corporal, ALFRED URMSON, 53121. 4th Battalion, 3rd NZ Rifle Brigade. Died 28 March 1918. Age 33. Son of William and Sarah Birchall, of 648 North Rd, North-East Valley, Dunedin. Born in New Zealand. Grevillers (NZ) Memorial, Pas de Calais, France.

BIRKETT, Sergeant, WILLIAM ARTHUR, 4/600, MM, Cross of Karageorge 1st Cl. with Swords (Serbia). Div. Signal Company, NZ Engineers. Died 28 March 1918. Age 24. Son of R.E.F. and Annie Birkett, of 'Rosewell', Collins St, Gisborne. Euston Road Cemetery, Colincamps, Somme, France. Grave or panel number: III.A.2.

BLACK, Corporal, ALFRED REGINALD, 10208. 1st Battalion, Wellington Regiment, NZEF. Died 30 March 1918. Age 31. Son of William and Mary Black, of Taranaki. Also served in Egypt. Mailly Wood Cemetery, Somme, France. Grave or panel number: I.N.I4.

BLACK, Sergeant, HARRY OSBORNE, IO/50. 2nd Battalion, Wellington Regiment, NZEF. Died 29 March 1918. Age 21. Son of John Henry and Mary

Black, of Dundooan, Coleraine, Ireland. Doullens Communal Cemetery Extension No. 1, Somme, France. Grave or panel number: V.C.38.

BLACKBURN, Gunner, REGINALD EVANS, 24972. NZ Field Artillery. Died 18 April 1918. Age 21. Son of Barnabas and Hannah Blackburn, of Wellington. Englebelmer Communal Cemetery Extension, Somme, France. Grave or panel number: P.7.

BLACKIE, Private, HERBERT WILLIAM, 58967. 1st Battalion, Otago Regiment, NZEF. Died 30 April 1918. Age 21. Son of William and Mabel Blackie, of Katea, Dunedin. Bagneux British Cemetery, Gezaincourt, Somme, France. Grave or panel number: I.D.29.

BLUETT, Private, CHARLES, 31942. 2nd Battalion, Auckland Regiment, NZEF. Died 27 March 1918. Son of Meraera Bluett, of Whakatane. Grevilliers (NZ) Memorial, Pas de Calais, France.

BLYTON, Lance Corporal, STEVEN, 22932. 1st Battalion, 3rd NZ Rifle Brigade. Died 5 April 1918. Age 36. Son of Mary Blyton, of 7 Vicar St, Coogee, Sydney, Australia, and the late Charles Blyton. Born in New South Wales. Grevillers (NZ) Memorial, Pas de Calais, France.

BODY, Private, FRANK, 48160. 2nd Battalion, Wellington Regiment, NZEF. Died 27 March 1918. Age 18. Son of Richard and Bessie Body, of Winslow, Ashburton. Native of Canterbury. Euston Road Cemetery, Colincamps, Somme, France. Grave or panel number: V.C.10.

BOGUN, Private, CHARLES PERCIVAL, 13723. 1st Battalion, Wellington Regiment, NZEF. Died 18 April 1918. Age 24. Son of Gottbred and Matilda Bogun, of Taihape. Etaples Military Cemetery, Pas de Calais, France. Grave or panel number: XXIX.G.3.

BOLTON, Private, WILLIAM HENRY, 12/3558. 2nd Battalion, Auckland Regiment, NZEF. Died 17 April 1918. Age 33. Son of Richard Bolton, of Silverdale Auckland, and Emma Bolton, of England; husband of Catherine Bolton, of 1 Servia St, Newton, Auckland. Grevillers (NZ) Memorial, Pas de Calais, France.

BOURK, Private, EDWARD MAGNUS, 6/777. 2nd NZ Entrenching Battalion, NZEF. Died 16 April 1918. Son of Mrs Lizzie Bourk, of 18 Hutchinson St, Sydenham, Christchurch. Messines Ridge (NZ) Memorial, Mesen, West-Vlaanderen, Belgium.

BOUSTEAD, Private, SAMUEL, 52034. 1st Battalion, Auckland Regiment, NZEF. Died 26 March 1918. Grevilliers (NZ) Memorial, Pas de Calais, France.

BOWLES, Sergeant, WILLIAM BERNARD, 24/978, MM. 2nd Battalion, 3rd NZ Rifle Brigade. Died 6 April 1918. Son of Mr and Mrs W.G. Bowles, of Waimate. Sucrerie Military Cemetery, Colincamps, Somme, France. Grave or panel number: I.I.7.

BOWYER, Lance Corporal, ARCHIBALD HERBERT OLIPHANT, 38335. 2nd Battalion, Auckland Regiment, NZEF. Died 1 April 1918. Age 29. Only son of

Clara Agnes Oliphant Bowyer and the late Edward Bowyer, of 26 Pompallier Tce, Ponsonby, Auckland. Native of New Zealand. Doullens Communal Cemetery Extension No. 1, Somme, France. Grave or panel number: VI.G.54.

BOYCE, Rifleman, JOHN STANLEY, 43911. 4th Battalion, 3rd NZ Rifle Brigade. Died 28 March 1918. Age 21. Son of David and Hannah Elizabeth Boyce, of corner of Manchester and Canon Sts, St Albans, Christchurch. Grevillers (NZ) Memorial, Pas de Calais, France.

BRACEWELL, Private, WALTER ARTHUR, 26780. NZ Machine Gun Battalion. Died 27 March 1918. Son of Mrs E. Bracewell, of 11 Yarborough St, Ponsonby, Auckland. Euston Road Cemetery, Colincamps, Somme, France. Grave or panel number: III.D.10.

BRADLEY, Private, RICHARD, 34016. 1st Battalion, Otago Regiment, NZEF. Died 28 April 1918. Age 19. Son of W.H. and Edith Bradley, of Ruanui Station, Mataroa, Rangitikei. Native of England. Euston Road Cemetery, Colincamps, Somme, France. Grave or panel number: I.J.2.

BRAMLEY, Private, HUDSON ARMOND, 54634. 1st Battalion, Canterbury Regiment, NZEF. Died 28 April 1918. Age 25. Son of James and Ada Bramley, of 27 Claremont St, Newmarket; husband of Annie Bramley, of 27 Claremont St, Newmarket, Auckland. Grevillers (NZ) Memorial, Pas de Calais, France.

BRANIGAN, Private, ALEXANDER, 11210. 2nd NZ Entrenching Battalion, NZEF. Died 16 April 1918. Age 45. Son of the late Robert and Barbara Branigan, of Wyndham, Invercargill. Messines Ridge (NZ) Memorial, Mesen, West-Vlaanderen, Belgium.

BRAZIL, Private, PATRICK JEREMIAH, 64616. 2nd NZ Entrenching Battalion, NZEF. Died 29 April 1918. Age 30. Son of John and Julia Brazil, of Cronadon, New Zealand. Born in Ireland. Perth Cemetery (China Wall), Ypres, West-Vlaanderen, Belgium. Grave or panel number: VI.F.20.

BREEZE, Private, WILLIAM HENRY, 39595. 2nd NZ Entrenching Battalion, NZEF. Died 17 April 1918. Son of Mr and Mrs Harry Breeze, of Lyndhurst, Canterbury. Messines Ridge (NZ) Memorial, Mesen, West-Vlaanderen, Belgium.

BRENNAN, Private, STEPHEN, 14378. 1st Battalion, Auckland Regiment, NZEF. Died 26 March 1918. Age 23. Son of Matthew and Ellen Brennan, of Victoria St, Onehunga, Auckland. Grevilliers (NZ) Memorial, Pas de Calais, France.

BREWER, Driver, G.T., 30470. 11th Battery, NZ Field Artillery. Died 5 April 1918. Forceville Communal Cemetery and Extension, Somme, France. Grave or panel number: 3.E.11.

BRIANT, Private, DANIEL, 46515. 1st Battalion, Otago Regiment, NZEF. Died 8 April 1918. Age 33. Son of Edward and Mary Ann Briant. Born at St George in the East, London. Mailly Wood Cemetery, Somme, France. Grave or panel number: I.K.32.

BRITTAN, Second Lieutenant, HAROLD ROLLESTON, 41213. 1st Battalion, 3rd NZ Rifle Brigade. Died 5 April 1918. Son of Mr and Mrs Francis H. Brittan, of Avonside, Christchurch. Euston Road Cemetery, Colincamps, Somme, France. Grave or panel number: IV.D.7.

BROOK, Lance Corporal, JOSEPH, 6/1788. 4th Battalion, 3rd NZ Rifle Brigade. Died 29 March 1918. Age 29. Son of D. and S.A. Brook, of Yorkshire, England. Native of Canterbury. Euston Road Cemetery, Colincamps, Somme, France. Grave or panel number: III.D.3.

BROWN, Private, FREDERICK ALEXANDER, 61035. 2nd Battalion, Canterbury Regiment, NZEF. Died 27 March 1918. Age 20. Son of James and Edith E.C. Brown, of Whakahua, Oxford, Christchurch. Grevilliers (NZ) Memorial, Pas de Calais, France.

BROWN, Private, JAMES, 62912. 2nd NZ Entrenching Battalion, NZEF. Died 16 April 1918. Age 29. Son of Thomas Christine Brown and Mary Ann Brown. Messines Ridge (NZ) Memorial, Mesen, West-Vlaanderen, Belgium.

BROWN, Sergeant, JAMES DOUGLAS, 12/948. No. 15 North Auckland Company, 2nd Battalion, Auckland Regiment, NZEF. Died 11 April 1918. Age 28. Son of David and Isabella Brown, of Reed St, Oamaru. Grevilliers (NZ) Memorial, Pas de Calais, France.

BROWN, Private, RODERICK, 47309. 2nd Battalion, Canterbury Regiment, NZEF. Died 24 April 1918. Age 24. Son of Mary and the late Alexander Brown, of Rakaia. Brookwood Military Cemetery, Surrey, United Kingdom. Grave or panel number: VIII.B.12.

BROWN, Corporal, SYDNEY VINCENT ANDREW, 212075. attd. 'X' Trench Mortar Battery, NZ Field Artillery. Died 5 April 1918. Age 22. Son of Andrew and Sarah G. Brown, of 43 Cameron Rd, Napier. Native of Wellington. Euston Road Cemetery, Colincamps, Somme, France. Grave or panel number: IV.G.5.

BROWN, Rifleman, WILLIAM, 53752. 3rd Battalion, 3rd NZ Rifle Brigade. Died 6 April 1918. Age 37. Son of John and the late Ann Forbes Brown. Mailly Wood Cemetery, Somme, France. Grave or panel number: I.J.28.

BROWNE, Private, EVELYN JAMES WILLIAM, 24485. NZ Cyclist Battalion. Died 17 April 1918. Son of Mrs J. D. Browne, of 42 Knolly's St, Suva, Fiji. Messines Ridge (NZ) Memorial, Mesen, West-Vlaanderen, Belgium.

BRUNT, Private, ARTHUR, 29341. 1st Battalion, Wellington Regiment, NZEF. Died 30 March 1918. Age 27. Son of John and Hannah R. Brunt, of Upper Symonds St, Auckland. Native of Melbourne, Australia. Euston Road Cemetery, Colincamps, Somme, France. Grave or panel number: Special Memorial A.16.

BUCHLER, Captain, FREDERICK LANCELOT, 23/1575. 'C' Company, 3rd Battalion, 3rd NZ Rifle Brigade. Died 6 April 1918. Age 26. Son of Arthur Buchler, formerly of Taranaki; and of Sarah Buchler, of Dromore, Ashburton. Also served in Egypt. Grevillers (NZ) Memorial, Pas de Calais, France.

BUFTON, Lance Corporal, SYDNEY LEWIS, 43950. 13th Company, 1st Battalion, Canterbury Regiment, NZEF. Died 18 April 1918. Age 25. Son of Mary Jane Bufton, of 267 Barbadoes St, Christchurch. Native of Greymouth. Sucrerie Military Cemetery, Colincamps, Somme, France. Grave or panel number: IV.E.1.

BULFIN, Rifleman, GEORGE FREDERICK, 41964. 2nd Battalion, 3rd NZ Rifle Brigade. Died 5 April 1918. Son of Mr and Mrs J. Bulfin, of Lawrence, Otago. Euston Road Cemetery, Colincamps, Somme, France. Grave or panel number: II.A.2.

BURDETT, Private, WILLIAM, 24459. 1st Battalion, Auckland Regiment, NZEF. Died 3 April 1918. Husband of Mrs E. Burdett, of Shoal Bay Rd, Devonport, Auckland. Grevilliers (NZ) Memorial, Pas de Calais, France.

BURN, Private, GORDON STANLEY, 11810. 2nd Battalion, Wellington Regiment, NZEF. Died 27 March 1918. Age 23. Son of Philip Edward and Emma Sarah Burn. Doullens Communal Cemetery Extension No. 1, Somme, France. Grave or panel number: V.D.24.

BURNARD, Private, HAROLD GORDON, 44826. 1st Battalion, Auckland Regiment, NZEF. Died 28 March 1918. Age 31. Abbeville Communal Cemetery Extension, Somme, France. Grave or panel number: I.D.29.

BURNES, Private, JAMES ALLEN, 9/584. NZ Machine Gun Corps. Died 27 March 1918. Age 23. Son of Charles and Annie Burnes, of 76 Surrey St, South Dunedin. Born at Wellington. Serre Road Cemetery No. 1, Pas de Calais, France. Grave or panel number V.C.27.

BURNETT, Rifleman, GEORGE FRANCIS, 23/86. 1st Battalion, 3rd NZ Rifle Brigade. Died 5 April 1918. Son of Mrs A.J. Burnett, of Christchurch. Euston Road Cemetery, Colincamps, Somme, France. Grave or panel number: IV.D.9.

BURROWES, Private, WILLIAM, 27160. NZ Cyclist Battalion. Died 17 April 1918. Age 32. Son of William Henry and Helena Marie Burrowes, of 221 Wainoni Rd, New Brighton, Christchurch. Native of Westland. Messines Ridge (NZ) Memorial, Mesen, West-Vlaanderen, Belgium.

BUTLER, Sapper, HERBERT EDWARD, 4/1898. Signal Company, NZ Engineers. Died 28 March 1918. Age 22. Son of Herbert Edward Ormond Butler and Mary Anne Butler, of 136 North Avon Rd, Richmond. Euston Road Cemetery, Colincamps, Somme, France. Grave or panel number: IV.A.2.

BUTLER, Private, JOSEPH CONNOR TAYLOR, 38655. 2nd Battalion, Wellington Regiment, NZEF. Died 27 March 1918. Age 37. Son of Joseph C.T. and Violetta Butler, of Blackhill, Victoria, Australia; husband of Ellen Ivy Butler, of Mangatawhiri Valley, Auckland. Euston Road Cemetery, Colincamps, Somme, France. Grave or panel number: III.D.6.

CAFFERY, Private, JOSEPH, 11404. 2nd Battalion, Auckland Regiment, NZEF. Died 29 March 1918. Son of Mrs Mary Ann Caffery, of 166 Neill St, Ponsonby,

Auckland. Grevilliers (NZ) Memorial, Pas de Calais, France.

CAIN, Gunner, ANDREW, 2/2790. 4th Battery, NZ Field Artillery. Died 14 April 1918. Age 26. Son of Samuel Cain, of Seadown, Temuka. Bertrancourt Military Cemetery, Somme, France. Grave or panel number: 2.A.24.

CAMERON, Private, JAMES, 33514. 1st Battalion, Wellington Regiment, NZEF. Died 31 March 1918. Age 44. Brother of Mrs Agnes Robinson, of Mornington, Dunedin. Gezaincourt Communal Cemetery Extension, Somme, France. Grave or panel number: II.H.14.

CAMERON, Rifleman, JOHN, 46518. 2nd Battalion, 3rd NZ Rifle Brigade. Died 26 March 1918. Son of the late Mr D. Cameron. Grevilliers (NZ) Memorial, Pas de Calais, France.

CAMERON, Rifleman, THOMAS, 25/1698. 4th Battalion, 3rd NZ Rifle Brigade. Died 30 April 1918. Age 36. Son of Isabella Hollingsworth (formerly Cameron), of 10 Dalziel St, Motherwell, Lanarkshire, Scotland, and the late Thomas Cameron. Les Baraques Military Cemetery, Sangatte, Pas de Calais, France. Grave or panel number: III.F.4A.

CAMERON, Gunner, THOMAS ALEXANDER, 10/2540. Attached 2nd Trench Mortar Battery, NZ Field Artillery. Died 26 April 1918. Son of Mr and Mrs A. Cameron, of Ngaere, Taranaki. Euston Road Cemetery, Colincamps, Somme, France. Grave or panel number: III.G.2.

CAMPBELL, Private, MURDOCK MCLEOD, 32129. 1st Battalion, Wellington Regiment, NZEF. Died 30 March 1918. Son of Mr and Mrs Simon Campbell, of Stoney Creek, Martinborough. Grevilliers (NZ) Memorial, Pas de Calais, France.

CAMPBELL, Gunner, WILLIAM JOHN, 13/2308. 3rd Battery, 1st Brigade, NZ Field Artillery. Died 8 April 1918. Son of Mr and Mrs P. Campbell, of Alexandra, Otago; husband of Florence L. Campbell, of Beach Rd, Thames. Bertrancourt Military Cemetery, Somme, France. Grave or panel number: 2.B.18.

CAPON, Corporal, MARTIN, 14398, MM. 2nd Battalion, Canterbury Regiment, NZEF. Died 21 April 1918. Age 24. Doullens Communal Cemetery Extension No. 1, Somme, France. Grave or panel number: VI.C.70.

CAPSTICK, Private, WILLIAM GEORGE, 41273. 1st Battalion, Auckland Regiment, NZEF. Died 26 March 1918. Father of John William George Capstick, of Te Aroha. Euston Road Cemetery, Colincamps, Somme, France. Grave or panel number: II.E.2.

CARLSON, Rifleman, ROLAND, 57028. 1st Battalion, 3rd NZ Rifle Brigade. Died 5 April 1918. Age 25. Only son of Mary Carlson, of Kaituna, Masterton, and the late Mr C. Carlson. Euston Road Cemetery, Colincamps, Somme, France. Grave or panel number: I.H.7.

CARPENTER, Private, WALTER JAMES, 52148. 1st Battalion, Auckland Regiment, NZEF. Died 27 March 1918. Age 22. Son of Walter William and

Ada Carpenter, of Papakura, Auckland. Euston Road Cemetery, Colincamps, Somme, France. Grave or panel number: III.B.1.

CARR, Lance Corporal, EDWARD MARTIN, 36406. 1st Battalion, 3rd NZ Rifle Brigade. Died 27 March 1918. Age 28. Auchonvillers Military Cemetery, Somme, France. Grave or panel number: II.L.43.

CARROLL, Corporal, FRANCIS, 14227. 4th Battalion, 3rd NZ Rifle Brigade. Died 30 March 1918. Grevillers (NZ) Memorial, Pas de Calais, France.

CARTER, Sapper, RICHARD, 13561. NZ Engineers. Died 6 April 1918. Age 27. Son of Henry and Julia Eliza Carter, of Hikurangi, Whangarei. Hédauville Communal Cemetery Extension, Somme, France. Grave or panel number: H.16.

CASAR, Private, JOHN RUDOLPH, 23/1582. 2nd Battalion, Auckland Regiment, NZEF. Died 31 March 1918. Age 25. Son of Joseph and Rose Casar, of Logan St, Mangawhare, Dargaville. Doullens Communal Cemetery Extension No. 1, Somme, France. Grave or panel number: V.A.38.

CASSIDY, Private, S.R., 51556. 1st Battalion, Wellington Regiment, NZEF. Died 30 March 1918. Age 34. Son of John Alexander and Mary Cassidy. Euston Road Cemetery, Colincamps, Somme, France. Grave or panel number: Special Memorial B.1.

CAVALIER, Private, VICTOR GEORGE, 49694. 1st Battalion, Auckland Regiment, NZEF. Died 31 March 1918. Age 25. Son of Alfred William and Susan Cavalier, of 35 Penge Rd, Upton Park, London, England. Native of Stepney. Englebelmer Communal Cemetery Extension, Somme, France. Grave or panel number: F.27.

CHAPMAN, Corporal, SIDNEY GIBSON, 28579. 1st Battalion, Auckland Regiment, NZEF. Died 26 March 1918. Age 23. Son of George C. and Elizabeth Chapman; husband of Ella Chapman, of 3 Wairere Rd, Remuera, Auckland. Born at Dunedin. Doullens Communal Cemetery Extension No. 1, Somme, France. Grave or panel number: V.E.16.

CHEYNE, Rifleman, GEORGE BARNETT, 53903. 1st Battalion, 3rd, NZ Rifle Brigade. Died 5 April 1918. Husband of Sarah Cheyne, of 254 Dyers Rd, Bromley, Christchurch. Euston Road Cemetery, Colincamps, Somme, France. Grave or panel number: III.E.4.

CHRISTIE, Private, MAXWELL, 53653. 1st Battalion, Auckland Regiment, NZEF. Died 27 March 1918. Age 21. Son of Maxwell Christie, of Scotland, and the late Alice Christie. Euston Road Cemetery, Colincamps, Somme, France. Grave or panel number: III.B.2.

CHRISTIE, Sapper, RUPERT JAMES, 35093. Div. Signals, NZ Engineers. Died 28 March 1918. Age 22. Son of Robert D. and Grace Christie, of 144 Britomart St, Berhampore, Wellington. Native of Newcastle, New South Wales, Australia. Euston Road Cemetery, Colincamps, Somme, France. Grave or panel number: IV.A.5.

New Zealanders in a strong point near Mailly-Maillet. The soldiers in the foreground are preparing a meal while a single man keeps watch, the Lewis gun ready for action. KIPPENBERGER MILITARY ARCHIVE AND RESEARCH LIBRARY H461

New Zealand medics help themselves to some milk at Courcelles village.
KIPPENBERGER MILITARY ARCHIVE AND RESEARCH LIBRARY H462

A batch of German prisoners taken by the New Zealand Division at the end of March 1918. KIPPENBERGER MILITARY ARCHIVE AND RESEARCH LIBRARY H452

The life-saver. Bringing up the rum ration to La Signy Farm in early April 1918. KIPPENBERGER MILITARY ARCHIVE AND RESEARCH LIBRARY H476

War trophies. Captured German machine guns being inspected by officers from New Zealand Division headquarters. KIPPENBERGER MILITARY ARCHIVE AND RESEARCH LIBRARY H482

The ruins of Hébuterne village, May 1918. KIPPENBERGER MILITARY ARCHIVE AND RESEARCH LIBRARY H578

Marcus David Smith soon after his return from the war and prior to taking up his law practice in Dannevirke in 1920. Lieutenant Smith was a newly commissioned officer thrown in the deep end at the Somme in 1918. ALASTAIR E.B. JONES

The Very Reverend Ronald G. Watson, MC, ED, MA, padre to the 1st Otago Battalion and one of the 'happy band of brothers' on the Somme. This photograph was taken in 1939, prior to several periods of Home Service in the Second World War. MALCOLM H. WATSON

The New Zealand soldiers were aware, even if it is typically understated in this cartoon, that they had played a key role in stopping the German spring offensive. CHRONICLES OF THE N.Z.E.F.

CLANACHAN, Private, WILLIAM, 52152. 1st Battalion, Auckland Regiment, NZEF. Died 27 March 1918. Son of Mr and Mrs P.S. Clanachan, of Auckland. Grevilliers (NZ) Memorial, Pas de Calais, France.

CLARK, Driver, FREDERICK ARTHUR, 50294. NZ Field Artillery. Died 10 April 1918. Son of Charles G. Clark, of Christchurch. Cite Bonjean (NZ) Memorial, Nord, France.

CLARK, Private, JAMES, 29746. 8th Company, 3rd Battalion, Otago Regiment, NZEF. Died 16 April 1918. Age 23. Son of David Fraser Clark and Sophia Clark, of Invercargill. Meteren Military Cemetery, Nord, France. Grave or panel number: II.M.321.

CLARK, Private, PERCY NEWTON, 49292. 1st Battalion, Wellington Regiment, NZEF. Died 30 March 1918. Age 36. Son of The Rev J.R. and Mrs S. Clark, of Wellington. Euston Road Cemetery, Colincamps, Somme, France. Grave or panel number: Special Memorial B.8.

CLARK, Rifleman, WILLIAM MCLEAN, 53318. 2nd Battalion, 3rd NZ Rifle Brigade. Died 6 April 1918. Age 21. Son of William and Elizabeth L. Clark, of The Triangle, Kelso, New Zealand. Native of Crichton, Lovell's Flat, Dunedin. Sucrerie Military Cemetery, Colincamps, Somme, France. Grave or panel number: I.I.5.

CLARK, Private, WILLIE HENRY, 51300. 1st Battalion, Wellington Regiment, NZEF. Died 21 April 1918. Age 44. Son of Edward Saunders and Suzan Clark, of New Zealand. Louvencourt Military Cemetery, Somme, France. Grave or panel number: 1.D.24.

CLARKE, Rifleman, JAMES CLIFFORD, 53475. 3rd Battalion. 3rd NZ Rifle Brigade. Died 31 March 1918. Age 28. Son of John and the late Laura Clarke, of Ngahauranga, Wellington. Gezaincourt Communal Cemetery Extension, Somme, France. Grave or panel number: II.H.21.

CLARKE, Private, JAMES SPENCER, 58978. 10th Company, 1st Battalion, Otago Regiment, NZEF. Died 9 April 1918. Age 27. Son of James and Annie Clarke, of Southall, Middlesex, England. Etaples Military Cemetery, Pas de Calais, France. Grave or panel number: XXXIII.F.12.

CLARKE, Gunner, RALPH JOHN, 12/320. attd. 'X' Trench Mortar Battery, NZ Field Artillery. Died 5 April 1918. Age 26. Son of Arthur Gale Clarke and Mary Grace Clarke, of 73 The Drive, Epsom, Auckland. Euston Road Cemetery, Colincamps, Somme, France. Grave or panel number: IV.G.4.

CLARKSON, Lance Corporal, WILLIAM FRANCIS, 6/2107. 1st Battalion, Canterbury Regiment, NZEF. Died 27 March 1918. Age 23. Son of Emerson Clarkson, of 34 Papanui Rd, Christchurch and the late Annie Clarkson. Grevilliers (NZ) Memorial, Pas de Calais, France.

CLEERE, Private, RICHARD, 49526. 1st Battalion, Canterbury Regiment, NZEF. Died 5 April 1918. Age 24. Son of Piree and Kate Cleere, of Brounstown Kilkenny, Ireland. Grevilliers (NZ) Memorial, Pas de Calais, France.

CLINTON, Private, THOMAS JAMES, 10783. NZ Cyclist Battalion. Died 18 April 1918. Age 25. Son of Mrs Mary Clinton, of Darfield, Canterbury, and the late William Francis Clinton. Messines Ridge (NZ) Memorial, Mesen, West-Vlaanderen, Belgium.

CLIVE, Private, PERCY DAVID, 31470. 2nd Battalion, Canterbury Regiment, NZEF. Died 14 April 1918. Age 29. Son of James and Mary Ann Clive. Doullens Communal Cemetery Extension No. 1, Somme, France. Grave or panel number: VI.C.33.

CLOTHIER, Rifleman, CHARLES AUGUSTUS, 30346. 2nd Battalion, 3rd NZ Rifle Brigade. Died 26 March 1918. Age 30. Son of Charles and Matilda Clothier, of Waiuku, Auckland. Born in New Zealand. Grevillers (NZ) Memorial, Pas de Calais, France.

COCHRANE, Rifleman, J., 53737. 1st Battalion, 3rd NZ Rifle Brigade. Died 27 March 1918. Auchonvillers Military Cemetery, Somme, France. Grave or panel number: II.L.42.

COCHRANE, Private, ROBERT, 54010. 2nd Battalion, Otago Regiment, NZEF. Died 28 April 1918. Age 33. Son of James and Helen Cochrane, of Ashburton. Mailly Wood Cemetery, Somme, France. Grave or panel number: I.J.27.

COLDICUTT, Gunner, GEORGE LAWRENCE, 2/2979. 9th Battery, 2nd Brigade, NZ Field Artillery. Died 28 April 1918. Age 21. Son of George Henry and Margaret Coldicutt, of 15 Murdoch Rd, Grey Lynn, Auckland. Boulogne Eastern Cemetery, Pas de Calais, France. Grave or panel number: IX.A.45.

COLE, Sergeant, KENNETH MCINTOSH, 12714, MM. 2nd Battery, NZ Field Artillery. Died 9 April 1918. Age 26. Son of Ellen Cole, of 18 Garrett St, Wellington, and the late George Cole. Also served in Samoa. Messines Ridge (NZ) Memorial, Mesen, West-Vlaanderen, Belgium.

COLEMAN, Second Lieutenant, HERBERT NAPIER, 36739. 1st Battalion, Canterbury Regiment, NZEF. Died 13 April 1918. Age 35. Son of J.H. and Hannah Coleman, of Waititirau, Napier; husband of B. Mary Coleman. Englebelmer Communal Cemetery Extension, Somme, France. Grave or panel number: F.21.

COLL, Lance Corporal, DANIEL, 29148. 2nd Battalion, Canterbury Regiment, NZEF. Died 28 March 1918. Age 33. Son of Mrs Catherine Coll, of Wilmhurst St, Temuka. Grevilliers (NZ) Memorial, Pas de Calais, France.

COLLETT, Rifleman, STANLEY BEACONSFIELD, 25/1689. 1st/3rd Battalion, NZ Rifle Brigade. Died 5 April 1918. Age 37. Son of Henry and Rosa Collett, of Chippenham, Wilts, England. Doullens Communal Cemetery Extension No. 1, Somme, France. Grave or panel number: VI.D.36.

CONDON, Private, VINCENT HENRY, 45478. 1st Battalion, Canterbury Regiment, NZEF. Died 19 April 1918. Age 32. Son of Arthur Henry and Clara Condon, of Awakino, New Zealand. Courcelles-Au-Bois Communal Cemetery Extension, Somme, France. Grave or panel number: F.11.

CONDON, Rifleman, WILLIAM FRANCIS, 18967. 'B' Company, 4th Battalion, 3rd NZ Rifle Brigade. Died 3 April 1918. Age 22. Son of John and Mary Condon, of Kororo, Greymouth. Etaples Military Cemetery, Pas de Calais, France. Grave or panel number: XXXIII.D.23.

CONLEY, Private, JACOB ADDEY, 40887. 1st Battalion, Otago Regiment, NZEF. Died 31 March 1918. Age 29. Son of George and Eliza Conley, of Dipton, Southland. Serre Road Cemetery No. 1, Pas de Calais, France. Grave or panel number: II.B.20.

CONNELL, Lance Corporal, HERBERT, 6/2984. 12th Company, 1st Battalion, Canterbury Regiment, NZEF. Died 27 March 1918. Age 42. Son of the late Basil and Amelia Connell, of Tapu, Thames. Served in the South African Campaign. Born at Nelson. Grevilliers (NZ) Memorial, Pas de Calais, France.

CONNELLY, Rifleman, JOHN THOMPSON, 49874. 2nd Battalion, 3rd NZ Rifle Brigade. Died 26 April 1918. Age 35. Brother of William Connelly, of Elizabeth St, Timaru. Brockenhurst (St Nicholas) Churchyard, Hampshire, United Kingdom. Grave or panel number: A.3.16.

CONNOR, Private, JOHN, 51106. 2nd Battalion, Wellington Regiment, NZEF. Died 2 April 1918. Age 30. Son of Hugh and Mary Connor, of 2 Lytton Rd, Gisborne. Native of Port Ahuriri, Napier. Sucrerie Military Cemetery, Colincamps, Somme, France. Grave or panel number: I.J.56.

COOPER, Lance Corporal, ARTHUR GEORGE, 11837. 2nd Battalion, Wellington Regiment, NZEF. Died 27 March 1918. Age 28. Son of William A. and Margret Cooper, of Rimu, Westland. Euston Road Cemetery, Colincamps, Somme, France. Grave or panel number: V.D.7.

COOPER, Private, MANCEL JOHN, 48174. 2nd Battalion, Canterbury Regiment, NZEF. Died 29 March 1918. Husband of Christina Cooper, of Porewa, Rata. Grevilliers (NZ) Memorial, Pas de Calais, France.

CORIN, Rifleman, WALTER HENRY, 25/1238. 3rd Battalion, 3rd NZ Rifle Brigade. Died 27 March 1918. Age 20. Son of Mrs Fanny St George, of Princes St, Otahuhu, Auckland. Born in New Zealand. Grevillers (NZ) Memorial, Pas de Calais, France.

CORK, Lance Corporal, HENRY RAYMOND, 38353. 2nd Battalion, Auckland Regiment, NZEF. Died 28 March 1918. Age 29. Son of Francis and Charlotte Cork, of 26 Elgin St, Grey Lynn, Auckland. Sucrerie Military Cemetery, Colincamps, Somme, France. Grave or panel number: I.J.57.

CORRIGAN, Private, MICHAEL, 13/2027. 2nd Battalion, Auckland Regiment, NZEF. Died 30 March 1918. Age 33. Son of Bernard and Sarah Corrigan, of Dirnan Lissan, Cookstown, County Tyrone, Ireland. Grevilliers (NZ) Memorial, Pas de Calais, France.

COSTER, Private, ALFRED CYRIL CLIFFORD, 52582. 1st Battalion, Wellington Regiment, NZEF. Died 30 March 1918. Age 27. Son of Alfred and Catherine Coster, of 29 The Rigi, Kelburn, Wellington. Euston Road Cemetery,

Colincamps, Somme, France. Grave or panel number: Special Memorial B.2.

COTTER, Private, HUMPHREY, 24/1962, 2nd Battalion, Canterbury Regiment, NZEF. Died 5 April 1918. Age 24. Son of Timothy and Ellen Cotter, of Wellington South. Auchonvillers Military Cemetery, Somme, France. Grave or panel number: II.L.29.

COTTINGHAM, Rifleman, HENRY JOHN, 58745. 4th Battalion, 3rd NZ Rifle Brigade. Died 5 April 1918. Age 28. Son of Susan Cottingham, of Weston, Oamaru, and the late George Cottingham. Euston Road Cemetery, Colincamps, Somme, France. Grave or panel number: V.I.6.

COURTNEY, Rifleman, ROBERT, 56747. 1st Battalion, 3rd NZ Rifle Brigade. Died 5 April 1918. Age 22. Son of Mrs M. Scott, of New Plymouth. Euston Road Cemetery, Colincamps, Somme, France. Grave or panel number: IV.D.4.

COX, Private, CLIFFORD, 47862. 1st Battalion, Auckland Regiment, NZEF. Died 26 March 1918. Age 37. Son of Benjamin William and Elizabeth Cox, of 62 Wainui Rd, Kaiti, Gisborne. Grevillers (NZ) Memorial, Pas de Calais, France.

COX, Lieutenant, WILFRED JAMES, 41180. 2nd Battalion, Auckland Regiment, NZEF. Died 27 March 1918. Age 24. Son of Robert George and Lydia Harriett Cox, of 208 Karangahape Rd, Auckland; husband of Doris Keys (formerly Cox). Grevilliers (NZ) Memorial, Pas de Calais, France.

CRAWFORD, Rifleman, GEORGE PHILIP, 24/1963. 'B' Company, 4th Battalion, 3rd NZ Rifle Brigade. Died 5 April 1918. Age 32. Son of Ruth Reid, of 129 Vivian St, Wellington. Euston Road Cemetery, Colincamps, Somme, France. Grave or panel number: II.B.3.

CREAMER, Rifleman, LEONARD, 46440. 2nd Battalion, 3rd NZ Rifle Brigade. Died 18 April 1918. Son of Mrs E. Creamer, of 9 Wanganui Ave, Ponsonby, Auckland. Serre Road Cemetery No. 1, Pas de Calais, France. Grave or panel number: I.K.14.

CRIPPS, Rifleman, VICTOR GEORGE, 56741. 3rd Battalion, 3rd NZ Rifle Brigade. Died 6 April 1918. Age 33. Son of George and Leah Cripps, of Rapanui, Wanganui. Born at Wimbledon, Napier. Grevillers (NZ) Memorial, Pas de Calais, France.

CROKER, Corporal, ERIC ROBERT IRVING, 39027. 2nd NZ Entrenching Battalion, NZEF. Died 16 April 1918. Age 32. Son of James Taylor Croker and Diana Valentine Croker, of 23 Waipapa Rd, Hataitai, Wellington. Native of Christchurch. Messines Ridge (NZ) Memorial, Mesen, West-Vlaanderen, Belgium.

CRONIN, Private, EDWARD JAMES, 51696. 2nd Battalion, Wellington Regiment, NZEF. Died 3 April 1918. Age 19. Son of Cornelius and Alice Louise Cronin, of 56 Malmesbury Tce, Canning Town, London, England. Sucrerie Military Cemetery, Colincamps, Somme, France. Grave or panel number: I.J.53.

CRONIN, Rifleman, THOMAS, 1/607. 4th Battalion, 3rd NZ Rifle Brigade. Died 30 March 1918. Age 25. Son of Michael and Mary Jane Cronin, of

Manawaru, Te Aroha. Born at Waiorongomai, Thames. Grevillers (NZ) Memorial, Pas de Calais, France.

CROPP, Private, ALFRED WILLIAM, 54015. 1st Battalion, Otago Regiment, NZEF. Died 27 April 1918. Age 28. Son of Benjamin and Sarah J. Cropp, New Zealand. Native of Wai-iti, Nelson. Euston Road Cemetery, Colincamps, Somme, France. Grave or panel number: I.T.1.

CROPP, Corporal, WALTER CHARLES, 51969. 2nd NZ Entrenching Battalion, NZEF. Died 14 April 1918. Meteren Military Cemetery, Nord, France. Grave or panel number: II.M.328.

CROWHURST, Private, FRANCIS ERNEST, 60080. 1st Battalion, Auckland Regiment, NZEF. Died 20 April 1918. Age 32. Son of Samuel George and Catherine Crowhurst, of 24 Eden St, Newmarket, Auckland. Bertrancourt Military Cemetery, Somme, France. Grave or panel number: 2.A.2.

CUFF, Private, ROBERT WILLIAM, 54121. 1st Battalion, Canterbury Regiment, NZEF. Died 5 April 1918. Age 21. Son of Clarence John and Annie Cuff, of Spencer St, Milton. Born at Geraldine. Grevilliers (NZ) Memorial, Pas de Calais, France.

CULLINGHAM, Sapper, ARTHUR JAMES, 4/1728. Div. Signal Company, NZ Engineers. Died 28 March 1918. Age 37. Son of James and Jane Cullingham, of Penge, London, England. Served with Royal Engineers in the Somaliland Expedition and the South African Campaign. Euston Road Cemetery, Colincamps, Somme, France. Grave or panel number: IV.A.1.

CUMMINS, Private, FRANK ROLAND, 43958. 1st Battalion, Canterbury Regiment, NZEF. Died 23 April 1918. Age 22. Son of Thomas F. and Rose Cummins, of 230 Norwood St, Beckenham, Christchurch. Colincamps Communal Cemetery, Somme, France.

CUNNINGHAM, Lance Corporal, FREDERICK JAMES, 13425. 1st Battalion, Canterbury Regiment, NZEF. Died 31 March 1918. Age 24. Son of James and the late Emma Cunningham, of Hilton, Canterbury. Etaples Military Cemetery, Pas de Calais, France. Grave or panel number: XXXIII.B.23.

CURTIS, Private, RONALD HENRY, 20110. NZ Cyclist Battalion. Died 27 April 1918. Age 27. Son of Robert Roland Curtis and Alice Mary Curtis, of Colyton, Feilding. Buttes New British Cemetery (NZ) Memorial, Polygon Wood, Zonnebeke, West-Vlaanderen, Belgium.

CUTHBERTSON, Captain, DOUGLAS MACPHERSON, 2/1384. 6th Howitzer Battery, NZ Field Artillery. Died 30 March 1918. Age 28. Son of the late Robert E. and Susan E. Cuthbertson, of Invercargill. Wimereux Communal Cemetery, Pas de Calais, France. Grave or panel number: IV.F.3.

DALLEY, Lance Corporal, STANLEY MILES CLIFFORD, 14952. 2nd Battalion, Canterbury Regiment, NZEF. Died 5 April 1918. Age 22. Son of Jonah and Florence Dalley, of Christchurch. Auchonvillers Military Cemetery, Somme,

France. Grave or panel number: II.A.35.

DANRELL, Private, SAMUEL INNIS, 28688. 2nd Battalion, Auckland Regiment, NZEF. Died 31 March 1918. Age 22. Brother of Mr A. Danrell of Ponsonby, Auckland. Gezaincourt Communal Cemetery Extension, Somme, France. Grave or panel number: II.H.9.

DAVIE, Second Lieutenant, HARRY PERCY CLAUDE, 11/243, MM. NZ Field Artillery. Died 23 April 1918. Age 28. Son of Geo. R. Davie, of Fox St, Woodville. Lijssenthoek Military Cemetery, Poperinge, West-Vlaanderen, Belgium. Grave or panel number: XXVI.GG.7.

DAVIES, Private, MILTON WILLIAM, 29229. 2nd Battalion, Canterbury Regiment, NZEF. Died 27 March 1918. Son of Mrs J. Davies, of 29 North Avon Rd, Christchurch. Grevilliers (NZ) Memorial, Pas de Calais, France.

DAVIS, Sapper, ALBERT EDWARD, 4/1913. 1st Field Company, NZ Engineers. Died 29 April 1918. Age 27. Son of William and Emma Davis, of Christchurch. Doullens Communal Cemetery Extension No. 2, Somme, France. Grave or panel number: I.A.27.

DAVIS, Sergeant, ERIC NATHANIEL, 8/2513. 1st Battalion, Otago Regiment, NZEF. Died 5 April 1918. Age 23. Son of Henry John and Grace M. Davis, of Pahiatua. Also served in Gallipoli. Auchonvillers Military Cemetery, Somme, France. Grave or panel number: II.L.27.

DAVIS, Private, JOHN, 47992. Canterbury Regiment, NZEF. Died 29 April 1918. Esquelbecq Military Cemetery, Nord, France. Grave or panel number: I.B.31.

DAVY, Private, ALFRED CHARLES, 31974. 1st Battalion, Auckland Regiment, NZEF. Died 26 March 1918. Husband of Flora Mary Davy, of Auckland. Grevilliers (NZ) Memorial, Pas de Calais, France.

DAWES, Private, JAMES, 49074. 1st Battalion, Auckland Regiment, NZEF. Died 27 March 1918. Age 24. Son of James and Esther Dawes, of 'Rosslyn', Park View Rd, Alphington, Victoria, Australia. Native of Melbourne, Victoria. Euston Road Cemetery, Colincamps, Somme, France. Grave or panel number: Special Memorial B.9.

DAWSON, Gunner, JAMES, 43473. NZ Field Artillery. Died 17 April 1918. Age 20. Son of Arthur and Hannah Maria Dawson, of Towai, North Auckland. Lijssenthoek Military Cemetery, Poperinge, West-Vlaanderen, Belgium. Grave or panel number: XXVII.G.8A.

DE CENT, Captain, KENNETH OWEN, 23471. 2nd Battalion, Otago Regiment, NZEF. Died 12 April 1918. Age 27. Son of Joseph Thomas and Sarah De Cent, of Gisborne. Doullens Communal Cemetery Extension No. 1, Somme, France. Grave or panel number: VI.A.34.

DE LUEN, Sergeant, FREDERICK, 12/2995, MM. 1st Battalion, Auckland Regiment, NZEF. Died 26 March 1918. Son of Mr and Mrs Frederick De Luen, of 19 Liverpool St, Wanganui. Grevilliers (NZ) Memorial, Pas de Calais, France.

DEED, Private, GUYLOTT HENRY JACKSON, 51698. 1st Battalion, Auckland Regiment, NZEF. Died 26 March 1918. Son of Mr and Mrs T.G. Deed, of Pukekohe. Euston Road Cemetery, Colincamps, Somme, France. Grave or panel number: Special Memorial B.12.

DELANEY, Rifleman, WILLIAM THOMAS, 53328. 4th Battalion, 3rd NZ Rifle Brigade. Died 30 March 1918. Grevillers (NZ) Memorial, Pas de Calais, France.

DELLOW, Lance Corporal, ARTHUR JOHN, 12148. 2nd Battalion, 3rd NZ Rifle Brigade. Died 5 April 1918. Age 25. Son of William and Elizabeth Dellow, of Tinwald, Ashburton. Born at Mayfield, Ashburton. Euston Road Cemetery, Colincamps, Somme, France. Grave or panel number: III.A.7.

DENT, Gunner, GEORGE BATES, 43076. NZ Field Artillery. Died 27 March 1918. Age 26. Son of Thomas and Cordelia Dent, of 24 Armidale St, Petone, Wellington. Mailly Wood Cemetery, Somme, France. Grave or panel number: I.E.23.

DERBYSHIRE, Lance Corporal, WILLIAM FREDERICK, 20974. 'C Company, 4th Battalion, 3rd NZ Rifle Brigade. Died 28 March 1918. Age 20. Son of Charles William and Elizabeth Derbyshire, of Nelson St, Papakura, Auckland. Grevillers (NZ) Memorial, Pas de Calais, France.

DEVITT, Private, JOHN, 45481. 2nd Battalion, Auckland Regiment, NZEF. Died 30 March 1918. Euston Road Cemetery, Colincamps, Somme, France. Grave or panel number: IV.B.8.

DEXTER, Private, ALBERT, 25209. 2nd Battalion, Auckland Regiment, NZEF. Died 27 March 1918. Age 26. Son of William and Maria Elizabeth Dexter, of 159 Tudor Rd, Leicester, England. Grevilliers (NZ) Memorial, Pas de Calais, France.

DICKESON, Lieutenant, COLIN ADDISON, 24/2128, MC. Acting Capt. NZ Cyclist Battalion. Died 26 April 1918. Age 30. Husband of Mrs L. E. Dickeson, of Mt Albert, Auckland. Lijssenthoek Military Cemetery, Poperinge, West-Vlaanderen, Belgium. Grave or panel number: XXVIII.C.5.

DICKIE, Gunner, ERIC STANLEY GORDON, 43960. 13th Battery, NZ Field Artillery. Died 22 April 1918. Age 22. Son of William and Clara Eliza Dickie, of Christchurch. Bertrancourt Military Cemetery, Somme, France. Grave or panel number: 2.B.2.

DICKIE, Private, JOHN DUNCAN, 51018. 2nd Battalion, Wellington Regiment, NZEF. Died 5 April 1918. Son of David and Eliza Dickie, of Ngahauranga, Wellington. Native of Kirkcaldy, Scotland. Sucrerie Military Cemetery, Colincamps, Somme, France. Grave or panel number: 1.J.49.

DICKSON, Private, HERBERT ALEXANDER, 12/2991. 2nd Battalion, Auckland Regiment, NZEF. Died 30 March 1918. Age 30. Son of Rebecca Dickson, of 271 Somme Parade, Aramoho, Wanganui, and the late George Henry Dickson. Grevilliers (NZ) Memorial, Pas de Calais, France.

DOAK, Lance Corporal, DAVID JOHN WILSON, 7/2376. 1st Battalion, Wellington Regiment, NZEF. Died 30 March 1918. Age 22. Son of David John and Sarah Doak, of Canterbury. Euston Road Cemetery, Colincamps, Somme, France. Grave or panel number: IV.C.9.

DOBSON, Sergeant, JOHN, 12158. 2nd Battalion, 3rd NZ Rifle Brigade. Died 5 April 1918. Age 42. Son of John and Catherine Dobson, of Heriot, Scotland; husband of Margaret Stevenson Dobson, of Baillie St, Thames. Euston Road Cemetery, Colincamps, Somme, France. Grave or panel number: III.A.6.

DOGGETT, Rifleman, ALFRED CEDRIC, 53329. 4th Battalion, 3rd NZ Rifle Brigade. Died 29 March 1918. Son of Margaret Doggett, of Hastings. Euston Road Cemetery, Colincamps, Somme, France. Grave or panel number: IV.C.4.

DOHERTY, Rifleman, CHARLES, 42479. 3rd Battalion, 3rd NZ Rifle Brigade. Died 7 April 1918. Age 27. Son of Francis and Eliza Doherty, of Balmoral, Outram, Dunedin. Grevillers (NZ) Memorial, Pas de Calais, France.

DONALDSON, Rifleman, IAN DOUGLAS, 25688. 'G' Company, 1st Battalion, 3rd NZ Rifle Brigade. Died 5 April 1918. Age 22. Son of Peter John Donaldson, of Ranganui, North Auckland, and the late Annabella Donaldson. Born at St Heliers Bay. Grevillers (NZ) Memorial, Pas de Calais, France.

DOUGLAS, Gunner, E.G., 11/2083. NZ Field Artillery. Died 17 April 1918. Lijssenthoek Military Cemetery, Poperinge, West-Vlaanderen, Belgium. Grave or panel number: XXVII.G.7.

DOUGLAS, Private, WILLIAM, 29750. 1st Battalion, Wellington Regiment, NZEF. Died 6 April 1918. Age 25. Son of the late Neil and Ellen Douglas, of Dunedin. Etaples Military Cemetery, Pas de Calais, France. Grave or panel number: XXXIII.D.7.

DOULL, Rifleman, JAMES, 53330. 2nd Battalion, 3rd NZ Rifle Brigade. Died 5 April 1918. Grevillers (NZ) Memorial, Pas de Calais, France.

DOWD, Rifleman, JOHN, 51356. 2nd Battalion, 3rd NZ Rifle Brigade. Died 26 March 1918. Son of Mrs N. Dowd, of 168 Edgeware Rd, St Albans, Christchurch. Euston Road Cemetery, Colincamps, Somme, France. Grave or panel number: III.A.4.

DOYLE, Rifleman, THOMAS FRANCIS, 49879. 4th Battalion, 3rd NZ Rifle Brigade. Died 31 March 1918. Age 33. Brother of John Doyle, of Wellington. Doullens Communal Cemetery Extension No. 1, Somme, France. Grave or panel number: VI.G.31.

DRAKE, Private, FRANCIS GEORGE, 42058. 1st Battalion, Auckland Regiment, NZEF. Died 27 March 1918. Age 45. Husband of T. Drake, of 8 Chamberlain Ave, Mt Eden, Auckland. Doullens Communal Cemetery Extension No. 1, Somme, France. Grave or panel number: V.A.40.

DRISCOLL, Private, THOMAS, 52972. 2nd Battalion, Wellington Regiment, NZEF. Died 27 March 1918. Age 28. Son of Thomas Driscoll, of Wellington. Euston Road Cemetery, Colincamps, Somme, France. Grave or panel number: V.A.9.

DRIVER, Private, BENJAMIN HENRY, 59510. 2nd Battalion, Otago Regiment, NZEF. Died 28 March 1918. Age 38. Son of James and Eliza Driver, of London, England. Euston Road Cemetery, Colincamps, Somme, France. Grave or panel number: III.A.5.

DRUMMOND, Rifleman, PETER, 45195. 2nd Battalion, 3rd NZ Rifle Brigade. Died 9 April 1918. Age 34. Son of Elizabeth Drummond, of North East Valley, Dunedin. Doullens Communal Cemetery Extension No. 1, Somme, France. Grave or panel number: VI.C.14.

DRYSDALE, Second Lieutenant, THOMAS JOHN HIRST, 4195A. 3rd Battalion, 3rd NZ Rifle Brigade. Died 6 April 1918. Age 34. Son of John Drysdale, M.D., and Alice Drysdale (née Dodson), of 2 Belhaven Tce, Rutherglen, Scotland. Born at Port Chalmers, New Zealand. Gezaincourt Communal Cemetery Extension, Somme, France. Grave or panel number: II.J.21.

DUFF, Lance Corporal, GEORGE KENNETH, 4/1041, Div. Signal Company, NZ Engineers. Died 28 March 1918. Age 25. Son of Neil and Cordelia Duff, of 134 Edgeware Rd, Christchurch. Also served in Egypt and Gallipoli. Euston Road Cemetery, Colincamps, Somme, France. Grave or panel number: III.A.1.

DUFFEY, Sergeant, FREDERICK, 23/739. 1st Battalion, 3rd NZ Rifle Brigade. Died 5 April 1918. Son of Mrs M. Duffey, of 74 Dundas St, Dunedin. Euston Road Cemetery, Colincamps, Somme, France. Grave or panel number: I.H.5.

DUGGAN, Private, JAMES, 33525. 1st Battalion, Wellington Regiment, NZEF. Died 30 March 1918. Euston Road Cemetery, Colincamps, Somme, France. Grave or panel number: Special Memorial B.3.

DUNBAR, Private, JOHN DAVID, 54123. 1st Battalion, Otago Regiment, NZEF. Died 7 April 1918. Age 24. Son of William and Grace A. Dunbar, of Totara, New Zealand. Auchonvillers Military Cemetery, Somme, France. Grave or panel number: II.M.28.

DUNCAN, Private, ALEXANDER, 47550. 2nd NZ Entrenching Battalion, NZEF. Died 14 April 1918. Age 25. Son of James and Mary Ellen Duncan, of Aickens, Westland. Native of Annat, Canterbury. Meteren Military Cemetery, Nord, France. Grave or panel number: III. D. 638.

DUNCAN, Rifleman, JOHN, 56568. 4th Battalion, 3rd NZ Rifle Brigade. Died 29 March 1918. Age 21. Son of Thomas S. and Annie Duncan, of Aria, Te Kuiti. Doullens Communal Cemetery Extension No. 1, Somme, France. Grave or panel number: VI.G.7.

DUNGEY, Rifleman, ALFRED HUGH, 47716. 3rd Battalion, 3rd NZ Rifle Brigade. Died 12 April 1918. Son of Maria Dungey, of Dunedin, and the late James Dungey. Grevillers (NZ) Memorial, Pas de Calais, France.

DUNNET, Captain, JOHN CLOUSTON, 21214. 12th Battery, 3rd Brigade, NZ Field Artillery. Died 5 April 1918. Age 29. Son of Mary and the late Charles F. Dunnet, of Kelso, Otago. Doullens Communal Cemetery Extension No. 1, Somme, France. Grave or panel number: VI.A.19.

DURAND, Staff Sergeant Major (WO.I), JAMES DOUGLAS GERALD HAY, 5/41. NZ Army Service Corps. Died 26 April 1918. Grevillers (NZ) Memorial, Pas de Calais, France.

DURNETT, Private, ROBERT, 63576. 2nd NZ Entrenching Battalion, NZEF. Died 14 April 1918. Son of Evelyn Beatrice Durnett, of Taranaki St, Wellington. Messines Ridge (NZ) Memorial, Mesen, West-Vlaanderen, Belgium.

DUROSE, Private, HAROLD, 37998. 1st Battalion, Wellington Regiment, NZEF. Died 23 April 1918. Age 27. Son of Benjamin and Jane Durose, of 1 Atiawa St, Petone, Wellington. Native of Oldham, England. Bagneux British Cemetery, Gezaincourt, Somme, France. Grave or panel number: I.C.17.

DWYER, Sergeant, THOMAS BYRNE, 611277. 1st Battalion, Canterbury Regiment, NZEF. Died 7 April 1918. Age 24. Son of John and Theresa Eileen Dwyer, of 555 Manchester St, Christchurch. Born at Oamaru. St Sever Cemetery Extension, Rouen, Seine-Maritime, France. Grave or panel number: P.IX.F.4A.

EBBITT, Rifleman, GEORGE, 42309. 4th Battalion, 3rd NZ Rifle Brigade. Died 5 April 1918. Age 27. Son of George and Caroline Ebbitt, of Wairoa, Hawke's Bay. Euston Road Cemetery, Colincamps, Somme, France. Grave or panel number: II.B.6.

EDGAR, Corporal, JESSE, 613308. 1st Battalion, Canterbury Regiment, NZEF. Died 27 April 1918. Age 31. Son of Mrs M. Edgar, of Islandmore Portrush, County Antrim, Ireland. Bagneux British Cemetery, Gezaincourt, Somme, France. Grave or panel number: I.D.16.

EDMONDSON, Private, TYSON, 48629. 1st Battalion, Auckland Regiment, NZEF. Died 28 March 1918. Age 26. Son of James and Hannah Edmondson, of Silverdale, Lancashire. Englebelmer Communal Cemetery Extension, Somme, France. Grave or panel number: F.19.

EDWARDS, Private, HERBERT JAMES, 41969. 1st Battalion, Auckland Regiment, NZEF. Died 26 March 1918. Age 39. Son of James and Margaret Edwards, of Arrowtown; husband of Eva M. Edwards, of Onerahi, Whangarei. Euston Road Cemetery, Colincamps, Somme, France. Grave or panel number: III.B.7.

EDWARDS, Private, RALPH CYRIL, 61128. 2nd NZ Entrenching Battalion, NZEF. Died 14 April 1918. Age 31. Son of Alfred Rutland Edwards and Harriett Edwards, of High St, Motueka. Messines Ridge (NZ) Memorial, Mesen, West-Vlaanderen, Belgium.

EGGLESTON, Corporal, WILLIAM DOBSON, 25993. 4th Battalion, 3rd NZ Rifle Brigade. Died 30 March 1918. Son of Mrs J.C. Eggleston, of 187 Daniell St, Newtown, Wellington. Grevillers (NZ) Memorial, Pas de Calais, France.

ELLIS, Private, JAMES, 63579. 2nd NZ Entrenching Battalion, NZEF. Died 27 April 1918. Son of Mr and Mrs George M. Ellis, of Islington, Christchurch. Cologne Southern Cemetery, Koln (Cologne), Nordrhein-Westfal, Germany. Grave or panel number: XI.B.21.

ELLISON, Private, JOHN, 38368. 1st Battalion, Auckland Regiment, NZEF. Died 26 March 1918. Age 35. Son of Elizabeth Ellison, of Whitstone House, Woodburne, Northumberland, England, and the late William Ellison; husband of Florence J.E. Ellison, of Tauranga. Born at Morpeth, England. Grevilliers (NZ) Memorial, Pas de Calais, France.

ENGELBRECHT, Corporal, JOHN, 15886. 3rd Battalion, 3rd NZ Rifle Brigade. Died 29 March 1918. Age 23. Son of John David and Ellen Jane Engelbrecht, of Waimate. Grevillers (NZ) Memorial, Pas de Calais, France.

ERICKSEN, Lance Corporal, ERIC AXEL CARL JOHANES, 30191. 3rd Battalion, Otago Regiment, NZEF. Died 31 March 1918. Age 24. Son of Diderick and Holga Ericksen, of Napier; formerly of Denmark. Haringhe (Bandaghem) Military Cemetery, Poperinge, West-Vlaanderen, Belgium. Grave or panel number: II.A.18.

ERLANDSSON, Private, FRANK GUSTAVE, 45169. 2nd Battalion, Otago Regiment, NZEF. Died 3 April 1918. Age 22. Son of Peter and Cecilia J. Erlandsson, of Clinton, Otago. Doullens Communal Cemetery Extension No. 1, Somme, France. Grave or panel number: VI.E.2.

ERNEST, Private, DAVID, 52398. 2nd Battalion, Wellington Regiment, NZEF. Died 3 April 1918. Age 27. Son of Thomas and Anne Ernest, of 48 Gillies Ave, Epsom, Auckland. Born at Whakatane. Grevilliers (NZ) Memorial, Pas de Calais, France.

EVANS, Rifleman, THOMAS HARRY, 32835. 4th Battalion, 3rd NZ Rifle Brigade. Died 30 March 1918. Euston Road Cemetery, Colincamps, Somme, France. Grave or panel number: Special Memorial A.2.

EWEN, Lance Corporal, GEORGE TAYLOR, 22960. 3rd Battalion, 3rd NZ Rifle Brigade. Died 7 April 1918. Grevillers (NZ) Memorial, Pas de Calais, France.

FABLING, Rifleman, JOHN, 251176. 'B' Company, 3rd Battalion, NZ Rifle Brigade. Died 5 April 1918. Age 23. Son of Henry and Catherine Fabling, of 30 Duncan Tce, Kilbirnie, Wellington. Gezaincourt Communal Cemetery Extension, Somme, France. Grave or panel number: II.J.24.

FABRIN, Private, PETER HANS JORGEN, 51157. 1st Battalion, Canterbury Regiment, NZEF. Died 27 April 1918. Age 23. Son of Hans P. H. and Maren J. Fabrin, of South Norsewood, Napier. Native of Bunnythorpe. Colincamps, Communal Cemetery, Somme, France.

FAIRLIE, Corporal, GODFREY ALEXANDER, 16/982. NZ Maori (Pioneer) Battalion. Died 5 April 1918. Age 20. Son of Herbert and Bessie Fairlie, of

Tokomaru Bay, New Zealand. Bertrancourt Military Cemetery, Somme, France. Grave or panel number: 2.B.5.

FAIRWEATHER, Private, WILLIAM FREDERICK, 48630. 2nd Battalion, Auckland Regiment, NZEF. Died 28 March 1918. Son of Mrs Margaret Fairweather, of Gladstone Rd, Mt Albert, Auckland. Grevilliers (NZ) Memorial, Pas de Calais, France.

FARRA, Private, EDWARD ST CLAIR, 32644. 3rd Battalion, Otago Regiment, NZEF. Died 2 April 1918. Age 32. Son of James Fawcett Farra and Mary Torrie Farra, of Oamaru. Born at Dunedin. Lijssenthoek Military Cemetery, Poperinge, West-Vlaanderen, Belgium. Grave or panel number: XXVI.E.11A.

FARRINGTON, Lance Corporal, MARTIN JOHN, 91442. Otago Mounted Rifles, NZEF. Died 26 April 1918. Son of Mr and Mrs Martin Parrington, of 17 Hatton St, Timaru. Buttes New British Cemetery (NZ) Memorial, Polygon Wood, Zonnebeke, West-Vlaanderen, Belgium.

FAUL, Private, MICHAEL JOSEPH, 59883. 2nd Battalion, Canterbury Regiment, NZEF. Died 27 March 1918. Son of M.J. and Theresa Faul, of Wellington. Grevilliers (NZ) Memorial, Pas de Calais, France.

FEATHER, Private, WILLIAM HENRY, 55462. 1st Battalion, Canterbury Regiment, NZEF. Died 27 March 1918. Age 32. Husband of Frances Eunice Feather, of High St, Mosgiel. Born at North Loburn, Christchurch. Grevilliers (NZ) Memorial, Pas de Calais, France.

FEEK, Private, GORDON STANLEY, 29381. 1st Battalion, Wellington Regiment, NZEF. Died 30 March 1918. Son of Mrs S.R. Feek, of 11 Edgeware Rd, Palmerston North. Euston Road Cemetery, Colincamps, Somme, France. Grave or panel number: II.E.9.

FEIERABEND, Private, PERCY HAROLD, 63847. 2nd Battalion, Auckland Regiment, NZEF. Died 13 April 1918. Hédauville Communal Cemetery Extension, Somme, France. Grave or panel number: H.25.

FENTON, Private, JOHN GILMORE, 52400. 2nd Battalion, Auckland Regiment, NZEF. Died 27 March 1918. Son of Mrs A. Fenton, of Rangiuru, Te Puke, and the late James Henry Fenton. Grevilliers (NZ) Memorial, Pas de Calais, France.

FIFIELD, Rifleman, EDWARD, 53768. 1st Battalion, 3rd NZ Rifle Brigade. Died 14 April 1918. Age 21. Son of William and Mary Fifield, of 77 Arthur St, Blenheim. Native of England. Knightsbridge Cemetery, Mesnil-Martinsart, Somme, France. Grave or panel number: C.37.

FISHER, Private, CHARLES FORBES, 62802. 1st Battalion, Canterbury Regiment, NZEF. Died 5 April 1918. Age 30. Son of the Rev. David K. and Mary Fisher, of The Manse, Lumsden. Born in Shetland Islands. Grevilliers (NZ) Memorial, Pas de Calais, France.

FISHER, Private, ORR, 251624. NZ Cyclist Battalion. Died 25 April 1918.

Brother of Mrs Jane McEwan, of 14 Victoria St, Timaru. Buttes New British Cemetery (NZ) Memorial, Polygon Wood, Zonnebeke, West-Vlaanderen, Belgium.

FITZELL, Private, ROBERT THOMAS, 47871. 2nd Battalion, Wellington Regiment, NZEF. Died 14 April 1918. Sucrerie Military Cemetery, Colincamps, Somme, France. Grave or panel number: I.J.46.

FITZGERALD, Rifleman, EDWARD, 53168. 4th Battalion, 3rd NZ Rifle Brigade. Died 30 March 1918. Age 30. Son of Edward and Catherine Fitzgerald, of 8 New St, Musselburgh, Dunedin; husband of Hyacinth Fitzgerald, of Dunedin. Etaples Military Cemetery, Pas de Calais, France. Grave or panel number: XXXIII.B.14.

FITZGIBBON, Private, EDWARD, 55467. 2nd Battalion, Canterbury Regiment, NZEF. Died 5 April 1918. Son of Mr and Mrs M. Fitzgibbon, of Rangiora. Serre Road Cemetery No. 1, Pas de Calais, France. Grave or panel number: II.B.6.

FITZPATRICK, Private, MICHAEL BERNARD, 39468. 1st Battalion, Canterbury Regiment, NZEF. Died 18 April 1918. Age 33. Son of William and Margaret Fitzpatrick, of Brunnerton, New Zealand. Sucrerie Military Cemetery, Colincamps, Somme, France. Grave or panel number: IV.E.2.

FLEMING, Lance Corporal, JOHN FURNESS, 12167. 2nd Battalion, 3rd NZ Rifle Brigade. Died 6 April 1918. Age 24. Son of Alexander and A.W. Fleming, of Kokatahi, New Zealand. Doullens Communal Cemetery Extension No. 1, Somme, France. Grave or panel number: VI.D.51.

FLETCHER, Private, HAROLD JOSEPH, 30194. 2nd NZ Entrenching Battalion, NZEF. Died 14 April 1918. Son of Mr and Mrs Joseph Fletcher, of Onga Onga, Waipawa. Messines Ridge (NZ) Memorial, Mesen, West-Vlaanderen, Belgium.

FOGARTY, Private, JOHN FRANCIS, 34572. NZ Machine Gun Battalion. Died 5 April 1918. Son of Mr and Mrs J. Fogarty, of Waimate. Ancre British Cemetery, Beaumont-Hamel, Somme, France. Grave or panel number II.D.50.

FOLEY, Sapper, WILLIAM, 28452. NZ Engineers. Died 6 April 1918. Age 28. Only son of Maurice and Brigid Foley, of Redwood St, Blenheim. Mailly Wood Cemetery, Somme, France. Grave or panel number: II.H.2.

FORBES, Sergeant, WILLIAM ROLAND, 25285. 2nd Battalion, Auckland Regiment, NZEF. Died 4 April 1918. Age 34. Son of Edward James and Mary Forbes, of Towai, New Zealand. Etaples Military Cemetery, Pas de Calais, France. Grave or panel number: XXXIII.D.20.

FORREST, Private, ERNEST ALBERT, 60098. 2nd Battalion, Auckland Regiment, NZEF. Died 27 March 1918. Husband of Addilet Forrest, of Auckland. Grevilliers (NZ) Memorial, Pas de Calais, France.

FOSTER, Private, BERTIE, 14090. 2nd Battalion, Canterbury Regiment, NZEF. Died 19 April 1918. Meteren Military Cemetery, Nord, France. Grave or panel number: IV.D.645.

FOTHERGILL, Private, FREDERICK JAMES, 38681. 'E' Company, 1st Battalion, Auckland Regiment, NZEF. Died 27 March 1918. Age 21. Son of Sarah Fothergill, of Otahuhu, Auckland, and the late William Fothergill. Euston Road Cemetery, Colincamps, Somme, France. Grave or panel number: Special Memorial B.13.

FOWLER, Private, WILLIAM RICHARD, 52405. 'E' (Ruahine) Company, 2nd Battalion, Wellington Regiment, NZEF. Died 5 April 1918. Age 40. Son of John and Jane Fowler, of Bunnythorpe, Wellington. Grevillers (NZ) Memorial, Pas de Calais, France.

FOX, Rifleman, BENJAMIN, 53171. 4th Battalion, 3rd NZ Rifle Brigade. Died 5 April 1918. Son of Mr and Mrs G.F. Fox, of Fortrose, Southland. Euston Road Cemetery, Colincamps, Somme, France. Grave or panel number: II.S.9.

FOX, Private, JAMES, 25504. 1st Battalion, Wellington Regiment, NZEF. Died 11 April 1918. Age 21. Son of Bernard and Christina Fox, of 14 Udy St, Petone, Wellington. Euston Road Cemetery, Colincamps, Somme, France. Grave or panel number: III.N.10.

FRANCE, Private, HERBERT, 42316. 1st Battalion, Auckland Regiment, NZEF. Died 26 March 1918. Son of Mr and Mrs Thomas France, of Crescent Rd, Birkenhead, Auckland. Grevillers (NZ) Memorial, Pas de Calais, France.

FRANCIS, Private, FRANK, 8/1984. 1st Battalion, Otago Regiment, NZEF. Died 13 April 1918. Age 30. Son of Francis James and Kate Francis, of Folkestone, England. Etaples Military Cemetery, Pas de Calais, France. Grave or panel number: XXIX.B.8.

FRANKE, Corporal, ALFRED, 12375. 2nd Battalion, Auckland Regiment, NZEF. Died 30 March 1918. Son of Mr and Mrs W. Franke, of Turakina Valley, Wanganui. Euston Road Cemetery, Colincamps, Somme, France. Grave or panel number: IV.B.4.

FRANKHAM, Rifleman, WALTER ETHELBERT, 52185. 2nd Battalion, 3rd NZ Rifle Brigade. Died 4 April 1918. Age 21. Son of C.H. and M. Frankham, of 199 Jervois Rd, Auckland. Wimereux Communal Cemetery, Pas de Calais, France. Grave or panel number: X.A.4A.

FRYER, Company Quartermaster Sergeant, WILLIAM, 25844. No. 2 NZ Entrenching Battalion, NZEF. Died 14 April 1918. Husband of Mrs F. A. Fryer, of Grey and Childers Rd, Gisborne. Bailleul Communal Cemetery Extension (Nord), Nord, France. Grave or panel number: III.G.62.

FULTON, Brigadier General, HARRY TOWNSEND, 23/1, CMG, DSO, Croix de Guerre. NZ Rifle Brigade. Died 29 March 1918. Age 49. Son of Lieutenant General John Fulton and Ellen Fulton, of India. Doullens Communal Cemetery Extension No. 1, Somme, France. Grave or panel number: 1915. VI.A.4.

FULTON, Private, SAMUEL, 49079. 2nd Battalion, Auckland Regiment, NZEF. Died 29 March 1918. Age 34. Son of Samuel and the late Jane Fulton, of Auckland. Doullens Communal Cemetery Extension No. 1, Somme, France. Grave or panel number: V.B.4.

FUNKE, Corporal, HAROLD HENRY, 12/4529. 2nd Battalion, Wellington Regiment, NZEF. Died 27 March 1918. Son of Mr H.F. and Mrs M. Funke, of 27 Thackeray St, Napier. Euston Road Cemetery, Colincamps, Somme, France. Grave or panel number: II.D.10.

FYFE, Private, JACOB, 45088. 2nd Battalion, Otago Regiment, NZEF. Died 9 April 1918. Son of Mr and Mrs J. Fyfe, of Pine Cottage, North Balclutha. Knightsbridge Cemetery, Mesnil-Martinsart, Somme, France. Grave or panel number: A.2.

GADD, Private, HERBERT, 31988. No. 3 Company, 1st Battalion, Auckland Regiment, NZEF. Died 27 March 1918. Age 21. Son of Herbert and Annie Gadd, of Te Aroha St, Claudelands, Hamilton. Native of Blackheath, Birmingham, England. Euston Road Cemetery, Colincamps, Somme, France. Grave or panel number: Special Memorial B.14.

GAFFANEY, Sergeant, PETER MICHAEL, 24/431, MM. 2nd Battalion, NZ Rifle Brigade Died 5 April 1918. Age 24. Son of Francis and Katherine Gaffaney, of Dunedin. Louvencourt Military Cemetery, Somme, France. Grave or panel number: 1.D.21.

GARMONSWAY, Private, HAROLD GORDON, 56589. 2nd Battalion, Auckland Regiment, NZEF. Died 27 March 1918. Son of Mr and Mrs T. Garmonsway, of Auckland. Grevilliers (NZ) Memorial, Pas de Calais, France.

GARRICK, Rifleman, JAMES, 49239. 2nd Battalion, 3rd NZ Rifle Brigade. Died 31 March 1918. Age 24. Son of Margaret Garrick, of Point Rd, Bluff, and the late Lawrence Garrick. Grevillers (NZ) Memorial, Pas de Calais, France.

GAYLOR, Rifleman, HENRY CHARLES DOUGLAS, 41188. 'H' Company, 1st Battalion, 3rd NZ Rifle Brigade. Died 27 March 1918. Age 21. Son of Henry C. and Janet A. Gaylor, of Woodstock. Auchonvillers Military Cemetery, Somme, France. Grave or panel number: II.L.38.

GEAR, Private, JAMES HENRY NICHOLSON, 53581. 1st Battalion, Otago Regiment, NZEF. Died 5 April 1918. Husband of Martha Gear, of Dunedin. Grevillers (NZ) Memorial, Pas de Calais, France.

GEISOW, Private, ROBERT WILLIAM, 34852. 3rd Battalion, Otago Regiment, NZEF. Died 19 April 1918. Age 37. Son of the late F.W.F. Geisow; brother of Miss I.G. Geisow, of Queenstown. Etaples Military Cemetery, Pas de Calais, France. Grave or panel number: XXIX.G.10A.

GEORGE, Private, BRET ROWLAND, 46332 1st Battalion, Auckland Regiment, NZEF. Died 26 March 1918. Age 30. Son of John and Lillie George, of Otway Estate, Waihou, Te Aroha, Piako. Mailly Wood Cemetery, Somme, France. Grave or panel number: I.N.8.

GEORGE, Lance Corporal, ERNEST JOHN, 22009. NZ Machine Gun Battalion. Died 27 March 1918. Age 21. Son of Herbert Edward and Elizabeth George, of Dunedin. Euston Road Cemetery, Colincamps, Somme, France. Grave or panel number V.D.8.

GIBB, Private, ROBERT, 32659. 1st Battalion, Otago Regiment, NZEF. Died 5 April 1918. Age 21. Son of Robert and Jane Gibb, of Invercargill, Southland. Mailly Wood Cemetery, Somme, France. Grave or panel number: I.P.I0.

GIBBS, Rifleman, JAMES ERNEST, 53773. 1st Battalion, 3rd NZ Rifle Brigade. Died 6 April 1918. Son of Mr and Mrs A. Gibbs, of Wakefield, Nelson. Euston Road Cemetery, Colincamps, Somme, France. Grave or panel number: III.E.7.

GIFFORD, Private, ARTHUR HAROLD, 46182. 1st Battalion, Canterbury Regiment, NZEF. Died 23 April 1918. Age 34. Son of William G. and Esther E. Gifford, of Spring Creek, Marlborough. Colincamps Communal Cemetery, Somme, France.

GILHAM, Private, WILLIAM CLAUDE, 60931. 2nd Battalion, Canterbury Regiment, NZEF. Died 29 March 1918. Age 28. Son of William and Louisa Gilham, of Allington St, Methven. A.I.F. Burial Ground, Flers, Somme, France. Grave or panel number: VI.G.I.

GILL, Private, BENJAMIN, 48634. 2nd Battalion, Auckland Regiment, NZEF. Died 30 March 1918. Son of Mrs J. Gill, of 64 Esplanade Rd, Mt Eden, Auckland. Grevilliers (NZ) Memorial, Pas de Calais, France.

GILL, Private, FREDERICK BENJAMIN, 29244. 2nd Battalion, Canterbury Regiment, NZEF. Died 14 April 1918. Age 28. Son of Alfred and Mary Ann Ainelia Gill, of Nelson. Hédauville Communal Cemetery Extension, Somme, France. Grave or panel number: H.26.

GILL, Rifleman, HARRY, 38153. 3rd Battalion, 3rd NZ Rifle Brigade. Died 5 April 1918. Son of John Henry and Sarah May Gill, of Oamaru. Euston Road Cemetery, Colincamps, Somme, France. Grave or panel number: IV.L.7.

GILMOUR, Sergeant, JOHN KENNETH MURRAY, 2/312. NZ Field Artillery. Died 24 April 1918. Age 22. Son of Robert T. and Mary Agnes Gilmour, of Victoria St, Hamilton. Bertrancourt Military Cemetery, Somme, France. Grave or panel number: 2.B.1.

GIRLING-BUTCHER, Lieutenant, WALTER LANCELOT, 8/4064. 2nd Battalion, Otago Regiment, NZEF. Died 31 March 1918. Son of Mr and Mrs G. Girling-Butcher, of Tinakori Rd, Wellington. Knightsbridge Cemetery, Mesnil-Martinsart, Somme, France. Grave or panel number: C.40.

GLENDINNING, Private, JOHN, 28460. 2nd Battalion, Wellington Regiment, NZEF. Died 27 March 1918. Age 32. Son of the late Joseph and Isabella Glendinning, of Waikari, North Canterbury. Euston Road Cemetery, Colincamps, Somme, France. Grave or panel number: II.D.8.

GODFREY, Rifleman, EDWARD FRANCIS, 25851. 1st Battalion, 3rd NZ

Rifle Brigade. Died 5 April 1918. Age 23. Son of Arthur and Kate Godfrey, of Papanui, Christchurch. Born at Hawera. Euston Road Cemetery, Colincamps, Somme, France. Grave or panel number: V.D.1.

GODLEY, Lance Corporal, WILLIAM PERCIVAL, 46335. 3rd Battalion, Auckland Regiment, NZEF. Died 3 April 1918. Age 31. Son of Robert John and Lena Godley, of Brighton, England. Longuenesse (St Omer) Souvenir Cemetery, Pas de Calais, France. Grave or panel number: V.A.2.

GOLD, Private, ALBERT, 25/1126. NZ Cyclist Battalion. Died 25 April 1918. Age 23. Son of James Gold, of 23 Selbourne St, Grey Lynn, Auckland. Buttes New British Cemetery (NZ) Memorial, Polygon Wood, Zonnebeke, West-Vlaanderen, Belgium.

GOLDSMITH, Rifleman, JOHN RICHARD, 54349. 2nd Battalion, 3rd NZ Rifle Brigade. Died 5 April 1918. Age 24. Son of Mr and Mrs J. Goldsmith, of Sussex St, Masterton. Euston Road Cemetery, Colincamps, Somme, France. Grave or panel number: III.A.9.

GOODWIN, Rifleman, REGINALD CHARLES, 54741. 1st Battalion, 3rd NZ Rifle Brigade. Died 5 April 1918. Age 20. Son of Robert and Sarah Jane Goodwin, of Lorne St, Morrinsville. Grevillers (NZ) Memorial, Pas de Calais, France.

GORDON, Sergeant, HERBERT THOMAS, 26/795. 'H' Company, 4th Battalion, 3rd NZ Rifle Brigade. Died 29 March 1918. Age 21. Son of William Shannon Gordon and Wilhelmina Gordon, of Ohinemutu, Rotorua. Euston Road Cemetery, Colincamps, Somme, France. Grave or panel number: II.A.8.

GOULSTONE, Private, JOHN WILLIAM, 48493. 17th Ruahine Company, 1st Battalion, Wellington Regiment, NZEF. Died 30 March 1918. Age 23. Son of William F. and Rose L. Goulstone, of Symonds St, Onehunga, Auckland. Euston Road Cemetery, Colincamps, Somme, France. Grave or panel number: III.C.2.

GRAHAM, Rifleman, FRANCIS JOSEPH, 45619. 1st Battalion, 3rd NZ Rifle Brigade. Died 5 April 1918. Son of Michael and Maria Graham, of Waipiata, Central Otago. Euston Road Cemetery, Colincamps, Somme, France. Grave or panel number: III.E.5.

GRAHAM, Lance Corporal, GEORGE HENNING, 18650. 1st Battalion, 3rd NZ Rifle Brigade. Died 6 April 1918. Son of Mr J. and Mrs J.G. Graham, of Long Acre, Okoia, Wanganui. Euston Road Cemetery, Colincamps, Somme, France. Grave or panel number: III.E.3.

GRAHAM, Rifleman, HUGH, 53350. 1st Battalion, 3rd NZ Rifle Brigade. Died 5 April 1918. Age 35. Son of Mr and Mrs Hugh Graham, of Achahoish, Ardrishaig, Argyllshire, Scotland. Euston Road Cemetery, Colincamps, Somme, France. Grave or panel number: I.H.6.

GRANT, Private ARNOLD ERIC, 31838. 9th (Hawkes Bay) Company, 2nd Battalion, Wellington Regiment, NZEF. Died 27 March 1918. Age 22. Son of Annie Elizabeth and the late James Grant, of 124 Vivian St, New Plymouth.

Euston Road Cemetery, Colincamps, Somme, France. Grave or panel number: II.D.2.

GRANT, Private, DAVID ALBERT, 27498. 2nd Battalion, Otago Regiment, NZEF. Died 7 April 1918. Age 29. Son of David Elder Grant and Margaret Grant, of Outram, Dunedin. Englebelmer Communal Cemetery Extension, Somme, France. Grave or panel number: F.24.

GRAY, Private, ERIC ANDREW, 15527. 1st Battalion, Canterbury Regiment, NZEF. Died 27 March 1918. Age 22. Son of Andrew and Emily Ann Gray. Martinsart British Cemetery, Somme, France. Grave or panel number: I.H.38.

GRAY, Lance Corporal, GEORGE PATRICK, 31628. 1st Battalion, Auckland Regiment, NZEF. Died 26 March 1918. Grevillers (NZ) Memorial, Pas de Calais, France.

GRAY, Sergeant, WILLIAM ALEXANDER, IO/2429, MM. 1st Battalion, Wellington Regiment, NZEF. Died 1 April 1918. Age 21. Son of Clare Makin, of 78 Tasman St, Wellington. Native of Sydney, New South Wales. Also served at Gallipoli. Sucrerie Military Cemetery, Colincamps, Somme, France. Grave or panel number: I.J.58.

GREEN, Captain, DONALD BENJAMIN, 3/324. 2nd Battalion, Canterbury Regiment, NZEF. Died 5 April 1918. Age 31. Son of Henry and Mary M. Green, of 463 Worcester St, Christchurch, New Zealand. Born at Lyttelton. Also served at Gallipoli and in Egypt. Serre Road Cemetery No. 1, Pas de Calais, France. Grave or panel number: II.B.1.

GREEN, Rifleman, EDWARD, 54499. 1st Battalion, 3rd NZ Rifle Brigade. Died 29 March 1918. Age 27. Son of Edward and Johannah Green, of Ruatangata, Wangaehu, New Zealand. Etaples Military Cemetery, Pas de Calais, France. Grave or panel number: XXXIII.A.20.

GREEN, Private, FRANCIS ALFRED, 47589. 2nd NZ Entrenching Battalion, NZEF. Died 19 April 1918. Age 25. Son of Francis Alfred and Margaret Green, of Ellerslie, Auckland. Meteren Military Cemetery, Nord, France. Grave or panel number: I.E.140.

GREENWOOD, Private, JOSEPH ELLIOT, 48494. Ruahine Company, 1st Battalion, Wellington Regiment, NZEF. Died 30 March 1918. Age 24. Son of Joseph and Anne Irving Greenwood, of Great North Rd, Henderson, Auckland. Born at Leigh, Auckland. Grevillers (NZ) Memorial, Pas de Calais, France.

GREIG, Lance Corporal, ARTHUR ERNEST, 46018. 2nd NZ Entrenching Battalion, NZEF. Died 13 April 1918. Son of Mr and Mrs William Greig, of Ngaere, Taranaki. Messines Ridge (NZ) Memorial, Mesen, West-Vlaanderen, Belgium.

GRIEBEL, Private, GEORGE JULIUS, 45002. 1st Battalion, Canterbury Regiment, NZEF. Died 5 April 1918. Age 21. Son of Mrs P.E. Griebel, of Kaiapoi, Christchurch. Born at Ohoka. Grevilliers (NZ) Memorial, Pas de Calais, France.

GROVES, Private, SIDNEY THOMAS JAMES, 52415. 1st Battalion, Auckland Regiment, NZEF. Died 26 March 1918. Age 35. Son of John and Elizabeth Groves, of Auckland. Mailly-Maillet Communal Cemetery Extension, Somme, France. Grave or panel number: D.50.

GRUBB, Sergeant, WILLIAM JOHN, 2/1348, MM. NZ Field Artillery. Died 18 April 1918. Age 32. Son of David and Carolina Grubb, of Lyttelton. Also served at Gallipoli. Lijssenthoek Military Cemetery, Poperinge, West-Vlaanderen, Belgium. Grave or panel number: XXVII.G.18.

GUBBINS, Second Lieutenant, LAUNCELOT RUSSELL, 2/746. NZ Field Artillery. Died 23 April 1918. Age 36. Son of John Russell Gubbins and Mary Margaret Gubbins (née Dickson), of 22 Carlton Hill, St John's Wood, London, England. Born at Lima, Peru, South America. Lijssenthoek Military Cemetery, Poperinge, West-Vlaanderen, Belgium. Grave or panel number: XXVI.GG.8.

GUEST, Lance Corporal, JOHN, 15714. 2nd Battalion, Wellington Regiment, NZEF. Died 18 April 1918. Age 26. Son of the late John and Mary Guest, of Hamilton. Doullens Communal Cemetery Extension No. 1, Somme, France. Grave or panel number: V.A.16.

GUILFORD, Rifleman, WALTER, 21820. 1st Battalion, 3rd NZ Rifle Brigade. Died 27 March 1918. Age 36. Son of William and Annie Guilford, of Geraldine; husband of Jean H. Guilford, of Ophir, Dunedin. Auchonvillers Military Cemetery, Somme, France. Grave or panel number: II.L.33.

GURR, Corporal, FRANK, 44638. 3rd Battalion, 3rd NZ Rifle Brigade. Died 29 March 1918. Son of Mrs E. Gurr, of 17 Cheltenham Rd, Devonport, Auckland. Euston Road Cemetery, Colincamps, Somme, France. Grave or panel number: V.I.9.

GUTHRIE, Private, LEONARD, 6/3723. 2nd Battalion, Canterbury Regiment, NZEF. Died 27 March 1918. Age 31. Son of Jane Guthrie, of Moorehouse Ave, Christchurch, and the late John Guthrie. Grevilliers (NZ) Memorial, Pas de Calais, France.

GUY, Private, WALTER ALEXANDER COCHRANE, 25996. 1st Battalion, Canterbury Regiment, NZEF. Died 27 March 1918. Son of Mr and Mrs John A. Guy, of Ngatimote, Nelson. Grevilliers (NZ) Memorial, Pas de Calais, France.

GWYNNE, Private, JAMES HERBERT, 63863. 1st Battalion, Auckland Regiment, NZEF. Died 4 April 1918. Age 24. Son of George and Helen Gwynne, of Highland Rd, Mt Albert, Auckland. Mailly-Maillet Communal Cemetery Extension, Somme, France. Grave or panel number: D.51.

HAINES, Sergeant, HENRY FRANCIS, 12/2313. Machine Gun Battalion, NZ Machine Gun Corps. Died 27 March 1918. Son of Mr and Mrs W. Haines, of 33 Karaka St, Newton, Auckland. Grevillers (NZ) Memorial Cemetery, Pas de Calais, France.

HAIR, Lieutenant, HAROLD GILBERT, 26/1549. 1st Battalion, Auckland Regiment, NZEF. Died 26 March 1918. Age 31. Son of James and Mary Clarissa Hair, of 'Culwulla', Mount St, Nelson. Mailly-Maillet Communal Cemetery Extension, Somme, France. Grave or panel number: D.49.

HALL, Corporal, WILLIAM GORDON, 26743. 14th Company, 1st Battalion, Otago Regiment, NZEF. Died 20 April 1918. Age 24. Son of Isaac and Lucy Hall, of 25 Dunn St, Spreydon, Christchurch. Native of Lancashire, England. Euston Road Cemetery, Colincamps, Somme, France. Grave or panel number: I.H.2.

HALLAM, Lance Sergeant, HERBERT JOHN, 30205. 3rd Battalion, Canterbury Regiment, NZEF. Died 18 April 1918. Age 21. Son of David and Delilah Hallam. Meteren Military Cemetery, Nord, France. Grave or panel number: I.E.139.

HALLIDAY, Private, JOHN, 27280. 1st Battalion, Auckland Regiment, NZEF. Died 27 March 1918. Son of Mr and Mrs John Halliday, of Pakaraka, Auckland. Grevilliers (NZ) Memorial, Pas de Calais, France.

HALLY, Lieutenant, COLIN, 23935, MC. NZ Machine Gun Battalion. Died 6 April 1918. Son of Mr and Mrs James Hally, of Cambridge, New Zealand. Euston Road Cemetery, Colincamps, Somme, France. Grave or panel number: IV.G.3.

HAMILTON, Private, ALBERT STANLEY, II/1803. 9th Company, 2nd Battalion, Wellington Regiment, NZEF. Died 3 April 1918. Age 22. Son of Robert and Susannah Hamilton, of Reservoi, Oamaru. Born at Oamaru. Doullens Communal Cemetery Extension No. 1, Somme, France. Grave or panel number: VI.E.18.

HAMILTON, Private, ARCHIBALD FERGUSON, 52201. 1st Battalion, Auckland Regiment, NZEF. Died 26 March 1918. Age 27. Son of James and Euphemia Hamilton, of Tuakau; husband of Helen M.A. Hamilton, of Tuakau, Auckland. Born in Westport. Grevilliers (NZ) Memorial, Pas de Calais, France.

HAMILTON, Private, NOEL, 39527. 2nd Battalion, Wellington Regiment, NZEF. Died 27 March 1918. Son of Mr W.B. and Mrs C.A. Hamilton, of Ruataniwha, Waipawa. Euston Road Cemetery, Colincamps, Somme, France. Grave or panel number: III.A.3.

HAMMOND, Private, LEWIS BENJAMIN, 12106. 1st Battalion, Canterbury Regiment, NZEF. Died 5 April 1918. Age 25. Son of Walter Benjamin and Catherine Hammond, of Takamatua, Banks Peninsula. Knightsbridge Cemetery, Mesnil-Martinsart, Somme, France. Grave or panel number: A.12.

HANDLEY, Private, THOMAS MICHAEL, 52419. 2nd Battalion, Wellington Regiment, NZEF. Died 3 April 1918. Age 23. Son of Michael and Mary Handley of Wharepoa, Thames. Grevilliers (NZ) Memorial, Pas de Calais, France.

HANSEN, Private, IVAN ROY, 31125. 1st Battalion, Auckland Regiment, NZEF. Died 26 March 1918. Age 22. Son of Jim and Laura Hansen. Born at

Tepuna, Bay of Islands. Mailly Wood Cemetery, Somme, France. Grave or panel number: I.N.I5.

HARNEY, Rifleman, DANIEL JOSEPH, 21833. 1st Battalion, 3rd NZ Rifle Brigade. Died 5 April 1918. Son of Mr and Mrs R. Harney, of Southbridge, Canterbury. Euston Road Cemetery, Colincamps, Somme, France. Grave or panel number: III.E.2.

HARPER, Sergeant, LAWRENCE ALFRED, 26/1188. 4th Battalion, 3rd NZ Rifle Brigade. Died 5 April 1918. Euston Road Cemetery, Colincamps, Somme, France. Grave or panel number: III.C.9.

HARPER, Second Lieutenant, NORMAN ROBERT, 6/645, MC. 3rd Battalion, Canterbury Regiment, NZEF. Died 15 April 1918. Age 30. Son of Benjamin Harper, of Dunedin; husband of L.Z. Harper, of New Plymouth. Haringhe (Bandaghem) Military Cemetery, Poperinge, West-Vlaanderen, Belgium. Grave or panel number: II.C12.

HARRIS, Rifleman, HUBERT RAYMOND, 22978. 1st Battalion, 3rd NZ Rifle Brigade. Died 5 April 1918. Son of Louisa Harris, of Waiti Rd, Hawera. Euston Road Cemetery, Colincamps, Somme, France. Grave or panel number: IV.D.5.

HARRIS, Private, RAYMOND EDWARD, 10827. NZ Cyclist Battalion. Died 18 April 1918. Age 21. Son of Edward and Pleasant Harris, of 25 Durham St, Sydenham, Christchurch. Lijssenthoek Military Cemetery, Poperinge, West-Vlaanderen, Belgium. Grave or panel number: XXVII.G.6A.

HARRIS, Captain, ROY, 3/3071. NZ Medical Corps. Died 5 April 1918. Son of Mr and Mrs T.A. Harris, of Raetihi. Knightsbridge Cemetery, Mesnil-Martinsart, Somme, France. Grave or panel number: A.11.

HARTLAND, Private, JOHN LESLIE, 56592. 2nd Battalion, Auckland Regiment, NZEF. Died 31 March 1918. Age 28. Son of John Ford Hartland and Francis H.S. Hartland, of Remuera, Auckland. Gezaincourt Communal Cemetery Extension, Somme, France. Grave or panel number: II.H.18.

HARVEY, Private, JAMES, 63150. 2nd Battalion, Otago Regiment, NZEF. Died 3 April 1918. Age 36. Son of the late John Harvey. Doullens Communal Cemetery Extension No. 1, Somme, France. Grave or panel number: VI.E.11.

HASLETT, Private, GEORGE, 10/3900. 2nd Battalion, Wellington Regiment, NZEF. Died 27 March 1918. Son of Mr and Mrs George Haslett, of Junction Rd, Inglewood. Grevillers (NZ) Memorial, Pas de Calais, France.

HASTIE, Private, GEORGE, 37815. 1st Battalion, Otago Regiment, NZEF. Died 12 April 1918. Age 36. Son of James and Margaret Hastie, of Dunedin. Born in Scotland. Etaples Military Cemetery, Pas de Calais, France. Grave or panel number: XXIX.A.15A.

HATWELL, Private, FRANCIS ALOYSIUS LIGOUIRI, 4/132. 1st Battalion, Canterbury Regiment, NZEF. Died 24 April 1918. Age 24. Son of Joseph and Mary Ann Hatwell, of Gorge Rd, Woodville. Advance guard to Samoa, August

1914. Colincamps Communal Cemetery, Somme, France.

HAYCOCK, Rifleman, ARTHUR, 26/449. 4th Battalion, 3rd NZ Rifle Brigade. Died 5 April 1918. Age 26. Son of Mr and Mrs Haycock, of Feilding. Euston Road Cemetery, Colincamps, Somme, France. Grave or panel number: II.B.2.

HAYES, Rifleman, WILLIAM JAMES, 8/4347. 1st Battalion, 3rd NZ Rifle Brigade. Died 27 March 1918. Age 25. Son of William and Rebecca Hayes, of Ireland. Doullens Communal Cemetery Extension No. 1, Somme, France. Grave or panel number: V.A.51.

HAYHOE, Private, JAMES PARKER, 12/3888. 2nd Battalion, Auckland Regiment, NZEF. Died 30 March 1918. Age 44. Son of James Parker Hayhoe and Matilda Hayhoe, of Stanton, Suffolk, England. Euston Road Cemetery, Colincamps, Somme, France. Grave or panel number: IV.B.5.

HEANEY, Driver, ROBERT THOMAS, 2/1353. NZ Field Artillery. Died 18 April 1918. Age 29. Husband of Mrs G. K. Heaney, of Wellington. Lijssenthoek Military Cemetery, Poperinge, West-Vlaanderen, Belgium. Grave or panel number: XXVI.G.7.

HEATON, Rifleman, EDWARD DENYS HORNBY, 40148. 4th Battalion, 3rd NZ Rifle Brigade. Died 28 March 1918. Son of the late Mrs Helen Marianne Heaton, of Palmerston North. Grevillers (NZ) Memorial, Pas de Calais, France.

HEDLUND, Private, ANDREW KENNITH, 40564. 2nd Battalion, Auckland Regiment, NZEF. Died 30 March 1918. Age 22. Son of Mrs Helen Henrietta Hedlund, of 259 Khyber Pass, Newmarket, Auckland. Grevilliers (NZ) Memorial, Pas de Calais, France.

HEGAN, Rifleman, GEORGE WILLIAM THOMAS, 32332. 'G' Company, 2nd Battalion, 3rd NZ Rifle Brigade. Died 6 April 1918. Age 36. Son of Joseph and Catherine Hegan, of 38 Sherborne St, St Albans, Christchurch. Sucrerie Military Cemetery, Colincamps, Somme, France. Grave or panel number: I.I.3.

HENDERSON, Private, WILLIAM ALEXANDER, 48876. 2nd Battalion, Canterbury Regiment, NZEF. Died 5 April 1918. Age 25. Son of Thomas and Jane Henderson, of Scotland; husband of Myrtle J. Henderson, of Auckland. Auchonvillers Military Cemetery, Somme, France. Grave or panel number: II.A.17.

HENDLE, Sergeant, LEONARD HENRY, 2/49. 6th Battery, NZ Field Artillery. Died 10 April 1918. Age 22. Son of William and Eliza Hendle, of Pickering Tce, Kaiwarra; husband of Eliza Agnes Hendle, of 1 Pickering Tce, Kaiwarra, Wellington. Also served on Gallipoli and in Samoa. Strand Military Cemetery, Comines-Warneton, Hainaut, Belgium. Grave or panel number: IX.P.6.

HENRY, Private, JAMES WALTON, 42844. 2nd Battalion, Otago Regiment, NZEF. Died 2 April 1918. Age 22. Son of James and Barbara A. Henry, of Invercargill. Doullens Communal Cemetery Extension No. 1, Somme, France. Grave or panel number: VI.E.8.

HERBERT, Rifleman, CHARLES LEICESTER JAMES, 40749. 4th Battalion,

3rd NZ Rifle Brigade. Died 1 April 1918. Age 20. Son of Henry Frederick and Annie Herbert, of Linwood, Christchurch. Doullens Communal Cemetery Extension No. 1, Somme, France. Grave or panel number: VI.F.34.

HERRON, Private, JOHN, 23491. 1st Battalion, Otago Regiment, NZEF. Died 16 April 1918. Age 28. Son of James and Agnes Herron, of Southland. Meteren Military Cemetery, Nord, France. Grave or panel number: II.B.88.

HEWITT, Rifleman, ARCHIBALD FRANK, 39051. 'D' Company, 4th Battalion, 3rd NZ Rifle Brigade. Died 5 April 1918. Age 33. Son of Frank Hewitt, of 82 Church St, Gainsborough, England. Enlisted voluntarily. Grevillers (NZ) Memorial, Pas de Calais, France.

HICKINBOTTOM, Sergeant, BRUCE GLOVER, 11667. 1st Battalion, Canterbury Regiment, NZEF. Died 23 April 1918. Age 20. Son of William James and Martha Hickinbottom, of 168 Huxley St, Sydenham, Christchurch. Colincamps Communal Cemetery, Somme, France.

HIGGIE, Private, COLIN LESLIE, 51255. Wellington Regiment, NZEF. Died 2 April 1918. Age 21. Light Trench Mortar Bty. Son of Robert and Jane H. Higgie, of Wanganui. Wimereux Communal Cemetery, Pas de Calais, France. Grave or panel number: IX.D.9.

HIGGINS, Private, JAMES, 53012. 1st Battalion, Wellington Regiment, NZEF. Died 11 April 1918. Age 36. Son of the late John and B. Higgins. Born in County Derry, Ireland. Grevilliers (NZ) Memorial, Pas de Calais, France.

HILL, Private, ALEXANDER, 59898. 2nd Battalion, Wellington Regiment, NZEF. Died 14 April 1918. Son of Mrs C.C. Hill, of Main Rd, Howick, Auckland. Sucrerie Military Cemetery, Colincamps, Somme, France. Grave or panel number: I.J.45.

HILL, Private, GEORGE DOMINIC, 55494. NZ Entrenching Battalion, NZEF. Died 19 April 1918. Age 21. Haringhe (Bandaghem) Military Cemetery, Poperinge, West-Vlaanderen, Belgium. Grave or panel number: V.D.2.

HILL, Private, GEORGE JOHN, 53859. 2nd Battalion, NZ Entrenching Battalion, NZEF. Died 14 April 1918. Age 26. Son of the late William and Mary Jane Hill, of Dobson; husband of Annie Hill, of Dobson, Brunnerton, Greymouth. Messines Ridge (NZ) Memorial, Mesen, West-Vlaanderen, Belgium.

HILL, Private, JAMES MCCLINTOCK, 12546. 2nd Battalion, Auckland Regiment, NZEF. Died 30 March 1918. Son of Mr and Mrs J. Hill, of Arthur St West, Onehunga, Auckland. Euston Road Cemetery, Colincamps, Somme, France. Grave or panel number: III.C.6.

HILL, Private, THOMAS MOODY, 40316. No. 16 Waikato Company, 1st Battalion, Auckland Regiment, NZEF. Died 26 March 1918. Age 21. Son of the late John and Margaret Hill, of Tamahana St, Matamata. Born in Scotland. Grevilliers (NZ) Memorial, Pas de Calais, France.

HILLOCK, Private, THOMAS, 47331. 1st Battalion, Canterbury Regiment,

NZEF. Died 29 March 1918. Age 29. Son of Alexander Hillock, of Townhead, Kinghorn, Fifeshire. Doullens Communal Cemetery Extension No. 1, Somme, France. Grave or panel number: V.B.20.

HINCHCO, Private, ALFRED, 14261, MM. 1st Battalion, Auckland Regiment, NZEF. Died 27 March 1918. Age 22. Son of John and Rachael Hinchco, of 53 Esplanade Rd, Mt Eden, Auckland. Native of Huntly, Waikato. St Hilaire Cemetery, Frevent, Pas de Calais, France. Grave or panel number: V.B.10.

HINTZ, Rifleman, AMIL, 51842. 3rd Battalion, 3rd NZ Rifle Brigade. Died 6 April 1918. Age 38. Son of August and Emily Hintz, of Kopane, Palmerston North. Born in New Zealand. Grevillers (NZ) Memorial, Pas de Calais, France.

HODGSON, Sergeant, THOMAS CORLESS, 10749. NZ Cyclist Battalion. Died 23 April 1918. Age 23. Son of George Brown Hodgson and Annie Hodgson, of Capernuray, Carnforth, England. Emigrated to New Zealand, August 1913. Boulogne Eastern Cemetery, Pas de Calais, France. Grave or panel number: IX.A.12.

HODSON, Private, VICTOR EMANUEL, 5/29. NZ Cyclist Battalion. Died 17 April 1918. Son of Mr and Mrs Albert Edward Hodson, of 112 Church St, Palmerston North. Messines Ridge (NZ) Memorial, Mesen, West-Vlaanderen, Belgium.

HOGBEN, Private, HERBERT MCLACHLAN, 62313. 2nd Battalion, Canterbury Regiment, NZEF. Died 27 March 1918. Son of Emily Francis Hogben, of 205 Clyde St, Island Bay, Wellington, and the late George Hogben. Grevilliers (NZ) Memorial, Pas de Calais, France.

HOGG, Private, JOHN ANTHONY, 52425. 2nd Battalion, Wellington Regiment, NZEF. Died 14 April 1918. Son of Mr and Mrs Anthony Hogg, of Kauaeranga, Thames. Sucrerie Military Cemetery, Colincamps, Somme, France. Grave or panel number: I.J.47.

HOGG, Private, THOMAS, 30948. 2nd Battalion, Auckland Regiment, NZEF. Died 27 March 1918. Euston Road Cemetery, Colincamps, Somme, France. Grave or panel number: V.H.4.

HOLLAND, Rifleman, JOHN PATRICK, 24/447. 2nd Battalion, 3rd NZ Rifle Brigade. Died 29 March 1918. Age 30. Son of William and Mary Ann Holland, of 135 Leet St, Invercargill. Hédauville Communal Cemetery Extension, Somme, France. Grave or panel number: H.22.

HONEY, Private, WILLIAM REDMUND, 49543. 2nd Battalion, Canterbury Regiment, NZEF. Died 5 April 1918. Husband of G.A. Honey, of 48 Fitzgerald Ave, Christchurch. Serre Road Cemetery No. 1, Pas de Calais, France. Grave or panel number: II.B.8.

HOOPER, Private, GEORGE SEPTIMUS, 3/3046. 2nd Field Ambulance, NZ Medical Corps. Died 24 March 1918. Age 33. Son of Capt. C.W. and Agnes Hooper, of Liverpool, England. His brother Frank fell at Gallipoli. Boulogne Eastern Cemetery, Pas de Calais, France. Grave or panel number: VIII.I.165.

HOOPER, Private, REGINALD, 12/4536. 2nd Battalion, Auckland Regiment, NZEF. Died 27 March 1918. Age 22. Son of Frank Arthur and Ellen Hooper, of Tokomaru Bay. Euston Road Cemetery, Colincamps, Somme, France. Grave or panel number: V.H.5.

HORAN, Rifleman, JOHN, 26621. 3rd Battalion, 3rd NZ Rifle Brigade. Died 16 April 1918. Son of Mrs Jane Horan, of Hura St, Onehunga. Auckland. Grevillers (NZ) Memorial, Pas de Calais, France.

HORNE, Fitter, JOHN CHARLES, 13189. NZ Field Artillery. Died 20 April 1918. Age 23. Son of William Stanley and Lilian L. Horne, of 14 Waterview Rd, Stanley Bay, Auckland. Born in London, England. Haringhe (Bandaghem) Military Cemetery, Poperinge, West-Vlaanderen, Belgium. Grave or panel number: III.E.13.

HOTHERSALL, Private, EDWARD JAMES, 39660. 1st Battalion, Auckland Regiment, NZEF. Died 3 April 1918. Age 23. Son of Edward Gregory Hothersall and Elizabeth Hothersall, of Whitburne House, Garstang Rd, Preston, Lancs, England. Grevillers (NZ) Memorial, Pas de Calais, France.

HOWARD, Rifleman, JAMES MANN, 52610. 3rd Battalion, 3rd NZ Rifle Brigade. Died 21 April 1918. Englebelmer Communal Cemetery Extension, Somme, France. Grave or panel number: E.15.

HUDSON, Private, GEORGE HENRY, 41557. 2nd Battalion, Canterbury Regiment, NZEF. Died 28 March 1918. Age 23. Son of John and Emma Hudson, of Main Rd, Lower Hutt, Wellington. Gezaincourt Communal Cemetery Extension, Somme, France. Grave or panel number: I.H.7.

HUGHES, Second Lieutenant, LIONEL MURRAY, 44935. 3rd Battalion, 3rd NZ Rifle Brigade. Died 27 March 1918. Son of Barbara Hughes, of Bealey St, Hokitika. Euston Road Cemetery, Colincamps, Somme, France. Grave or panel number: V.D.4.

HUGHES, Rifleman, MATTHEW, 62573. 4th Battalion, 3rd NZ Rifle Brigade. Died 6 April 1918. Age 29. Son of James and Susan Hughes, of Ballybeg, Littleton, Thurles, County Tipperary, Ireland. Euston Road Cemetery, Colincamps, Somme, France. Grave or panel number: V.B.4.

HULLTEN, Rifleman, JOHN GUSTAVE, 21017. 4th Battalion, 3rd NZ Rifle Brigade. Died 30 March 1918. Son of Martin and Bertha Hullten, of Papatoetoe, Auckland. Grevillers (NZ) Memorial, Pas de Calais, France.

HUNT, Rifleman, ROBERT HERMAN WALTER THOMAS, 53020. 2nd Battalion, 3rd NZ Rifle Brigade. Died 5 April 1918. Euston Road Cemetery, Colincamps, Somme, France. Grave or panel number: III.A.8.

HUNTER, Private, ALBERT WILLIAM, 10837. NZ Cyclist Battalion. Died 17 April 1918. Age 38. Son of William and Susan Hunter, of 82 Antiqua St, Sydenham, Christchurch. Messines Ridge (NZ) Memorial, Mesen, West-Vlaanderen, Belgium.

HUNTER, Private, ANDREW, 38026. 2nd Battalion, Wellington Regiment,

NZEF. Died 16 April 1918. Age 36. Son of Peter and Ann Hunter, of Inglewood. Englebelmer Communal Cemetery Extension, Somme, France. Grave or panel number: F.6.

HUNTER, Private, DANIEL, 24016. 2nd Battalion, Auckland Regiment, NZEF. Died 30 March 1918. Husband of Susanna Mary Hunter, of Auckland. Grevilliers (NZ) Memorial, Pas de Calais, France.

HUNTINGTON, Second Lieutenant, STANLEY HUSTLER, 44550. 1st Battalion, 3rd NZ Rifle Brigade. Died 6 April 1918. Age 25. Son of J.H. and Mary H. Huntington, of William St, Ngaio, Wellington. Native of Bradford, England. Gezaincourt Communal Cemetery Extension, Somme, France. Grave or panel number: II.J.16.

HURLEY, Corporal, JAMES GRAVERS, 261812. 2nd NZ Entrenching Battalion, NZEF. Died 17 April 1918. Age 25. Son of Mary Hurley, of Taiaotea, Browns Bay, Auckland, and the late Henry Hurley. Messines Ridge (NZ) Memorial, Mesen, West-Vlaanderen, Belgium.

HUTT, Corporal, WILLIAM FREDERICK, 47338. 2nd Battalion, Canterbury Regiment, NZEF. Died 28 March 1918. Age 26. Son of Alfred and Margaret Hutt, of Merry St, Waimate. Grevilliers (NZ) Memorial, Pas de Calais, France.

HYSLOP, Private, JAMES ROBB, 49190. 2nd Battalion, Otago Regiment, NZEF. Died 10 April 1918. Son of Mr and Mrs James Hyslop, of Waterside, Greenfield, Otago. Knightsbridge Cemetery, Mesnil-Martinsart, Somme, France. Grave or panel number: A.5.

IRVINE, Lance Sergeant, JOSEPH SINCLAIR, 26/819. 'A' Company, 4th Battalion, 3rd NZ Rifle Brigade. Died 29 March 1918. Age 24. Son of John and Mary Irvine, of Otahuhu, Auckland. Euston Road Cemetery, Colincamps, Somme, France. Grave or panel number: H.A.7.

IRVING, Sergeant, CHARLES, 23/463. 1st Battalion, 3rd NZ Rifle Brigade. Died 5 April 1918. Son of Robert and Jessie Irving, of 85 Wright St, Wellington. Grevillers (NZ) Memorial, Pas de Calais, France.

IZETT, Rifleman, ANDREW SIGURD, 53500. 4th Battalion, 3rd NZ Rifle Brigade. Died 5 April 1918. Husband of Mrs A. Izett, of 81 Constable St, Newtown, Wellington. Euston Road Cemetery, Colincamps, Somme, France. Grave or panel number: II.B.1.

JACKSON, Rifleman, J., 31287. 4th Battalion, 3rd NZ Rifle Brigade. Died 29 March 1918. Age 30. Son of John and Margaret Elizabeth Jackson, of Crossnacole, Kiltegan, Baltinglass, County Wicklow. Euston Road Cemetery, Colincamps, Somme, France. Grave or panel number: III.D.5.

JACKSON, Lieutenant, JOHN KENNETH EDWARD, IO/395. 2nd Battalion, Wellington Regiment, NZEF. Died 28 March 1918. Age 23. Son of Robert

Jackson, of St Helens, England. Also served at Gallipoli. Englebelmer Communal Cemetery Extension, Somme, France. Grave or panel number: F.17.

JAMES, Private, CECIL ROY, 60132. 1st Battalion, Auckland Regiment, NZEF. Died 30 March 1918. Age 21. Son of George T. and Grace A. James. Englebelmer Communal Cemetery Extension, Somme, France. Grave or panel number: E.12.

JAMIESON, Sergeant, JOHN GIDEON, 26/454. 4th Battalion, 3rd NZ Rifle Brigade. Died 30 March 1918. Age 31. Son of Annie Jamieson, of 'Pine Holm', Awapuni, Palmerston North. Euston Road Cemetery, Colincamps, Somme, France. Grave or panel number: IV.C.3.

JEFFERY, Private, JAMES BEVINGTON, 39245. 1st Battalion, Otago Regiment, NZEF. Died 28 April 1918. Age 22. Son of Thomas and Alice S. Jeffery, of Dunedin. Euston Road Cemetery, Colincamps, Somme, France. Grave or panel number: I.J.3.

JENKINS, Private, JAMES, 56931. 2nd Battalion, Otago Regiment, NZEF. Died 1 April 1918. Age 38. Son of the late William and Mary Ann Jenkins, of Arrowtown. Doullens Communal Cemetery Extension No. 1, Somme, France. Grave or panel number: VI.F.38.

JENKINS, Lance Corporal, WILLIAM ROBERT, 2475. Machine Gun Battalion, NZ Machine Gun Corps. Died 5 April 1918. Age 22. Son of Robert and Annie Jenkins, of Packington St, Westport. Grevillers (NZ) Memorial Cemetery, Pas de Calais, France.

JENSEN, Private, CHRISTOFFER, 27903. 2nd Battalion, Wellington Regiment, NZEF. Died 27 March 1918. Son of Christoffer Jensen, of Haumoana, Hawkes Bay. Euston Road Cemetery, Colincamps, Somme, France. Grave or panel number: II.D.6.

JOHNSON, Bombardier, CHARLES STEPHEN, 2/273. NZ Field Artillery. Died 31 March 1918. Age 34. Son of William Ford Johnson and Ellen Mary Johnson, of Wellington. Also served at Gallipoli. Englebelmer Communal Cemetery Extension, Somme, France. Grave or panel number: P.3.

JOHNSTON, Lance Corporal, ALFRED HENRY, 32955. 3rd Battalion, 3rd NZ Rifle Brigade. Died 5 April 1918. Age 26. Husband of Ivy I. Johnston, of Murchison. Mailly Wood Cemetery, Somme, France. Grave or panel number: I.O.I5.

JOHNSTON, Lance Corporal, EDWARD COSLETT, 31293, MM. 2nd Battalion, Wellington Regiment, NZEF. Died 3 April 1918. Age 32. Son of Coslett and Annie Johnston, of Normanby, New Plymouth. Born at Taranaki. Grevilliers (NZ) Memorial, Pas de Calais, France.

JOHNSTON, Driver, JOHN, G/1876. NZ Field Artillery. Died 5 April 1918. Age 31. Hédauville Communal Cemetery Extension, Somme, France. Grave or panel number: H.29.

JOHNSTON, Lance Corporal, ROBERT NORRIES, 3/1168. 1st Field Ambulance, NZ Medical Corps. Died 6 April 1918. Age 26. Son of Helen C. and the late William Johnston, of Devonport, Auckland. Doullens Communal Cemetery Extension No. 1, Somme, France. Grave or panel number: VI.D.6.

JONES, Rifleman, ARTHUR DAVID, 44288. 3rd Battalion, 3rd NZ Rifle Brigade. Died 29 March 1918. Son of Mr W. Jones, of Upper Hutt, Wellington. Euston Road Cemetery, Colincamps, Somme, France. Grave or panel number: III.N.1.

JONES, Gunner, DANIEL WILLIAM, 13/2454. 7th Battery, NZ Field Artillery. Died 5 April 1918. Age 25. Son of Sydney Hezekiah and the late Jane Ellison Jones, of 57 Carlyle St, Napier. Bertrancourt Military Cemetery, Somme, France. Grave or panel number: 2.A.23.

JONES, Private, WILLIAM, 10/3616. 2nd Battalion, Wellington Regiment, NZEF. Died 16 April 1918. Son of Mr and Mrs T. Jones, of Kakahi, Auckland. Sucrerie Military Cemetery, Colincamps, Somme, France. Grave or panel number: I.J.42.

JOYCE, Private, THOMAS, 32858. 3rd Battalion, Otago Regiment, NZEF. Died 15 April 1918. Age 43. Son of Christina Joyce, of Otago and the late Hampden Thomas Joyce. Born at Waikouaiti. Grevillers (NZ) Memorial, Pas de Calais, France.

JUNO, Private, WILLIAM HENRY PHILLIP, 27908. 1st Battalion, Canterbury Regiment, NZEF. Died 27 March 1918. Son of Mary Carroll (formerly Juno), of Wellington, and the late Philip Juno, of Masterton. Grevilliers (NZ) Memorial, Pas de Calais, France.

KARA, Private, TAHA, 16/937. NZ Maori (Pioneer) Battalion. Died 5 April 1918. Age 22. Son of Hemi Kara and Mahara Kara, of Murwai, Gisborne. Bertrancourt Military Cemetery, Somme, France. Grave or panel number: 2.B.9.

KATTERSON, Rifleman, J., 54644. 2nd Battalion, 3rd NZ Rifle Brigade. Died 2 April 1918. Age 28. Son of James and Margaret Katterson, of Pollyamon, Castleburg, County Tyrone, Ireland. Euston Road Cemetery, Colincamps, Somme, France. Grave or panel number: V.D.6.

KAY, Sergeant, STANLEY ANGUS, G/1695, MM. Machine Gun Battalion, NZ Machine Gun Corps. Died 27 March 1918. Age 24. Son of Angus Colquonn and Jessie Lindsay Kay, of Lisbon St, Milton, Dunedin. Born at Balfour, Invercargill. Grevillers (NZ) Memorial Cemetery, Pas de Calais, France.

KEANE, Rifleman, GEORGE WILLIAM, 26629. 4th Battalion, 3rd NZ Rifle Brigade. Died 31 March 1918. Son of the late Daniel Keane, of 32 St Paul St, Auckland. Grevillers (NZ) Memorial, Pas de Calais, France.

KEARNEY, Rifleman, JOHN CHARLES, 45700. 'A' Company, 4th Battalion, 3rd NZ Rifle Brigade. Died 29 March 1918. Age 37. Son of James and Annie Kearney, of 114 Cathedral St, Sydney. Native of Culcairn, New South Wales. Euston Road Cemetery, Colincamps, Somme, France. Grave or panel number: I.H.9.

KEARNEY, Private, LESLIE GEORGE, 27306. 2nd NZ Entrenching Battalion, NZEF. Died 16 April 1918. Age 28. Son of Victoire Rose Kearney, of 20 Stratford St, Fendalton, Christchurch, and the late George Miles Kearney. Native of Gough's Bay, Banks Peninsula. Previously wounded at Messines. Messines Ridge (NZ) Memorial, Mesen, West-Vlaanderen, Belgium.

KEARNEY, Rifleman, M., 53788. 4th Battalion, 3rd NZ Rifle Brigade. Died 5 April 1918. Son of Francis Kearney, of Ballinacourty, Oranmore, Galway, Ireland. Euston Road Cemetery, Colincamps, Somme, France. Grave or panel number: II.B.4.

KEEN, Private, WILLIAM, 43990. 3rd Battalion, Canterbury Regiment, NZEF. Died 21 April 1918. Age 22. Son of George and Elizabeth Keen, of 61 Le Cren St, Timaru. Born at Peebles, Scotland. Doullens Communal Cemetery Extension No. 1, Somme, France. Grave or panel number: VI.C.80.

KEIG, Private, JOHN, 10356. NZ Machine Gun Battalion. Died 5 April 1918. Mailly Wood Cemetery, Somme, France. Grave or panel number 1.N.13.

KELEHER, Private, JOHN JOSEPH, 44387. 2nd Battalion, NZ Entrenching Battalion, NZEF. Died 29 April 1918. Son of Mrs Catherine Keleher, of Te Puke. Buttes New British Cemetery (NZ) Memorial, Polygon Wood, Zonnebeke, West-Vlaanderen, Belgium.

KELL, Private, FRANK ARCHIBALD, 40577. 2nd Battalion, Auckland Regiment, NZEF. Died 27 March 1918. Husband of Mrs F.A. Kell, of Auckland. Grevilliers (NZ) Memorial, Pas de Calais, France.

KELLAND, Private, CHARLES CORNISH, 27307. 1st Battalion, Canterbury Regiment, NZEF. Died 28 April 1918. Age 44. Son of the late William and Mary Kelland, of Orton, Rangitata; husband of the late Amelia Kelland. Served in the South African Campaign with the 7th New Zealand Contingent. Euston Road Cemetery, Colincamps, Somme, France. Grave or panel number: V.B.6.

KELLY, Private, STEPHEN HENRY, 44740. No. 15 North Auckland Company, 2nd Battalion, Auckland Regiment, NZEF. Died 27 March 1918. Age 24. Son of William and Mary J. Kelly, of 15 Bellwood Ave, Mt Eden, Auckland. Grevilliers (NZ) Memorial, Pas de Calais, France.

KELSALL, Private, GEORGE HENRY, 60138. 2nd Battalion, Auckland Regiment, NZEF. Died 30 March 1918. Englebelmer Communal Cemetery Extension, Somme, France. Grave or panel number: E.11.

KENDALL, Sergeant, JOHN THOMAS, 8/3304. 2nd Battalion, Otago Regiment, NZEF. Died 5 April 1918. Age 28. Son of Henry and Sarah Kendall, of Thames. Englebelmer Communal Cemetery, Somme, France. Grave or panel number: I.E.4.

KENNEDY, Private, ALBERT FRANCIS, 55505. 2nd Battalion, Canterbury Regiment, NZEF. Died 5 April 1918. Age 32. Son of William Kennedy of Annat, Canterbury. Etaples Military Cemetery, Pas de Calais, France. Grave or panel number: XXXII.A.1A.

KENNEDY, Rifleman, SAMUEL, 39058. 'B Company, 4th Battalion, 3rd NZ Rifle Brigade. Died 6 April 1918. Age 27. Son of Robert and Margaret Hood Kennedy, of 126 Clarence Rd, Lower Riccarton, Christchurch. Euston Road Cemetery, Colincamps, Somme, France. Grave or panel number: V.B.5.

KERMODE, Gunner, BERT, 7/1858. 5th Battery, 2nd Brigade, NZ Field Artillery. Died 18 April 1918. Age 31. Son of Jane Louisa and the late George Edwin Kermode, of 25 William St, Hataitai, Wellington. Lijssenthoek Military Cemetery, Poperinge, West-Vlaanderen, Belgium. Grave or panel number: XXVI.G.10.

KERR, Rifleman, W.G., 13040. 3rd Battalion, 3rd NZ Rifle Brigade. Died 28 March 1918. Husband of Mrs Sorenson (formerly Kerr), of 12 Carscadden St, Glasgow, Scotland. Euston Road Cemetery, Colincamps, Somme, France. Grave or panel number: II.C.3.

KIBBLEWHITE, Private, EDWARD, 43991. 2nd NZ Entrenching Battalion, NZEF. Died 17 April 1918. Husband of Mrs Evelyn Gladys Kibblewhite, of 102 Edward Ave, St Albans, Christchurch. Messines Ridge (NZ) Memorial, Mesen, West-Vlaanderen, Belgium.

KIELY, Corporal, ROBERT DALE, 44123. 4th Battalion, 3rd NZ Rifle Brigade. Died 29 March 1918. Age 29. Son of Ellen Kiely, of Westport; and the late William Overton Kiely. Born in Napier. Grevillers (NZ) Memorial, Pas de Calais, France.

KIELY, Rifleman, THOMAS, 47152. NZ Rifle Brigade Died 29 March 1918. Age 27. Son of Thomas and Margaret Kiely, of Dunedin. Bertrancourt Military Cemetery, Somme, France. Grave or panel number: 2.B.8.

KINAHAN, Rifleman, EDWIN, 42125. 'C' Company, 2nd Battalion, 3rd NZ Rifle Brigade. Died 26 March 1918. Age 33. Son of the late James Beluah and Alice Kinahan, of Clarence St, Ponsonby, Auckland. Grevillers (NZ) Memorial, Pas de Calais, France.

KING, Private, ARTHUR FREDERICK, 58545. 1st Battalion, Canterbury Regiment, NZEF. Died 28 March 1918. Age 23. Son of William and Julia King, of 100 Carlyle St, Sydenham, Christchurch. Grevilliers (NZ) Memorial, Pas de Calais, France.

KING, Rifleman, ARTHUR WILLIAM, 59126. 1st Battalion, 3rd NZ Rifle Brigade. Died 5 April 1918. Age 20. Son of John King, of Feilding. Grevilliers (NZ) Memorial, Pas de Calais, France.

KING, Private, GEORGE WALTER ERNEST, 60141. 2nd NZ Entrenching Battalion, NZEF. Died 29 April 1918. Perth Cemetery (China Wall), Ypres, West-Vlaanderen, Belgium. Grave or panel number: VI.D.I.

KING, Private, JOHN SMYTH, 48859. 2nd NZ Entrenching Battalion, NZEF. Died 14 April 1918. Age 28. Son of Mary Hamilton King, of North Canterbury and the late Thomas King. Messines Ridge (NZ) Memorial, Mesen, West-Vlaanderen, Belgium.

KING, Rifleman, THOMAS, 35169. 4th Battalion, 3rd NZ Rifle Brigade. Died 30 March 1918. Born at Wellington. Grevillers (NZ) Memorial, Pas de Calais, France.

KIRCHER, Private, CECIL SMART, 55510. 2nd NZ Entrenching Battalion, NZEF. Died 14 April 1918. Son of Mr and Mrs Henry William Kircher, of 20 Opawa Rd, Opawa, Christchurch. Messines Ridge (NZ) Memorial, Mesen, West-Vlaanderen, Belgium.

KIRK, Private, EDWARD WILLIAM, 7/1372. 2nd Battalion, Canterbury Regiment, NZEF. Died 7 April 1918. Age 26. Son of Aaron and Caroline Kirk, of Eketahuna. St Hilaire Cemetery Extension, Frevent, Pas de Calais, France. Grave or panel number: D.12.

KITTO, Private, HERBERT FRANCIS, 8/3658. 1st Battalion, Otago Regiment, NZEF. Died 28 March 1918. Age 23. Son of Jane and the late Francis Kitto, of Lowburn Ferry, Otago. Auchonvillers Military Cemetery, Somme, France. Grave or panel number: II.L.37.

KITTOW, Private, OTHO JONATHAN, 33561. 1st NZ Light Trench Mortar Battery. Died 30 March 1918. Age 31. Son of Jonathan and Catherine Kittow, of Tirau, Rotorua. Native of Cornwall, England. Euston Road Cemetery, Colincamps, Somme, France. Grave or panel number: V.B.9.

KLINK, Lance Corporal, CHARLES AMBROSE, 25890. 1st Battalion, 3rd NZ Rifle Brigade. Died 27 March 1918. Age 24. Son of Frederick and Martha Klink, of Pohangina, Wellington. Grevillers (NZ) Memorial, Pas de Calais, France.

KNAPPING, Private, CHRISTOPHER JOHN, 30817. 2nd Battalion, Auckland Regiment, NZEF. Died 30 March 1918. Age 27. Son of Ernest and Rosa Knapping, of East Tamaki, Auckland. Native of Otahuhu, Auckland. Euston Road Cemetery, Colincamps, Somme, France. Grave or panel number: III.C.7.

KNIGHT, Corporal, NORMAN RAGLAN, 31302, MM. 2nd Battalion, Wellington Regiment, NZEF. Died 16 April 1918. Age 31. Son of Mr and Mrs J. F. Knight, of Victoria St, Hawera; husband of Gertrude Elizabeth Flack (formerly Knight), of Caledonia St, Hawera. Sucrerie Military Cemetery, Colincamps, Somme, France. Grave or panel number: I.J.44.

KONUKE, Private, PAT, 16/552. NZ Maori (Pioneer) Battalion. Died 14 April 1918. Age 24. Son of Huka and Aui Konuke, of Post Office, Wairoa. Born at Petane, New Zealand. Etaples Military Cemetery, Pas de Calais, France. Grave or panel number: XXIX.R.16A.

KUPLI, Rifleman, M., 55979. 4th Battalion, NZ Rifle Brigade. Died 29 March 1918. Brother of Mr J. E. Kupli, of 74 Leeside Crescent, Golders Green, London. Euston Road Cemetery, Colincamps, Somme, France. Grave or panel number: V.A.2.

LACEY, Rifleman, EDWARD, 52844. 2nd Battalion, 3rd NZ Rifle Brigade.

Died 13 April 1918. Age 27. Son of George and Elizabeth Lacey, of 157 Meadow Lane, Loughborough, England. Messines Ridge (NZ) Memorial, Mesen, West-Vlaanderen, Belgium.

LAFFEY, Rifleman, JOHN TIMOTHY, 15921. 3rd Battalion, 3rd NZ Rifle Brigade. Died 29 March 1918. Age 23. Son of John and Ellen Laffey, of South St, Ashburton. Grevillers (NZ) Memorial, Pas de Calais, France.

LAIDLAW, Second Lieutenant, ARTHUR FREDERICK, 35642. 2nd Battalion, Auckland Regiment, NZEF. Died 27 March 1918. Husband of Mrs M. Laidlaw, of Epsom, Auckland. Sucrerie Military Cemetery, Colincamps, Somme, France. Grave or panel number: I.I.2.

LAING, Corporal, JAMES DUNCAN, 32862. 4th Battalion, 3rd NZ Rifle Brigade. Died 30 March 1918. Son of Charlotte Walker (formerly Laing), of Dipton, Southland. Grevillers (NZ) Memorial, Pas de Calais, France.

LAIRD, Private, CHARLES WILLIAM, 13771. 1st Battalion, Auckland Regiment, NZEF. Died 2 April 1918. Age 31. Son of the late Charles Richard and Maria Laird. Etaples Military Cemetery, Pas de Calais, France. Grave or panel number: XXXIII.C.19.

LAND, Rifleman, ALFRED FREDERICK, 31418. 2nd Battalion, 3rd NZ Rifle Brigade. Died 26 March 1918. Son of Mr and Mrs Edmund George Land, of Manawaru, Thames. Grevillers (NZ) Memorial, Pas de Calais, France.

LANG, Private, WILLIAM, 40338. 2nd Battalion, Auckland Regiment, NZEF. Died 27 March 1918. Son of Mr and Mrs William Lang, of Te Puke. Euston Road Cemetery, Colincamps, Somme, France. Grave or panel number: III.E.9.

LARNACH, Corporal, MAGNUS JAMES, 38840. 1st Battalion, Auckland Regiment, NZEF. Died 26 March 1918. Age 33. Son of David Larnach, of Dunedin. Euston Road Cemetery, Colincamps, Somme, France. Grave or panel number: III.B.9.

LAVERTY, Rifleman, JAMES, 47043. 3rd Battalion, 3rd NZ Rifle Brigade. Died 30 March 1918. Husband of Mrs M.M. Peat (formerly Laverty), of 22 Herbert St, North Invercargill. Grevillers (NZ) Memorial, Pas de Calais, France.

LAVIN, Gunner, ANDREW MARK, 50882. 1st Battery, NZ Field Artillery. Died 31 March 1918. Englebelmer Communal Cemetery Extension, Somme, France. Grave or panel number: F.4.

LAWSON, Corporal, CLIFFORD PETER, IO/2671. 1st Battalion, Wellington Regiment, NZEF. Died 30 March 1918. Age 24. Son of Peter and Cathrine Annie Lawson, of Mangamaire, New Zealand. Also served in Gallipoli and Egypt. Euston Road Cemetery, Colincamps, Somme, France. Grave or panel number: III.B.4.

LAWTON, Lance Corporal, N.A., 21031. 4th Battalion, 3rd NZ Rifle Brigade. Died 29 March 1918. Age 36. Son of Joseph and Mary Hardie Lawton, of Union St, Friockheim, Arbroath, Forfarshire. Hédauville Communal Cemetery Extension, Somme, France. Grave or panel number: H.23.

LAY, Private, HAROLD GEORGE, 20541. 3rd Battalion, Wellington Regiment, NZEF. Died 16 April 1918. Meteren Military Cemetery, Nord, France. Grave or panel number: V.J.833.

LEAH, Lance Corporal, HENRY LAWSON, 12209. 'A' Company, 4th Battalion, 3rd NZ Rifle Brigade. Died 29 March 1918. Age 24. Son of Joseph Andrew and Martha Jane Leah, of Timaru. Euston Road Cemetery, Colincamps, Somme, France. Grave or panel number: III.V.1.

LEASK, Private, P.F., 64645. Canterbury Regiment, NZEF. Died 14 April 1918. Mendinghem Military Cemetery, Poperinge, West-Vlaanderen, Belgium. Grave or panel number: IX.F.I.

LEEN, Private, JOHN EDWARD, 63354. 2nd Battalion, Auckland Regiment, NZEF. Died 10 April 1918. Age 27. Son of Michael and Johanna Leen, of East Gore, Southland. Grevilliers (NZ) Memorial, Pas de Calais, France.

LEES, Lance Corporal, HENRY JOHN, 15925. 3rd Battalion, 3rd NZ Rifle Brigade. Died 27 March 1918. Age 26. Son of John and Margaret Lees, of Kohukohu, Hokianga. Euston Road Cemetery, Colincamps, Somme, France. Grave or panel number: III.N.3.

LEMMER, Gunner, ADOLF JULIUS, 2/2859. 15th Battery, NZ Field Artillery. Died 6 April 1918. Age 20. Son of Julius B. and Amy Lemmer, of 20 Van Diemen St, Nelson. Gezaincourt Communal Cemetery Extension, Somme, France. Grave or panel number: II.J.10.

LENNOX, Lance Corporal, ERIC, 1st Battalion, Canterbury Regiment, NZEF. Died 23 April 1918. Age 26. Son of John and Sarah Lennox, of 23 Broadway Terrace, Wellington. Colincamps Communal Cemetery, Somme, France.

LE ROY, Lance Corporal, GORDON, 4877. 2nd NZ Entrenching Battalion, NZEF. Died 16 April 1918. Age 21. Son of Edward and Gertrude Le Roy, of 21 Queen St, Auckland. Messines Ridge (NZ) Memorial, Mesen, West-Vlaanderen, Belgium.

LEWIS, Private, ANDREW JONATHAN, 29423. 1st Battalion, Wellington Regiment, NZEF. Died 29 March 1918. Euston Road Cemetery, Colincamps, Somme, France. Grave or panel number: Special Memorial B.7.

LEWIS, Lieutenant, SAMUEL ELDRIDGE, 22906. 'G' Company, 4th Battalion, 3rd NZ Rifle Brigade. Died 5 April 1918. Age 35. Son of Sarah Elizabeth and the late William Lewis; husband of Emma Lewis, of 118 Onepu Rd, Lyall Bay, Wellington. Grevillers (NZ) Memorial, Pas de Calais, France.

LEYS, Captain, JAMES ROBERT RUXTON, 15/557A, MC. 3rd Battalion, Otago Regiment, NZEF. Died 17 April 1918. Age 22. Son of Robert Ruxton Leys and Florence Amelia Mary Leys, of 228 Happy Valley Rd, Brooklyn, Wellington. Also served in Gallipoli. Haringhe (Bandaghem) Military Cemetery, Poperinge, West-Vlaanderen, Belgium. Grave or panel number: V.D.21.

LIDDELL, Gunner, VERNARD CLIFTON, 2/2667. 15th Heavy Battery, NZ

Field Artillery. Died 24 April 1918. Age 24. Son of James and Kate Liddell, of Palmerston North. Louvencourt Military Cemetery, Somme, France. Grave or panel number: I.D.23.

LIDDELL, Private, WILLIAM, 55765. 2nd Battalion, Otago Regiment, NZEF. Died 12 April 1918. Son of Mr and Mrs James Liddell, of King Edward Rd, South Dunedin. Knightsbridge Cemetery, Mesnil-Martinsart, Somme, France. Grave or panel number: F.68.

LINDBOM, Corporal, ALBERT WILLIAM, 39440. 2nd NZ Entrenching Battalion, NZEF. Died 14 April 1918. Age 34. Son of Frederick and Emily Lindbom, of Cardwell St, Cobden, Greymouth. Native of Kumara, Greymouth. Messines Ridge (NZ) Memorial, Mesen, West-Vlaanderen, Belgium.

LISSAMAN, Private, ALARIC DISRAELI, 23401. 1st Battalion, Auckland Regiment, NZEF. Died 30 March 1918. Age 23. Son of A.A. and A.E. Lissaman, of Palmerston North. Englebelmer Communal Cemetery Extension, Somme, France. Grave or panel number: E.10.

LOCKE, Rifleman, JOHN EDWARD, 261113. 4th Battalion, 3rd NZ Rifle Brigade. Died 28 March 1918. Euston Road Cemetery, Colincamps, Somme, France. Grave or panel number: IV.A.4.

LOCKSTONE, Gunner, REGINALD HUNTER WARD, 10620. 15th Howitzer Battery, 1st Brigade, NZ Field Artillery. Died 8 April 1918. Age 26. Son of Edward and Barbara Lockstone, of 14 Duke St, Dunedin. Bertrancourt Military Cemetery, Somme, France. Grave or panel number: 2.B.19.

LOFTUS, Sapper, WILLIAM JACKSON, 26640. NZ Engineers. Died 29 March 1918. Age 31. Son of Henry Loftus and Marion Leah Jackson (his wife), of Parnell, Auckland. Hazebrouck Communal Cemetery, Nord, France. Grave or panel number: III.E.3.

LONGNEY, Private, GRAHAM JOHN, 64538. NZ Entrenching Battalion, NZEF. Died 16 April 1918. Age 36. Son of Frederick John and Eliza Longney, of Longney, Gloucester, England. Meteren Military Cemetery, Nord, France. Grave or panel number: V.J.840.

LOVE, Lance Corporal, DAVID, 26/1632. 2nd Battalion, 3rd NZ Rifle Brigade. Died 2 April 1918. Age 32. Son of David Love and Hannah Jane Love, of Kilcreen, Glarryford, County Antrim, Ireland. Grevillers (NZ) Memorial, Pas de Calais, France.

LOVELL, Lance Corporal, WILLIAM GEORGE, 64539. 2nd NZ Entrenching Battalion, NZEF. Died 16 April 1918. Age 28. Son of George Thomas and Marion Lovell; husband of Bertha Lovell, of 'Ormland', 8 Victor Rd, East Malvern, Melbourne, Victoria, Australia. Native of Melbourne. Messines Ridge (NZ) Memorial, Mesen, West-Vlaanderen, Belgium.

LOWENDALE, Private, ERIK, 13943. 1st Battalion, Otago Regiment, NZEF. Died 11 April 1918. Age 27. Son of Johan Alfred Lowendale and Hulda Maria Anderson his wife, of Stromhagen, 5 Addevalla, Sverige. Born at Lovendal.

Englebelmer Communal Cemetery Extension, Somme, France. Grave or panel number: E.3.

LOWTHER, Rifleman, ALBERT EDWARD, 12/2019. 2nd Battalion, 3rd NZ Rifle Brigade. Died 2 April 1918. Age 40. Son of Mary Jane Lowther, of Papatoetoe, Auckland, and the late Edward Lowther. Also served at Gallipoli. Grevillers (NZ) Memorial, Pas de Calais, France.

LUCAS, Lance Corporal, GEORGE ROBERT, 11892. 1st Battalion, Wellington Regiment, NZEF. Died 30 March 1918. Son of Mr and Mrs G.H. Lucas, of Awahuri, Manawatu. Euston Road Cemetery, Colincamps, Somme, France. Grave or panel number: V.E.11.

LUPTON, Corporal, FREDERICK, 28742. 1st Battalion, Auckland Regiment, NZEF. Died 18 April 1918. Age 35. Son of Elizabeth Lupton, of 36 3rd Avenue, Kingsland, Auckland. Native of Auckland. Bertrancourt Military Cemetery, Somme, France. Grave or panel number: II.B.20.

LUSTY, Private, FELIX MATTHEW, 38294. 2nd NZ Entrenching Battalion, NZEF. Died 14 April 1918. Age 24. Son of Arthur and Caroline Lusty, of Richmond, Nelson. Messines Ridge (NZ) Memorial, Mesen, West-Vlaanderen, Belgium.

LYONS, Rifleman, GEORGE MATTHEW, 48976. 4th Battalion, 3rd NZ Rifle Brigade. Died 29 March 1918. Age 40. Son of Matthew and Augustina Lyons, of Christchurch. Euston Road Cemetery, Colincamps, Somme, France. Grave or panel number: III.D.4.

LYONS, Private, JOHN MITCHELL, 60954. 2nd Battalion, Canterbury Regiment, NZEF. Died 28 March 1918. Husband of Mrs J.M. Lyons, of 23 South Tce, Geraldine. Grevilliers (NZ) Memorial, Pas de Calais, France.

LYONS, Private, THOMAS, 41406. NZ Machine Gun Battalion. Died 8 April 1918. Age 21. Son of Michael and Ellen Lyons, of Taikorea, New Zealand. Late of Ireland. Doullens Communal Cemetery Extension No. 1, Somme, France. Grave or panel number: B.A. VI.C.19.

McALISTER, Lieutenant, DOUGLAS WILLIAM, 22667. 1st Battalion, Otago Regiment, NZEF. Died 5 April 1918. Age 35. Son of E. and Mary McAlister, of Pyramid, Southland. Englebelmer Communal Cemetery Extension, Somme, France. Grave or panel number: F.22.

McALLISTER, Private, WILLIAM MCCLURE, 47280. 14th Company, 2nd Battalion, Otago Regiment, NZEF. Died 9 April 1918. Age 26. Son of James and Agnes McAllister, of Mataura, Southland. Doullens Communal Cemetery Extension No. 1, Somme, France. Grave or panel number: VI.C.20.

McANALLY, Private, SAMUEL CLERY, 46374. 1st Battalion, Auckland Regiment, NZEF. Died 27 March 1918. Age 38. Son of the late Alexander and Margaret McAnally, of Scottsdale, Tasmania; husband of Ethel May McAnally, of Hardington St, Onehunga, Auckland. Served in the South African Campaign.

Left New Zealand with the 25th Reinforcements. Doullens Communal Cemetery Extension No. 1, Somme, France. Grave or panel number: V.A.48.

McARTHUR, Sergeant, ARCHIBALD, 8/433. 1st Battalion, Otago Regiment, NZEF. Died 11 April 1918. Age 24. Son of Archibald and Emily McArthur, of Woodlands, New Zealand. Served in Egypt and France. Doullens Communal Cemetery Extension No. 1, Somme, France. Grave or panel number: VI.B.5.

McARTHUR, Captain, ARTHUR KEIRBY, 12/2623. 2nd Battalion, Auckland Regiment, NZEF. Died 30 March 1918. Age 23. Son of Mr and Mrs A.F. McArthur, Auckland, New Zealand; husband of Margot M. McArthur, of 'The Black Horse', Sheen Rd, Richmond, Surrey, England. Etaples Military Cemetery, Pas de Calais, France. Grave or panel number: XXVIII.F.1.

McARTHUR, Rifleman, JOHN FINDLAY, 47028. 1st Battalion, 3rd NZ Rifle Brigade. Died 5 April 1918. Son of Mr and Mrs James Neil McArthur, of Main St, Gore. Grevillers (NZ) Memorial, Pas de Calais, France.

McAULAY, Private, ARCHIBALD, 60969. 2nd Battalion, Canterbury Regiment, NZEF. Died 28 April 1918. Age 38. Son of William and Marion McAulay, of Paisley, near Glasgow, Scotland. Etaples Military Cemetery, Pas de Calais, France. Grave or panel number: LXVI.A.8.

McCALL, Private, ALFRED, 64562. 2nd NZ Entrenching Battalion, NZEF. Died 16 April 1918. Son of Mr and Mrs James William McCall, of 20 Moxham Ave, Hataitai, Wellington. Messines Ridge (NZ) Memorial, Mesen, West-Vlaanderen, Belgium.

McCARTHY, Corporal, HUGH, 6/4634. 2nd Battalion, Canterbury Regiment, NZEF. Died 26 March 1918. Serre Road Cemetery No. 1, Pas de Calais, France. Grave or panel number: V.C.16.

McCOID, Private, JOHN, 26653. 1st Battalion, Auckland Regiment, NZEF. Died 26 March 1918. Age 20. Son of the late William John and Elizabeth Jane McCoid, Turua, of Thames River, Auckland. Euston Road Cemetery, Colincamps, Somme, France. Grave or panel number: III.B.10.

McCONAUGHY, Private, FREDERICK EDWARD, 46376. 2nd Battalion, Auckland Regiment, NZEF. Died 30 March 1918. Age 21. Son of James and Elizabeth McConaughy, of Grey Ave, Mangere Crossing, Otahuhu, Auckland. Euston Road Cemetery, Colincamps, Somme, France. Grave or panel number: V.B.10.

MacCONNACHIE, Driver, D., 43443. NZ Field Artillery. Died 17 April 1918. Lijssenthoek Military Cemetery, Poperinge, West-Vlaanderen, Belgium. Grave or panel number: XXVII.G.8.

McCUSKER, Private, HENRY MURDOCH, 13964. 2nd NZ Entrenching Battalion, NZEF. Died 19 April 1918. Age 37. Son of Mary McCusker. Native of Christchurch. Lijssenthoek Military Cemetery, Poperinge, West-Vlaanderen, Belgium. Grave or panel number: XXVI.G.15A.

McDERMOTT, Private, BRYAN PETER, 42139. 2nd Battalion, Auckland

Regiment, NZEF. Died 30 March 1918. Age 27. Son of Peter and Bridget McDermott, of Onetea, North Auckland. Euston Road Cemetery, Colincamps, Somme, France. Grave or panel number: II.C.6.

MACDONALD, Private, HORATIO ARNOLD, 45876. 2nd Battalion, Wellington Regiment, NZEF. Died 27 March 1918. Age 19. Son of Margaret McCallum Bowie (formerly Macdonald), and the late John Alexander Macdonald. Native of Petone. Euston Road Cemetery, Colincamps, Somme, France. Grave or panel number: III.D.8.

McDONALD, Private, HERMAN CECIL, 26872. 2nd Battalion, Auckland Regiment, NZEF. Died 30 March 1918. Age 21. Son of Thomas and Eliza McDonald, of Rosebank Rd, Avondale, Auckland. Euston Road Cemetery, Colincamps, Somme, France. Grave or panel number: IV.B.6.

MACE, Lance Corporal, GUY GEORGE, 41844. 4th Battalion, 3rd NZ Rifle Brigade. Died 29 March 1918. Age 32. Son of Walter and Emma Mace; husband of Noeline Mace, of Masterton. Euston Road Cemetery, Colincamps, Somme, France. Grave or panel number: III.B.3.

McFADDEN, Rifleman, JOSEPH EDWARD, 51859. Lewis Gun Section, 'A' Company, 3rd Battalion, 3rd NZ Rifle Brigade. Died 27 March 1918. Age 25. Son of Thomas and Annie McFadden, of Estuary Rd, New Brighton, Christchurch. Grevillers (NZ) Memorial, Pas de Calais, France.

McGINNIS, Private, JOSEPH AUGUSTINE, 49913. 2nd Battalion, Auckland Regiment, NZEF. Died 30 March 1918. Age 34. Son of the late Michael Joseph and Mary Jane McGinnis, of Earnscleugh Flat, Dunedin. Euston Road Cemetery, Colincamps, Somme, France. Grave or panel number: II.C.7.

McGOUGH, Private, PATRICK, 58572. 1st Battalion, Canterbury Regiment, NZEF. Died 27 March 1918. Age 32. Son of Pat and Alice McGough, of Kilnacranfy, Culloville, County Monaghan, Ireland. Grevilliers (NZ) Memorial, Pas de Calais, France.

McGREGOR, Second Lieutenant, JOHN, 39400. 2nd Battalion, Otago Regiment, NZEF. Died 16 April 1918. Age 24. Son of John and Rachel Jane McGregor, of 58 York Place, Dunedin. Native of Dunback, Otago. Messines Ridge (NZ) Memorial, Mesen, West-Vlaanderen, Belgium.

McGUINNESS, Private, JAMES OWEN, 29177. 2nd Battalion, Canterbury Regiment, NZEF. Died 27 March 1918. Age 25. Son of Owen and Kate McGuinness, of Longbeach, Ashburton. Born at Longbeach. Grevilliers (NZ) Memorial, Pas de Calais, France.

McINDOE, Lance Sergeant, GORDON FRANK, 32959. 2nd Battalion, Canterbury Regiment, NZEF. Died 5 April 1918. Age 22. Son of William and Mary McIndoe, of Seddonville, Westport. Serre Road Cemetery No. 1, Pas de Calais, France. Grave or panel number: II.B.4.

McINTOSH, Lance Corporal, C., 12/3110, MM. 1st Battalion, Auckland Regiment, NZEF. Died 20 April 1918. Age 36. Son of John and the late Georgina

Mitchell McIntosh, of Schoolcroft, Garvock, Laurencekirk, Scotland. Bertrancourt Military Cemetery, Somme, France. Grave or panel number: II.B.3.

McINTOSH, Private, JAMES, 54145. 2nd Battalion, Canterbury Regiment, NZEF. Died 29 March 1918. Son of Mr and Mrs James McIntosh, of 10 Musselburgh Rise, Dunedin. A.I.F. Burial Ground, Flers, Somme, France. Grave or panel number: VI.G.2.

McINTOSH, Rifleman, STANLEY HERBERT, 12443. 4th Battalion, 3rd NZ Rifle Brigade. Died 29 March 1918. Age 23. Son of John and Jane McIntosh, of Timaru. Doullens Communal Cemetery Extension No. 1, Somme, France. Grave or panel number: V.C.39.

McINTOSH, Corporal, WILLIAM GARROW, 55081. 1st Battalion, 3rd NZ Rifle Brigade. Died 5 April 1918. Age 42. Son of Grace McIntosh, of Southbrook, Canterbury; and the late Kenneth McIntosh. Euston Road Cemetery, Colincamps, Somme, France. Grave or panel number: IV.D.10.

MACKAY, Rifleman, ALEXANDER, 23402. 4th Battalion, 3rd NZ Rifle Brigade. Died 6 April 1918. Son of Murdock and Mary Mackay, of Te Maire, Wairoa. Grevillers (NZ) Memorial, Pas de Calais, France.

MACKAY, Rifleman, DONALD, 62117. 4th Battalion, 3rd NZ Rifle Brigade. Died 29 March 1918. Euston Road Cemetery, Colincamps, Somme, France. Grave or panel number: V.A.3.

MACKAY, Lance Corporal, NEIL, 31691. 1st Battalion, Auckland Regiment, NZEF. Died 27 March 1918. Age 26. Son of Mr and Mrs R. Mackay, of Auckland; husband of Lilian Mackay, of 480 Church St, Parramatta North, New South Wales. Doullens Communal Cemetery Extension No. 1, Somme, France. Grave or panel number: V.A.56.

MACKAY, Private, RODERICK, 58576. 1st Battalion, Canterbury Regiment, NZEF. Died 5 April 1918. Age 21. Son of Finlay and Isabella Mackay, of Kirkton, Balmacara, Kyle, Ross-shire, Scotland. Serre Road Cemetery No. 1, Pas de Calais, France. Grave or panel number: IV.G.13.

McKAY, Gunner, GEORGE, 2/3051. NZ Field Artillery. Died 9 April 1918. Son of Jean McKay, of Waikanae. Messines Ridge (NZ) Memorial, Mesen, West-Vlaanderen, Belgium.

McKAY, Private, LEONARD HAROLD, 37935. NZ Machine Gun Corps. Died 7 April 1918. Age 24. Only son of Thomas and Eliza McKay, of 1 Worman Rd, Gisborne. St Sever Cemetery Extension, Rouen, Seine-Maritime, France. Grave or panel number: P.IX.F.8A.

MACKENZIE, Lance Corporal, JOHN SMITH, 14285. 1st Battalion, Auckland Regiment, NZEF. Died 26 March 1918. Age 43. Son of Donald Hugh and Margaret A. Mackenzie, of Scotland. St Hilaire Cemetery, Frevent, Pas de Calais, France. Grave or panel number: V.E.4.

MACKENZIE, Rifleman, KENNETH WILLIAM, 44647. 3rd Battalion, 3rd NZ Rifle Brigade. Died 21 April 1918. Age 25. Son of Alexandrina and the late Colin Mackenzie, of Waipu. Etaples Military Cemetery, Pas de Calais, France. Grave or panel number: XXIX.J.7A.

McKENZIE, Rifleman, JOHN, 37002. 4th Battalion, 3rd NZ Rifle Brigade. Died 30 March 1918. Age 31. Grevillers (NZ) Memorial, Pas de Calais, France.

McKENZIE, Rifleman, WILLIAM, 47034. 3rd Battalion, 3rd NZ Rifle Brigade. Died 30 March 1918. Husband of Mrs W. McKenzie, of 32 Bowmont St, Invercargill. Grevillers (NZ) Memorial, Pas de Calais, France.

McKINLAY, Corporal, WILLIAM DAVID, 4/1978, MM. 1st Company, NZ Engineers. Died 12 April 1918. Age 36. Son of David and Euphemia McKinlay, of Scotland. Doullens Communal Cemetery Extension No. 1, Somme, France. Grave or panel number: VI.B.II.

McKINNA, Private, WILLIAM JOHN, 47568. 2nd Battalion, Wellington Regiment, NZEF. Died 28 March 1918. Age 22. Son of John W. and Joanna W. McKinna, of Collingwood, Nelson. Doullens Communal Cemetery Extension No. 1, Somme, France. Grave or panel number: V.D.I.

McKINNON, Gunner, JAMES EDWIN, 42921. NZ Field Artillery. Died 17 April 1918. Age 36. Son of Robert and Mary McKinnon, of Gonville Ave, Wanganui. Westoutre British Cemetery, Heuvelland, West-Vlaanderen, Belgium. Grave or panel number: E.6.

MACKINTOSH, Private, NEIL JOHN, 51285. 1st Battalion, Canterbury Regiment, NZEF. Died 28 March 1918. Age 27. Son of Ewen and Marjory Mackintosh, of 121 Parke St, St Albans, Christchurch. Born at North Canterbury. Grevilliers (NZ) Memorial, Pas de Calais, France.

McLACHLAN, Rifleman, CLEMENT ROTHERY, 53711. 2nd Battalion, 3rd NZ Rifle Brigade. Died 18 April 1918. Age 24. Son of the late Alexander and Elizabeth McLachlan, of 'Strathlachlan', Doyleston, New Zealand. Englebelmer Communal Cemetery Extension, Somme, France. Grave or panel number: F.5.

McLAREN, Private, HUGH, 56334. 1st Battalion, Auckland Regiment, NZEF. Died 26 March 1918. Age 33. Son of Mrs Mary McLaren, of Manukau Rd, Onehunga, Auckland. Born at Falkirk, Scotland. Grevillers (NZ) Memorial, Pas de Calais, France.

McLAREN, Private, THOMAS CORBET, 64325. 2nd NZ Entrenching Battalion, NZEF. Died 17 April 1918. Age 29. Son of the late Thomas and Margaret McLaren; husband of Margaret Mabel McLaren, of 31 Beaconsfield St, Grey Lynn, Auckland. Messines Ridge (NZ) Memorial, Mesen, West-Vlaanderen, Belgium.

McLAREN, Rifleman, WILLIAM WHITE, 46236. 2nd Battalion, 3rd NZ Rifle Brigade. Died 5 April 1918. Age 25. Son of George Dickson McLaren and Christina McLaren, of Lower Kaimai, Tauranga. Native of Scotland. Euston Road Cemetery, Colincamps, Somme, France. Grave or panel number: III.A.10.

McLAY, Private, PETER, 54568. 2nd Battalion, Auckland Regiment, NZEF. Died 31 March 1918. Doullens Communal Cemetery Extension No. 1, Somme, France. Grave or panel number: VI.G.42.

MacLEAN, Corporal, CLARENCE, IO/4481. 'B' Company, 2nd Battalion, Wellington Regiment, NZEF. Died 27 March 1918. Age 21. Son of Peter and Annie MacLean, of Okaramio, Blenheim. Euston Road Cemetery, Colincamps, Somme, France. Grave or panel number: III.D.7.

McLEAN, Private, DONALD, 30624. 2nd Battalion, Wellington Regiment, NZEF. Died 29 March 1918. Age 32. Son of Angus and Annie McLean, of Clashmore, Clashnessie, Lochinver, Sutherlandshire. Doullens Communal Cemetery Extension No. 1, Somme, France. Grave or panel number: V.B.45.

McLEAN, Private, WILLIAM ROBERT, 20208. NZ Machine Gun Battalion. Died 24 April 1918. Age 22. Son of Robert T. McLean, of 9 Swan St, Napier. Boulogne Eastern Cemetery, Pas de Calais, France. Grave or panel number: IX.A.16.

McLEOD, Rifleman, JOHN, 42696. 3rd Battalion, NZ Rifle Brigade Died 7 April 1918. Age 34. Son of George and Marion McLeod, of Taramoa, New Zealand. St Hilaire Cemetery Extension, Frevent, Pas de Calais, France. Grave or panel number: G.5.

McLEOD, Rifleman, LOUIS AUGUSTINE BERNARD, 31875. 4th Battalion, 3rd NZ Rifle Brigade. Died 15 April 1918. Age 23. Son of James and Annie McLeod of New Zealand. Doullens Communal Cemetery Extension No. 1, Somme, France. Grave or panel number: VI.B.38.

McLEOD, Corporal, WILLIAM ERNEST, 36836. 1st Battalion, 3rd NZ Rifle Brigade. Died 5 April 1918. Age 26. Son of William and Isabella McLeod, of Mosgiel. Euston Road Cemetery, Colincamps, Somme, France. Grave or panel number: III.E.6.

McMILLAN, Corporal, FREDERICK THOMAS, 10/3679. 2nd Battalion, Wellington Regiment, NZEF. Died 4 April 1918. Age 22. Son of Thomas and Elizabeth McMillan, of 3 Line, Wanganui East. Sucrerie Military Cemetery, Colincamps, Somme, France. Grave or panel number: I.3.50.

McNEIL, Rifleman, ARCHIBALD, 58783. 3rd Battalion, 3rd NZ Rifle Brigade. Died 20 April 1918. Age 33. Son of Mary Jamieson (formerly McNeil), of Coromandel, and the late Archibald McNeil. Knightsbridge Cemetery, Mesnil-Martinsart, Somme, France. Grave or panel number: D.63.

McNOE, Lance Corporal, WILLIAM ANDREW, 27096. 2nd Battalion. 3rd NZ Rifle Brigade. Died 6 April 1918. Age 24. Son of Samuel and Agnes McNoe, of Balclutha. Native of Otago. Sucrerie Military Cemetery, Colincamps, Somme, France. Grave or panel number: I.I.6.

McPHERSON, Private, ROBERT COCHRANE, 40612. No. 3 Company, 2nd Battalion, Auckland Regiment, NZEF. Died 30 March 1918. Age 25. Son of Agnes McPherson, of Mt Albert Rd, Auckland. Euston Road Cemetery,

Colincamps, Somme, France. Grave or panel number: II.T.4.

McQUEEN, Lance Corporal, ROBERT HAROLD, 39872. 1st Battalion, Wellington Regiment, NZEF. Died 11 April 1918. Age 26. Son of Charles and Christina Rose McQueen, of New Zealand. Euston Road Cemetery, Colincamps, Somme, France. Grave or panel number: III.C.8.

McQUEEN, Corporal, WILLIAM ALEXANDER, 2311108. 1st Battalion, 3rd NZ Rifle Brigade. Died 26 March 1918. Age 28. Son of Laclan and Rhoda J. McQueen, of 68 Sefton St, Timaru. Served also in Egypt. Mailly Wood Cemetery, Somme, France. Grave or panel number: I.N.I.

MACRAE, Private, ALICK, 51286. 2nd Battalion, Canterbury Regiment, NZEF. Died 27 March 1918. Brother of Mr C. Macrae, of Otira, West Coast. Serre Road Cemetery No. 1, Pas de Calais, France. Grave or panel number: III.B.5.

McRAE, Lance Corporal, HUGH, 10/3342. 1st Battalion, Wellington Regiment, NZEF. Died 30 March 1918. Grevilliers (NZ) Memorial, Pas de Calais, France.

MACSHANE, Lance Corporal, CHARLES EUGENE, 33205. 2nd Battalion, Auckland Regiment, NZEF. Died 4 April 1918. Age 38. Son of the late Mrs Mary MacShane, of Picton. St Pol Communal Cemetery Extension, Pas de Calais, France. Grave or panel number: H.24.

McSWEENEY, Private, BERNARD BRIAN, 57427. 1st Battalion, Otago Regiment, NZEF. Died 22 April 1918. Age 29. Son of John and Ellen Roache McSweeney; husband of Margaret Scott McSweeney, of Auckland. Euston Road Cemetery, Colincamps, Somme, France. Grave or panel number: I.H.3.

McWHA, Private, DUPREE WILLIAM, 6/3394. 1st Battalion, Canterbury Regiment, NZEF. Died 18 April 1918. Age 24. Son of Francis and Alice McWha, of Murchison. Sucrerie Military Cemetery, Colincamps, Somme, France. Grave or panel number: IV.E.3.

MALCOLM, Second Lieutenant, GEORGE, 41981. 4th Battalion, 3rd NZ Rifle Brigade. Died 28 March 1918. Age 22. Son of Alex and Mary J. Malcolm, of Enfield, Otago. Euston Road Cemetery, Colincamps, Somme, France. Grave or panel number: IV.C.5.

MALONE, Lieutenant, EDMOND LEO, 11/699, MC. 1st Battalion, 3rd NZ Rifle Brigade. Died 6 April 1918. Son of the late Lt. Col. and Mrs W.G. Malone, of Stratford, Taranaki; husband of Mary H. Malone of 29 Longworth Rd, Horwich, Lancs. Wimereux Communal Cemetery, Pas de Calais, France. Grave or panel number: IV.D.2.

MAPP, Private, RICHARD, 34407. 1st Battalion, Auckland Regiment, NZEF. Died 30 April 1918. Age 39. Son of Richard and the late Emma Mapp, of Midhurst, Taranaki. Etaples Military Cemetery, Pas de Calais, France. Grave or panel number: LXVI.A.34.

MARCHANT, Rifleman, ALEXANDER BARBER, 23/1434. 1st Battalion, 3rd NZ Rifle Brigade. Died 27 March 1918. Age 32. Son of Francis Septimus and Elizabeth Marchant, of Hastings. Served also in Egypt. Mailly Wood Cemetery, Somme, France. Grave or panel number: I.N.2.

MARTEN, Rifleman, CARL, 12436. 4th Battalion, 3rd NZ Rifle Brigade. Died 29 March 1918. Son of Mr and Mrs John Marten, of 11 Violet St, Eden Terrace, Auckland. Euston Road Cemetery, Colincamps, Somme, France. Grave or panel number: I.H.8.

MARTIN, Private, CYRIL JESSE GIBSON, 61142. 2nd NZ Entrenching Battalion, NZEF. Died 29 April 1918. Age 22. Son of Frederick and Georgina Martin, of Islington, Blenheim. Perth Cemetery (China Wall), Ypres, West-Vlaanderen, Belgium. Grave or panel number: VI.C.3.

MARTIN, Private, HENRY SAVILLE, 51573. 1st Battalion, Auckland Regiment, NZEF. Died 30 March 1918. Age 31. Son of Henry H. and Annie M. Martin, of Howick, Auckland. Born at Chatham Islands. Doullens Communal Cemetery Extension No. 1, Somme, France. Grave or panel number: V.B.35.

MARTIN, Sapper, JAMES HORACE, 4/1973. Light Railway Operating Section, NZ Engineers. Died 25 April 1918. Age 29. Son of James and Louisa Martin, of Upper Hutt, Wellington. Served at Samoa. Poperinghe New Military Cemetery, Poperinge, West-Vlaanderen, Belgium. Grave or panel number: II.K.9.

MARTIN, Private, JOHN WILLIAM, 27337. 2nd Battalion, Canterbury Regiment, NZEF. Died 26 March 1918. Age 22. Son of Elizabeth Evans, of Ely, England. Mailly Wood Cemetery, Somme, France. Grave or panel number: I.N.4.

MARTIN, Private, LEONARD, 61700. 1st Battalion, Canterbury Regiment, NZEF. Died 27 April 1918. Age 21. Son of James and Caroline Martin, of Moreton Rd, Carterton. Colincamps Communal Cemetery, Somme, France.

MARTIN, Private, ROBERT FREDERICK, 48661. 2nd Battalion, Auckland Regiment, NZEF. Died 30 March 1918. Age 24. Son of Frederick Thomas and Annie E. Martin, of Taniwha, Te Kauwhata. Euston Road Cemetery, Colincamps, Somme, France. Grave or panel number: IV.B.9.

MASON, Private, ALBERT CHERNELL, 25558. NZ Machine Gun Battalion. Died 27 March 1918. Son of Mr and Mrs A. Mason, of New Plymouth. Euston Road Cemetery, Colincamps, Somme, France. Grave or panel number V.D.9.

MASON, Lance Sergeant, WILLIAM, 25/507. 'A' Company, 3rd Battalion, 3rd NZ Rifle Brigade. Died 29 March 1918. Age 36. Son of the late William and Ellen Mason, of Auckland. Euston Road Cemetery, Colincamps, Somme, France. Grave or panel number: V.I.10.

MASON, Rifleman, WILLIAM PATRICK, 24/2243. 4th Battalion, 3rd NZ Rifle Brigade. Died 5 April 1918. Age 22. Son of James and Margaret Mason, of 53 Kent Tce, Wellington. Born at Victoria Place, Wellington. Courcelles-au-Bois Communal Cemetery Extension, Somme, France. Grave or panel number: F.8.

MATTHEWSON, Private, HUGH HENDERSON, 48659. 2nd Battalion, Auckland Regiment, NZEF. Died 1 April 1918. Age 36. Son of James and the late Mary Matthewson, of Dunedin; husband of B.J. Matthewson, of 'Marlow', Albert St, Petersham, Sydney, New South Wales, Australia. Etaples Military Cemetery, Pas de Calais, France. Grave or panel number: XXXII.A.13A.

MAULE, Rifleman, JAMES, 52851. 1st Battalion, 3rd NZ Rifle Brigade. Died 16 April 1918. Age 56. Son of Captain and Ellen Maule, of Wellington. Mendinghem Military Cemetery, Poperinge, West-Vlaanderen, Belgium. Grave or panel number: IX.F.39.

MAUNDER, Private, ALFRED ROY, 40348. 2nd Battalion, Wellington Regiment, NZEF. Died 25 April 1918. Age 26. Only son of Alfred H. and Annie Maunder. Born at Hamilton. Euston Road Cemetery, Colincamps, Somme, France. Grave or panel number: V.P.9.

MAXWELL, Rifleman, CHARLES, 15928. 3rd Battalion, 3rd NZ Rifle Brigade. Died 28 March 1918. Son of Sarah Maxwell, of Beautiful Valley, Geraldine, and the late R.F. Maxwell. Grevillers (NZ) Memorial, Pas de Calais, France.

MAXWELL, Private, THEODORE HENRY, 24029. 1st Battalion, Auckland Regiment, NZEF. Died 27 March 1918. Age 23. Son of Mr L.S. and Mrs A.E. Maxwell, of Northcote, Auckland. St Pol British Cemetery, St Pol-sur-Ternoise, Pas de Calais, France. Grave or panel number: I.A.5.

MAYLEN, Private, WILLIAM, 49638. 2nd Battalion, Canterbury Regiment, NZEF. Died 28 March 1918. Age 23. Son of Mrs Maylen, of Caithness, Scotland. Doullens Communal Cemetery Extension No. 1, Somme, France. Grave or panel number: V.C.18.

MAYO, Private, CHARLES EDWARD, 44069. 2nd Battalion, Canterbury Regiment, NZEF. Died 14 April 1918. Meteren Military Cemetery, Nord, France. Grave or panel number: III.D.633.

MEADWAY, Private, EDWIN LAURENCE, 45534. 2nd Battalion, Auckland Regiment, NZEF. Died 30 March 1918. Age 24. Son of William Edwin and Jane Meadway, of Paterangi, Hamilton. Grevilliers (NZ) Memorial, Pas de Calais, France.

MENZIES, Rifleman, DUNCAN, 25/779. 3rd Battalion, 3rd NZ Rifle Brigade. Died 27 March 1918. Son of Mr and Mrs Thomas Menzies, of Lumsden. Euston Road Cemetery, Colincamps, Somme, France. Grave or panel number: III.N.7.

MENZIES, Private, WILLIAM GREIG , 32532. 1st Battalion, Auckland Regiment, NZEF. Died 26 March 1918. Age 35. Son of Jean Menzies, of 58 St Asaph St, Christchurch, and the late Adam Menzies; husband of Bessie G. Menzies, of Waverley, Wellington. Grevilliers (NZ) Memorial, Pas de Calais, France.

MENZIES, Private, WILLIAM RUTLEDGE, 46654. 1st Battalion, Canterbury Regiment, NZEF. Died 5 April 1918. Age 21. Son of William and C.I.

Menzies. Martinsart British Cemetery, Somme, France. Grave or panel number: I.H.37.

MERCER, Private, EDGAR JOSEPH, 47504. 2nd NZ Entrenching Battalion, NZEF. Died 14 April 1918. Age 32. Son of Thomas and Margaret Mercer, of Makikihi, Timaru. Messines Ridge (NZ) Memorial, Mesen, West-Vlaanderen, Belgium.

METCALFE, Rifleman, ERNEST, 39270. 2nd Battalion, 3rd NZ Rifle Brigade. Died 28 April 1918. Age 28. Son of Thomas and Mary Metcalfe, of Otatara, Invercargill. Etaples Military Cemetery, Pas de Calais, France. Grave or panel number: LXVI.A.23.

METTAM, Corporal, FREDERICK JAMES, 12/3421. 2nd Battalion, Auckland Regiment, NZEF. Died 6 April 1918. Age 23. Son of John Tunnard Mettam and Lavinia Mettam, of Swanson, Auckland. Thrice wounded. Etaples Military Cemetery, Pas de Calais, France. Grave or panel number: XXXIII.D.5.

MILES, Lance Corporal, HENRY ERNEST OSBORNE, 44000. 2nd Battalion, Canterbury Regiment, NZEF. Died 5 April 1918. Age 26. Son of Samuel and Mary Miles, of 44 Ranfurley St, Christchurch. Serre Road Cemetery No. 1, Pas de Calais, France. Grave or panel number: II.D.5.

MILLAR, Rifleman, JOHN REGINALD, 39074. 3rd Battalion, 3rd NZ Rifle Brigade. Died 5 April 1918. Age 20. Son of John and Elizabeth Millar, of Beach Rd, Ashburton. Grevillers (NZ) Memorial, Pas de Calais, France.

MILLER, Private, WILLIAM ARTHUR, 17933. NZ Machine Gun Corps. Died 7 April 1918. Age 21. Son of Rudolph and Jessie Miller. Born at Invercargill. Hédauville Communal Cemetery Extension, Somme, France. Grave or panel number H.24.

MILLIGAN, Corporal, WALTER GEORGE, 10/3350. 1st NZ Entrenching Battalion, NZEF. Died 14 April 1918. Age 30. Son of Isaac and Mary Milligan, late of Oxford, Canterbury. Native of Oxford. Messines Ridge (NZ) Memorial, Mesen, West-Vlaanderen, Belgium.

MILLS, Private, RONGO, 47914. 2nd Battalion, Canterbury Regiment, NZEF. Died 5 April 1918. Son of Mrs Pimia Mills, of Gisborne. Serre Road Cemetery No. 1, Pas de Calais, France. Grave or panel number: II.D.6.

MILNE, Corporal, THOMAS ANDREW, 53393. 'J' Company, 1st Battalion, 3rd NZ Rifle Brigade. Died 5 April 1918. Age 21. Son of John and Alice May Milne, of Raes Junction, Dunedin. Grevillers (NZ) Memorial, Pas de Calais, France.

MITCHELL, Sergeant, ARCHIBALD CLEMENT, 8/3360. 1st Battalion, Otago Regiment, NZEF. Died 28 April 1918. Age 34. Son of Adam and Annie Mitchell, of Epsom, Auckland. Euston Road Cemetery, Colincamps, Somme, France. Grave or panel number: I.J.4.

MITCHELL, Private, VALENTINE PATRICK, 11903. 1st Battalion, Wellington Regiment, NZEF. Died 31 March 1918. Age 22. Son of the late Timothy and Alice Mitchell, of Dover, England. Englebelmer Communal Cemetery Extension, Somme, France. Grave or panel number: E.13.

MOHAN, Rifleman, EDWARD, 45712. 2nd Battalion, 3rd NZ Rifle Brigade. Died 26 March 1918. Age 42. Son of Micheal and Mary Mohan, of 13 Hand St, Drogheda, County Louth, Ireland. Grevillers (NZ) Memorial, Pas de Calais, France.

MOHR, Corporal, KEITH, 13/3185. Machine Gun Battalion, NZ Machine Gun Corps. Died 26 March 1918. Son of Mr and Mrs P.H. Mohr, of Auckland. Grevillers (NZ) Memorial, Pas de Calais, France.

MOIR, Gunner, GORDON, 50220. 5th Battery, NZ Field Artillery. Died 18 April 1918. Age 21. Son of Leslie John and Ann Catherine Moir, of Mangawai. Lijssenthoek Military Cemetery, Poperinge, West-Vlaanderen, Belgium. Grave or panel number: XXVI.G.10A.

MONAGHAN, Private, JOHN, 33920. 2nd Battalion, Auckland Regiment, NZEF. Died 27 March 1918. Age 26. Son of Patrick and Bridget Monaghan, of 4 Devon St, Auckland. Mailly Wood Cemetery, Somme, France. Grave or panel number: I.P.22.

MONTAGU, Sergeant, ELLWOOD CHARLES DOUGLAS, 23/212. 1st Battalion, 3rd NZ Rifle Brigade. Died 5 April 1918. Age 25. Son of Charles E. and Ida Montagu, of Chesterfield, West Coast. Enlisted January 1915. Euston Road Cemetery, Colincamps, Somme, France. Grave or panel number: IV.D.8.

MOORE, Rifleman, ALFRED KETTLEY, 41096. 'A' Company, 3rd Battalion, 3rd NZ Rifle Brigade, Died 29 March 1918. Age 26. Son of Harriet Moore, of Christchurch, and the late William Keetley Moore. Euston Road Cemetery, Colincamps, Somme, France. Grave or panel number: III.N.2.

MOORE, Private, KENNETH STUART, 31680, MM. 1st Battalion, Auckland Regiment, NZEF. Died 27 March 1918. Age 32. Husband of Ethel Moore, of Alfriston, Auckland. Doullens Communal Cemetery Extension No. 1, Somme, France. Grave or panel number: V.A.46.

MOORE, Corporal, SUNNY, 16/555. NZ Maori (Pioneer) Battalion. Died 24 April 1918. Brother of W. Moore, of Whananaki, Auckland. St Sever Cemetery Extension, Rouen, Seine-Maritime, France. Grave or panel number: IX.D.6A.

MORGAN, Private, JOHN SAMUEL, 45891. 1st Battalion, Canterbury Regiment, NZEF. Died 31 March 1918. Age 22. Son of William John and Sarah Morgan, of Cornwall, England. Etaples Military Cemetery, Pas de Calais, France. Grave or panel number: XXXIII.B.20.

MORGAN, Rifleman, RENELD, 54553. 4th Battalion, 3rd NZ Rifle Brigade. Died 30 March 1918. Age 20. Son of John and Delia Morgan, of Te Horo, Wellington. Doullens Communal Cemetery Extension No. 1, Somme, France. Grave or panel number: VI.G.44.

MORONEY, Rifleman, PETER, 55991. 'G' Company, 3rd Battalion, 3rd NZ

Rifle Brigade. Died 7 April 1918. Age 39. Son of the late Peter Morrissey and Mary Moroney, of Normandale, Lower Hutt, Wellington. Born at Oamaru. Grevillers (NZ) Memorial, Pas de Calais, France.

MORRIS, Private, GEORGE ARTHUR, 53597. 1st Battalion, Auckland Regiment, NZEF. Died 18 April 1918. Age 39. Son of George A. and Catherine Morris, of Douglas St, Highfield, Timaru. Grevillers British Cemetery, Pas de Calais, France. Grave or panel number: XII.F.37.

MORRISON, Private, EVAN WILLIAM, 31320. 1st Battalion, Wellington Regiment, NZEF. Died 5 April 1918. Age 24. Son of A. and F. Morrison, of 62 Cambridge Terrace, Wellington. Doullens Communal Cemetery Extension No. 1, Somme, France. Grave or panel number: VI.D.3.

MORTON, Private, JOHN CASTLE, 52355, 1st Battalion, Auckland Regiment, NZEF. Died 19 April 1918. Age 33. Son of Clara and the late W.H. Morton, of Waihi. Doullens Communal Cemetery Extension No. 1, Somme, France. Grave or panel number: V.A.14.

MOTHERWELL, Sergeant, JAMES PATTISON, 38419. 2nd Battalion, Auckland Regiment, NZEF. Died 27 March 1918. Grevilliers (NZ) Memorial, Pas de Calais, France.

MOWBRAY, Private, WILLIAM ERNEST, 22063. 4th Company, 2nd Battalion, Otago Regiment, NZEF. Died 4 April 1918. Age 32. Son of William and Rosetta Mowbray. Martinsart British Cemetery, Somme, France. Grave or panel number: I.H.33.

MUIR, Private, MATTHEW THOMAS, 59534. 1st Battalion, Otago Regiment, NZEF. Died 30 March 1918. Age 38. Son of James and Mary Muir, of Havelock North. Doullens Communal Cemetery Extension No. 1, Somme, France. Grave or panel number: VI.F.22.

MULCAHY, Private, DAVID, 24/2043. NZ Cyclist Battalion. Died 29 April 1918. Son of Mrs M. Mulcahy, of Tyndall St, Pahiatua. Wytschaete Military Cemetery, Heuvelland, West-Vlaanderen, Belgium. Grave or panel number: VI.B.I.

MULLANY, Rifleman, JOHN, 24/2045. 3rd Battalion, 3rd NZ Rifle Brigade. Died 6 April 1918. Age 21. Son of Louis and Susan Mullany, of 42 Richmond St, Petone. Sucrerie Military Cemetery, Colincamps, Somme, France. Grave or panel number: I.AA.22.

MUNNOCH, Private, JOHN, 8/4182. 1st Battalion, Otago Regiment, NZEF. Died 8 April 1918. Age 31. Son of William Munnoch, of Cowane St, Stirling, Scotland. Gezaincourt Communal Cemetery Extension, Somme, France. Grave or panel number: I.K.23.

MUNRO, Private, HECTOR JOHN, 54926. 1st Battalion, Auckland Regiment, NZEF. Died 27 March 1918. Son of Catherine Munro, of Pokeno, Auckland. Grevillers (NZ) Memorial, Pas de Calais, France.

MURPHY, Sergeant, DENIS, 25145. 2nd Battalion, Otago Regiment, NZEF.

Died 5 April 1918. Martinsart British Cemetery, Somme, France. Grave or panel number: I.H.36.

MURPHY, Driver, EDDIE, 28006. 6th Battery, NZ Field Artillery. Died 10 April 1918. Age 22. Son of Alfred Edward and Ada Murphy, of 10 Owens Rd, Epsom, Auckland. Native of Lichfield, Waikato. Strand Military Cemetery, Comines-Warneton, Hainaut, Belgium. Grave or panel number: IX. P.7.

MURPHY, Private, GEORGE ALEXANDER, 14296. 2nd Battalion, Auckland Regiment, NZEF. Died 2 April 1918. Age 32. Son of Hull Ingram Murphy and Mary Jane Murphy, of Dublin, Ireland. Etaples Military Cemetery, Pas de Calais, France. Grave or panel number: XXIX.A.5A.

MURPHY, Private, THOMAS, 34403. 1st Battalion, Auckland Regiment, NZEF. Died 26 March 1918. Grevilliers (NZ) Memorial, Pas de Calais, France.

MURRAY, Gunner, LINCOLN BISHOP, 17314. 15th Battery, 1st Brigade, NZ Field Artillery. Died 13 April 1918. Age 21. Only son of John Lincoln Murray and Mary Ellen Murray, of 48 Church St, Masterton. Etaples Military Cemetery, Pas de Calais, France. Grave or panel number: XXIX.B.17.

MURRAY, Lance Corporal, MARTIN, 1312599. 4th Battalion, 3rd NZ Rifle Brigade. Died 28 March 1918. Age 39. Son of Bridget Bodkin (formerly Murray), of Auckland, and the late John Murray. Euston Road Cemetery, Colincamps, Somme, France. Grave or panel number: IV.C.2.

NAPIER, Private, NORMAN CAMPBELL, 57130. 2nd Battalion, Otago Regiment, NZEF. Died 9 April 1918. Son of Mrs Mary Napier, of Strath Eden, Eketahuna. Knightsbridge Cemetery, Mesnil-Martinsart, Somme, France. Grave or panel number: A.4.

NASH, Sergeant, HECTOR FREDERICK, 23081. 3rd Battalion, 3rd NZ Rifle Brigade. Died 5 April 1918. Mailly Wood Cemetery, Somme, France. Grave or panel number: I.N.I6.

NEAL, Sergeant, ALFRED, 23/1761. 2nd Battalion, Wellington Regiment, NZEF. Died 23 April 1918. Age 21. Son of Moses and Marion Neal, of Birkenhead, Auckland. Wimereux Communal Cemetery, Pas de Calais, France. Grave or panel number: XI.F.9.

NEILSON, Lieutenant, ALEXANDER ROBERT, 22690. 3rd Battalion, 3rd NZ Rifle Brigade. Died 28 March 1918. Age 30. Son of Robert Neilson, of Ohaeawai, Bay of Islands. St Pol British Cemetery, St Pol-Sur-Ternoise, Pas de Calais, France. Grave or panel number: II.A.3.

NEILSON, Shoeing Smith Corporal, VICTOR FRANCIS, 2/2225. NZ Field Artillery. Died 15 April 1918. Longuenesse (St Omer) Souvenir Cemetery, Pas de Calais, France. Grave or panel number: V.A.52.

NELSON, Private, HARRY, 10145. 1st Battalion, Canterbury Regiment, NZEF. Died 6 April 1918. Grevillers (NZ) Memorial, Pas de Calais, France.

NELSON, Second Lieutenant, WILLIAM THOMAS, 2/584. NZ Field Artillery. Died 18 April 1918. Age 24. Son of W. T. Nelson, of Napier. Lijssenthoek Military Cemetery, Poperinge, West-Vlaanderen, Belgium. Grave or panel number: XXVI.G.8.

NEWELL, Lance Corporal, D'ARCY ROYCROFT, 8/2687. 1st Battalion, Otago Regiment, NZEF. Died 13 April 1918. Age 22. Son of Frederic Thomas and Alice Maud Newell, of 232 Powderham St, New Plymouth. Brockenhurst (St Nicholas) Churchyard, Hampshire, United Kingdom. Grave or panel number: A.4.13.

NEWNHAM, Private, THOMAS, 52099. 1st Battalion, Canterbury Regiment, NZEF. Died 27 March 1918. Son of Mr and Mrs Thomas Newnham, of 70 Allen St, Upper Riccarton. Christchurch. Grevillers (NZ) Memorial, Pas de Calais, France.

NEWPORT, Lance Sergeant, JONATHAN HOWARD, 15585. 2nd Battalion, Canterbury Regiment, NZEF. Died 5 April 1918. Age 38. Son of Joseph and Sarah Newport, of 114 Nile St, East Nelson. Serre Road Cemetery No. 1, Pas de Calais, France. Grave or panel number: III.C.21.

NICHOLSON, Private, GERALD, 23/1766. 2nd Battalion, Auckland Regiment, NZEF. Died 12 April 1918. Age 22. Son of J.E. and E.S. Nicholson, of Farrar St, Auckland. Born at Port Albert, Auckland. St Sever Cemetery Extension, Rouen, Seine-Maritime, France. Grave or panel number: P.IX.H.4B.

NICOLAS, Sapper, LOUIS OSWALD, 911593, MM. NZ Engineers. Died 5 April 1918. Mailly Wood Cemetery, Somme, France. Grave or panel number: II.F.I4.

NICOLSON, Rifleman, DAVID, 51890. 2nd Battalion, 3rd NZ Rifle Brigade. Died 31 March 1918. Age 23. Son of David and Esther Emma Nicolson, of Christchurch. Native of Perthshire, Scotland. Euston Road Cemetery, Colincamps, Somme, France. Grave or panel number: IV.D.3.

NIXON, Private, ALFRED ERNEST, 38899. 4th NZ Machine Gun Battalion. Died 7 April 1918. Age 27. Son of William Nixon, of Henderson, Auckland. Wimereux Communal Cemetery, Pas de Calais, France. Grave or panel number: X.A.15.

NORCROSS, Private, JAMES THOMAS, 56989. Otago Regiment, NZEF. Died 30 March 1918. Age 38. Son of Alice E. and the late Thomas Norcross, of 32 Weka St, Nelson. Doullens Communal Cemetery Extension No. 1, Somme, France. Grave or panel number: V.B.17.

NUTTER, Second Lieutenant, EDWARD ROLAND, 38849. 2nd Battalion, 3rd NZ Rifle Brigade. Died 30 March 1918. Husband of Elizabeth Penlington (formerly Nutter), of 602 Grays Rd, Hastings. Grevillers (NZ) Memorial, Pas de Calais, France.

OBERG, Private, JAMES ALBERT, 25295. 2nd Battalion, Canterbury Regiment, NZEF. Died 26 March 1918. Son of Jonas and Mary Oberg, of 15 Elmwood Rd, Fendalton, Christchurch. Grevillers (NZ) Memorial, Pas de Calais, France.

O'CONNOR, Rifleman, MICHAEL, 36883. 3rd Battalion, 3rd NZ Rifle Brigade. Died 20 April 1918. Son of Mrs C. O'Connor, of John St, Gore. Mesnil Communal Cemetery Extension, Somme, France. Grave or panel number: II.A.8.

O'CONNOR, Second Lieutenant, MICHAEL BERNARD, 18582. 3rd Battalion, Canterbury Regiment, NZEF. Died 5 April 1918. Age 23. Son of Maurice and Elizabeth O'Connor, of County Kerry, Ireland. Auchonvillers Military Cemetery, Somme, France. Grave or panel number: II.M.27.

O'KEEFE, Private, PATRICK, 49736. 2nd Battalion, Auckland Regiment, NZEF. Died 30 March 1918. Son of Mrs E. O'Keefe, of Broadford, County Clare, Ireland. Grevilliers (NZ) Memorial, Pas de Calais, France.

OLD, Lance Sergeant, HAROLD EDWARD, 10/1940. 1st Battalion, Wellington Regiment, NZEF. Died 3 April 1918. Age 23. Son of William and Emma Jane Old, of Wanganui. Also served at Gallipoli. Etaples Military Cemetery, Pas de Calais, France. Grave or panel number: XXXIII.C.5A.

OLDRIDGE, Rifleman, THOMAS SMART DAVEY, 56831. 3rd Battalion, 3rd NZ Rifle Brigade. Died 27 March 1918. Grevillers (NZ) Memorial, Pas de Calais, France.

OLIVER, Rifleman, THOMAS FRANCIS, 41010. 4th Battalion, 3rd NZ Rifle Brigade. Died 6 April 1918. Age 21. Son of Thomas and Elizabeth Oliver, of Pine Bush, Southland. Gezaincourt Communal Cemetery Extension, Somme, France. Grave or panel number: I.J.21.

O'MEARA, Rifleman, JAMES, 23/865. 4th Battalion, 3rd NZ Rifle Brigade. Died 29 March 1918. Age 26. Son of John and Elizabeth O'Meara, of Swanson, Auckland. Euston Road Cemetery, Colincamps, Somme, France. Grave or panel number: II.A.6.

O'NEILL, Private, THOMAS, 29065. 1st Battalion, Canterbury Regiment, NZEF. Died 5 April 1918. Age 37. Son of Edward and Mary O'Neill, of 57 Macandrew Rd, South Dunedin. Serre Road Cemetery No. 1, Pas de Calais, France. Grave or panel number: IV.G.14.

ORANGE, Private, RAYMOND LIONEL, 40837. 2nd Battalion, Canterbury Regiment, NZEF. Died 5 April 1918. Age 25. Son of Albert Edward and Helena B. Orange; husband of Lilian L. Orange, of 32 Esplanade, Sumner, Christchurch. Auchonvillers Military Cemetery, Somme, France. Grave or panel number: II.M.26.

ORCHARD, Private, CHARLES JAMES, 21316. 1st Battalion, Auckland Regiment, NZEF. Died 26 March 1918. Age 43. Son of James Orchard and Ellen Jillard Vodden Orchard. Grevilliers (NZ) Memorial, Pas de Calais, France.

O'SULLIVAN, Rifleman, P., 55616. 2nd Battalion, 3rd NZ Rifle Brigade. Died 5 April 1918. Gezaincourt Communal Cemetery Extension, Somme, France. Grave or panel number: I.J.27.

OWEN, Private, JOHN, 12/3119, MM. 1st Battalion, Auckland Regiment, NZEF. Died 5 April 1918. Age 32. Son of John and Anne Owen, of 'Norwood', 54 Gt South Rd, Remuera, Auckland. Bertrancourt Military Cemetery, Somme, France. Grave or panel number: 2.B.4.

OWEN, Rifleman, WILLIAM JOSEPH, 14853. 4th Battalion, 3rd NZ Rifle Brigade. Died 29 March 1918. Age 22. Son of Susan Halpin (formerly Owen), of Gisborne, and the late William Joseph Owen. Euston Road Cemetery, Colincamps, Somme, France. Grave or panel number: V.A.1.

PACEY, Rifleman, WILLIAM, 41106. 3rd Battalion, 3rd NZ Rifle Brigade. Died 27 March 1918. Age 25. Son of William and Annie Pacey, of Taieri Rd, Halfway Bush, Wakari, Dunedin, husband of Mary Elizabeth Pacey, of Girton, Newark, England. Born at Bingham, Nottingham, England. Grevillers (NZ) Memorial, Pas de Calais, France.

PAGE, Rifleman, THOMAS ALBERT JAMES, 51893. 'A' Company, 1st Battalion, 3rd NZ Rifle Brigade. Died 5 April 1918. Age 27. Son of William and Sarah Page, of Hororata, Canterbury. Euston Road Cemetery, Colincamps, Somme, France. Grave or panel number: IV.D.6.

PALLANT, Private, ARTHUR ERNEST, 14732. 2nd NZ Entrenching Battalion, NZEF. Died 15 April 1918. Age 22. Son of Arthur and Annie Pallant, of Pinfold Rd, Woodville. Native of Dannevirke. Messines Ridge (NZ) Memorial, Mesen, West-Vlaanderen, Belgium.

PALMER, Private, JAMES DARCY, 19172. 1st Battalion, Auckland Regiment, NZEF. Died 27 March 1918. Age 24. Son of Robert and Agnes Palmer, of Normanby, Hawera; husband of Mary J. Carmichael (formerly Palmer), of Regent St, Hawera. St Hilaire Cemetery, Frevent, Pas de Calais, France. Grave or panel number: V.E.8.

PATCHETT, Rifleman, EDWARD ERNEST, 58800. 4th Battalion, 3rd NZ Rifle Brigade. Died 29 March 1918. Age 23. Son of Mrs Mary Patchett, of Customhouse St, Blenheim. Grevillers (NZ) Memorial, Pas de Calais, France.

PATERSON, Private, ALAN MCLEAN, 30635. 1st Battalion, Canterbury Regiment, NZEF. Died 27 March 1918. Son of Mrs F.I. Paterson, of 148 Adelaide Rd, Wellington. Grevillers (NZ) Memorial, Pas de Calais, France.

PATTISON, Corporal, HERBERT CAMPBELL, 11/1208. 2nd Battalion, Wellington Regiment, NZEF. Died 23 March 1918. Son of R. Pattison, of Kumeroa, Hawke's Bay. Hazebrouck Communal Cemetery, Nord, France. Grave or panel number: III.C.40.

PAVITT, Private, REGINALD, 48563. 2nd Battalion, Auckland Regiment, NZEF. Died 30 March 1918. Age 31. Son of the late George and Eliza Pavittt.

Grevilliers (NZ) Memorial, Pas de Calais, France.

PEAKE, Rifleman, FRANK ROWLAND, 52268. 1st Battalion, NZ Rifle Brigade Died 8 April 1918. Age 24. Son of William and Edith Peake, of 109 Great North Rd, Grey Lynn, Auckland. St Hilaire Cemetery Extension, Frevent, Pas de Calais, France. Grave or panel number: D.15.

PEARCE, Corporal, VICTOR WILLIAM, 24/1167, MM. 2nd Battalion, 3rd NZ Rifle Brigade. Died 26 March 1918. Age 27. Son of William Pearce, of 'Leostan', Wick Rd, Devizes, Wilts, England. Twice previously wounded. One of three brothers who served. Grevillers (NZ) Memorial, Pas de Calais, France.

PEARSON, Gunner, RUPERT LESLIE, 50560. NZ Field Artillery. Died 19 April 1918. Age 20. Son of Agnes E. Pearson and stepson of Peter Pearson, of Sealey St, Thames. Haringhe (Bandaghem) Military Cemetery, Poperinge, West-Vlaanderen, Belgium. Grave or panel number: I.P.15.

PEMBERTON, Private, DAVID AUTUMN, 32893. 2nd Battalion, Otago Regiment, NZEF. Died 2 April 1918. Age 21. Son of Mr H.J. Pemberton, of Limehills, Southland. Gezaincourt Communal Cemetery Extension, Somme, France. Grave or panel number: II.H.6.

PENZER, Private, ESAU JOSEPH, 59712. 2nd Battalion, Canterbury Regiment, NZEF. Died 5 April 1918. Age 40. Son of Elizabeth Knight (formerly Penzer), of 163 Grey St, Auckland. Born at Alton, Wellington. Grevillers (NZ) Memorial, Pas de Calais, France.

PERRY, Lance Corporal, EDWARD JEVAN HERBERT, 25121. NZ Machine Gun Battalion. Died 31 March 1918. Age 29. Son of James Lewis and Susan Perry; husband of Louisa H. Perry, of 17 Innes Rd, Merivale, Christchurch. Sucrerie Military Cemetery, Colincamps, Somme, France. Grave or panel number: I.J.51.

PERRY, Rifleman, JAMES, 42570. 'D' Company, 3rd Battalion, 3rd NZ Rifle Brigade. Died 6 April 1918. Age 39. Son of William and Mary Perry, of Sawyers Bay, Dunedin. Grevillers (NZ) Memorial, Pas de Calais, France.

PERRY, Lance Corporal, WILLIAM ALFRED, IO/1617. 'C' Company, 4th Battalion, 3rd NZ Rifle Brigade. Died 28 March 1918. Age 25. Son of George Henry and Mahala Perry, of Hale Edge, South Nutfield, Surrey, England. Euston Road Cemetery, Colincamps, Somme, France. Grave or panel number: IV.D.2.

PERYMAN, Corporal, LEONARD WESLEY, 29071. 3rd Battalion, 3rd NZ Rifle Brigade. Died 6 April 1918. Age 33. Son of Henry Edward and Catherine Mary Peryman, of Tai Tapu, Canterbury. Hédauville Communal Cemetery Extension, Somme, France. Grave or panel number: H.15.

PETERSEN, Rifleman, HAROLD LEWIS CHRISTIAN, 20562. 2nd Battalion, 3rd NZ Rifle Brigade. Died 7 April 1918. Age 19. Son of Martin and Ellen Petersen, of Wellington. Gezaincourt Communal Cemetery Extension, Somme, France. Grave or panel number: II.J.4.

PETERSON, Private, FREDERICK CREIGHTON, 13/3299. 2nd Battalion,

Wellington Regiment, NZEF. Died 27 March 1918. Age 22. Youngest son of Peter and Matilda Jane Peterson, of Napier. Euston Road Cemetery, Colincamps, Somme, France. Grave or panel number: V.C.8.

PETRIE, Second Lieutenant, ARNOLD JAMES, 6th (Hauraki) Company, 1st Battalion, Auckland Regiment, NZEF. Died 18 April 1918. Age 24. Son of Isaac L. and Jessie A. Petrie, of Invercargill. Also served in Gallipoli and Egypt. Wounded while leading his platoon into front line near Colincamps. Doullens Communal Cemetery Extension No. 1, Somme, France, Grave or panel number: VI.A.36.

PHELPS, Private, EDGAR ERNEST, 52006. 1st Battalion, Canterbury Regiment, NZEF. Died 18 April 1918. Age 26. Son of Mr and Mrs Charles Phelps, of Leeds, England; husband of Rose Amelia Phelps, of 33 Myrtle Crescent, Wellington. Sucrerie Military Cemetery, Colincamps, Somme, France. Grave or panel number: IV.E.4.

PHILLIS, Lance Corporal, FREDERICK JOHN, 32962. 3rd Battalion, 3rd NZ Rifle Brigade. Died 29 March 1918. Age 25. Son of Thomas Frederick and Mary Ellen Phillis, of 62 Whiteleigh Ave, Addington, Christchurch. Etaples Military Cemetery, Pas de Calais, France. Grave or panel number: XXXI.L.4A.

PIERSON, Rifleman, FRANK, 14858. 4th Battalion, 3rd NZ Rifle Brigade. Died 5 April 1918. Age 36. Son of Carl and Ellen Pierson, of Okato, New Plymouth. Born at Patea, Wellington. Grevillers (NZ) Memorial, Pas de Calais, France.

PILCHER, Private, CHARLES STEPHEN, 13800. 1st Battalion, Auckland Regiment, NZEF. Died 26 March 1918. Age 30. Son of Edward and Rose Pilcher, of Stanway, Halcombe, Wellington; husband of Hazel Dorothy McKay (formerly Pilcher), of 27 South Road, Masterton. Grevilliers (NZ) Memorial, Pas de Calais, France.

PLASKETT, Private, WALTER, 60986. 2nd Battalion, Canterbury Regiment, NZEF. Died 29 March 1918. Age 30. Son of William and Elizabeth Plaskett, of Fernside, North Canterbury. A farmer. Serre Road Cemetery No. 1, Pas de Calais, France. Grave or panel number: II.B.9.

POLGLASE, Private, JOHN, 37652. 1st Battalion, Otago Regiment, NZEF. Died 5 April 1918. Englebelmer Communal Cemetery Extension, Somme, France. Grave or panel number: E.18.

POMEROY, Private, FRANCIS EDWARD, 55790. 2nd NZ Entrenching Battalion, NZEF. Died 16 April 1918. Age 22. Son of Phillipa Williams (formerly Pomeroy), of 12 Wesley St, South Dunedin. Messines Ridge (NZ) Memorial, Mesen, West-Vlaanderen, Belgium.

PORTEOUS, Lance Corporal, T., 36790. 3rd Battalion, 3rd NZ Rifle Brigade. Died 27 March 1918. Euston Road Cemetery, Colincamps, Somme, France. Grave or panel number: IV.D.1.

POWER, Private, EDMOND JOSEPH, 41620. Otago Regiment, NZEF. Died

30 March 1918. Age 26. Son of Richard and Margaret Power, of Westmere, Wanganui. Doullens Communal Cemetery Extension No. 1, Somme, France. Grave or panel number: VI.F.3.

POWER, Private, THOMAS EDWARD, 10887. NZ Cyclist Battalion. Died 18 April 1918. Age 28. Son of J. and M. Power, of 13 Mathers Rd, Spreydon, Christchurch. Messines Ridge (NZ) Memorial, Mesen, West-Vlaanderen, Belgium.

PRATT, Private, CHARLES EDWARD, 44775. 1st Battalion, Auckland Regiment, NZEF. Died 26 March 1918. Age 27. Husband of Lillan Margaret Pratt, of Dunedin. Grevilliers (NZ) Memorial, Pas de Calais, France.

PREBBLE, Lance Corporal, ERNEST KENNETH, 41991. 4th Battalion, 3rd NZ Rifle Brigade. Died 31 March 1918. Age 25. Son of John and Emily Prebble, of Barrhill, Rakaia. Euston Road Cemetery, Colincamps, Somme, France. Grave or panel number: II.D.5.

PRICE, Gunner, DUDLEY EVERARD OWEN, 9/1722. 9th Battery, 2nd Brigade, NZ Field Artillery. Died 14 April 1918. Age 23. Son of Thomas Owen Price and Florence Helen Price, of Dunedin. Native of Braemar, Waihao Downs, Waimate. Locre Hospice Cemetery, Heuvelland, West-Vlaanderen, Belgium. Grave or panel number: II.C.7.

PRICTOR, Rifleman, JAMES ALFRED, 49261. 4th Battalion, 3rd NZ Rifle Brigade. Died 28 March 1918. Grevillers (NZ) Memorial, Pas de Calais, France.

PRIEST, Rifleman, EDWARD JAMES, 44152. 4th Battalion, 3rd NZ Rifle Brigade. Died 29 March 1918. Age 22. Son of John and Catherine Priest, of Baxters Siding, New Zealand. Doullens Communal Cemetery Extension No. 1, Somme, France. Grave or panel number: V.B.14.

PRINGLE, Corporal, ALEXANDER MERRIFORD, 33437. 2nd NZ Entrenching Battalion, NZEF. Died 14 April 1918. Age 30. Son of the late Alexander and Sarah Pringle. Native of Ashhurst, Wellington. Messines Ridge (NZ) Memorial, Mesen, West-Vlaanderen, Belgium.

PRYDE, Private, ALEXANDER, 23239. 2nd Light Trench Mortar Battery, Otago Regiment, NZEF. Died 10 April 1918. Age 34. Son of William and Isabella Pryde, of Pilmuir St, Lower Hutt, Wellington. Born at Glasgow, Scotland. Knightsbridge Cemetery, Mesnil-Martinsart, Somme, France. Grave or panel number: A.8.

PURDY, Major, ROBERT GLEADOW, 23/10, MC and Bar, Croix de Guerre. 3rd NZ Rifle Brigade. Died 28 March 1918. Doullens Communal Cemetery Extension No. 1, Somme, France. Grave or panel number: VI.A.7.

QUAID, Private, WILLIAM SILVESTER, 36486. 2nd Battalion, Canterbury Regiment, NZEF. Died 5 April 1918. Son of Mr and Mrs Kyran Quaid, of Pleasant Valley, Canterbury. Serre Road Cemetery No. 1, Pas de Calais, France. Grave or panel number: II.B.7.

QUINLAN, Lance Corporal, GEORGE AMBROSE, 23314. 1st Battalion, Auckland Regiment, NZEF. Died 26 March 1918. Son of Mr and Mrs P. Quinlan, of Taihoa, Matamata. Grevilliers (NZ) Memorial, Pas de Calais, France.

QUINLAN, Private, THOMAS MICHAEL, 51776. 1st Battalion, Auckland Regiment, NZEF. Died 28 April 1918. Son of Mr and Mrs John Quinlan, of North Loburn, Rangiora. Hébuterne Military Cemetery, Pas de Calais, France. Grave or panel number: III.B.3.

RADFORD, Rifleman, RAYMOND CYRIL, 41355. 4th Battalion, 3rd NZ Rifle Brigade. Died 30 March 1918. Son of Mr and Mrs Joseph George Radford, of Palmerston North. Grevillers (NZ) Memorial, Pas de Calais, France.

RAE, Private, ROBERT ERNEST, 44415. Otago Regiment, NZEF. Died 2 April 1918. Age 32. Son of George and Mary Rae, of Hawera; husband of Annie Pauline Rae, of Broadway North, Stratford. Etaples Military Cemetery, Pas de Calais, France. Grave or panel number: XXXIII.C.9.

RAMSAY, Private, HAROLD VIVIAN, 18080. NZ Medical Corps. Died 2 April 1918. Age 28. Son of John and Mary Ramsay, of Auckland. A Schoolmaster. Native of Forfar, Scotland. Englebelmer Communal Cemetery Extension, Somme, France. Grave or panel number: F.20.

RAMSEY, Gunner, ALEXANDER, 2/1899. 6th Howitzer Battery, NZ Field Artillery. Died 17 April 1918. Age 24. Son of Donald and Agnes Ramsey, of Rangiotu, Manawatu. La Clytte Military Cemetery, Heuvelland, West-Vlaanderen, Belgium. Grave or panel number: V.C.20.

RANDALL, Rifleman, BERTRAM ROBERT, 54080. 1st Battalion, 3rd NZ Rifle Brigade. Died 19 April 1918. Age 21. Son of Mr T.W. Randall, of 17 Hall St, South Dunedin. Lijssenthoek Military Cemetery, Poperinge, West-Vlaanderen, Belgium. Grave or panel number: XXVI.G.14.

RAVLICH, Lance Corporal, JACK, 12/3790. 2nd Battalion, Auckland Regiment, NZEF. Died 29 March 1918. Son of Jim Ravlich, of Yakau, Ravlich, Kozica, Dalmatia. Grevilliers (NZ) Memorial, Pas de Calais, France.

RAY, Rifleman, ROBERT, 26/1689, MM. 4th Battalion, 3rd NZ Rifle Brigade. Died 30 March 1918. Age 45. Son of John and Kathleen Ray. Euston Road Cemetery, Colincamps, Somme, France. Grave or panel number: II.D.4.

READ, Private, GEORGE DUNBAR, 55792. 1st Battalion, Otago Regiment, NZEF. Died 24 April 1918. Age 38. Son of George and Jessie Read, of Omimi, Seacliffe, Otago. Euston Road Cemetery, Colincamps, Somme, France. Grave or panel number: I.J.15.

REDMOND, Private, JAMES, 27960. 1st Battalion, Otago Regiment, NZEF. Died 5 April 1918. Mailly Wood Cemetery, Somme, France. Grave or panel number: I.P.9.

REED, Private, SIDNEY HERBERT, 38981. 1st Battalion, Canterbury Regiment, NZEF. Died 4 April 1918. Son of Mrs E. Reed, of Christchurch. Grevillers (NZ) Memorial, Pas de Calais, France.

REEVE, Private, CHARLES STUART JACKSON, 13990. 1st Battalion, Otago Regiment, NZEF. Died 5 April 1918. Age 39. Brother of Miss Emily Reeve, of Fairfield, Dunedin. Born in Dunedin. Auchonvillers Military Cemetery, Somme, France. Grave or panel number: II.L.28.

REEVE, Rifleman, GEORGE SPENCER, 30407. 3rd Battalion, 3rd NZ Rifle Brigade. Died 6 April 1918. Age 33. Husband of Minnie Reeve, of New Plymouth. Euston Road Cemetery, Colincamps, Somme, France. Grave or panel number: IV.E.1.

REEVE, Second Lieutenant, WILLIAM ALFRED CAMPBELL, 24/660. 2nd Battalion, 3rd NZ Rifle Brigade. Died 29 March 1918. Son of Bertha Violet Reeve, of Taranaki; and the late William Jesse Reeve. Grevillers (NZ) Memorial, Pas de Calais, France.

REID, Private, HORACE ERNEST GEORGE, 38748. 1st Battalion, Auckland Regiment, NZEF. Died 29 March 1918. Age 21. Youngest son of Walter and Mary Reid, of Auckland. Doullens Communal Cemetery Extension No. 1, Somme, France. Grave or panel number: V.C.12.

REID, Rifleman, JOHN, 42709. 3rd Battalion, 3rd NZ Rifle Brigade. Died 19 April 1918. Age 28. Son of Jane and the late Alex Watson Reid, of Edward St, Te Kuiti. Doullens Communal Cemetery Extension No. 1, Somme, France. Grave or panel number: VI.C.49.

REID, Private, STUART, 23431. 1st Battalion, Auckland Regiment, NZEF. Died 27 March 1918. Son of Mrs H.C. Hillman, of Te Puke. Euston Road Cemetery, Colincamps, Somme, France. Grave or panel number: Special Memorial B.10.

RENNIE, Sergeant, JOHN WESLEY, 6/3842, MM. 2nd Battalion, Canterbury Regiment, NZEF. Died 5 April 1918. Son of Mr and Mrs George Rennie, of Beach Rd, Westport. Serre Road Cemetery No. 1, Pas de Calais, France. Grave or panel number: II.B.2.

REVILL, Private, MARMADUKE, 46082. 2nd NZ Entrenching Battalion, NZEF. Died 14 April 1918. Age 27. Son of Maria Revill, of 9 Nayland St, Sumner, Christchurch, and the late Oliver Revill. Messines Ridge (NZ) Memorial, Mesen, West-Vlaanderen, Belgium.

REYNOLDS, Private, DENCIL GEORGE, 40057. 2nd Battalion, Canterbury Regiment, NZEF. Died 28 March 1918. Age 29. Son of George and Eliza Jane Reynolds, of Havelock North. Grevillers (NZ) Memorial, Pas de Calais, France.

REYNOLDS, Rifleman, G.S., 53413. 1st Battalion, 3rd NZ Rifle Brigade. Died 28 March 1918. Auchonvillers Military Cemetery, Somme, France. Grave or panel number: II.L.41.

RICHARDS, Corporal, FRANK HAROLD, 11945. 1st Battalion, Wellington Regiment, NZEF. Died 19 April 1918. Age 36. Haringhe (Bandaghem) Military Cemetery, Poperinge, West-Vlaanderen, Belgium. Grave or panel number: II.F.37.

RICHARDSON, Private, LEONARD COLVILLE, 25593. 2nd Battalion, Wellington Regiment, NZEF. Died 12 April 1918. Age 21. Son of William and Kathleen Richardson, of Ohakune Rd, Raetihi. Etaples Military Cemetery, Pas de Calais, France. Grave or panel number: XXXIII.G.3.

RIVERS, Rifleman, JOHN PETER, 23437. 3rd Battalion, 3rd NZ Rifle Brigade. Died 7 April 1918. Age 24. Son of John and Mary Elizabeth Rivers, of Russell, Bay of Islands. Euston Road Cemetery, Colincamps, Somme, France. Grave or panel number: IV.C.10.

ROBERTS, Private, ALBERT MOSES, 58923. 1st Battalion, Otago Regiment, NZEF. Died 5 April 1918. Age 40. Son of Elizabeth Roberts, of Caversham, Dunedin; and the late J.T. Roberts. Mailly Wood Cemetery, Somme, France. Grave or panel number: I.P.II.

ROBERTSHAW, Private, FREDERICK ARTHUR, 58924. 2nd Battalion, Otago Regiment, NZEF. Died 16 April 1918. Meteren Military Cemetery, Nord, France. Grave or panel number: IV.N.974.

ROBERTSON, Lieutenant, DOUGLAS LESLIE, 37054. 2nd Battalion, Wellington Regiment, NZEF. Died 27 March 1918. Age 28. Husband of the late Elizabeth Swanson Robertson. Native of Lovell's Flat, Dunedin. Euston Road Cemetery, Colincamps, Somme, France. Grave or panel number: V.D.5.

ROBERTSON, Private, HARRY BRYDEN, 54085. 2nd Battalion, Otago Regiment, NZEF. Died 5 April 1918. Age 21. Son of John and Maggie Robertson of Ashburton. Auchonvillers Military Cemetery, Somme, France. Grave or panel number: II.M.5.

ROBERTSON, Rifleman, WILLIAM JOHN, 47038. 3rd Battalion, 3rd NZ Rifle Brigade. Died 20 April 1918. Son of Mr and. Mrs J. Robertson, of 67 Ann St, Invercargill. Knightsbridge Cemetery, Mesnil-Martinsart, Somme, France. Grave or panel number: D.62.

ROBINSON, Private, ANDREW HENRY, 59543. 9th Battalion, Otago Regiment, NZEF. Died 5 April 1918. Age 22. Son of Henry Thomas and Sophia Robinson, of England. Born at Fairlie, New Zealand. Doullens Communal Cemetery Extension No. 1, Somme, France. Grave or panel number: VI.D.30.

ROBINSON, Private, FREDERICK GEORGE, 33769. 2nd Battalion, Canterbury Regiment, NZEF. Died 7 April 1918. Age 23. Son of Robert James and Mary Jane Robinson, of Waikuku, North Canterbury. Etaples Military Cemetery, Pas de Calais, France. Grave or panel number: XXXIII.D.3.

ROBINSON, Private, JAMES JOSEPH, 40638. No. 16 (Waikato) Company, 1st Battalion, Auckland Regiment, NZEF. Died 26 March 1918. Age 20. Son of James Joseph and Katherine J. Robinson, of Auckland. Grevilliers (NZ) Memorial, Pas de Calais, France.

ROBINSON, Private, JOHN HENRY, 53611. 1st Battalion, Canterbury Regiment, NZEF. Died 5 April 1918. Age 30. Husband of M. Robinson, of Waipawa, Napier. Martinsart British Cemetery, Somme, France. Grave or panel number: I.H.40.

ROBINSON, Gunner, R.C., 18031, NZ Field Artillery. Died 13 April 1918. Etaples Military Cemetery, Pas de Calais, France. Grave or panel number: XXIX.F.4.

ROBINSON, Lance Corporal, ROY GEORGE, 40161. 1st Battalion, Wellington Regiment, NZEF. Died 30 March 1918. Age 26. Son of John William and Margaret Robinson, of Wellington. Euston Road Cemetery. Colincamps, Somme, France. Grave or panel number: Special Memorial B.6.

ROBSON, Private, NINIAN, G/1351. 1st Battalion, Otago Regiment, NZEF. Died 10 April 1918. Son of Mrs E. Robson, of Lovell's Flat, Otago. Knightsbridge Cemetery, Mesnil-Martinsart, Somme, France. Grave or panel number: A.7.

ROGERS, Private, JOHN HENRY, 58601. 2nd NZ Entrenching Battalion, NZEF. Died 17 April 1918. Brother of William Rogers, of Townsend Island, Yeppoon, Queensland, Australia. Messines Ridge (NZ) Memorial, Mesen, West-Vlaanderen, Belgium.

ROLLS, Sapper, GEORGE WILLIAM, 55628. NZ Engineers. Died 12 April 1918. Age 30. Son of Sidney and Ellen Rolls, of Canterbury. Dainville Communal Cemetery, Pas de Calais, France. Grave or panel number: B.6.

ROSA, Rifleman, HUBERT, 60270. 4th Battalion, 3rd NZ Rifle Brigade. Died 29 March 1918. Son of Sarah Rosa, of 73 Darling St, Glebe, Sydney, New South Wales, Australia. Euston Road Cemetery, Colincamps, Somme, France. Grave or panel number: V.A.4.

ROSS, Private, ALEXANDER, 34432. 1st Battalion, Auckland Regiment, NZEF. Died 26 March 1918. Son of Mrs R. Ross, of 47 Ferguson St West, Palmerston North. Grevilliers (NZ) Memorial, Pas de Calais, France.

ROSS, Rifleman, ROY MCLEOD, 54601. 1st Battalion, 3rd NZ Rifle Brigade. Died 5 April 1918. Age 21. Son of Alexander and Emma Ross, of Rangiotu, Palmerston North. Euston Road Cemetery, Colincamps, Somme, France. Grave or panel number: III.E.8.

ROSS, Private, WILLIAM, 56794. 1st Battalion, Canterbury Regiment, NZEF. Died 28 March 1918. Age 30. Son of the late Mary Ross, of Clinton, Otago. Mesnil Communal Cemetery Extension, Somme, France. Grave or panel number: II.A.7.

ROSSITER, Private, ALBERT ARTHUR, 23879, MM. 2nd Battalion, Wellington Regiment, NZEF. Died 23 March 1918. Brother of E. Rossiter, of Murphy St, Wellington. Hazebrouck Communal Cemetery, Nord, France. Grave or panel number: III.C.39.

ROULSTON, Rifleman, HERBERT LEWIS, 56031. 4th Battalion, 3rd NZ

Rifle Brigade. Died 5 April 1918. Age 33. Son of Samuel and Elizabeth Roulston, of 15 Patanga Crescent, Wellington. Euston Road Cemetery, Colincamps, Somme, France. Grave or panel number: II.Q.2.

ROWE, Corporal, MARK WILMOT, 6/3449. 1st Battalion, Canterbury Regiment, NZEF. Died 27 March 1918. Son of Mrs Kathleen Rowe, of Ocean View, Tauranga. Grevilliers (NZ) Memorial, Pas de Calais, France.

RUCK, Lance Corporal, FREDERICK THOMAS, 31895. 4th Battalion, NZ Rifle Brigade. Died 30 March 1918. Grevillers (NZ) Memorial, Pas de Calais, France.

RUSSELL, Second Lieutenant, NEIL RUFFELL, 32542. 1st Battalion, Auckland Regiment, NZEF. Died 26 March 1918. Age 29. Son of J.R. and M.E. Russell, of New Zealand; husband of Molly Russell, of Dannevirke. Euston Road Cemetery, Colincamps, Somme, France. Grave or panel number: III.B.6.

RUTHERFORD, Lance Corporal, STANLEY, 8/3392. 1st Battalion, Otago Regiment, NZEF. Died 6 April 1918. Age 23. Youngest son of Peter and Sarah Rutherford, of Caversham, Dunedin. Auchonvillers Military Cemetery, Somme, France. Grave or panel number: II.L.26.

RUTTER, Lance Corporal, WILLIAM ARTHUR, 12/3804. 2nd Battalion, Auckland Regiment, NZEF. Died 30 March 1918. Age 26. Son of William C. and Mary J. Rutter, of England. Doullens Communal Cemetery Extension No. 1, Somme, France. Grave or panel number: VI.G.25.

RYAN, Private, THOMAS PADDY, 39105. 6th (Hauraki) Company, 2nd Battalion, Auckland Regiment, NZEF. Died 2 April 1918. Age 37. Son of Mary and Edmond Dougherty, of Normanby, Taranaki. St Sever Cemetery Extension, Rouen, Seine-Maritime, France. Grave or panel number: IX.I.13A.

SANDERSON, Private, ROBERT, 24064. 2nd Battalion, Auckland Regiment, NZEF. Died 30 March 1918. Age 26. Native of Okupu, Great Barrier Island. Son of Eliza Jane Sanderson, of Mt Eden, Auckland, and the late Benjamin Sanderson. Euston Road Cemetery, Colincamps, Somme, France. Grave or panel number: IV.B.2.

SANGWELL, Private, WALTER HAROLD PERCY, 6/2746. 1st Battalion, Canterbury Regiment, NZEF. Died 5 April 1918. Age 29. Son of John and Isabella Sangwell, of 258 Palmerston Rd, Gisborne. Born at Westport. Grevillers (NZ) Memorial, Pas de Calais, France.

SCADDEN, Rifleman, CLIVE THEODORE AORANGI, 56859. 4th Battalion, 3rd NZ Rifle Brigade. Died 10 April 1918. Age 21. Son of Phoebe and the late George William Scadden, of Lady's Mile, Foxton. Born at Clive, Hawke's Bay. Boulogne Eastern Cemetery, Pas de Calais, France. Grave or panel number: VIII.I.184.

SCANLAN, Rifleman, WILLIAM WEBBER WILSON, 38074. 4th Battalion, 3rd NZ Rifle Brigade. Died 5 April 1918. Age 25. Son of Josephine and the late Francis Scanlan. Euston Road Cemetery, Colincamps, Somme, France. Grave or panel number: II.Q.1.

SCHENK, Private, FREDERICK LUDWIG, 28805. 2nd Battalion, Auckland Regiment, NZEF. Died 29 March 1918. Age 36. Son of Bendix and Catherine Schenk, of 7 Harbour St, Ponsonby, Auckland. St Pol British Cemetery, St Pol-sur-Ternoise, Pas de Calais, France. Grave or panel number: II.A.9.

SCHUMACHER, Private, FREDERICK WILLIAM, 55550. 2nd Battalion, Canterbury Regiment, NZEF. Died 14 April 1918. Age 29. Husband of V.K. Schumacher, of Rapanui, Christchurch. Doullens Communal Cemetery Extension No. 1, Somme, France. Grave or panel number: VI.B.29.

SCOTT, Private, ALLAN ROY, 28806. 2nd Battalion, Auckland Regiment, NZEF. Died 27 March 1918. Age 24. Son of the late A.J. and J.W.A. Scott, of Paterangi, Waikato. Euston Road Cemetery, Colincamps, Somme, France. Grave or panel number: V.B.2.

SCOTT, Corporal, ARTHUR TENNYSON, 12/243. 1st Battalion, Auckland Regiment, NZEF. Died 26 March 1918. Age 26. Son of Isabella Scott, of 8 King's View Rd, Mt Eden, Auckland, and the late Edward John Scott. Also served in Egypt and at Gallipoli. Grevilliers (NZ) Memorial, Pas de Calais, France.

SCOTT, Private, CHARLES RODERICK LESLIE, 39331. 2nd Battalion, Otago Regiment, NZEF. Died 15 April 1918. Age 22. Son of James G. and Charlotte S. Scott, of Dunedin. Gezaincourt Communal Cemetery Extension, Somme, France. Grave or panel number: II.L.18.

SCOTT, Private, EDWARD ANDREW, 56365. 1st Battalion, Auckland Regiment, NZEF. Died 28 March 1918. Englebelmer Communal Cemetery Extension, Somme, France. Grave or panel number: F.18.

SCOTT, Rifleman, FRANK HERBERT, 30413. 4th Battalion, 3rd NZ Rifle Brigade. Died 29 March 1918. Age 39. Son of the late George Scott, of Leeston, Canterbury. Euston Road Cemetery, Colincamps, Somme, France. Grave or panel number: I.H.10.

SCOTT, Sergeant, ROBERT, 121459. 2nd NZ Entrenching Battalion, NZEF. Died 16 April 1918. Age 24. Son of Robert and Jane Lockhart Scott, of The Ranch, Ngarua, Waitoa, Hamilton. Native of Lesmahagow, Scotland. Messines Ridge (NZ) Memorial, Mesen, West-Vlaanderen, Belgium.

SCOTT, Private, WILLIAM JOHN, 49753. 2nd Battalion, Auckland Regiment, NZEF. Died 11 April 1918. Age 25. Son of Jane Vickers (formerly Scott), of Mangalepara, Morrinsville; and the late Robert Scott. Euston Road Cemetery, Colincamps, Somme, France. Grave or panel number: IV.O.6.

SCOTT, Rifleman, WILLIAM KENNETH, 40379. 2nd Battalion, 3rd NZ Rifle Brigade. Died 6 April 1918. Age 23. Son of William and Bridget Scott, of Paeroa Rd, Waihi. Gezaincourt Communal Cemetery Extension, Somme, France. Grave or panel number: I.K.10.

SCOULLAR, Second Lieutenant, WILLIAM ARTHUR, 24/946. 3rd Battalion, 3rd NZ Rifle Brigade. Died 6 April 1918. Son of Mr and Mrs Joseph Gordon Scoullar, of Dunedin. Also served in Samoa. Grevillers (NZ) Memorial, Pas de Calais, France.

SCULLIN, Private, FELIX, 57156. 2nd Battalion, Auckland Regiment, NZEF. Died 27 March 1918. Age 30. Son of John and Mary Scullin, of Napier. Mailly Wood Cemetery, Somme, France. Grave or panel number: I.P.2I.

SEED, Corporal, GILBERT JOHN, 12/2836. 2nd Battalion, Auckland Regiment, NZEF. Died 27 March 1918. Age 33. Son of William and Isabella Seed, of 19 Devon Rd, Frankton Junction. St Pol British Cemetery, St Pol-sur-Ternoise, Pas de Calais, France. Grave or panel number: I.A.4.

SEXTON, Private, JAMES, 49552. 1st Battalion, Canterbury Regiment, NZEF. Died 28 March 1918. Age 40. Son of William and Bridget Sexton, of Palmerston St, Westport. Born at Charleston. Grevillers (NZ) Memorial, Pas de Calais, France.

SHADRACH, Private, WALTER, 44025. 2nd NZ Entrenching Battalion, NZEF. Died 17 April 1918. Son of Mrs J. Shadrach, of 31 Aylmer St, Beckenham, Christchurch. Outtersteene Communal Cemetery Extension, Bailleul, Nord, France. Grave or panel number: II.H.27.

SHANKLAND, Rifleman, JOHN, 19056. 4th Battalion, 3rd NZ Rifle Brigade. Died 29 March 1918. Age 25. Son of Jane A. Shankland, of Tokanui, Southland, and the late John Shankland. Euston Road Cemetery, Colincamps, Somme, France. Grave or panel number: III.D.2.

SHARP, Rifleman, HERBERT, 62645. 4th Battalion, 3rd NZ Rifle Brigade. Died 21 April 1918. Age 25. Son of Alfred W. and Jane Sharp, of 21 Waverley St, Auckland; husband of Olive Sharp, of 25 Belgium St, Auckland. Born at Maryborough, Queensland. Grevillers (NZ) Memorial, Pas de Calais, France.

SHARP, Private, WILLIAM CAMPBELL, 12/3818. 1st Battalion, Auckland Regiment, NZEF. Died 26 March 1918. Son of Humprey Ewing and Margaret Sharp, of Oratia, Auckland. Grevillers (NZ) Memorial, Pas de Calais, France.

SHAW, Lieutenant, DAVID JOHN, 14023. 4th Battalion, 3rd NZ Rifle Brigade. Died 30 March 1918. Age 25. Son of John W. and Mary M. Shaw, of Gore. Born at Geraldine. Grevillers (NZ) Memorial, Pas de Calais, France.

SHEAD, Private, ERNEST WILLIAM, 61426. 15th Company, 2nd Battalion, Auckland Regiment, NZEF. Died 11 April 1918. Age 24. Son of Louisa Lee, of 131 Richardson St, St. Kilda, Dunedin. Gezaincourt Communal Cemetery Extension, Somme, France. Grave or panel number: II.K.1.

SHEED, Private, WILLIAM ROBERT, 61810. 2nd Battalion, Wellington Regiment, NZEF. Died 27 March 1918. Husband of Margaretha Sheed, of 39 Hillcourt Rd, East Dulwich, London, England. Euston Road Cemetery, Colincamps, Somme, France. Grave or panel number: V.A.8.

SHENNAN, Rifleman, JOHN JAMES, 45245. 3rd Battalion, NZ Rifle Brigade. Died 23 April 1918. Age 22. Son of Robert and Ellen Shennan, of Berwick, Otago. Doullens Communal Cemetery Extension No. 1, Somme, France. Grave or panel number: VI.B.58.

SHEPHERD, Lance Corporal, ROBERT FREW, 46532. 3rd Battalion, 3rd NZ Rifle Brigade. Died 27 March 1918. Age 35. Son of Mrs J. Shepherd, of Southland. Euston Road Cemetery, Colincamps, Somme, France. Grave or panel number: III.N.4.

SHEPHERD, Private, VIVIAN ARNOLD, 31440. 2nd Battalion, Auckland Regiment, NZEF. Died 27 March 1918. Age 21. Son of Charles Parry and Mabel Anne Isabella Shepherd, of Whangaroa, Auckland. Grevillers (NZ) Memorial, Pas de Calais, France.

SHEPPARD, Driver, GEORGE FINNIS, IO/3391. NZ Army Service Corps. Died 22 April 1918. Age 22. Son of Henry and Susan Sheppard, of Lenham Heath, Maidstone, England. Englebelmer Communal Cemetery Extension, Somme, France. Grave or panel number: F.9.

SHIELDS, Private, GEORGE HERBERT, 35045. 2nd NZ Entrenching Battalion, NZEF. Died 12 April 1918. Son of Mr and Mrs R. Shields, of Wyndham, Southland. Messines Ridge (NZ) Memorial, Mesen, West-Vlaanderen, Belgium.

SHIPLEY, Driver, HENRY, 5/815. NZ Army Service Corps. Died 5 April 1918. Age 27. Son of Thomas and Mary Jane Shipley, of Derbyshire, England. Bertrancourt Military Cemetery, Somme, France. Grave or panel number: 2.B.15.

SHRIMPTON, Gunner, NORMAN, 43459. 9th Battery, NZ Field Artillery. Died 12 April 1918. Age 22. Son of Edward A. and Florence J. Shrimpton, of 38 Rongotai Terrace, Miramar, Wellington. Wulverghem-Lindenhoek Road Military Cemetery, Heuvelland, West-Vlaanderen, Belgium. Grave or panel number: II.D.30.

SIEGEL, Private, CHARLES CHRISTIAN, 49849. 1st Battalion, Wellington Regiment, NZEF. Died 30 March 1918. Son of Mr and Mrs Christian Siegel, of Halcombe, Oroua, New Zealand. Euston Road Cemetery, Colincamps, Somme, France. Grave or panel number: II.E.10.

SIMMS, Private, FREDERICK, 28809. 2nd Battalion, Auckland Regiment, NZEF. Died 1 April 1918. Age 35. Son of James and Ellen Simms, of Remuera, Auckland. Etaples Military Cemetery, Pas de Calais, France. Grave or panel number: XXXIII.C.23A.

SIMONS, Gunner, CHARLES EDWARD, 2/2540. NZ Field Artillery. Died 18 April 1918. Age 26. Son of Robert Henry and Margaret Simons, of Station House, Lower Rattray St, Dunedin. Lijssenthoek Military Cemetery, Poperinge, West-Vlaanderen, Belgium. Grave or panel number: XXVI.G.9A.

SIMPSON, Lance Corporal, JAMES WALKER, 26/216. 4th Battalion, 3rd NZ Rifle Brigade. Died 5 April 1918. Age 21. Son of James and Elizabeth

Walker Simpson, of 15 McGregor's Rd, East Linwood, Christchurch. Born at Leith, Scotland. Grevillers (NZ) Memorial, Pas de Calais, France.

SIMPSON, Private, WILLIAM HART, 64671. 1st Battalion, Canterbury Regiment, NZEF. Died 24 April 1918. Age 21. Son of Mrs E. Simpson, of Grey Lynn, Auckland. Doullens Communal Cemetery Extension No. 1, Somme, France. Grave or panel number: VI.B.66.

SINCLAIR, Second Lieutenant, JOHN, 36761. 2nd Battalion, Canterbury Regiment, NZEF. Died 27 March 1918. Son of Mrs M. Sinclair, of High St, Milton. Grevilliers (NZ) Memorial, Pas de Calais, France.

SINCLAIR, Rifleman, ROBERT MARCUS, 15425. 3rd Battalion, 3rd NZ Rifle Brigade. Died 7 April 1918. Son of Alfred Sinclair, of Belmont, Wantage, Berks, England. Grevillers (NZ) Memorial, Pas de Calais, France.

SINTON, Private, JAMES, 54989. 'E' Company, 1st Battalion, Auckland Regiment, NZEF. Died 26 March 1918. Age 23. Son of Annie Margaret Sinton, of Patumahoe, Franklin, and the late George Sinton. Born at Devonport. Grevilliers (NZ) Memorial, Pas de Calais, France.

SKINNER, Lance Corporal, JAMES, 32907. 2nd NZ Entrenching Battalion, NZEF. Died 16 April 1918. Son of Mr and Mrs Peter Skinner, of Papakaio, Oamaru. Messines Ridge (NZ) Memorial, Mesen, West-Vlaanderen, Belgium.

SLIGHT, Bombardier, FRANK, 2/2722. 12th Battery, 3rd Brigade, NZ Field Artillery. Died 6 April 1918. Age 26. Son of James and Christina Slight, of Scotland. Bertrancourt Military Cemetery, Somme, France. Grave or panel number: 2.A.3.

SMAIL, Private, WILLIAM JOHN, 32240. 1st Battalion, Canterbury Regiment, NZEF. Died 3 April 1918. Age 35. Son of Thomas and Mary Ann Smail. Brockenhurst (St Nicholas) Churchyard, Hampshire, United Kingdom. Grave or panel number: A.3.15.

SMALL, Private, ALBERT ERNEST, 48864. 2nd NZ Entrenching Battalion, NZEF. Died 14 April 1918. Age 21. Son of Albert Ernest and James Small, of Milton Farm, Ashburton, Canterbury. Messines Ridge (NZ) Memorial, Mesen, West-Vlaanderen, Belgium.

SMALL, Rifleman, LEONARD ERNEST, 23/283. 1st Battalion, 3rd NZ Rifle Brigade. Died 28 March 1918. Age 25. Son of Mrs K. Small, of 14 Western Springs Rd, Morningside, Auckland. Euston Road Cemetery, Colincamps, Somme, France. Grave or panel number: Special Memorial B.15.

SMEED, Rifleman, EDMUND, 41368. 1st Battalion, 3rd NZ Rifle Brigade. Died 19 April 1918. Age 23. Son of Thomas and Edith Smeed. Meteren Military Cemetery, Nord, France. Grave or panel number: IV.D.648.

SMITH, Private, ALBERT ARTHUR, 55553. 1st Battalion, Canterbury Regiment, NZEF. Died 27 March 1918. Son of Mr and Mrs William Arthur Smith, formerly of Kaikoura. Grevillers (NZ) Memorial, Pas de Calais, France.

SMITH, Private, CHARLES, 44876. 1st Battalion, Auckland Regiment, NZEF. Died 26 March 1918. Grevillers (NZ) Memorial, Pas de Calais, France.

SMITH, Sergeant, CHARLES, 22377. 4th Battalion, 3rd NZ Rifle Brigade. Died 6 April 1918. Age 26. Son of Edward and Emma Smith, of 26 Hawke St, New Brighton, Christchurch. Native of Oamaru. Gezaincourt Communal Cemetery Extension, Somme, France. Grave or panel number: II.J.27.

SMITH, Private, ERNEST EDWARD, 8/4024. 2nd Battalion, Otago Regiment, NZEF. Died 5 April 1918. Martinsart British Cemetery, Somme, France. Grave or panel number: I.H.35.

SMITH, Rifleman, F.L., 23/910. 2nd Battalion, 3rd NZ Rifle Brigade. Died 30 March 1918. Age 29. Son of Brian and Alice Smith, of Braintree, Essex, England. Euston Road Cemetery, Colincamps, Somme, France. Grave or panel number: V.P.1.

SMITH, Lance Corporal, GEORGE FREDERICK, 13534. 2nd Battalion, Wellington Regiment, NZEF. Died 27 March 1918. Son of the late W.J. Smith, of Masterton. Euston Road Cemetery, Colincamps, Somme, France. Grave or panel number: II.D.7.

SMITH, Private, HERBERT, 26326. 2nd Battalion, Otago Regiment, NZEF. Died 9 April 1918. Son of Mr and Mrs H.O. Smith, of Kaikoura. Knightsbridge Cemetery, Mesnil-Martinsart, Somme, France. Grave or panel number: A.6.

SMITH, Private, HOANI, 19394. NZ Maori (Pioneer) Battalion. Died 11 April 1918. Age 21. Son of Mrs H. Smith, of Ruhaka, Hawke's Bay. Gezaincourt Communal Cemetery Extension, Somme, France. Grave or panel number: II.K.3.

SMITH, Private, JOHN PHILLIP, 59471. 1st Battalion, Wellington Regiment, NZEF. Died 29 April 1918. Age 29. Son of John Smith, of 35 Molesworth St, Wellington. Louvencourt Military Cemetery, Somme, France. Grave or panel number: I.D.30.

SMITH, Private, JOSEPH, 46094. 2nd NZ Entrenching Battalion, NZEF. Died 16 April 1918. Son of Mr and Mrs William Smith, of Oroua Downs, Palmerston North. Messines Ridge (NZ) Memorial, Mesen, West-Vlaanderen, Belgium.

SMITH, Rifleman, ROBERT, 44165. 4th Battalion, 3rd NZ Rifle Brigade. Died 27 March 1918. Age 34. Son of Young and Mary J. Smith, of Ashton Farm, Aylesbury, Canterbury. Boulogne Eastern Cemetery, Pas de Calais, France. Grave or panel number: VIII.I.168.

SMITH, Private, VICTOR JUBILEE, 48683. 2nd Battalion, Auckland Regiment, NZEF. Died 30 March 1918. Son of Mrs M.J. Ashdown, of Tauranga. Euston Road Cemetery, Colincamps, Somme, France. Grave or panel number: IV.B.10.

SMITH, Bombardier, WALTER, II/1971. NZ Field Artillery. Died 18 April 1918. Age 22. Haringhe (Bandaghem) Military Cemetery, Poperinge, West-Vlaanderen, Belgium. Grave or panel number: II.F.20.

SMITH, Rifleman, WILLIAM, 53273. 1st Battalion, 3rd NZ Rifle Brigade. Died 5 April 1918. Son of Mrs E.J. Smith, of Brown St, South Invercargill. Grevillers (NZ) Memorial, Pas de Calais, France.

SNELL, Corporal, GEORGE DANIEL, 23300. 4th Battalion, 3rd NZ Rifle Brigade. Died 29 March 1918. Son of Mr and Mrs J.B. Snell, of Gordon St, Mosgiel. Euston Road Cemetery, Colincamps, Somme, France. Grave or panel number: II.A.9.

SNODGRASS, Corporal, WILLIAM JOSEPH, 42718. 'A' Company, 3rd Battalion, 3rd NZ Rifle Brigade. Died 7 April 1918. Age 21. Son of William and Margaret Teresa Snodgrass, of Kennington, Southland. Born at Lake Te Anau. Grevillers (NZ) Memorial, Pas de Calais, France.

SNOW, Private, FREDERICK JAMES, 41419. NZ Machine Gun Battalion. Died 27 March 1918. Son of Mr and Mrs C.H. Snow, of 292 Tinakori Rd, Wellington. Euston Road Cemetery, Colincamps, Somme, France. Grave or panel reference number III.F.7.

SORENSON, Rifleman, MALCOLM JOHN, 60316. 3rd Battalion, 3rd NZ Rifle Brigade. Died 9 April 1918. Age 29. Son of S. and A. Sorenson, of Vancouver, British Columbia; husband of C.E. Sorenson, of Mangonui Hotel, Mangonui. Etaples Military Cemetery, Pas de Calais, France. Grave or panel number: XXXIII.F.15A.

SOUTER, Lance Sergeant, PATRICK, 24/2095. 2nd Battalion, Canterbury Regiment, NZEF. Died 5 April 1918. Age 32. Son of John Pearson Souter and Margaret Souter, of Hokitika. Serre Road Cemetery No. 1, Pas de Calais, France. Grave or panel number: II.B.3.

SPARK, Corporal, ROBERT TWELVETREE, 24/590. 'B' Company, 2nd Battalion, 3rd NZ Rifle Brigade. Died 15 April 1918. Age 25. Son of George and Louisa M. Spark, of Toira, Clutha County, Otago. Auchonvillers Military Cemetery, Somme, France. Grave or panel number: II.M.29.

SPARROW, Private, PHILIP, 26/138. 3rd Battalion, Otago Regiment, NZEF. Died 29 April 1918. Age 28. Son of William and Elizabeth Sparrow, of Wellington. Auxi-Le-Chateau Churchyard, Pas de Calais, France.

SPECK, Rifleman, HAROLD JAMES, 51500. 3rd Battalion, 3rd NZ Rifle Brigade. Died 5 April 1918. Age 21. Son of Richard John and Agnes Emma Speck, of 14 Richmond St, Glenmore, Auckland. Grevillers (NZ) Memorial, Pas de Calais, France.

SPOWART, Private, JOHN JASPER, 24/1821. 2nd Battalion, Otago Regiment, NZEF. Died 4 April 1918. Age 30. Son of Mr and Mrs David Spowart, of 28 Erskine St, Alloa, Scotland. Martinsart British Cemetery, Somme, France. Grave or panel number: I.H.34.

STAINES, Private, JACK LESLIE, 37949. NZ Machine Gun Battalion. Died 31 March 1918. Age 22. Son of Robert and Ellen Staines, of Waipukurau, Hawke's Bay. Sucrerie Military Cemetery, Colincamps, Somme, France. Grave or panel number: I.J.52.

STANSELL, Private, JACK ALEXANDER, 41655. 2nd Battalion, Otago Regiment, NZEF. Died 5 April 1918. Age 21. Son of Robert and Louie C. Stansell, of Kennedy's Bay, Auckland. Born at Levin. Grevillers (NZ) Memorial, Pas de Calais, France.

STANTON, Private, ALFRED LITTLEDYKE, 47606. 1st Battalion, Auckland Regiment, NZEF. Died 26 March 1918. Age 37. Son of George Lyttledyke Stanton and Caroline Madeline Stanton. Mailly Wood Cemetery, Somme, France. Grave or panel number: I.N.9.

STAUNTON, Rifleman, JOHN FRANCIS, H/49937. 2nd Battalion, 3rd NZ Rifle Brigade. Died 12 April 1918. Age 36. Son of Thomas and Bridget Staunton, of Galway, Ireland. Doullens Communal Cemetery Extension No. 1, Somme, France. Grave or panel number: VI.C.30.

STAVELEY, Private, ROBERT GEORGE, 56863. 2nd NZ Entrenching Battalion, NZEF. Died 23 April 1918. Age 29. Son of Robert Jones and Mrs H. Staveley, of 20 Duppa St, Berhampore, Wellington; husband of Nora Elizabeth Revell (formerly Staveley), of Upper Hutt, Wellington. Messines Ridge (NZ) Memorial, Mesen, West-Vlaanderen, Belgium.

STEEL, Private, MALCOLM, 48289. 2nd Battalion, Canterbury Regiment, NZEF. Died 5 April 1918. Age 21. Auchonvillers Military Cemetery, Somme, France. Grave or panel number: II.M.25.

STEPHENS, Private, ERNEST EDWARD, 41. 1st Battalion, Otago Regiment, NZEF. Died 6 April 1918. Age 26. Son of Horace and Kate Stephens; husband of Grace Hamilton Stephens, of Dunedin. Gezaincourt Communal Cemetery Extension, Somme, France. Grave or panel number: I.J.20.

STEPHENS, Rifleman, JOHN, 53434. 4th Battalion, 3rd NZ Rifle Brigade. Died 30 March 1918. Age 27. Son of Mark and Mary Jane Stephens, of Parkyns Tce, St Columb Rd, Fraddon, Cornwall, England. Grevillers (NZ) Memorial, Pas de Calais, France.

STEVENS, Private, JOHN JAMES, 6/3480. 2nd Battalion, Canterbury Regiment, NZEF. Died 5 April 1918. Son of the late Mrs Jessie Stevens. Grevillers (NZ) Memorial, Pas de Calais, France.

STEVENSON, Rifleman, WILLIAM, 44319. 3rd Battalion, 3rd NZ Rifle Brigade. Died 29 March 1918. Age 39. Son of Stuart and Charlotte Stevenson, of Kapuka, Southland. Etaples Military Cemetery, Pas de Calais, France. Grave or panel number: XXXIII.A.19A.

STEWART, Sergeant, ARTHUR, 12/4279. No. 15 North Auckland Company, 1st Battalion, Auckland Regiment, NZEF. Died 26 March 1918. Age 34. Son of the late George and Isabella Stewart, of Dorsincilly Cottage, Glen Muick, Ballater, Scotland. Grevilliers (NZ) Memorial, Pas de Calais, France.

STEWART, Rifleman, JAMES WILLIAM, 42719. 3rd Battalion, 3rd NZ Rifle Brigade. Died 6 April 1918. Son of Mr and Mrs J. Stewart, of Whenuakoa, Dunedin. Grevillers (NZ) Memorial, Pas de Calais, France.

STORRIER, Private, STANLEY, 37888. 2nd Battalion, Otago Regiment, NZEF. Died 3 April 1918. Age 20. Son of John and Isabella Storrier, of 46 South St, Feilding. Born at Timaru. Ancre British Cemetery, Beaumont-Hamel, Somme, France. Grave or panel number: VII.C.8.

STOUT, Private, THOMAS WILLIAM, 29880. 2nd Battalion, Otago Regiment, NZEF. Died 17 April 1918. Age 26. Son of William Anderson Stout and Louisa Helen Stout, of 9 Filleul St, Gladstone, Invercargill. Etaples Military Cemetery, Pas de Calais, France. Grave or panel number: XXIX.E.14A.

STRACHAN, Trooper, DOUGLAS, 9/206. Otago Mounted Rifles, NZEF. Died 29 April 1918. Age 28. Son of John and Mary Strachan, of Tapanui, Otago Central. Buttes New British Cemetery (NZ) Memorial, Polygon Wood, Zonnebeke, West-Vlaanderen, Belgium.

STUART, Warrant Officer Class II, ALEXANDER, 26/282. 4th Battalion, NZ Rifle Brigade. Died 5 April 1918. Grevillers (NZ) Memorial, Pas de Calais, France.

STYLES, Private, WILLIAM JAMES MITCHELL, 34746. 2nd Battalion, Canterbury Regiment, NZEF. Died 27 March 1918. Age 23. Son of George and Eliza Styles, of Timaru. Doullens Communal Cemetery Extension No. 1, Somme, France. Grave or panel number: V.A.52.

SUTHERLAND, Lance Corporal, ARTHUR ROBERT, 31742. 1st Battalion, Auckland Regiment, NZEF. Died 26 March 1918. Son of the late Mrs H. Sutherland, of Auckland. Grevilliers (NZ) Memorial, Pas de Calais, France.

SUTHERLAND, Rifleman, OSCAR ROBERT, 52702. 3rd Battalion, NZ Rifle Brigade. Died 30 March 1918. Age 22. Son of the late Eric and Sophia Sutherland. Gezaincourt Communal Cemetery Extension, Somme, France. Grave or panel number: II.H.20.

SWAN, Sergeant, DAVID GORDON, 33192. 6th Company, 1st Battalion, Auckland Regiment, NZEF. Died 26 March 1918. Age 39. Son of David and Mary Swan, of Anderson's Bay, Dunedin. Auchonvillers Military Cemetery, Somme, France. Grave or panel number: II. L. 44.

SWEETAPPLE, Corporal, ERNEST THEODORE, 25647. 4th Battalion, 3rd NZ Rifle Brigade. Died 30 March 1918. Son of Mrs Annie Sweetapple, of Napier. Grevillers (NZ) Memorial, Pas de Calais, France.

SWINNEY, Corporal, WILLIAM THOMAS, 36693. 3rd Battalion, 3rd NZ Rifle Brigade. Died 7 April 1918. Son of Mr and Mrs William Swinney, of Dunedin. Grevillers (NZ) Memorial, Pas de Calais, France.

SYMES, Private, FRANCIS ERNEST, 31369. 1st Battalion, Wellington Regiment, NZEF. Died 30 March 1918. Age 19. Son of Charles and Hannah Symes, of 228 Willis St, Wellington. Sucrerie Military Cemetery, Colincamps, Somme, France. Grave or panel number: I.J.55.

SYMONS, Corporal, ARTHUR, 15797. 2nd Battalion, Wellington Regiment, NZEF. Died 27 March 1918. Son of Mr and Mrs M.C. Symons, of Waipukurau.

Euston Road Cemetery, Colincamps, Somme, France. Grave or panel number: V.C.7.

SYMONS, Private, JOHN, 23258. 2nd NZ Entrenching Battalion, NZEF. Died 13 April 1918. Age 23. Son of Nathaniel and Elizabeth Symons, of England. Born in New Zealand. Meteren Military Cemetery, Nord, France. Grave or panel number: II.E.160.

TAMAUAHI, Corporal, PAPERA, 16/963. 'C' Company, NZ Maori (Pioneer) Battalion. Died 5 April 1918. Age 21. Son of Pineha and Keita Tamauahi, of Ruatorea, East Coast. Bertrancourt Military Cemetery, Somme, France. Grave or panel number: 2.B.6.

TANNER, Private, FREDERICK ARTHUR, 25613. 2nd Battalion, Wellington Regiment, NZEF. Died 16 April 1918. Age 33. Son of Frederick and Eleanor Tanner, of Vogel St, Fitzroy, New Plymouth. Sucrerie Military Cemetery, Colincamps, Somme, France. Grave or panel number: I.J.43.

TATTERSALL, Private, THOMAS NORMAN, 48584. No. 16 (Waikato) Company, 1st Battalion, Auckland Regiment, NZEF. Died 26 March 1918. Age 26. Son of Lawrence and Martha Tattersall, of 76 Prospect Terrace, Mt Eden, Auckland. Grevillers (NZ) Memorial, Pas de Calais, France.

TAYLOR, Private, CHAS BRIAN, 28007. 2nd Battalion, Auckland Regiment, NZEF. Died 30 March 1918. Age 21. Son of William and Bessie Taylor, of Taikorea, Manawatu. Previously wounded on the Somme, 1916. Believed to be buried in Euston Road Cemetery, Colincamps, Somme, France. Grave or panel number: IV.B.3.

TAYLOR, Private, SYDNEY THOMAS, 34456. 'E' Company, 1st Battalion, Auckland Regiment, NZEF. Died 26 March 1918. Age 20. Son of Mabel Maud Taylor, of Peachgrove Rd, Claudelands, Hamilton, and the late William Taylor. Born at Brisbane, Queensland. Grevillers (NZ) Memorial, Pas de Calais, France.

TAYLOR, Private, WILLIAM PETER, 34947. 3rd Battalion, Otago Regiment, NZEF. Died 14 April 1918. Age 22. Son of Simon and Helen Taylor, of Kia Ora, Oamaru. Meteren Military Cemetery, Nord, France. Grave or panel number: II.M.327.

TE HAU, Private, PERA, 16/964. NZ Maori (Pioneer) Battalion. Died 5 April 1918. Age 36. Son of Pita and Kiwa Te Hau, of Muriwai, New Zealand. Bertrancourt Military Cemetery, Somme, France. Grave or panel number: 2.B.10.

TERRY, Private, JOHN MCLENNAN, 44033. 2nd Battalion, Canterbury Regiment, NZEF. Died 28 March 1918. Age 28. Son of William and Annie Terry, of Norton Rd, Frankton Junction. Native of Dunedin. Auchonvillers Military Cemetery, Somme, France. Grave or panel number: II.L.31.

THOMPSON, Private, CHRISTOPHER, 12/4106. 2nd Battalion, Auckland Regiment, NZEF. Died 16 April 1918. Meteren Military Cemetery, Nord, France. Grave or panel number: II.M.323.

THOMPSON, Rifleman, GEORGE, 37038. 4th Battalion, 3rd NZ Rifle Brigade. Died 16 April 1918. Age 44. Foster son of Mrs G.C. Williams, of Rangiora. St Sever Cemetery Extension, Rouen, Seine-Maritime, France. Grave or panel number: P.IX.P.3A.

THOMPSON, Lance Corporal, GEORGE CHARLES, 33971. 2nd Battalion, Auckland Regiment, NZEF. Died 27 March 1918. Age 31. Son of William and Wilhelmina Thompson, of 4 Cockburn St, Grey Lynn, Auckland. Grevillers (NZ) Memorial, Pas de Calais, France.

THOMPSON, Lance Sergeant, GEORGE WILLIAM, 23/299. 4th Battalion, 3rd NZ Rifle Brigade. Died 7 April 1918. Age 30. Son of Joseph and Hannah Thompson, of 10 Grantham Place, Bradford, Yorks, England. Doullens Communal Cemetery Extension No. 1, Somme, France. Grave or panel number: VI.D.54.

THOMPSON, Gunner, JAMES RICHARD, 9/1243. NZ Field Artillery. Died 18 April 1918. Age 25. Son of James and Margaret Thompson, of Nimihau, Wyndham, Southland. Lijssenthoek Military Cemetery, Poperinge, West-Vlaanderen, Belgium. Grave or panel number: XXVI.G.9.

THOMPSON, Rifleman, OSWALD CHARLES, 32972. 4th Battalion, 3rd NZ Rifle Brigade. Died 29 March 1918. Age 38. Son of Charles and Mary Ann Thompson, of Forster, New South Wales, Australia. Grevillers (NZ) Memorial, Pas de Calais, France.

THOMPSON, Corporal, ROBERT WILLIAM, 26013. 1st Battalion, Auckland Regiment, NZEF. Died 26 March 1918. Age 38. Son of the late Archibald and Eliza Thompson; husband of Agnes Thompson, of 183 Strickland St, Spreydon, Christchurch. Born at Hokitika, Greymouth. Grevilliers (NZ) Memorial, Pas de Calais, France.

THOMSON, Private, BASIL HERBERT BELL, 49754. 1st Battalion, Auckland Regiment, NZEF. Died 26 March 1918. Age 34. Son of John Bell Thomson and Annie Thomson, of Auckland. Euston Road Cemetery, Colincamps, Somme, France. Grave or panel number: III.B.8.

THOMSON, Corporal, J.H., 3/453. NZ Medical Corps. Died 5 April 1918. Doullens Communal Cemetery Extension No. 1, Somme, France. Grave or panel number: VI.E.50.

THORBURN, Rifleman, CHARLES SIDNEY, 25651. 2nd Battalion, 3rd NZ Rifle Brigade. Died 28 March 1918. Son of Mrs L. Thorburn, of Hamilton. Euston Road Cemetery, Colincamps, Somme, France. Grave or panel number: IV.A.3.

THORBURN, Private, GORDON KEITH, 38459. 2nd Battalion, Auckland Regiment, NZEF. Died 30 March 1918. Son of Mr and Mrs A. Thorburn, of Auckland. Grevillers (NZ) Memorial, Pas de Calais, France.

THURSTON, Rifleman, WILLIAM PETER, 49942. 4th Battalion, 3rd NZ Rifle Brigade. Died 5 April 1918. Euston Road Cemetery, Colincamps, Somme, France. Grave or panel number: II.B.5.

TIBBOTT, Private, JAMES, 37510. 1st Battalion, Otago Regiment, NZEF. Died 5 April 1918. Age 41. Husband of Ada Florence Tibbott, of 64 Bridge House, George Row, Bermondsey, London, England. Englebelmer Communal Cemetery Extension, Somme, France. Grave or panel number: E.1.

TILLER, Private, SAMUEL JOHN, 62415. 2nd Battalion, Canterbury Regiment, NZEF. Died 28 March 1918. Age 22. Son of Samuel and Alice Louisa Tiller, of Colville, Coromandel. Grevillers (NZ) Memorial, Pas de Calais, France.

TILSLEY, Lance Corporal, WALTER ALEXANDER, 31766. 1st Battalion, Auckland Regiment, NZEF. Died 28 March 1918. Son of Mrs J. Tilsley, of 191 Hobson St, Auckland. Euston Road Cemetery, Colincamps, Somme, France. Grave or panel number: III.E.10.

TIPENE, Private, WIPARATA, 19572. NZ Maori (Pioneer) Battalion. Died 11 April 1918. Husband of Mrs Te Kirihan Tipene, of Kohu Kohu, Auckland. Etaples Military Cemetery, Pas de Calais, France. Grave or panel number: XXXIII.G.15A.

TOBECK, Rifleman, LEONARD WILLIAM, 49030. 3rd Battalion, 3rd NZ Rifle Brigade. Died 27 March 1918. Age 21. Son of J.H. and A. Tobeck, of Tai Tapu, Canterbury. Euston Road Cemetery, Colincamps, Somme, France. Grave or panel number: III.N.5.

TOBIN, Rifleman, WILLIAM MCINTOSH, 42724. 3rd Battalion, 3rd NZ Rifle Brigade. Died 8 April 1918. Age 35. Son of Helen Tobin, of Dunedin, and the late Henry Tobin. Born at Owaka. Grevillers (NZ) Memorial, Pas de Calais, France.

TODD, Private, ERNEST ASHLEY, 44609. 1st Battalion, Canterbury Regiment, NZEF. Died 6 April 1918. Age 22. Son of Joseph William and Margaret Todd, of Coutts Island, New Zealand. Knightsbridge Cemetery, Mesnil-Martinsart, Somme, France. Grave or panel number: A.13.

TOLE, Private, JOHN, 47256. 1st Battalion, Auckland Regiment, NZEF. Died 23 April 1918. Age 23. Son of William Richard and Mary L. Tole, of Onehunga, Auckland. Doullens Communal Cemetery Extension No. 1, Somme, France. Grave or panel number: VI.B.45.

TRAINOR, Private, PETER JAMES, 45934. 'B' Company, 1st Battalion, Wellington Regiment, NZEF. Died 22 April 1918. Age 24. Son of Charles and Mary Trainor, of 19 Pitt St, Wanganui. Courcelles-Au-Bois Communal Cemetery Extension, Somme, France. Grave or panel number: F.2.

TREGEAR, Gunner, RAY THOMSON, 17/298. NZ Field Artillery. Died 9 April 1918. Age 25. Son of Charles and Annie Tregear, of 2 Princes St, St Kilda, Victoria, Australia. Native of Geelong, Victoria, Australia. Messines Ridge (NZ) Memorial, Mesen, West-Vlaanderen, Belgium.

TREMAINE, Trooper, HUBERT HENRY HORRELL, G/222. Otago Mounted Rifles, NZEF. Died 26 April 1918. Age 25. Son of William Henry Horrell Tremaine and Margaret Tremaine, of Kaweku, Riversdale, Southland. Native of Gore. Buttes New British Cemetery (NZ) Memorial, Polygon Wood, Zonnebeke, West-Vlaanderen, Belgium.

TROWER, Rifleman, EDWARD WALE, 44174. 3rd Battalion, 3rd NZ Rifle Brigade. Died 7 April 1918. Son of Mrs J. Trower, of Vanguard St, Nelson. Grevillers (NZ) Memorial, Pas de Calais, France.

TRUBSHOE, Private, GEORGE OSBORNE, 40087. 2nd Battalion, Canterbury Regiment, NZEF. Died 5 April 1918. Age 30. Son of Poulton Trubshoe and Martha Trubshoe, of 11 Shamrock St, Napier. Born in London, England. Serre Road Cemetery No. 1, Pas de Calais, France. Grave or panel number: II.B.5.

TUCKER, Rifleman, LEONARD, 54616. 4th Battalion, 3rd NZ Rifle Brigade. Died 5 April 1918. Son of Frank Tucker and Agnes Tucker, of Hall Farm, Wedmore, Cheddar, Somerset, England. Euston Road Cemetery, Colincamps, Somme, France. Grave or panel number: II.B.7.

TUOHY, Rifleman, ANDREW, 40088. 2nd Battalion,3rd NZ Rifle Brigade. Died 6 April 1918. Son of Mr Andrew Tuohy, of Patutahi, Gisborne. Sucrerie Military Cemetery, Colincamps, Somme, France. Grave or panel number: I.I.4.

TURCHIE, Private, JOSEPH, 13140. 1st Battalion, Wellington Regiment, NZEF, NZ Light Trench Mortar Battery. Died 6 April 1918. Age 40. Son of Santina and Carlo Turchie. Gezaincourt Communal Cemetery Extension, Somme, France. Grave or panel number: II.J.3.

TURNBULL, Rifleman, CHRISTIE MACKAY, 45264. 2nd Battalion, 3rd NZ Rifle Brigade. Died 5 April 1918. Age 30. Son of James and Elizabeth Turnbull (née Walker). Euston Road Cemetery, Colincamps, Somme, France. Grave or panel number: II.A.4.

TURNBULL, Private, JOSEPH GREEN WATSON, 35050. 2nd NZ Entrenching Battalion, NZEF. Died 16 April 1918. Age 28. Son of James and Elizabeth Walker Turnbull, of Joseph St, Gore. Messines Ridge (NZ) Memorial, Mesen, West-Vlaanderen, Belgium.

TURNER, Sergeant, WILLIAM HENRY ARTHUR, 2/2948. NZ Field Artillery. Died 5 April 1918. Son of Mrs E. Turner, of Christchurch. Bertrancourt Military Cemetery, Somme, France. Grave or panel number: 2.B.17.

TUSON, Private, JAMES, 20462. 1st Battalion, Wellington Regiment, NZEF. Died 30 March 1918. Age 27. Son of William and Mary Tuson, of 846 Hollins Rd, Hollinwood, Oldham. Euston Road Cemetery, Colincamps, Somme, France. Grave or panel number: Special Memorial B.4.

TYE, Private, A.J., 25/833. 3rd Light Trench Mortar Battery, NZ Field Artillery. Died 5 April 1918. Age 22. Son of Alfred J. and Elizabeth Tye, of 104 Newton Rd, Sparkhill, Birmingham. Euston Road Cemetery, Colincamps, Somme, France, Grave or panel number: IV.C.8.

TYSON, Gunner, JOHN VICKERS, 13/2381. NZ Field Artillery. Died 16 April 1918. Age 31. Son of Margaret and the late William Tyson, of Windermere,

England. Etaples Military Cemetery, Pas de Calais, France. Grave or panel number: XXIX.E.10.

URE, Lance Sergeant, JOHN HENRY, 29321. 3rd Battalion, Canterbury Regiment, NZEF. Died 29 April 1918. Age 22. Son of Robert and Mary Ure, of Herbert, North Otago. Lijssenthoek Military Cemetery, Poperinge, West-Vlaanderen, Belgium. Grave or panel number: XXVIII.E.4A.

VAGUE, Rifleman, WILLIAM EDMUND, 21915. 'A' Company, 4th Battalion, 3rd NZ Rifle Brigade. Died 29 March 1918. Age 35. Son of Edmund and Margaret Patton Vague, of 24 North Rd, Papanui, Christchurch. Born at Crest, North Canterbury. Doullens Communal Cemetery Extension No. 1, Somme, France. Grave or panel number: V.B.13.

VALENTINE, Gunner, STACY GEORGE, 211683. NZ Field Artillery. Died 17 April 1918. Age 21. Son of Hammond Fraser Valentine and Edith May Valentine, of Devonport, Auckland; husband of Zita E. Valentine, of 31 Hastings Parade, Devonport, Auckland. La Clytte Military Cemetery, Heuvelland, West-Vlaanderen, Belgium. Grave or panel number: V.A.28.

VAUGHAN, Rifleman, JOSEPH, 56875. 3rd Battalion, 3rd NZ Rifle Brigade. Died 29 March 1918. Son of Mrs Margaret C. Vaughan, of 247 Audubon Ave, New York, U.S.A. Grevillers (NZ) Memorial, Pas de Calais, France.

VICKERS, Private, HARRY, 45579. 2nd Battalion, Auckland Regiment, NZEF. Died 30 March 1918. Age 34. Son of Thomas and Emma Vickers, of Kaipaki, Ohaupo, Auckland. Euston Road Cemetery, Colincamps, Somme, France. Grave or panel number: IV.N.6.

WAAKA, Private, HOHEPA, 20816. NZ Maori (Pioneer) Battalion. Died 12 April 1918. Age 21. Son of Sam Waaka, of Waihopo, Auckland. Doullens Communal Cemetery Extension No. 1, Somme, France. Grave or panel number: VI.B.19.

WADDELL, Corporal, GEORGE HENRY, 44038. 2nd Battalion, Canterbury Regiment, NZEF. Died 23 April 1918. Age 26. Son of Andrew John and Emily Waddell, of Tullyrush, Seskanore, County Tyrone, Ireland. Sucrerie Military Cemetery, Colincamps, Somme, France. Grave or panel number: I.AA.8.

WAINWRIGHT, Private, CHARLES, 64815. 2nd NZ Entrenching Battalion, NZEF. Died 16 April 1918. Son of Mrs Caroline Barrett (formerly Wainwright), of Wellington St, Launceston, Tasmania, and the late William Wainwright. Messines Ridge (NZ) Memorial, Mesen, West-Vlaanderen, Belgium.

WAKEFIELD, Private, SYDNEY HERBERT, 56694. 2nd Battalion, Auckland Regiment, NZEF. Died 31 March 1918. Age 34. Son of Sydney and Jane Wakefield, of Auckland. Doullens Communal Cemetery Extension No. 1, Somme, France. Grave or panel number: VI.G.34.

WAKELIN, Lance Corporal, LEOPOLD TOCKER, 24/1511. 4th Battalion, 3rd NZ Rifle Brigade. Died 30 March 1918. Age 35. Husband of May A. Wakelin, of Mill Rd, New Plymouth. Born in Wellington. Grevillers (NZ) Memorial, Pas de Calais, France.

WALKER, Private, ERIC TREVOR LOGIER, 38462. 2nd Battalion, Auckland Regiment, NZEF. Died 30 March 1918. Age 21. Son of Maxwell and Ellen L. Walker, of 4 Wynyard St, Auckland. Euston Road Cemetery, Colincamps, Somme, France. Grave or panel number: IV.H.7.

WALKER, Private, JAMES JEFFREYS, S/798. 1st Battalion, Auckland Regiment, NZEF. Died 11 April 1918. Age 26. Son of the Rev James E. Walker, of St Chad's Vicarage, West Coseley, and the late Mary Elizabeth Katon, Walker. Sedgley (All Saints) Churchyard West Extension, Staffordshire, United Kingdom. Grave or panel number: IV. South.

WALKER, Private, WILLIAM, 49131. 2nd Battalion, Auckland Regiment, NZEF. Died 30 March 1918. Age 31. Son of William Walker (Sen.), of 7 Bridge St, Cambuslang, Lanarkshire. Doullens Communal Cemetery Extension No. 1, Somme, France. Grave or panel number: VI.G.46.

WALKER, Rifleman, WILLIAM, 41055. 4th Battalion, 3rd NZ Rifle Brigade. Died 5 April 1918. Husband of Mrs N. Walker, of 8 Adams St, Brooklyn, Wellington. Grevilliers (NZ) Memorial, Pas de Calais, France.

WALKER, Rifleman, WILLIAM, 42727. 2nd Battalion, 3rd NZ Rifle Brigade. Died 5 April 1918. Son of the late John and Christina Walker. Euston Road Cemetery, Colincamps, Somme, France. Grave or panel number: II.A.3.

WALL, Rifleman, PERCIVAL, 56885. 4th Battalion, 3rd NZ Rifle Brigade. Died 28 March 1918. Grevillers (NZ) Memorial, Pas de Calais, France.

WALLACE, Private, GEORGE, 17738. 1st Battalion, Wellington Regiment, NZEF. Died 30 March 1918. Age 35. Son of John and Ellen Wallace, of Rangiotiu, Palmerston North. Euston Road Cemetery, Colincamps, Somme, France. Grave or panel number: Special Memorial B.5.

WALSH, Private, JOHN EDMUND, 54998. 2nd Battalion, Auckland Regiment, NZEF. Died 30 March 1918. Son of Mr and Mrs James Henry Walsh, of Mackay St, Waihi. Grevillers (NZ) Memorial, Pas de Calais, France.

WANDEN, Corporal, HERBERT WINN, 21734. 'C' Company, 2nd Battalion, Canterbury Regiment, NZEF. Died 27 March 1918. Age 35. Son of Richard and Elizabeth M. Wanden, of Blenheim. Auchonvillers Military Cemetery, Somme, France. Grave or panel number: II.L.40.

WARD, Private, FRANK, 60020. 2nd Battalion, Wellington Regiment, NZEF. Died 17 April 1918. Age 23. Son of Sylvester L. and Margaret Ward, late of Farnworth, Lancs., England. Doullens Communal Cemetery Extension No. 1, Somme, France. Grave or panel number: V.A.29.

WARD, Rifleman, WALTER JAMES, 39918. 3rd Battalion, 3rd NZ Rifle Brigade. Died 5 April 1918. Age 38. Husband of Letitia May Ward, of 25 Elm

Row, Dunedin. Born in Sunderland, England. Grevillers (NZ) Memorial, Pas de Calais, France.

WARN, Private, FRANK, 58632. 2nd Battalion, Canterbury Regiment, NZEF. Died 26 April 1918. Age 25. Son of Charles B. and Ellen Warn, of Yarmouth, England; husband of C.E. Warn, of 7 Whiteleigh Ave, Lower Riccarton, Christchurch. Doullens Communal Cemetery Extension No. 1, Somme, France. Grave or panel number: VI.A.56.

WARNER, Private, LESLIE CHARLES, 46814. 2nd Battalion, Otago Regiment, NZEF. Died 28 March 1918. Age 23. Only son of Charles and Mabel Warner, of Wilson St, Wanganui. Euston Road Cemetery, Colincamps, Somme, France. Grave or panel number: IV.A.6.

WARREN, Private, HAROLD JAMES, 28837. 1st Battalion, Auckland Regiment, NZEF. Died 26 March 1918. Grevilliers (NZ) Memorial, Pas de Calais, France.

WATKINS, Rifleman, RICHARD WILLIAM, 58948. 'D' Company, 3rd Battalion, 3rd NZ Rifle Brigade. Died 29 March 1918. Age 21. Son of Richard William and Barbara Watkins, of 105 Malvern St, Dunedin. Euston Road Cemetery, Colincamps, Somme, France. Grave or panel number: V.I.8.

WATKINS, Private, WILLIAM ARTHUR, 24087. 2nd Battalion, Auckland Regiment, NZEF. Died 25 April 1918. Age 30. Son of Rhoda and the late Edwin Watkins, of Kakahi, Main Trunk Line, New Zealand. Brookwood Military Cemetery, Surrey, United Kingdom. Grave or panel number: VIII.B.13.

WATSON, Private, ANDREW, 32767. 2nd NZ Entrenching Battalion, NZEF. Died 14 April 1918. Age 44. Son of Alexander and Euphemia Spiden Watson, of Tyne St, Oamaru; husband of Mary M. B. Watson, of 79 Forth St, Dunedin. Messines Ridge (NZ) Memorial, Mesen, West-Vlaanderen, Belgium.

WATSON, Rifleman, WALTER COULSON, 53453. 1st NZ Rifle Brigade. Died 5 April 1918. Age 32. Son of William and Elizabeth Watson, of St Bathans, New Zealand. Doullens Communal Cemetery Extension No. 1, Somme, France. Grave or panel number: VI.D.4.

WATT, Corporal, JOHN WILLIAM, 24421. 14th (South Otago) Company, 2nd NZ Entrenching Battalion, NZEF. Died 14 April 1918. Age 24. Son of John and Isabella Watt, of Charleston, Otekaieke, Oamaru. Messines Ridge (NZ) Memorial, Mesen, West-Vlaanderen, Belgium.

WATT, Private, P., 41681. 1st Battalion, Otago Regiment, NZEF. Died 2 April 1918. Age 26. Son of Jessie Watt, of Hangingshaw Farm, Heriot, Midlothian; husband of J.G. Brown (formerly Watt). Mailly Wood Cemetery, Somme, France. Grave or panel number: I.K.33.

WATTERS, Lance Corporal, ALEXANDER, IO/3771. 2nd Battalion, Wellington Regiment, NZEF. Died 27 March 1918. Age 28. Son of the late Alexander and Annie Elizabeth Watters, of Kumara, New Zealand. Euston Road Cemetery, Colincamps, Somme, France. Grave or panel number: IV.A.8.

WATTS, Private, JOHN CYRIL ROSS, 29528. 2nd Battalion, Auckland Regiment, NZEF. Died 30 March 1918. Age 40. Son of J. Ross Watts and Sybella M. Watts, of New Zealand; husband of Edith A. Watts, of Morrinsville. Euston Road Cemetery, Colincamps, Somme, France. Grave or panel number: IV.B.7.

WEDDALL, Driver, ROBERT, 5/142B. NZ Field Artillery. Died 10 April 1918. Son of Mrs E. Weddall, of 269 Anlaby Rd, Hull, England. Westhof Farm Cemetery, Heuvelland, West-Vlaanderen, Belgium. Grave or panel number: Special Memorial 5.

WEIR, Rifleman, FRANCIS, 34762. 1st Battalion, 3rd NZ Rifle Brigade. Died 21 April 1918. Englebelmer Communal Cemetery Extension, Somme, France. Grave or panel number: E.8.

WEIR, Rifleman, HENRY, 51935. 3rd Battalion, 3rd NZ Rifle Brigade. Died 27 March 1918. Son of Mrs S. Weir, of 214 Upper Riccarton, Christchurch. Euston Road Cemetery, Colincamps, Somme, France. Grave or panel number: III.N.6.

WEIR, Sergeant, KEITH MUNRO, 2/2564. 11th Battery, NZ Field Artillery. Died 24 April 1918. Age 21. Son of James and Jessie Weir, of Pumping Station, Heathcote Valley, Christchurch. Haringhe (Bandaghem) Military Cemetery, Poperinge, West-Vlaanderen, Belgium. Grave or panel number: V.B.16.

WEIR, Private, ROBERT WILLIAM, 53291. 2nd NZ Entrenching Battalion, NZEF. Died 17 April 1918. Meteren Military Cemetery, Nord, France. Grave or panel number: V.A.562.

WELLS, Private, FRED BERTIE ARTHUR, 12/3865. 2nd Battalion, Auckland Regiment, NZEF. Died 29 March 1918. Age 34. Son of Fred Harold and Martha Wells, of 18 Domain St, Devonport, Auckland. Grevilliers (NZ) Memorial, Pas de Calais, France.

WELSH, Private, JACK DARLING, 10930. NZ Cyclist Battalion. Died 26 April 1918. Age 21. Son of Minnie Welsh, of 22 Windsor Place, Wellington, and the late James Welsh. Buttes New British Cemetery (NZ) Memorial, Polygon Wood, Zonnebeke, West-Vlaanderen, Belgium.

WELSH, Corporal, ROBERT FRANCIS, 9/234. Otago Mounted Rifles, NZEF. Died 29 April 1918. Age 30. Son of Margaret Welsh, of 37 Ravelston St, Anderson's Bay, Dunedin, and the late Michael Welsh. Native of Clifton, Invercargill. Buttes New British Cemetery (NZ) Memorial, Polygon Wood, Zonnebeke, West-Vlaanderen, Belgium.

WESTBROOK, Rifleman, FREDERICK VICTOR, 55268. 2nd Battalion, 3rd NZ Rifle Brigade. Died 23 April 1918. Age 26. Son of Ellen Goddard, of Wellington. Abbeville Communal Cemetery Extension, Somme, France. Grave or panel number: IV.A.15.

WESTON, Rifleman, JAMES ELLIOTT, 44327. 'H' Company, 3rd Battalion, 3rd NZ Rifle Brigade. Died 7 April 1918. Son of Harold and Matilda Weston, of Opotiki. Born in Gisborne. Grevillers (NZ) Memorial, Pas de Calais, France.

WHELAN, Gunner, ALFRED, 43846. 5th Battery, NZ Field Artillery. Died 10 April 1918. Age 21. Son of Thomas and Helena Whelan, of 25 Springhill Rd, Mornington, Dunedin. Westhof Farm Cemetery, Heuvelland, West-Vlaanderen, Belgium. Grave or panel number: Special Memorial 4.

WHISKER, Corporal, LESLIE JOHN, 23/953, MM. 1st Battalion, 3rd NZ Rifle Brigade. Died 21 April 1918. Age 23. Son of Charles and Eliza Whisker, of Newmarket, Auckland. St Sever Cemetery Cemetery Extension, Rouen, Seine-Maritime, France. Grave or panel number: P.VI.N.4A.

WHITAKER, Private, ADRIAN, 63980. 1st NZ Entrenching Battalion, NZEF. Died 15 April 1918. Age 21. Son of Agnes and the late Bernard Whitaker. Perth Cemetery (China Wall), Ypres, West-Vlaanderen, Belgium. Grave or panel number: II.B.13.

WHITAKER, Private, FREDERICK JOHN, 47537. 1st Battalion, Otago Regiment, NZEF. Died 24 April 1918. Age 23. Son of Thomas F. and Mary E. Whitaker, of 78 Hull St, Oamaru. Euston Road Cemetery, Colincamps, Somme, France. Grave or panel number: I.H.4.

WHITE, Private, ALEXANDER MCGREGOR, 56388. 2nd Battalion, Auckland Regiment, NZEF. Died 28 March 1918. Age 25. Son of David and Catherine Ann White, of Eglinton Ave, Mt Eden, Auckland. Gezaincourt Communal Cemetery Extension, Somme, France. Grave or panel number: II.G.14.

WHITE, Sergeant, ARTHUR, 10283. 2nd NZ Entrenching Battalion, NZEF. Died 16 April 1918. Age 25. Brother of Edmonston White, of 57 Amesbury Rd, Penylan, Cardiff, South Wales. Messines Ridge (NZ) Memorial, Mesen, West-Vlaanderen, Belgium.

WHITE, Private, ARTHUR EDWARD, 31755. 1st Battalion, Auckland Regiment, NZEF. Died 16 April 1918. Age 22. Son of William and Emily White, of Wiltshire, England. Doullens Communal Cemetery Extension No. 1, Somme, France. Grave or panel number: V.A.31.

WHITE, Lance Sergeant, GODFREY DAVID, 1013444. 2nd Battalion, Wellington Regiment, NZEF. Died 27 April 1918. Age 27. Son of Henry Joseph and Marian White, of Worcester, England. St Sever Cemetery Extension, Rouen, Seine-Maritime, France. Grave or panel number: XI.H.7A.

WHITE, Gunner, ROY KESSELL, 18270, NZ Field Artillery. Died 9 April 1918. Age 24. Son of Charles Kessell White and Alice Maude Whites of 25 King Edward Ave, Epsom, Auckland. Messines Ridge (NZ) Memorial, Mesen, West-Vlaanderen, Belgium.

WHITTLE, Private, WILLIAM, 35445. NZ Machine Gun Battalion. Died 27 March 1918. Son of Mr and Mrs T. Whittle, of Puketitiri, Hawke's Bay. Euston Road Cemetery, Colincamps, Somme, France. Grave or panel number: V.A.10.

WICKINS, Private, FREDERICK GEORGE, 37904. 2nd Battalion, Canterbury Regiment, NZEF. Died 29 March 1918. Age 36. Son of William and

Emily Wickins, of Hill House, Lime Tree Hill, Burford, Oxon, England. Grevillers (NZ) Memorial, Pas de Calais, France.

WIGZELL, Sergeant, JAMES OLIVER FRANCIS, 28055. 1st Battalion, Canterbury Regiment, NZEF. Died 5 April 1918. Age 23. Son of Francis and Margaret Wigzell, of Grey St, Woodville. Knightsbridge Cemetery, Mesnil-Martinsart, Somme, France. Grave or panel number: A.9.

WILDS, Private, JOHN EMERY, 5374. 2nd Battalion, Canterbury Regiment, NZEF. Died 22 April 1918. Age 21. Son of J.H. and Eliza Wilds, of Atipua Rd, Timaru. Born at Timaru. Wimereux Communal Cemetery, Pas de Calais, France. Grave or panel number: XI.F.2.

WILES, Rifleman, THOMAS ALFRED, 47189. 1st Battalion, 3rd NZ Rifle Brigade. Died 5 April 1918. Age 19. Son of William and Minnie Wiles, of 24 Randolph St, Newton, Auckland. Euston Road Cemetery, Colincamps, Somme, France. Grave or panel number: IV.A.9.

WILLIAMS, Private, ALBERT OLIVER, 41692. 2nd Battalion, Canterbury Regiment, NZEF. Died 29 March 1918. Age 34. Son of Oliver and Mary Ann Williams, of Whakamara, New Plymouth; husband of Maud Williams, of Dives Ave, Hawera. Grevilliers (NZ) Memorial, Pas de Calais, France.

WILLIAMS, Second Lieutenant, ALLEN DOUGLAS, 32555. 2nd Battalion, Canterbury Regiment, NZEF. Died 27 March 1918. Age 36. Son of Allen Marsh and Isabel Buchanan Williams; husband of Clara Olive Williams, of Havelock North. Born at Hawkes Bay. Grevilliers (NZ) Memorial, Pas de Calais, France.

WILLIAMS, Gunner, COLIN SYDNEY, 23/647. 6th Battery, NZ Field Artillery. Died 10 April 1918. Age 23. Son of T.S. and Agnes L. Williams, of Tuparoa, Gisborne. Strand Military Cemetery, Comines-Warneton, Hainaut, Belgium. Grave or panel number: IX.P.3.

WILLIAMS, Private, FREDERICK, 14710. 1st Battalion, Otago Regiment, NZEF. Died 18 April 1918. Age 40. Etaples Military Cemetery, Pas de Calais, France. Grave or panel number: XXIX.F.15.

WILLIAMS, Driver, GEORGE HARMAN, 18310. NZ Field Artillery. Died 5 April 1918. Age 24. Son of W.F.J. and S. Williams, of Romilly St, Westport. Hédauville Communal Cemetery Extension, Somme, France. Grave or panel number: H.28.

WILLIAMS, Private, HENRY RICHARD, 24/1864. NZ Cyclist Battalion. Died 27 April 1918. Age 32. Son of Thomas and Eliza Williams, of Nelson. Longuenesse (St Omer) Souvenir Cemetery, Pas de Calais, France. Grave or panel number: V.A.76.

WILLIAMS, NORMAN VIVIAN, 55003. 2nd Battalion, Wellington Regiment, NZEF. Died 6 April 1918. Age 24. Son of George and Ruth Williams, of Myrtle Cottage, Llandogo, Chepstow, Wales. Courcelles-Au-Bois Communal Cemetery Extension, Somme, France. Grave or panel number: F.9.

WILLIAMS, Rifleman, RICHARD HENRY, 45583. 1st Battalion, 3rd NZ Rifle Brigade. Died 27 March 1918. Age 33. Son of Richard and Ellen Williams, of Te Puke. Native of County Kerry, Ireland. Auchonvillers Military Cemetery, Somme, France. Grave or panel number: II.L.34.

WILLIAMS, Lance Corporal, THOMAS JOHN, 34960. 2nd NZ Entrenching Battalion, NZEF. Died 17 April 1918. Son of Mr and Mrs W. S. Williams, of Middlemarsh, Otago Central. Messines Ridge (NZ) Memorial, Mesen, West-Vlaanderen, Belgium.

WILLIAMSON, Private, PERCY CHARLES, 55025. 1st Battalion, Canterbury Regiment, NZEF. Died 5 April 1918. Husband of Mrs Myrtle Miller (formerly Williamson), of 60 Howe St, Auckland. Knightsbridge Cemetery, Mesnil-Martinsart, Somme, France. Grave or panel number: A.14.

WILLIS, Private, THOMAS WALTER, 46153. 2nd Bn, Auckland Regiment, NZEF. Died 8 April 1918. Englebelmer Communal Cemetery Extension, Somme, France. Grave or panel number: F.25.

WILLIS, Rifleman, WILLIAM HENRY, 59177. 4th Battalion, 3rd NZ Rifle Brigade. Died 28 March 1918. Husband of Kate M.F. Beagley (formerly Willis), of Pirongia, Hamilton. Grevillers (NZ) Memorial, Pas de Calais, France.

WILSON, Rifleman, ALBERT, 39135. 4th Battalion, 3rd NZ Rifle Brigade. Died 29 March 1918. Age 31. Son of George Edward and Jane Wilson, of 10 Cranley St, Bromley, Christchurch. Euston Road Cemetery, Colincamps, Somme, France. Grave or panel number: II.A.10.

WILSON, Private, HAROLD THOMAS, 38473. 2nd Battalion, Auckland Regiment, NZEF. Died 17 April 1918. Son of Mrs M. J. Wilson, of 109 Wellesley St West, Auckland. Grevillers (NZ) Memorial, Pas de Calais, France.

WILSON, Lance Corporal, HUGH LAMBIE, 28259. 1st Battalion, Auckland Regiment, NZEF. Died 26 March 1918. Age 21. Son of Hugh and Emma Buchanan Wilson, of 41 Grove Rd, Kelburn, Wellington. Born in New Zealand. Grevillers (NZ) Memorial, Pas de Calais, France.

WILSON, Rifleman, JOHN, 52120. 4th Battalion, 3rd NZ Rifle Brigade. Died 5 April 1918. Son of Mrs F. Phipps (formerly Wilson), of Cook St, Havelock, Blenheim. Grevillers (NZ) Memorial, Pas de Calais, France.

WILSON, Lance Corporal, WILLIAM JAMES, 39385. 3rd Battalion, 3rd NZ Rifle Brigade. Died 6 April 1918. Son of Mr and Mrs S. Wilson, of 37 Edwards St, Rangiora. Euston Road Cemetery, Colincamps, Somme, France. Grave or panel number: IV.E.5.

WINSKILL, Sergeant, GEORGE, 6/1431. NZ Machine Gun Battalion. Died 27 March 1918. Son of G. Winskill, of Bank St, Amberley, Canterbury. Euston Road Cemetery, Colincamps, Somme, France. Grave or panel number: V.D.3.

WOOD, Trooper, ALFRED, 9/487. Otago Mounted Rifles, NZEF. Died 17 April 1918. Age 27. Son of Charles S. and Helena Wood, of 31 Walburgh St,

St George-in-the-East, London, England. Ypres Reservoir Cemetery, Ypres, West-Vlaanderen, Belgium. Grave or panel number: VI.H.47.

WOOD, Lance Corporal, FINLEY CAMPBELL, 12525. 1st Battalion, Wellington Regiment, NZEF. Died 5 April 1918. Age 22. Son of George and Catherine Wood, of Dannevirke. Bertrancourt Communal Cemetery, Somme, France.

WOOLLEY, Corporal, WILLIAM FRANCIS, 22902. 2nd Battalion, Otago Regiment, NZEF. Died 3 April 1918. Age 22. Son of Frank and Jane Woolley, of Koromiko, New Zealand. Doullens Communal Cemetery Extension No. 1, Somme, France. Grave or panel number: VI.E.22.

WRIGHT, Rifleman, JOHN, 59178. 3rd Battalion, 3rd NZ Rifle Brigade. Died 5 April 1918. Son of Mr and Mrs J. Wright, of 25 Harman St, Addington, Christchurch. Grevillers (NZ) Memorial, Pas de Calais, France.

WRIGHT, Private, ROBERT JAMES, 59086. 8th Company, 2nd Battalion, Otago Regiment, NZEF. Died 11 April 1918. Age 35. Son of Joseph and Ellen Wright, of Croydon, Siding Gore, New Zealand. Wimereux Communal Cemetery, Pas de Calais, France. Grave or panel number: X.B.15.

YEARBURY, Rifleman, FRANK WILLIAM, 53736. 1st Battalion, 3rd NZ Rifle Brigade. Died 5 April 1918. Age 23. Son of George and Emily Yearbury, of Whangarei; husband of Lillian Mabel Yearbury (now Mitchell), of Kopok Putaruru, North Auckland. Euston Road Cemetery, Colincamps, Somme, France. Grave or panel number: III.E.1.

YOUNG, Private, DAVID LOGAN, 51585. 2nd Battalion, Auckland Regiment, NZEF. Died 27 March 1918. Son of the late Hugh Young, of Opotiki. Grevilliers (NZ) Memorial, Pas de Calais, France.

YOUNG, Rifleman, LEONARD SAMUEL, 42858. 2nd Battalion, 3rd NZ Rifle Brigade. Died 31 March 1918. Age 24. Eldest son of Alice Young, of 59 Victoria St, Petone, Wellington, and the late Mr E. Young. Born at Petone, Wellington. Englebelmer Communal Cemetery Extension, Somme, France. Grave or panel number: E.14.

YOUNGMAN, Private, REGINALD JOHN, 51812. 1st Battalion, Auckland Regiment, NZEF. Died 27 March 1918. Son of Mr and Mrs J.R. Youngman, of Charing Cross, Kirwell, North Canterbury. Euston Road Cemetery, Colincamps, Somme, France. Grave or panel number: Special Memorial B.11.

ZIMMERMAN, Private, FRANCIS XAVIER, 23468. 2nd Battalion, Auckland Regiment, NZEF. Died 30 March 1918. Son of Mrs Mary Zimmerman, of Waitara, New Plymouth. Grevilliers (NZ) Memorial, Pas de Calais, France.

Appendix 2

Structure of the
New Zealand Division

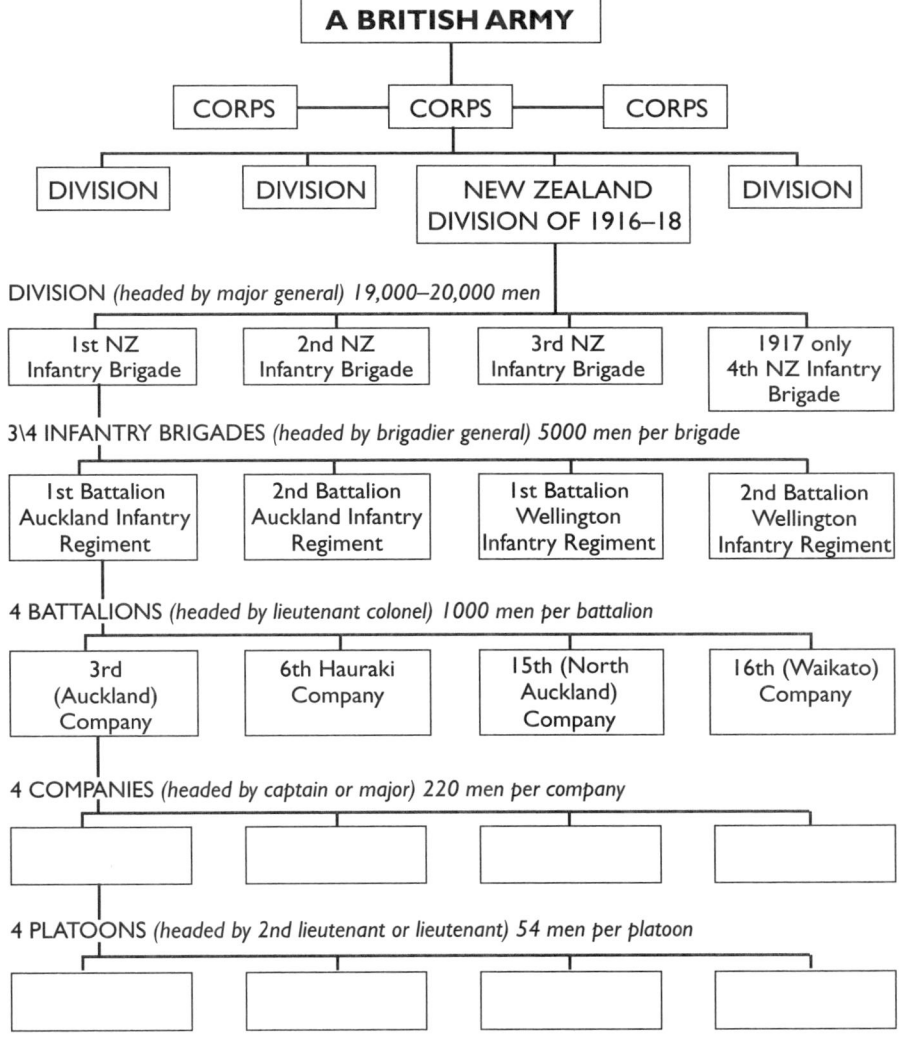

A BRITISH ARMY

CORPS — CORPS — CORPS

DIVISION | DIVISION | NEW ZEALAND DIVISION OF 1916–18 | DIVISION

DIVISION *(headed by major general)* 19,000–20,000 men

| 1st NZ Infantry Brigade | 2nd NZ Infantry Brigade | 3rd NZ Infantry Brigade | 1917 only 4th NZ Infantry Brigade |

3\4 INFANTRY BRIGADES *(headed by brigadier general)* 5000 men per brigade

| 1st Battalion Auckland Infantry Regiment | 2nd Battalion Auckland Infantry Regiment | 1st Battalion Wellington Infantry Regiment | 2nd Battalion Wellington Infantry Regiment |

4 BATTALIONS *(headed by lieutenant colonel)* 1000 men per battalion

| 3rd (Auckland) Company | 6th Hauraki Company | 15th (North Auckland) Company | 16th (Waikato) Company |

4 COMPANIES *(headed by captain or major)* 220 men per company

4 PLATOONS *(headed by 2nd lieutenant or lieutenant)* 54 men per platoon

4 SECTIONS *(headed by corporal or sergeant)* 10–12 men per section

271

The Infantry Units of the New Zealand Division: An Explanatory Note

When the New Zealand Expeditionary Force (NZEF) left New Zealand in October 1914 the infantry units consisted of the Auckland, Wellington, Canterbury and Otago battalions. The four military districts into which the dominion was then divided had each provided a battalion. In 1916, with the decision to expand New Zealand's commitment to a full division for service in France, the original battalions were split into two and four new battalions were formed carrying the designation 2nd in front of their name (2nd Auckland Battalion or 2nd Otago Battalion, for example). The numbers in all the battalions were brought up to full establishment by the arrival of reinforcements.

The third brigade needed to complete a division was formed in New Zealand and called the 3rd New Zealand Rifle Brigade. Its battalions were numbered one to four. As this was the last brigade formed, the soldiers were said to be 'fair dinkum' about their motives for enlisting so they became known as 'the Dinks'. As the brigade's honorary colonel was the Governor, Lord Liverpool, the Rifle Brigade was also designated The Earl of Liverpool's Own.

Initially all of the battalions designated '2nd' were placed in the 2nd Brigade, which seemed to be a logical solution. In January 1917, however, the 1st and 2nd Brigades were reorganised so that all the North Island units were placed in the 1st Brigade and all those from the South Island in the 2nd Brigade. From most accounts, this reorganisation was not very popular, partly because the South Island lacked the numbers to sustain a full brigade and many North Island soldiers found themselves serving in units from Otago and Canterbury. Later in the year, surplus reinforcements from New Zealand enabled the establishment of a fourth infantry brigade consisting of the 3rd Auckland, Wellington, Canterbury and Otago Battalions. The Fourth New Zealand Infantry Brigade fought at Passchendaele on 4 October 1917, its only action of the war. The brigade was disbanded on 7 February 1918.

Battle Order of the British Third Army

This appendix lists all the divisions that were part of the British Third Army (under the control of General Sir Julian Byng) during the Second Battle of the Somme. It details when additional divisions were added to the Army in order to boost its flagging numbers. The New Zealand Division joined the Third Army on 25 March 1918 and remained with it for the duration of the war.

Front: 28 miles. *Divisions:* 14. *Guns:* 1120 including 461 heavies

XVII Corps (Lieutenant General Charles Fergusson)
15th (Scottish) Division, 4th Division

VI Corps (Lieutenant General Sir J. Haldane)
3rd Division, 34th Division, 59th (2nd North Midland) Division

IV Corps (Lieutenant General Sir George Harper)
6th Division, 51st (Highland) Division

V Corps (Lieutenant General Sir E. Fanshawe)
47th (2nd London) Division, 63rd (Royal Naval) Division, 17th (Northern) Division

All the above divisions were in the line on 21 March.

Reserves under Byng's command:
Guards Division, near Arras; 25th Division at Bapaume; 19th and 2nd Divisions behind IV and V Corps

Reserves under the command of GHQ and placed behind Third Army:
40th Division in old Somme battle area and the 41st Division some 20 miles behind the line

Additional reserves committed to aid Third Army during March:
31st Division (from evening March 22); 42nd Division (24 March); 12th Division, 62nd Division (25 March); **New Zealand Division** and 4th Australian Division (25–26 March); 3rd Australian Division (27 March)

French reserves sent to the aid of the Fifth Army during the crisis:
125th Division (22 March); 9th, 10th and 1st Dismounted Cavalry (23 March); 55th Division (24 March); 1st, 56th and 35th Divisions (25 March); elements of two divisions (26 March)

The 22nd and 62nd French cavalry divisions also came into action in the area around March 24.

(From William Moore, *See How They Ran. The British Retreat of 1918*, p. 280)

Bibliography

Primary Sources

Three centres of research provided the bulk of the primary source material for this book: the Alexander Turnbull Library, the National Archives of New Zealand — both in Wellington — and the Kippenberger Military Archive and Research Library at Waiouru. Of these, the Alexander Turnbull Library proved to be the most fruitful. The Manuscript and Archives Collection alone had 144 separate records of the New Zealand Division in France in 1918. The Turnbull's Oral History Centre also provided much useful material.

Other primary sources consulted included:

Glyn Harper (ed.), *Letters from the Battlefield. New Zealand Soldiers Write Home 1914-18*, Auckland, HarperCollins, 2001.

List of Casualties and a Summary of Casualties in Order of Units Reported from 15 February to 14 May, 1918, Wellington, Marcus F. Marks, Government Printer, 1918.

Chrissie Ward, (ed.), *Dear Lizzie. A Kiwi Soldier Writes from the Battlefields of World War One*, Auckland, HarperCollins, 2000.

Nigel M. Watson (ed.), *Letters from a Padre. A Record of the War Service of Ronald S. Watson MC, ED, MA, 1891–1959*, Melbourne, 1970.

Unpublished Manuscripts

Stewart Collis and Graham Langton (eds), *Les Collis First World War Diaries*, Palmerston North, 1999.

Secondary Sources

Books

Lieutenant Colonel S.S. Allen, *2/Auckland, 1918*, Auckland, Whitcombe and Tombs Limited, 1920.

Lieutenant Colonel W.S. Austin, *The Official History of the New Zealand Rifle Brigade*, Wellington, L.T. Watkins Ltd, 1924.

C.E.W. Bean, *The Australian Imperial Force in France during the Main German Offensive, 1918*, Sydney, Angus and Robertson, 1943.

C.E.W. Bean, *Anzac to Amiens*, Melbourne, Penguin Books, 1993.

Gregory Blaxland, *Amiens: 1918*, London, W.H. Allen & Co. Ltd, 1981.

Brian Bond (ed.), *The First World War and British Military History*, Oxford, Clarendon Press, 1991.

Brian Bond and Nigel Cave (eds), *Haig. A Reappraisal 70 Years On*, Barnsley, Leo Cooper, 1999.

Malcolm Brown, *The Imperial War Museum Book of the First World War*, London, Sidgwick and Jackson, 1991.

John Buchan, *Nelson's History of the War. Volume XXII The Darkest Hour*, London, Thomas Nelson and Sons, n.d.

O.E. Burton, *The Auckland Regiment, N.Z.E.F. 1914–1918*, Auckland, Whitcombe and Tombs, 1922.

O.E. Burton, *The Silent Division. New Zealanders at the Front: 1914–1919*, Sydney, Angus and Robertson, 1935.

A.E. Byrne, *Official History of the Otago Regiment, N.Z.E.F. in the Great War 1914–1918*, Dunedin, J.Wilkie and Co, 1921.

J.R. Byrne, *New Zealand Artillery in the Field 1914–18*, Auckland, Whitcombe and Tombs Ltd, 1922.

A.D. Carbery, *The New Zealand Medical Service in the Great War 1914-1918*, Auckland, Whitcombe & Tombs Ltd, 1924.

Winston S. Churchill, *The World Crisis 1916–1918 Part II*, London, Thornton Butterworth Limited, 1927.

John Coates, *An Atlas of Australia's Wars*, Melbourne, Oxford University Press, 2001.

James Cowan, *'Te Hokowhitu a Tu'. The Maoris in the Great War*, Auckland, Whitcombe and Tombs, 1926.

W.H. Cunningham, C.A.L. Treadwell and J.S. Hanna, *The Wellington Regiment N.Z.E.F. 1914–1919*, Wellington, Ferguson and Osborn Ltd, 1923.

Peter Dennis and Jeffrey Grey (eds), *1918. Defining Victory*, Canberra, The Army History Unit, 1999.

Brigadier Sir James E. Edmonds, *History of the Great War. Military Operations France and Belgium, 1918 Volume I*, London, Macmillan and Co., 1935.

Brigadier Sir James E. Edmonds, *History of the Great War. Military Operations France and Belgium, 1918 Volume II*, London, Macmillan and Co., 1937.

Cyril Falls, *The Great War*, New York, G.P. Putmans, 1959.

Anthony Farrar-Hockley, *Goughie. The Life of General Sir Hubert Gough CGB, GCMG, KCVO*, London, MacGibbon, 1975.

David Ferguson, *The History of the Canterbury Regiment, N.Z.E.F. 1914–1919*, Auckland, Whitcombe and Tombs, 1921.

General Sir Hubert Gough, Soldiering On, *London, Arthur Barker Ltd, 1954.*

Jeffrey Grey, *A Military History of Australia*, Melbourne, Cambridge University Press, 1999.

Richard Holmes, *The Western Front*, London, BBC Worldwide Ltd, 1999.

J.H. Johnson, *1918. The Unexpected Victory*, London, Arms and Armour Press, 1997.

Ernst Junger, *The Storm of Steel. From the Diary of a German Storm-Troop Officer on the Western Front*, London, Chatto & Windus, 1929.

John Keegan, *The First World War*, London, Hutchinson, 1998.

M. Knox and W. Murray (eds), *The Dynamics of Military Revolution 1300–2050*, Cambridge, Cambridge Press, 2001.

John Laffin, *Guide to Australian Battlefields of the Western Front 1916–1918*, Sydney, Kangaroo Press and the Australian War Memorial, 1992.

David Lloyd George, *War Memoirs of David Lloyd George Volume II*, London, Odhams Press Limited, 1936.

Gerhard Loose, *Ernst Junger*, New York, Twayne Publishers, 1974.

General Ludendorff, *My War Memories 1914-1918 Volume II*, London, Hutchinson & Co, 1919.

J.H. Luxford, *With the Machine Gunners in France and Palestine*, Auckland, Whitcombe and Tombs Ltd, 1923.

Ian McGibbon (ed.), *The Oxford Companion to New Zealand Mili-*

tary History, Auckland, Oxford University Press, 2000.

Ian McGibbon, *New Zealand Battlefields and Memorials of the Western Front*, Auckland, Oxford University Press, 2001.

Cecil Malthus, *ANZAC. A Retrospect*, Auckland, Reed Publishing, 2002.

Cecil Malthus, *Armentieres and the Somme*, Auckland, Reed Publishing, 2002.

Martin and Mary Middlebrook, *The Somme Battlefields. A Comprehensive Guide from Crecy to the Two World Wars*, London, Viking, 1991.

William Moore, *See How They Ran. The British Retreat of 1918*, London, Sphere Books, 1975.

John Mosier, *The Myth of the Great War. A New Military History of World War I*, New York, HarperCollins Publishers, 2001.

Officers & NCO's, *Official History of the New Zealand Engineers during the Great War 1914–1919*, Wanganui, Evans, Cobb and Sharpe, n.d.

Albert Palazzo, *Seeking Victory on the Western Front. The British Army & Chemical Warfare in World War I*, Lincoln, University of Nebraska Press, 2000.

Christopher Pugsley, *On the Fringe of Hell. New Zealanders and Military Discipline in the First World War*, Auckland, Hodder & Stoughton, Auckland, 1991.

Geoffrey Serle, *John Monash. A Biography*, Melbourne, Melbourne University Press, 1982.

Gary Sheffield, *Forgotten Victory. The First World War: Myths and Realities*, London, Headline Book Publishing, 2001.

H. Stewart, *The New Zealand Division 1916–1919*, Auckland, Whitcombe and Tombs Ltd, 1921.

Hew Strachan, *The Oxford Illustrated History of the First World War*, Oxford, Oxford University Press, 1998.

John Terraine, *To Win a War. 1918 The Year of Victory*, London, Cassell & Co, 2000.

Craig Wilcox (ed.), *The Great War. Gains and Losses — ANZAC and Empire*, Canberra, The Australian National University and The Australian War Memorial, 1995.

Jay Winter and Blaine Baggett, *1914–1918. The Great War and the Shaping of the 20th Century*, London, BBC Books, 1996.

Articles

Barrie Pitt, 'Germany: 1918. New strategy, new tactics', in *History of the First World War* Volume 6, Number 14, London, 1971, p. 2616.

Barrie Pitt, 'The Ludendorff Offensive Phase 1', in *History of the First War* Volume 6, Number 15, London, 1971, p. 2638

Christopher Pugsley, 'Russell of the New Zealand Division', in *New Zealand Strategic Management*, Autumn 1995, pp. 47–50.

Christopher Pugsley, 'Russell. Commander of Genius', in *New Zealand Defence Quarterly*, Number. 23, Summer 1998, pp. 25–29.

Index

Index

283